CLIMATE MIGRATION

This book explores the complex literature on climate migration and investigates the epistemological and ethical challenges the topic poses for anyone who takes an interest in the relationship between climate change and human migration.

At the heart of the contemporary preoccupation with climate change is a concern for its societal impacts. Among these, its presumed effect on human migration is perhaps the most politically resonant, regardless of whether that politics is oriented towards human or national security.

There is, however, a problem: research on the causal link between climate change and migration has shown it to be a highly equivocal one. By extension, it remains unclear what – if any – response is required from law and policy.

Carefully structured to guide the reader through the issue of climate migration in a logical and rigorous manner, this book is the first to bring together key critiques, caveats and cautions in order to systematically examine the challenges facing law, policy and research on the topic.

At a time in which both the effects of climate change and the causes of migration are of great public and political interest, and in which these interests are often fraught with sentiment and freighted with politics, the book brings dispassionately critical perspectives to bear on a topic that desperately needs it.

Climate Migration

Critical Perspectives for Law, Policy and Research

Edited by
Calum TM Nicholson
and
Benoit Mayer

•HART•
OXFORD • LONDON • NEW YORK • NEW DELHI • SYDNEY

HART PUBLISHING

Bloomsbury Publishing Plc

Kemp House, Chawley Park, Cumnor Hill, Oxford, OX2 9PH, UK

1385 Broadway, New York, NY 10018, USA

29 Earlsfort Terrace, Dublin 2, Ireland

HART PUBLISHING, the Hart/Stag logo, BLOOMSBURY and the Diana logo are trademarks of Bloomsbury Publishing Plc

First published in Great Britain 2023

A catalogue record for this book is available from the British Library.

A catalogue record for this book is available from the Library of Congress.

ISBN: HB: 978-1-50996-174-0
ePDF: 978-1-50996-176-4
ePub: 978-1-50996-175-7

Typeset by Compuscript Ltd, Shannon

For Elizabeth
&
For Peixi

FOREWORD

Editors Calum Nicholson and Benoit Mayer are to be congratulated for pulling together this thoughtful and important book on *Climate Migration: Critical Perspectives for Law, Policy, and Research*. It comes at a critical moment. Whether or not one believes the earth has entered a new geological era of the Anthropocene, the effects of anthropogenic climate change are real, visible, and visceral except to the most hard-core denialist. Climate change is now one of the defining issues of our time. As such, it has become a sort of discursive magnet, attracting and attaching to it other major environmental, social, economic, and political concerns. Primary among them is human migration.

I first became aware of this phenomenon while researching the evolution and impact of environmental conflict ideas which circulated widely in international security circles in the 1990s. I found that at the root of most of them was a simplistic neo-Malthusian causality that claimed that population pressures and poverty in developing countries precipitate environmental degradation and resource scarcities. These, in turn, would lead people to migrate as 'environmental refugees' either to other rural areas or to cities where they stimulate ethnic unrest or violent conflict.

In the early 2000s I watched with unease as these narratives began to shift to fears of 'climate conflict' and 'climate refugees' employing the same basic logic. Defence think-tanks and intelligence agencies took up the mantle, warning of threats to Western security and borders posed by mass migrations of climate refugees. More often than not, these narratives and their accompanying images were applied to Africans. Racist stereotypes of violent young black men became a stock of the trade.

Twenty years have passed since this first burst of interest in climate conflict and climate refugees. In the meantime, social scientists and legal scholars have thankfully turned a more discerning eye on the subject, challenging the fundamental premise that climate change and migration are directly and causally linked. The contributors to this volume are among the most informed and incisive critics.

Here in one book academics, policymakers, legal experts, and students in climate, migration, and related fields can find answers to the key questions about 'Climate Migration'. Is there solid evidence that climate change induces or forces migration? In the absence of that evidence, does the term 'Climate Migration' itself constrain our understanding and divert research efforts away from more productive paths? What are the impacts of 'Climate Migration' in Western policy circles, law, media, and popular culture?

Furthermore, what is the role of racism in constructing 'climate refugees' and fomenting fears of them in national and international security circles as well as in dystopian cli-fi fiction and films? How does 'Climate Migration' bolster the border control industry and anti-immigrant politics on the Right? How does one respond to the arguments of more liberal environmentalists and development agencies that 'Climate Migration', even if not a scientifically sound concept, helps awaken the public to the urgency of addressing both the climate change and migration crises? What if migrants themselves identity as 'climate migrants', as in the recent case of Ioane Teitiota, national of the Pacific island of Kiribati, who sought to remain in New Zealand on that basis?

And finally, what should researchers, policymakers, and jurists do to not only challenge the problematic causality inherent in discussions of 'Climate Migration', but to chart alternative knowledge pathways that would better serve the development of migration law and policies in the era of climate change?

This book is not only a guide through the now voluminous and complex literature and epistemologies that address these pressing questions, but also an indispensable resource for building a more equitable, just, and sustainable future.

Betsy Hartmann

ACKNOWLEDGEMENTS

Assembling this book has been a two-year journey, and one not entirely free of adventures. We have therefore had the immense good fortune to have kept excellent company throughout.

Were it not for the support of the team at Hart Publishing – in particular Roberta Bassi, Rosie Mearns, and Verity Stuart – it goes without saying that this collection would not exist. They have backed up their enthusiasm for the original proposal with nothing but good-natured professionalism ever since.

Throughout the process, we have also been lucky to work for institutions that both understand the importance of writing and the time commitment involved. In Calum's case, Dr Dezső Tamás and the Danube Institute and Dr Szalai Zoltán and the Mathias Corvinus Collegium have gone out of their way to provide the space and conditions to work on the book. In Benoit's case, the Chinese University of Hong Kong and Prof Lutz-Christian Wolff have done similarly.

In the final months of editing, we have been particularly fortunate to have received outstanding research assistance from Mateusz Slowik. Like a player thrown onto the pitch late in the game, he brought fresh legs and an enthusiasm to leave no page unturned, no 'i' undotted, and no 't' uncrossed.

We were also honoured when Betsy Hartmann – an early influence on us both – agreed to write the Foreword. Her final piece manages to be at once comprehensive and succinct, and is an eloquent distillation of the book's core themes and ultimate purpose.

Most importantly, we owe thanks to the eight other authors – Ilan, Gunvor, Greg, Sarah, David, Andrew, Giovanna, and Carol – for producing such a range of thoughtful and thought-provoking critical pieces on 'climate migration'. Long-time fans of all their scholarship, we were delighted when they each signed on and, even more so, when they signed off on their chapters. Every single one brings something distinct and important to the book.

Finally, we would like to thank the reader for picking up this book. We hope you find it as interesting to read as it was to conceive.

CONTENTS

PART III
IMPLICATIONS FOR RESEARCH, POLICY, AND LAW

CONTRIBUTORS

Andrew Baldwin is Associate Professor of Human Geography at Durham University. He is the author of *The Other of Climate Change: Racial Futurism, Migration, Humanism* (Rowman & Littlefield, 2022) and co-editor of *Life Adrift: Climate Change, Migration, Critique* (Rowman & Littlefield, 2017) and *Climate Change, Migration and Human Rights: Law and Policy Perspectives* (Routledge, 2017).

David Durand-Delacre is a senior researcher in the Environment and Migration: Interactions and Choices section of the UN University Institute for Environment and Human Security in Bonn, Germany. As a human geographer and critical migration scholar, his work explores the political, cultural, and epistemological controversies arising from growing concern about climate change's impact on human mobilities. On this basis, he aims to promote more inclusive and equitable migration policies as well as support a diversity of new, nuanced, and thought-provoking media representations about the intersection of climate change and human mobilities.

Carol Farbotko is a human geographer based at Griffith University in Australia. Her research interests include the politics and cultures of climate change, particularly climate mobilities, with a focus on justice and equity among climate-affected people. She currently holds an Australian Research Council Future Fellowship focused on indigenous solutions to global challenges in the Pacific Islands Her work has been published widely, including in *Nature Climate Change* and *Global Environmental Change.*

Betsy Hartmann is professor emerita of Development Studies at Hampshire College in Amherst, MA, US. Her research, writing, and advocacy focus on the nexus between population, environment, climate, migration, and security concerns. Among her books are *Reproductive Rights and Wrongs: The Global Politics of Population Control* and *The America Syndrome: Apocalypse, War and Our Call to Greatness*, and she is co-editor of the anthology *Making Threats: Biofears and Environmental Anxieties*. Betsy has consulted for the United Nations Environment Programme and UN Women; in Spring 2015 she was a Fulbright-Nehru Distinguished Chair in New Delhi, India.

Gunvor Jónsson is a trained anthropologist and interdisciplinary scholar who has conducted both independent and collaborative research on migration and mobilities in West Africa and more recently, western Europe. She works at the Centre for International Migration, Office for National Statistics (UK), and is an Honorary Research Associate in Sociology at the Open University. She has taught courses in migration studies at SOAS and the University of Oxford and was formerly a key member of the team at the International Migration Institute, University of Oxford. Gunvor is the author of several articles, book chapters, a special journal issue and an edited book. Her monograph, *Terminus: Urban Displacement and Trade in a Senegalese Market*, is forthcoming with UCL Press and the International Africa Institute.

Ilan Kelman is Professor of Disasters and Health at University College London, England, and a Professor at the University of Agder, Kristiansand, Norway. His research explores the links between disasters and health, and the relationship of climate change to both. Three main areas are: (i) disaster diplomacy and health diplomacy; (ii) island sustainability involving safe and healthy communities in isolated locations; and (iii) risk education for health and disasters.

Giovanna Lauria has a master's degree in Law from the University of Bologna and a PhD in Law from the University of Macerata with a thesis on 'the international protection regime in the age of climate change'. During her studies, she has been a visiting student at the University of Groningen and at the Complutense University in Madrid. She was admitted to the Italian Bar Association in September 2019. She is currently working as a law clerk at the Court of Padua, Italy.

Benoit Mayer is Associate Professor at the Faculty of Law of the Chinese University of Hong Kong, where he teaches climate, environmental, and international law. His research focuses on various aspects of climate law, including international law obligations on climate change mitigation, the development of environmental assessments as a tool for climate change mitigation, and the climate–migration nexus. He is the author of *The International Law on Climate Change* (Cambridge University Press, 2018) and *International Law Obligations on Climate Change Mitigation* (Oxford University Press, 2022). He is also a member of the UNFCCC roster of experts.

Sarah Louise Nash is a political scientist and currently holds the position of senior scientist at the Platform for Sustainable Development of the University for Continuing Education Krems, in Austria. Her first book, *Governing Migration in the Context of Climate Change, International Policy and Discourse*, was published in 2019 with Bristol University Press. Since then, she has specialised on European politics and policy at the crossroads of climate change and migration.

Calum TM Nicholson read social anthropology at Trinity College, Cambridge, migration studies at St Antony's College, Oxford, and holds a PhD in human geography from Swansea University. He teaches courses on international migration and international development at the Institute of Continuing Education at the University of Cambridge, and is a former Visiting Fellow of the Danube Institute, and a current Visiting Fellow at the Mathias Corvinus Collegium, both in Budapest. His work on 'climate migration' critically explores both the role of science in society, and the assumptions that inform the way society's governing institutions think.

Gregory White is the Mary Huggins Gamble Chair of Government at Smith College, Northampton, Massachusetts, in the United States, where he currently directs the Environmental Science & Policy Program. He holds a PhD in Political Science and African Studies from the University of Wisconsin-Madison, and held Fulbright scholarships to both Tunisia and Morocco. White is the former editor of the Journal of North African Studies. He is the author of *Climate Change and Migration: Security and Borders in a Warming World* (Oxford University Press, 2011) and co-editor (with Yahia Zoubir) of *North Africa: Continuity and Change* (Routledge, 2015). He is currently at work on a monograph, titled *Refugees of the Apocalypse: A Critique of the Concept of 'Climate Refugees.*

ABBREVIATIONS

AFD	Agence Française de Développement
BMZ	Federal Ministry for Economic Cooperation and Development (Germany)
CIA	Central Intelligence Agency
COP	Conference of the Parties to the United Nations Framework Convention on Climate Change
CRID	Centre de Recherche et d'Information pour le Développement
DPPDM	Des Ponts Pas des Murs
ECtHR	European Court of Human Rights
EUROSUR	European Border Surveillance system
GHG	Greenhouse gas
GIZ	German Society for International Development
HRC	United Nations Human Rights Committee
ICCPR	International Covenant on Civil and Political Rights
IOM	International Organisation for Migration
IPCC	Intergovernmental Panel on Climate Change
NGO	Non-governmental organisation
NLC	National League of Cities
OSCE	Organization for Security and Co-operation in Europe
SIVE	Sistema Integrado de Vigilancia del Exterior
UNFCCC	United Nations Framework Convention on Climate Change
UNHCR	United Nations High Commissioner for Refugees

Introduction

CALUM TM NICHOLSON AND BENOIT MAYER

> How can I present a proposal intended not to say what is, or what ought to be, but to provoke thought; one that requires no other verification than the way in which it is able to 'slow down' reasoning and create an opportunity to arouse a slightly different awareness of the problems and situations mobilizing us?[1]

I. Context

A. The Discourse on 'Climate Migration'

In the three decades since the end of the Cold War, there have been few emergent issues that have proven as emotive and as politically charged in western culture as climate change, and as human migration. Initially of interest mostly to those on the political left, but rapidly gaining mainstream orthodoxy, climate change is now widely perceived as an unparalleled threat that will overwhelm society's capacity to cope, and thereby undermine the economic and, inevitably, political order of things. Initially of interest to those on the political right, but likewise gaining popular and electoral resonance, immigration is increasingly viewed as a nonpareil force for cultural and thus political change. In the popular mind, these two 'apolitical' phenomena preoccupy, inflame, and divide the public sphere just as the political ideologies of the Cold War once did.

Understandably, in the course of the last three decades, the two themes have dovetailed in the form of a concern for 'climate migration', and the various cognate categories that – whatever their superficial differences – assume the same basic causal articulation, such as 'climate refugee' or 'climate mobility'. This thematic fusing is hardly a surprise. On the one hand, in migration studies, 'climate migration' feeds a discourse about a presumed *effect* of the most politically charged area of the natural sciences: climate change. On the other hand, in climate studies, the same concept identifies climate change as a *cause* of perhaps the most politically

[1] Isabelle Stengers, 'The Cosmopolitical Proposal', in Bruno Latour and Peter Weibel (eds), *Making Things Public: Atmospheres of Democracy* (Cambridge, Massachusetts, MIT Press 2005) 994, at 994.

charged area of the social sciences: migration. The former discourse appeals as it is presumed to be a 'clear cut' case of the consequences of climate change – a 'canary in the coalmine', providing would-be tangible, incontrovertible evidence of the reality and perils associated with climate change. The appeal of the latter is because 'climate migration' is assumed to be a less political and more analytically tractable form of migration, anchored 'objectively' in the science on climate change.

While the two issues resonate on their own terms, when folded together in this way they occupy an almost unique[2] place in Western culture – and in the international institutions that reflect and express the orthodoxies of that culture – lying as they do simultaneously at the intersection between science and social science, between academia and policy-making, and between formal knowledge (*episteme*) and public opinion (*doxa*). As such, 'climate migration' may be taken not only as 'a standard element of climate-change discourse',[3] but also as something of a bellwether for the intellectual culture that is preoccupied with that discourse, for it distils – perhaps more succinctly than any other theme or topic – the epistemological and ethical norms of Western society.

This discourse on 'climate migration', however, relies on simple causal assumptions that, as the following shows, cannot be substantiated.

B. Underlying Causal Assumptions

While the discourse around the concept is various and multifaceted, it ultimately reduces – by definition – to a pair of quite simple claims:

(a) that it is possible to *determine* a distinct causal relationship between climate change and human migration;
(b) that it is therefore possible to *distinguish* a 'climate migrant' from any other migrant or person.

No matter how one approaches the subject, or what data or definition one draws upon, at its foundations the concept is concerned with causality. The discourse on 'climate migration' may encompass a great deal of complexity and variety of circumstance, but, at the most basic level, it pivots on this fundamentally simple causal claim. One cannot meaningfully speak about 'climate migration' without assuming that climate change causes specific instances of migration, and that these instances are identifiable.

The imaginative appeal of 'climate migration' is derived precisely from this putative simplicity. Who is not curious about the societal effects of climate change? Who is not interested in the causes of migration? 'Climate migration' promises – again, by definition – a pleasingly straightforward and efficient answer to

[2] Akin, perhaps, only to contemporary discourses around 'mental health'.
[3] Andrew Baldwin, 'Racialisation and the Figure of the Climate-Change Migrant' (2013) 45(6) *Environmental and Planning A: Economy and Space* 1474, 1475, available at doi.org/10.1068/a45388.

both questions, with implications for climate and migration policy alike. But simultaneously, the very centrality of the causal assumption to 'climate migration' means that a great deal depends on the *integrity* of that assumption. The simple causal claim at the heart of the issue is, in a sense, an analytically load-bearing one.

If the causal claim's structural integrity as an epistemological position is proven, the reward is a tool of inestimable value for lawyers and policy-makers who seek to understand the societal effects of climate change and the environmental causes of migration, regardless of whether one's interest is in the well-being of, in the implications of climate change for the prosperity or security of nations, or both.

If, however, the causal assumption cannot be substantiated, then logically we must forfeit any claim to be able to speak meaningfully, and usefully, about the relationship between climate and migration as a distinct phenomenon (as opposed to a mere statistical relation). Any such failure would, by extension, tell us a great deal about ourselves, revealing a fault-line in our culture – a chasm between what we wish to know, and what we can. There is value in this of a different sort: it is the sort of conclusion that might encourage us to reconsider our assumptions, or, perhaps, to realise how many assumptions we make when we think about the world and our relationship to it. It would have implications for how we – and particularly our institutions – formulate policy, and act in and upon the world.

C. Debunked Assumptions

A critical approach to 'climate migration' therefore has potentially much to tell about the epistemology and ethics of the culture that takes an interest in the topic. This is because the discourse on 'climate migration' has thrived despite the widely acknowledged fact that the causal assumption on which it relies cannot be substantiated. For at least a decade, there has been a general consensus among migration scholars, and other researchers working closely with the theme, that 'climate migration' is a misconception, given that causality in migration is never so simple: migration decisions 'are always mediated through complex political, social and economic structures';[4] and migrants have agency, and are not simply passive victims in the face of environmental hazards.[5]

Indeed, it is broadly agreed that 'no accepted definition of "climate migration" … actually exists'.[6] Attempts to quantify 'climate migrants' are 'on shaky ground methodologically, and fail to recognise the multi-causality of migration

[4] Mike Hulme, 'Attributing Weather Extremes to "Climate Change": A Review' (2014) 38(4) *Progress in Physical Geography: Earth and Environment* 499, 509, available at doi.org/10.1177/0309133314538644.

[5] Francois Gemenne, 'Why the Numbers Don't Add Up: A Review of Estimates and Predictions of People Displaced by Environmental Changes' (2011) 22 *Global Environmental Change* 541, available at doi.org/10.1016/j.gloenvcha.2011.09.005.

[6] Sarah Louise Nash, *Negotiating Migration in the Context of Climate Change: International Policy and Discourse* (Policy Press 2019) 8.

and … climate change adaptation efforts';[7] and such attempts give 'the illusion of a deeper understanding of [causal linkage]'.[8] Indeed, it is widely accepted that it is 'not empirically possible in most, if not all, circumstance' to identify 'climate migrants',[9] for climate change 'is [best] understood as a threat or impact multiplier, rather than being a tangible risk that a person can be exposed and vulnerable to'.[10] As such, 'climate migration' is an 'intrinsically equivocal concept',[11] perennially unmoored from any actual constituency. There are migrants, but there are no *climate* migrants: 'there is no solution to "climate migration" because "climate migration" is not an issue in and by itself'.[12]

There is, thus, a tension between, on the one hand, the emotiveness of the discussion around 'climate migration', and on the other hand, the pattern of inconclusion and equivocation that is the hallmark of the empirical literature on the topic.[13] In light of that tension, this volume offers perspectives on 'climate migration' that are critical, in three senses of the word. First, the volume is an exercise in dispassionate, rigorous, and scholarly analysis of 'climate migration', in order to demonstrate its contexts of relevance, hidden assumptions, and conceptual flaws. Second, it mounts a critique of the way in which the topic has typically been handled. Third, it argues that a more systematic and rigorous approach to the supposed 'climate–migration nexus' is of critical importance in a time in which the consequences or climate change and the causes of migration are of great public and political interest.

II. Content

In service of these critical objectives, the contributions to this volume are arranged in three parts, which loosely progress concatenating arguments. Part I outlines the problems with how 'climate migration' is conceptualised – namely with what 'climate migration', in its implicit *content*, actually *is*. Part II then details the problems with how 'climate migration' is used and abused expediently in relation to the broader political, economic, and social milieu – that is, what 'climate migration', in its explicit *context*, actually *does*. Finally, part III presents arguments

[7] ibid 6.

[8] ibid.

[9] Ingrid Boas and others, 'Climate Migration Myths' (2019) 9 *Nature Climate Change* 901, 902, available at doi.org/10.1038/s41558-019-0633-3.

[10] Matthew Scott, *Climate Change, Disasters and the Refugee Convention* (Cambridge, Cambridge University Press 2020) 10.

[11] Calum TM Nicholson, '"Climate-Induced Migration": Ways Forward in the Face of an Intrinsically Equivocal Concept', in Benoit Mayer and François Crépeau (eds), *Research Handbook on Climate Change, Migration and the Law* (Cheltenham, Edward Elgar 2017) 49.

[12] Benoit Mayer, *The Concept of Climate Migration: Advocacies and its Prospects* (Cheltenham, Edward Elgar 2016) 301.

[13] Calum TM Nicholson, 'Climate Change and the Politics of Causal Reasoning: The Case of Climate Change and Migration' (2014) 180(2) *Geographical Journal* 151, available at doi.org/10.1111/geoj.12062.

for what researchers, policy-makers, and jurists might do instead, if they are to formulate, interpret, or apply laws and policies on migration against the backdrop of concerns for climate change, but in a manner that avoids lapsing into the epistemological and ethical problems outlined in parts I and II.

As such, part I offers a range of analytical critiques of the content of the discourse on 'climate migration'; part II presents a range of political critiques of the effect that discourse has on its cultural context; and part III considers what empirical and legal scholars, as well as law- and policy-makers, ought to do instead if they are to avoid the paradoxes outlined in part I and unintended consequences laid out in part II.

A. What 'Climate Migration' *Is*

In examining why 'climate migration' is so problematic as an analytical concept, part I explores the nature of the causal assumption that lies, by definition, at its heart.

In chapter one, social anthropologist and human geographer Calum Nicholson demonstrates how any concern for 'climate migration' reduces to a causal claim. Having done this, he argues that establishing a causal linkage between climate change and migration remains elusive and suggests that the literature has little hope in remedying this, as the problem is less one of data or definition, and more to do with the assumptions being made, and the questions being asked. Having done this, he outlines its implications for how lawyers, policy-makers, and researchers approach understanding not just the theme of 'climate migration', but also the societal consequences of climate change more generally.

In chapter two, disaster risk reduction specialist Ilan Kelman draws on insights from his discipline to examine the extent to which we can isolate, and should understand, climate change as an independent variable that shapes societal outcomes, not least migration. In doing so, he challenges the causal determinism underlying much of the discussion of climate change, particularly in discussions of climate change adaptation. He argues that we must remember to begin not from what we believe *ought to be*, but from what the science tells *is* in fact the case, and that we must be as conscious of what we stand to lose – in our understanding of and sensitivity to prevailing political and economic conditions – as we are of what we stand to gain, when we privilege climate change in analyses of society.

In chapter three, migration scholar Gunvor Jónsson draws on insights from political ecology and migration studies to examine the extent to which we can and should ever understand migration as a direct effect of climate change. In doing, she traces the evolution of the discussion on 'climate migration' and critiques the causal determinism and neo-Malthusian assumptions which lie at its heart. Drawing on empirical findings of migration scholarship on the Sahel, she demonstrates how analyses of 'climate migration' are often founded not just on a misunderstanding, but an exclusion, of much that has otherwise been discovered about the nature and causes of human migration.

B. What 'Climate Migration' *Does*

Having, in part I, critically and analytically examined the epistemological *content* of the literature on 'climate migration', part II considers the ethics of the literature's relationship to its broader political, economic, and cultural milieu – that is, the *context* in which it exists.

In chapter four, political scientist Gregory White examines John Lanchester's 2019 novel, The Wall. Identifying it as a work of climate fiction ('cli-fi'), he highlights the ways in which the novel portrays migrants fleeing climate change, depicted in the novel as 'the Others'. He notes that, while these characters are central to the story, they are thinly drawn and rarely encountered by the protagonists. They are presented as a racialised threat requiring the construction of a wall around an island nation, ostensibly Great Britain. White encourages us to ask whether it is constructive for this to be the understanding of 'climate migrants' that is being inculcated into the public consciousness by works of art.

In chapter five, human geographer and critical migration scholar David Durand-Delacre draws on the perspectives of international development and migrant solidarity organisations in France to illustrate that, while policy stakeholders may study, debate, and discuss the concept of 'climate migration', this rarely leads to any concrete action. He explains this is in no small part due to 'perhaps insurmountable' analytical and political ambiguities that appear to be inherent to any discussion of the topic in France. Having done this, he reflects on what uses the topic can still serve despite these ambiguities.

In chapter six, political scientist Sarah Louise Nash examines how policy actors in European nation states are understanding, and beginning to develop governance responses to, the links between climate change and migration. Using the cases of Austria, Germany, Denmark, and Sweden, she explores the framing, management, and regulation of climate change and migration as linked phenomena. Specifically, she scrutinises the European mode of governing climate change and migration as part of an overarching project of migration prevention.

In chapter seven, human geographer Andrew Baldwin argues that the scientific and policy discourse on 'climate migration' is rooted in a complicated politics of race and racism. But whereas climate change, migration and race often converge on issues of transnational migration, borders, and sovereignty, Baldwin argues that they also stand to materialise around questions of property and land use, particularly in the US urban context.

C. Beyond 'Climate Migration'

The last three chapters, in part III, put forward arguments for how scholars, policy-makers, and jurists can hope to proceed, if they are to both avoid the causal pitfalls and paradoxes that are the hallmark of the content of the empirical and normative literature on 'climate migration', as outlined in part I, and avoid the negative effects that 'climate migration' has in relation to the broader political, economic, and cultural context in which it is discussed, as outlined in part II.

In chapter eight, human geographer Carol Farbotko explores the implications for knowledge and public policy of the recent case of a national of Kiribati, Ioane Teitiota, who made headlines as the first person to claim in a court of law to be a 'climate migrant' through an appeal to his own lived experience and the simple act of self-identification. Farbotko considers the reasons for this and its implications for future law, policy, and research.

In chapter nine, international law scholar Giovanna Lauria analyses how the Human Rights Committee has approached the relation between climate change and migration in its views on the case brought by Mr Teitiota. She shows that the Committee's decision is open to two different interpretations, one of which recognises the multicausality of migration.

Finally, in chapter ten, legal scholar Benoit Mayer seeks to understand a persistent disconnect between what is known of the climate–migration nexus and the law-and-policy discourse on 'climate migration'. Building on a review of the literature and a personal account of the evolution of his own views, he identifies the risk of scholarship becoming part and parcel of post-truth politics.

III. Purpose of the Book

The purpose of this volume is to provide a single resource with which scholars and students may orient themselves when they seek to examine this emotive and often disorienting topic.

Dispassion, and the epistemological humility to acknowledge our limited ability to understand the world we live in, are crucial when we discuss this topic, as it is with most if not all issues with implications for public policy. If one is to invest time in studying the subject, let alone formulating policy and law about it, it is surely crucial to have a sense of two things. First, we need to understand *what*, precisely, the object of concern is when we take an interest in 'climate migration'. Second, we also need to know *why* we care to have this concern, in the specific formulations that mobilises us.

Often, with issues such as 'climate migration', the answers to both these questions are presumed to be known, and so the questions themselves are rarely asked to begin with. Yet, if we take the time to reflect upon these questions – of what is at issue, and why we care about it – the answers we tend to give dissolve into platitude or the arbitrary.[14] One problem is that it is easy to imagine 'climate migration' – in the mind's eye we can easily picture a 'climate migrant'. But this does not give any assurance that actually distinguishing 'them', in the real world, from any other sort of migrant, or indeed from any other sort of person, is remotely straightforward.

[14] ibid.

This matters, because the context in which 'climate migrants' are discussed with any practical implication is within our collective national and international institutions, which – if they are not simply to act arbitrarily – require sound conceptual and empirical foundations to guide and justify their action, and the cost incurred on us all to fund those actions. As a consequence, a rigorous, dispassionate, and logically structured approach to the topic is crucial, and it is that which this volume seeks to provide.

Crucially, the volume aims to bring together critiques that are typically seen as distinct and often intended for different audiences. Thus, in part I, the critiques are more 'analytical' in their spirit. In part II, they are 'critical' in the 'continental' sense: that is, they bring to bear political and interpretative critiques.[15] Yet throughout, the purpose is to use both forms of criticism to 'pincer' the topic so that, notwithstanding whether readers are arriving at the subject for the first time or seeking guidance in order to act upon it, they are cautioned about the epistemological and ethical dangers that attend any engagement with it.

Ultimately, the purpose of the collection is not necessarily to provide definitive answers, be they of an empirical variety (ie about what 'climate migration' is) or a normative one (ie about what ought to be done about 'it'). There is a voluminous literature that attempts to do both of these things, even if the answers themselves remain notoriously opaque.[16] Rather, the purpose of this volume is, as the opening quote suggests, to 'provoke thought', and to '"slow down" our reasoning' so we might 'arouse a slightly different awareness of the problems and situations mobilizing us'.[17] As such, this is not critique as an end in itself, but critique as a means to an end. In this case, the end is one whereby lawyers, policy-makers, and researchers are, on the one hand, as rigorous and dispassionate as possible, and, on the other hand, as conscious of the limits on what we can know as they are of the imperatives regarding what we must do.

We live in an age of heightened rhetoric, which is both flush with noble ideals and awash with a fear of that which cannot be controlled. None of these intellectual fashions are timeless, and all of them may lead to ethical and epistemological carelessness. The need for a more dispassionate, rigorous, and critical approach to the examination of the societal consequences of climate change is important, not

[15] David Held, *Introduction to Critical Theory: Horkheimer to Habermas* (Berkeley, University of California Press 1980).

[16] Etienne Piguet, Antoine Pecoud, and Paul de Guchteneire, *Migration and Climate Change* (Cambridge, Cambridge University Press 2011); Gregory White, *Climate Change and Migration: Security and Borders in a Warming World* (New York, Oxford University Press 2011); Jane McAdam, *Climate Change, Forced Migration, and International Law* (Oxford, Oxford University Press 2012); Robert A McLeman, *Climate and Human Migration: Past Experiences, Future* (Cambridge, Cambridge University Press 2013); Mayer (n 11); Sarah Louise Nash, *Negotiating Migration in the Context of Climate Change: International Policy and Discourse* (Bristol, Bristol University Press 2019); Matthew Scott, *Climate Change, Disasters, and the Refugee Convention* (Cambridge, Cambridge University Press 2020).

[17] Stengers (n 1) 994.

because we needn't worry about climate change, but precisely because we should. If it is true that the climate is changing at an accelerated rate due to human action, we owe it to ourselves not simply to conduct social science on all the possible areas of its societal consequence, but also to ensure that the investigations we conduct are careful to avoid leaping *to* any wrong answers – or, perhaps more problematically, leaping *from* the wrong questions to begin with.

Laden as they are with sentiment, moral significance, and political currency, the topics of climate change and migration are, independent of each other, already ones that demand a more dispassionate perspective. Linked together, the need for scrutiny, caution, and perspective is all the more urgent. It is hoped that, on completing this volume, the reader will have gained a clearer view of what we do and do not know about the societal consequences of climate change, of the consequences of presuming we know what we do not, and of the nature of our institutions and their capacity to meet the crises that define our time.

PART I

Content

1

Conceptualising 'Climate Migration'

CALUM TM NICHOLSON

> We cannot confine our attention to the great impersonal forces, natural and man-made, which act upon us. The goals and motives that guide human action must be looked at in the light of all that we know and understand; their roots and growth, their essence, and above all their validity, must be critically examined with every intellectual resource that we have.[1]

I. Introduction

Throughout history, and across culture, human societies have found many ways to organise themselves, from feudal systems to city-states, acephalous societies to thalasocracies, tribes to empires.

The end of the era of European imperialism, however, saw another system – originally emerging as a regional reaction to the chaos that characterised the long period of post-Reformation liminality which culminated in the Thirty Years' War – go global, and become a worldwide standard. This system of the 'nation-state' is distinct in at once emphasising the strict geographical demarcation of territory, the principle of state sovereignty, and the centralisation of government.

In the wake of the decades of decolonisation following World War II, this system was so widely adopted by former colonies that it quickly became the de facto universal geopolitical 'operating system', more or less contiguously spanning the globe, and encompassing (with a few exceptions that otherwise prove the rule) all the world's societies and habitable land.

In doing, this system established a common framework of norms and governmental structures that – in principle at least – continue to allow otherwise culturally diverse and often normatively divergent societies to be, at worst,

[1] Isaiah Berlin, 'The Pursuit of the Ideal', in *The Proper Study of Mankind: An Anthology of Essays* (New York, Farrar, Straus and Giroux 1998) 2.

mutually intelligible and, at best, mutually tolerant. As a result, an emergent property of this universal nation-state 'operating system' is the suite of international institutions and agencies brought into existence precisely to facilitate the coordination and cooperation of nation-states in the face of shared challenges and to provide a means by which they may resolve their differences without resort to violence.

According to the anthropologist James Scott, a key feature of these modern nation-states – and by extension the international entities wrought in their image – is the impulse to render both the territory and the population 'legible' to the state and its institutions, allowing land and people to become subject to classification and quantification, processes which themselves require the imposition of standardised categories and units of measurement.[2]

The purpose of seeking such legibility is, of course, to allow states to establish an evidence base that may inform law- and policy-making, the better to serve whatever the state determines to be its strategic interests – typically reducible to the health of the political economy, which is generally deemed to be at once the measure, means, and ends of the state's general activity.

* * *

It is against the backdrop of this global frame of reference, and in the context of this worldwide system of contiguous nation-states that share an operating system of norms and institutions, that we have seen, in recent decades, the concept of anthropogenic global climate change emerge as an issue of popular and political concern, discussed at both the national and international level as an object of law and policy. This timing may be more than simple coincidence; arguably, 'climate change' is itself only conceivable, and indeed, only meaningful, against precisely such a backdrop, and precisely in the context of such an operating system.

It is important to remember that the concept of global climate change is not a directly observable phenomenon, but a statistical abstraction. By definition, the concept refers not to the climate at a point in time, but to a thirty-year rolling average.[3] Additionally, in being a global frame of reference, it further refers not to the climate in one place, but to a worldwide average. As such, to talk of climate change presupposes the existence of both a worldwide standard (or at least comparable standards) of measurement, and – as a prerequisite for even that – a degree of institutional uniformity across the globe that would allow us to even begin to think at that level of abstraction about anything, climate change not least.

[2] James C Scott, *Seeing Like a State: How Certain Schemes to Improve the Human Condition Have Failed* (New Haven, Yale University Press 1992).

[3] Ulrich Cubasch and others, 'Introduction', in IPCC Fifth Assessment Report, *The Physical Science Basis* (Cambridge, Cambridge University Press 2013) 119.

Climate change, in short, is not a concept that has emerged, immaculately conceived, in a cultural or geopolitical vacuum. Rather, it is best understood as a concept that, precisely in being an abstraction, reflects as much the culture of which it is an artefact as it does the natural world of which it is an analysis. The planet has always been there, but humanity having a planetary frame of reference has not. While this planetary frame of reference has provided us a new way of understanding the natural world, it also reveals something of the culture that has produced it, specifically what it believes itself capable of both being, and doing.

* * *

There is a further way in which climate change is inextricably linked to societal context. It is that we care about climate change because we are concerned it will not only change society, but change it in ways that will, on the whole, be unwelcome. Among the many forms such changes might take, those pertaining to the pattern, rate, trajectory and thus nature of human migration are among the most frequently discussed.

The appeal of this particular type of supposed climate-induced societal change is that it is presumed to be relatively 'low-hanging fruit' for state action: of all the varied and complex impacts of climate change on society, it is easy to imagine that the impact on migration will be relatively discernible and discrete. As temperatures rise, the thinking goes, people will flee climate 'hotspots'; changing migration statistics will then confirm this thinking; and as a result, it will then become possible to identify a distinct group of people who may be classified as 'climate migrants'.

Thus quantified and classified, the 'problem' of 'climate migration' would be rendered legible, and thus amenable to the art of government through judiciously wrought policies and laws, whether to mitigate the causes of 'climate migration', adapt to the arrival of 'climate migrants', stop 'climate migrants' coming 'here', or provide humanitarian support for those who have been forced to become 'climate migrants'. Whatever the purpose and politics of engaging the issue, the same set of presumptions are shared by all who do so: (i) that climate will affect migration; (ii) that the nature and scale of this impact may be discovered; and (iii) that this information may be operationalised by states and their institutions. While perhaps not often made explicit in this way, most scholars would likely agree that these have nevertheless been the orienting assumptions behind much of the political and popular interest in 'climate migration'.

Yet, perhaps counter-intuitively, or at least surprisingly, the literature on 'climate migration' is notable less for its conclusions than for how uniformly inconclusive it has been. Whether one is an academic or a practitioner, whether one is a governmental or non-governmental actor, and whether one is interested in migration from a human or national security perspective,[4] reading the literature on 'climate migration' can be disorienting. It is characterised by circular reasoning, a cacophony of categories, and a welter of case studies whose meaning and implication are equivocal at best. Despite all the words written on the topic, the plain fact is that the questions 'who is a climate migrant?' and 'what is climate migration?' have still not been answered.

* * *

In light of all the above, this opening chapter offers a means by which anyone who has experienced a sense of disorientation when reading the empirical or normative literature on 'climate migration' may, hopefully, steady themselves.

Ultimately, the purpose of this chapter is neither to say anything new, nor to simply rehearse things that have long been known. It will not provide a definition of 'climate migration', still less evidence of 'it', nor will the chapter suggest how 'it' might be addressed in law or policy. Rather, the chapter's purpose is to simply help the reader see the issue of 'climate migration' in its full and proper context. Alongside taking into account what we know of the world about which the concept is believed to refer, the chapter also reflects on what we know about ourselves – that is, the people who are interested in generating such concepts. While the chapter will detail the pattern of the *content* of the debate on 'climate migration', it will also set this debate in *context*. The latter is particularly important, as only by doing so can lawyers, policy-makers, and researchers hope to gain not only a clear perspective on the debate, but also a clear sense of their relationship to it.

To this end, section II argues that, no matter what terminology is used, no matter what figures are cited, and no matter what case study is examined, to talk of 'climate migration' is inevitably and necessarily to presume that a clear and distinct causal relationship between whatever we define as 'climate' and whatever we define as 'migration' not only exists, but can be discovered. Furthermore, section II argues that this causal relationship is not sought as an end in itself, but as a means to an end, namely so that governments and institutions can write law and fashion policy in response to the issue.

Section III assesses how well the effort to empirically substantiate the supposed causal nexus has gone. Arguing that it has not gone at all well, section III goes on to suggest why this may be.

Lastly, section IV considers the implications of the arguments of sections II and III for how we think about migration as a specific effect of climate change, how we think about climate change as a general cause of any societal outcomes, and how we think, reflexively, about our own frames of reference, which inform not only our thinking about the previous two issues, but also how we react to them.

[4] It is worth noting that human and national security concerns are not necessarily mutually exclusive.

II. The Centrality of Causality

A. The History of the 'Climate Migration' Concept

The history of the 'climate migration' concept has been well rehearsed and is reasonably well known.[5] However, a few facts are worth repeating and a few patterns worth pointing out.

While a small number of isolated studies were published at a rate of one every decade or so throughout the early to mid-twentieth century,[6] it was only in the late 1970s to 1980s that a steady trickle of papers on the general relationship between environmental factors and human migration began to appear, at a rate of not quite one per year from 1976 to 1988.[7] Initially, this was largely a consequence of the emergence of the modern environmental movement, which in its early years in the 1970s had a strong neo-Malthusian spirit, believing that the greatest risk to society was the possibility of the population outstripping the natural resources available, leading to an ecological crisis.

In the context of a neo-Malthusian frame of reference, human migration in the face of limited resources was seen as a primary source of systemic risk, and thus worthy of study. Furthermore, the neo-Malthusian frame of reference was one that construed migration not just as problematic, but also as aberrant. This is because it adopted – however unwittingly – the sedentary bias of the nation-state itself.[8]

[5] It is also covered in Benoit Mayer, 'De-Conceptualising "Climate Migration"', ch 10 in this volume.

[6] See Harry L Shapiro, *Migration and Environment* (Oxford, Oxford University Press 1939); John R Mather, 'The Effect of Climate on the New World Migration of Primitive Man' (1954) 10(3) *Southwestern Journal of Anthropology* 304; Julian Wolpert, 'Migration as an Adjustment to Environmental Stress' (1966) *Journal of Social Issues* 92, available at doi.org/10.1111/j.1540-4560.1966.tb00552.x.

[7] See Lester R Brown, Patricia L McGrath, and Bruce Stokes, *Twenty-Two Dimensions of the Population Problem* (Washington, DC, World Watch Institute 1976); Larry M Svart, 'Environmental Preference Migration: A Review' (1976) 66(3) *Geographical Review* 314, available at doi.org/10.2307/213888; Philip E Graves, 'A Life-Cycle Empirical Analysis of Migration and Climate, by Race' (1979) 6 *Journal of Urban Economics* 135; Philip E Graves, 'Migration and Climate' (1980) 20(2) *Journal of Regional Science* 227, available at ssrn.com/abstract=1438711; Donald R Haurin, 'The Regional Distribution of Population, Migration and Climate' (1980) 95(2) *The Quarterly Journal of Economics* 293, available at doi.org/10.2307/1885501; Lloyd Timberlake, *Environmental Wars and Environmental Refugees: The Political Background to the Cartagena Convention* (London, Earthscan 1983), cited in Bogumil Terminski, 'Environmentally-Induced Displacement: Theoretical Frameworks and Current Challenges' (Centre d'étude de l'ethnicité et des migrations Research Paper, 2012), available at ssrn.com/abstract=2027858; Essam El-Hinnawi, 'Environmental Refugees' (UNEP 1985); Suhair S Khalil, 'The Socio-Economic and Political Implications on the Environmental Refugees in the Vicinity of Omdurman' (Institute of Environmental Studies 1987) 132; Shridath S Ramphal, 'The Environment and Sustainable Development' (1987) 135(5376) *Journal of the Royal Society of Arts* 879; Jodi L Jacobson, 'Environmental Refugees: A Yardstick of Habitability' (1988) 8(3) *Bulletin of Science, Technology and Society* 257; Richard Black, *Refugees, Environment and Development* (Abingdon, Routledge 1998); Crispin Tickell, 'Environmental Refugees' (London, National Environmental Research Council Annual Lecture, 1989); Jodi L Jacobson, 'Abandoning Homelands', in Lester R Brown (ed), 'State of the World' (Washington, DC, Worldwatch Institute 1989) 59.

[8] The understanding of migration as aberrant and inherently problematic is not a recent phenomenon. As early as 1931, Etienne Dennery claimed that 'appalling visions of a sudden eruption of

According to James Scott, such a bias was not itself natural or inevitable, but rather a product of the state's wish to render populations legible:

> The more I examined efforts at sedentarization, the more I came to see them as a state's attempt to make a society legible, to arrange the population in ways that simplified the classic state functions of taxation, conscription, and prevention of rebellion. Having begun to think in these terms, I began to see legibility as a central problem in statecraft. The pre-modern state was, in many crucial respects, particularly blind; it knew precious little about its subjects, their wealth, their landholdings and yields, their location, their very identity. It lacked anything like a detailed 'map' of its terrain and its people.[9]

From the 1970s until the early 1990s, migration was therefore used as a sort of synecdoche – a narrow case that was presumed to illustrate the broader problem of the consequences of the pressure that population growth was expected, by neo-Malthusians, to put on environmental systems. In 1988, for instance, Jodi Jacobson argued that the (apparent) decline in the planet's habitability was increasingly evidenced by the numbers of 'environmental refugees', the existence of which she insisted ought to be taken as a 'yardstick of habitability'.[10] As James Morrissey has explained:

> Around the time that the term 'environmental refugee' came into use, the environmental lobby was dominated by the conservation paradigm, and the emotive notion of 'environmental refugees' was very likely employed to stir up support for increased efforts at conservation and environmental protection.[11]

By the 1990s, however, the world had changed. The Intergovernmental Panel on Climate Change was formed in 1988 and, with the publication of its first report in 1990, the first step had been taken towards 'a widespread acceptance of "global warming" as the dominant influence' in environmental change.[12] Then, with the collapse of the Soviet Union the following year came a reorientation – in the capitalist West – regarding what was understood to constitute a problem for national security.

Specifically, the 1990s saw a rapid shift away from an exclusive concern with *political threats* (as in a newly unipolar world, and for a period of time now long since over, the Euro-American West faced no credible existential threat from a state actor), towards a concern for *apolitical risks.* It is no coincidence that, in the post-Cold War era, both climate change and migration emerged, separately, as

Asiatic peoples on to the white man's country have haunted the minds of the West since the days of Attila and Genghis Khan'. See Etienne Dennery, *Asia's Teeming Millions and its Problems for the West* (Port Washington, Kennikat Press 1931) 229. Gilles Deleuze and Felix Guattari have commented that 'history is always written from a sedentary point of view and in the name of a unitary State apparatus, at least a possible one, even when the topic is nomads'. See Gilles Deleuze and Felix Guattari, *A Thousand Plateaus: Capitalism and Schizophrenia* (Brian Massumi translation, Minneapolis, University of Minnesota Press 1987) 23.

[9] Scott (n 2) 2.

[10] Jacobson, 'Environmental Refugees' (n 7).

[11] James Morrissey, 'Environmental Change and Forced Migration: A State of the Art Review' (Refugee Studies Centre Background Paper 8, 2009), available at perma.cc/RS9Y-MMU7.

[12] Patricia L Saunders, 'Environmental Refugees: The Origins of a Construct', in Philip Stott and Sian Sullivan (eds), *Political Ecology: Science, Myth, Power* (New York, Arnold 2000) 218.

popular and political concerns. Whereas neither would previously have decided elections in the liberal democratic West, in the decades since, few issues have been able to compete with them in their power to contour and contort the body politic.

The emergence of climate change as a distinct theme of concern, in combination with the geopolitical changes wrought by the end of the Cold War, laid the conditions for scholars and institutions to begin examining the security implications of climate change, and particularly its possible relationship to conflict. Building on the existing (if small) literature on 'environmental refugees' established by the previous neo-Malthusian enthusiasm, this topic rapidly gained a new-found impetus among the security community, vigilantly looking for new challenges as they traversed the wake of the Soviet Union.[13]

Thomas Homer-Dixon, for instance, wrote in 1991 of his fear that environmental degradation would produce 'waves of environmental refugees that spill across borders with destabilizing effects' on both the domestic order and international stability.[14] He later added that 'large population movements caused by environmental stress [will] induce "group identity" conflicts, especially ethnic clashes'.[15] Similarly, writing in the 1990s Norman Myers claimed that 'developed countries cannot isolate themselves from distress and disaster in developing countries', and saw the 'threat' taking the form of 'environmental refugees', who would come to the Organization for Security and Co-operation in Europe (OSCE) countries 'usually illegally'.[16] He emphasised how 'today's stream will surely be regarded as a trickle when compared with the floods that will ensue in decades ahead'.[17] As Patricia Saunders has noted, the term 'environmental refugee' was, in the 1990s, therefore 'deeply embedded in the globalisation agenda of its American originators and contemporary geopolitical preoccupations'.[18]

While the literature on 'climate migration' continued to grow, averaging approximately seven new pieces annually from 1989–2005, in 2006 the number of publications suddenly exploded. From 2006–2017 the average rate of publication

[13] Johan Galtung, 'Global Migration: A Thousand Years' Perspective', in Nicholas Polunin (ed), *Population and Global Security* (Cambridge, Cambridge University Press 1998) 173; Thomas F Homer-Dixon, 'On the Threshold: Environmental Change as Causes of Violent Conflict' (1991) 16(2) *International Security* 76, available at doi.org/10.2307/2539061; Thomas F Homer-Dixon, 'Environmental Scarcities and Violent Conflict: Evidence from Cases' (1994) 19 *International Security* 5, available at doi.org/10.2307/2539147; Thomas F Homer-Dixon and Jessica Blitt (eds), *Ecoviolence: Links among Environmental Population and Security* (Lanham, Rowman & Littlefield, 1999); Norman Myers, 'Environmental Refugees in a Globally Warmed World: Estimating the Scope of What Could Well Become a Prominent International Phenomenon' (1993) 43(11) *Bioscience* 752, available at doi.org/10.2307/1312319; Norman Myers, 'Environmental Refugees' (1997) 19(2) *Population and Environment* 167, available at doi.org/10.1023/A:1024623431924; Norman Myers, 'Environmental Refugees: An Emergent Security Issue' (13th Economic Forum, Prague, 2005); Norman Myers and Jennifer Kent, *Environmental Exodus: An Emergent Crisis in the Global Arena* (Washington, DC, Climate Institute 1995).

[14] Homer-Dixon, 'On the Threshold' (n 13) 77.

[15] ibid 6–7.

[16] Myers, 'Environmental Refugees: An Emergent Security Issue' (n 13) 3–4.

[17] ibid.

[18] Saunders (n 12) 240.

jumped to at least seventeen papers a year – an estimate that is likely very low. Indeed, at the time of writing, according to one frequently updated database, there are at least 1,412 papers on 'climate migration' including 590 empirical case studies, and 147 legal papers, with the vast majority of these having been published in the previous few years.[19]

The determining factor in this 'big bang' in research on 'environmental' or 'climate' migration appears to be, once again, contextual. Prior to 2006, climate change had been regarded as a relatively niche preoccupation, without broad mainstream resonance. Yet, due to a number of factors – not least the release in 2006 of the Oscar-winning documentary *An Inconvenient Truth* and the subsequent awarding of the Nobel Peace Prize jointly to the Intergovernmental Panel on Climate Change (IPCC) and to the documentary's star, Al Gore – climate change 'went mainstream'. In subsequent years, media coverage of climate change only intensified, which has in turn driven interest in 'climate migration'.[20]

Such prominent processes as the 2005 Global Commission for Migration, the September 2006 UN General Assembly High-Level Dialogue on International Migration and Development, and the July 2007 Global Forum on Migration and Development barely mentioned the topic. However, by February 2008, at a UN General Assembly Thematic Debate, it was stated that 'climate change has implications across a broad range of policy issues from the environment, health, security, and migration'.[21] In the same year, Graeme Hugo was able to state that 'environment and international migration and their relationship with development are among the most pressing issues on the contemporary global agenda'.[22] In late 2009, Roger Zetter published a chapter on 'the role of legal and normative frameworks for the protection of environmentally displaced people'.[23] His work is notable for being explicit that his analysis was in relation to those who move due to *climatic variables*, rather than generic environmental change,[24] thereby implicitly recognising that the recent discussion of 'environmental' migrants is in relation to the increasing concern with climate change.

It is against this backdrop that the discussion and concern about the relationship between environmental – and particularly climatic – variables and human migration has gained impetus. It has come to occupy the attention of 'mainstream'

[19] 'Welcome to Climig Database Project!' (Climig, 2023), available at climig.com/#about (last accessed 27 January 2023).

[20] Alexander Betts, 'Substantive Issue-Linkage and the Politics of Migration', in Corneliu Bjola and Markus Kornprobst (eds), *Arguing Global Governance* (Abingdon, Routledge 2010) 85, 91.

[21] '"Addressing Climate Change: The United Nations and the World at Work" Theme, as General Assembly Opens Two-Day Debate at Headquarters' (United Nations, 11 February 2008), available at perma.cc/5K5W-44C8.

[22] Graeme Hugo, 'Migration, Development and Environment' (Workshop on Migration and the Environment: Developing a Global Research Agenda, Munich, 2008) 2.

[23] Roger Zetter, 'The Role of Legal and Normative Frameworks for the Protection of Environmentally Displaced People', in Frank Laczko and Christine Aghazarm (eds), *Migration, Environment and Climate Change: Assessing the Evidence* (International Organization for Migration 2009) 385, 388.

[24] ibid.

epistemic communities, notably those whose work is oriented to, and framing concerns derived from, international institutions such as the International Organisation for Migration (IOM) and the office of the UN High Commissioner for Refugees (UNHCR). These institutions have themselves produced a torrent of publications on the topic.[25]

Today, the 'migration and climate change nexus' may be said to be a highly versatile concept, regularly discussed in combination with myriad other concerns, ranging from health to development; climate mitigation to adaptation; community resilience to vulnerability, loss and damage, disaster and risk; national to human security; mobility to displacement – all 'depending on the speaker'.[26] 'Climate migration' has, in short, become a key element in not only how we see the world, but how we hope to act upon it.

B. The Content of the 'Climate Migration' Concept

Given the topic's currency and the proliferation of research papers exploring it over the last ten to fifteen years, it is surprising that, far from this resulting in clarity, it is leading to growing opacity. It cannot escape the notice of any reader that the object of discussion proves elusive, as evidenced by the panoply of categories and labels that circulate within the discourse, which collectively suggests a semantic uncertainty indicating an area of research ill at ease with itself.

These categories and labels include, but are not limited to, 'environmental refugee', 'environmental migrant', 'environmental displacement', 'climate refugee', 'climate migration', 'climate displacement', 'environmentally induced migration', 'climate induced migration', 'environmental mobility', 'climate mobility', 'climate mobilities', migration or mobility 'in the context of climate change', 'climigration', 'climate migrant-to-be', 'climate change migration', 'climate-forced migration', 'climate-related migration', climate or environmental 'movement', the 'relation between migration and climate change',[27] and the 'climate/migration nexus' or

[25] For IOM publications from the period of 2007–09 alone, see: 'Discussion Note: Migration and Environment' (IOM Ninety-Fourth Session, MC/INF/288, 2007); Graeme Hugo, 'Migration, Development and Environment' (IOM 2008); 'Expert Seminar: Migration and the Environment' (IOM International Dialogue on Migration No 10, 2008); Oli Brown, 'Migration and Climate Change' (IOM World Migration Report Series 2008); Dominik Kniveton and others, 'Climate Change and Migration: Improving Methodologies to Estimate Flows' (IOM World Migration Report Series 2008); Laczko and Aghazarm (n 23); 'Migration, Climate Change and Environmental Degradation' (IOM 2009); 'Compendium on IOM's Activities in Migration, Climate Change, and the Environment' (IOM 2009). For UNHCR from 2006 to 2009, see 'The State of the World's Refugees 2006: Human Displacement in the New Millennium' (UNHCR 2006); Etienne Piguet, 'New Issues in Refugee Research: Climate Change and Forced Migration' (UNHRC Research Paper No 153, 2008); 'Climate Change, Natural Disasters and Human Displacement' (UNHCR Policy Paper, August 2009); 'UNHCR and Climate Change: Involvement, Challenges and Responses' (UNHCR 2009).

[26] Sarah Louise Nash, *Negotiating Migration in the Context of Climate Change: International Policy and Discourse* (Bristol, Bristol University Press 2019) 135.

[27] ibid 6.

'migration and climate change nexus'.[28] One edited collection employed at least seventeen different phrases throughout its pages.[29]

This cacophony of categories provokes some obvious questions. First, are these terms merely synonyms, trading in distinctions without differences? If so, why are so many even required? Or do the terms in fact refer to separate phenomena? And if so, what is the nature of the separation?

Be they a scholar or student, a lawyer or policy-maker, or a governmental or non-governmental actor, anyone looking for answers to these questions in the literature should brace for disappointment. For all the interest in making people in the real world 'legible' to the state, the literature on the topic is a sort of conceptual 'wild west', with little consideration given to reconciling the different terms in circulation across the literature, and sometimes in circulation within a single paper. Where one would wish for clarity of meaning and certainty of data, there is only confusion and chaos. As one French NGO representative laments, in David Durand-Delacre's chapter in this volume, 'the words we were using were very vague, it wasn't very clear between climatic, environmental, migrants, refugees, displaced persons, all of that'.[30]

As such, the use of terms like 'climate', 'environment', 'induced', 'related', 'refugee', 'migration', 'displacement', 'movement', or 'mobility' may be regarded as 'sketchy', in both senses of the word. First, they tend to be used very loosely – to figuratively sketch a theme rather than engage in an analytically literal, exact and unambiguous set of claims which are collectively comprehensive yet mutually exclusive. Second, in as much as their inexactness and ambiguity limits the concepts' analytical value, these characteristics also allow papers that rely on them to, in disguising their own limitations and lacunae, avoid difficult questions and critiques.

As a result of all this, for a reader engaging not only with multiple papers, but sometimes with the very same paper, it is often unclear what the object of study in fact is.[31] Who are the people in question? What is the 'phenomenon' at issue? And ultimately, what does all this literature amount to? What coherent and consistent knowledge can be gleaned from the literature, if there is little clarity regarding whether the publications that make it up are all talking about the same object, and indeed, if the individual pieces do little to spell out what their object in fact may be?

***

There is, however, a way to ground oneself in the face of this cacophony of categories and welter of words. To do so, it is perhaps useful to draw on an analogy

[28] ibid 9.

[29] Jane McAdam (ed), *Climate Change and Displacement: Multidisciplinary Perspectives* (London, Hart Publishing 2010).

[30] Durand-Delacre, 'Obstacles to Action on "Climate Migration"', ch 5 in this volume.

[31] This may be because the writer, too, was not sure what their object was.

with the biological distinction between 'phenotype' and 'genotype'. 'Phenotype' describes an organism's observable characteristics, while the 'genotype' describes the underlying genetic code or structure.

In the case of the discussion at hand, the wide range of terms and labels may be understood as phenotypic – words that are meant to *describe* some observable phenomena in the real world. However, logically speaking, we may also say that, regardless of their surface-level 'phenotypic' variety, all these terms share the same underlying 'genetic' structure. That is, they are all, fundamentally and necessarily, claims to *explain* the world, and specifically, to explain it *causally*.

Whatever the *descriptive* concept, category, label, or term, when the interest is in migration, displacement, or mobility as an outcome of environmental or climatic processes – and no matter whether our intention is to assist migrants or arrest migration, or whether we see migration as a societal pathology, or symptom, or cure – the analysis must necessarily be about *explanation* and causality. Indeed, what could it possibly mean to be interested in distinguishing a 'climate migrant' from any other sort of migrant or person, if the interest does *not* presume that we may determine the causal impact of climate upon migration, exclusive of other impacts? Why, indeed, would we care to talk in those terms – 'climate migration' and the like – if not to understand the causal link between them? To connect the natural environment (inclusive of climate change) and human migration together is, logically speaking, to assume that (i) the former can be distinguished from other 'causes', and (ii) the latter can be distinguished from other 'effects'; and, thus, that we can determine the exclusive causal relationship between these two terms.

As such, when we take an interest in 'climate migration', what we are interested in explaining is a causal relationship. In a sense, the descriptive 'phenotype' ('climate migration'; 'environmental migration'; 'climate mobility', etc) is arbitrary, and of secondary importance to the explanatory 'genetic' claim that is always implied: a concern less for how we phenotypically *describe* the world in a static sense, but how we 'genetically' *explain* its dynamics. Questions of categorisation, still less data, are simply downstream of the triple assumption (i) that causality exists, (ii) that we may discern it, and (iii) that we may then act upon this knowledge.

C. The Context of the 'Climate Migration' Concept

The latter point – that we may act upon a causal understanding of the relationship between climate change and human migration (hereafter 'climate migration') once it has been secured – may be seen as simply a derivation, albeit a welcome one, from the exploration of causality. However, this would be to miss just how central *utility* is to this interest in causality, or rather, just how intrinsic an interest in utility is to the context in which discussing the causality of 'climate migration' has any consequence.

It is important to make explicit that the *interest* is itself not simply an idle one, but one that – if it has any relevance at all – is in relation to a *concern*. As noted at the outset, the reason that climate change has become both a popular and political preoccupation is precisely because it is presumed that it will lead not only to societal changes, but ones that will be unwelcome. A change in not only the quantity but the nature of migration is seen as one consequence among many of climate change, albeit one that has generally been assumed to be relatively straightforward to identify.

In the face of the societal changes that are expected to be wrought by future climate change, and the fear that these changes will constitute a problem for the stability of society, there is – logically enough – an interest in finding solutions for these problems.

With regard to 'climate migration', the literature is populated by various perspectives on the nature of the 'problem'.

First, there are those who are primarily concerned with *climate change* as a pathology. In relation to this, they view migration as either its *symptom* or its *cure*. Those who see migration as a symptom of climate change interpret it as sign of society's *failure to adapt* to climate change, and thus an indication that a cure to climate change is needed. Conversely, those who see migration as a cure for climate change interpret it as itself being a form of *successful adaptation* – a way of coping with the ills of climate change.

Second, there are also those who are primarily concerned with *migration* as a pathology. This view of migration takes two forms. On the one hand, there are those who have a more 'emic' interest in the agency and experience of migrants themselves, regarding migration as a potentially fraught undertaking for the person in question, impinging on their freedoms and infringing on their rights and dignity. On the other hand, there are those whose interest is more 'etic', oriented to structured factors, seeing *emigration* as either a (developmental, often 'brain-drain') problem for migrants' countries of origin, or *immigration* as a challenge to societal stability and even national security for the country of reception.

As has already been outlined, at the heart of all these problems is a belief that a causal relationship exists and can be discovered. Yet these problems do not simply have a presumption relating to their *content*, but also their *context*. That is, in construing them as problems, there is a framing interest in solving them.

To solve such problems, we do not mean to do so in the granular, arbitrary instance of a particular case, nor in the tractionless, abstract instance of a purely theoretical or universal case, but in the context of the actual societal milieu in which we live. Today, this means to talk about life under the prevailing hegemony of the nation-state system. And as such, when we talk of solutions, we are necessarily talking about ones to be found through the collective mechanisms that are available through that system of nation-states and the suite of international institutions that are emergent from them. We must conceive of solutions in this context not because this system is necessarily the best means imaginable to achieve them, but rather because it is the proverbial water we swim in.

If the institutional mechanisms of the state are to act both prudently and defensibly – that is, with intended rather than unintended consequences, and with an effective and efficient use of finite resources in the face of essentially infinite challenges – is it not enough for them to simply know (in this case) that climate change might impact human migration in some general or vague sense. Rather, it is necessary to know the actual nature, modalities, timing, scope, scale, and trajectory of the impact. That is, they require a theory of causality and evidence of 'climate migration' on the basis of that theory in order to model policy responses and to budget for any such responses, regardless of what the response may be and of what view of climate change or migration those responses may serve.[32]

As such, to state that causality is central to the concept of 'climate migration' is not simply a statement about its *content*. It is also a statement about the *context* in which the concept has any utility and practical consequence. As a result, although we can see that the 'phenotypic', descriptive plurality of the 'climate migration' topic may often be confusing, it disguises the 'genetically' monistic nature of all such concepts. They are about causality, or they are about nothing at all. The consequences of this observation are explored in section III.

III. The Paradoxes of Causality

A. The State of the Art on 'Climate Migration'

Section II argued that causality is not only necessarily central and intrinsic to the content of any discussion on the migratory effects of climate change, but that it is also crucial to the actual context in which the topic is discussed with any utility or practical consequence as an object of policy and law.

We may therefore ask how the substantiation of causality by research has gone. The short answer is, quite simply, 'not well'. Indeed, this has been so widely acknowledged that, in November 2019, *Nature Climate Change*, perhaps the leading journal on climate change, published a Special Issue on 'climate migration'. The most prominent paper in this collection, entitled 'Climate Migration Myths', was signed by 31 co-authors, almost all of whom are leading names in the study of the supposed causal linkage.

The paper was notable because its premise was rather startling, at least to those who have not spent much time engaging with the literature on the topic. It began

[32] It is of course inevitably the case that policy is often informed less by evidence than by what is performatively and politically expedient. This does not change the point, however, that the policy-making process – at least in a democratic context where there is an expectation of accountability – gains its legitimacy by the claim to be evidence-based. But in either case, if acquiring an evidence base does not matter, then what purpose does conducting research on 'climate migration' serve? Without an evidence base, the best impact that policy can hope to have is arbitrary, which strictly speaking is no better than doing nothing at all.

by arguing that we need to question, not affirm, the 'assumption that climate change causes mass human migration', because 'migration is not solely driven by climate change' but instead by a 'mix of climatic, socio-economic, cultural and political factors'.[33] It went on to note that 'even when climate change does play a role, it remains difficult to determine the extent of its influence'.[34]

From this, it made clear that 'categorizing climate migrants as distinguishable from "non-climate migrants" is not empirically possible in most, if not all, circumstances. As a consequence, predictions of mass climate-induced migration are inherently flawed'.[35]

In a 2019 monograph, one of the paper's co-authors (and a contributor to this volume),[36] Sarah Louise Nash, further argued that 'no accepted definition of "climate migration" … actually exists',[37] and explained that attempts at 'quantification … give the illusion of a deeper understanding of [causal linkage]', and that such attempts are 'on shaky ground methodologically, and fail to recognise both the multi-causality of migration and … climate change adaptation efforts'.[38] She later noted that there is no 'easily identifiable community of affected people' at the 'centre of the phenomenon'.[39]

While perhaps perplexing for those unfamiliar with this area of research, such claims are rather 'old hat' for those who work within it, and are in keeping with excellent empirical and analytical work done on the topic over the last two decades.[40] Indeed, perhaps the most consistent and clear conclusion of the vast literature on the causal linkage between environmental or climate change and displacement or migration is, precisely, that *nothing* consistent or clear has been, or indeed can be, concluded.

[33] Ingrid Boas and others, 'Climate Migration Myths' (2019) 9 *Nature Climate Change* 901, 902, available at doi.org/10.1038/s41558-019-0633-3.

[34] ibid.

[35] ibid.

[36] Sarah Louise Nash, 'The View from the Fortress: European Governance Perspectives on Climate Change and Migration', ch 6 in this volume.

[37] Nash (n 26) 8.

[38] ibid 6.

[39] ibid 137.

[40] Giovanni Bettini, 'Climate Barbarians at the Gate? A Critique of Apocalyptic Narratives on "Climate Refugees"' (2013) 45 *Geoforum* 63, available at doi.org/10.1016/j.geoforum.2012.09.009; Alexander Betts, 'Survival Migration: A New Protection Framework' (2010) 16 *Global Governance* 361, available at www.jstor.org/stable/29764952; Alexander Betts and A Pilath, 'The Politics of Causal Claims: The Case of Environmental Migration' (2017) 20(4) *Journal of International Relations and Development* 782, available at doi.org/10.1057/s41268-016-0003-y; Richard Black, 'Environmental Refugees: Myth or Reality?' (UNHCR Working Paper No 34, 2001); Stephen Castles, 'Environmental Change and Forced Migration: Making Sense of the Debate' (UNHCR Working Paper No 70, 2002); Andrew Baldwin and Francois Gemenne, 'The Paradoxes of Climate Change and Migration', in *World Social Science Report* (Paris, UNESCO 2013) 265; Betsy Hartmann, 'Rethinking Climate Refugees and Climate Conflict: Rhetoric, Reality and the Politics of Policy Discourse' (2010) 22(2) *Journal of International Development* 233, available at doi.org/10.1002/jid.1676; Ilan Kelman, 'Imaginary Numbers of Climate Change Migrants?' (2019) 8(5) *Social Sciences* 131; Benoit Mayer, *The Concept of Climate Migration: Advocacy and its Prospects* (Cheltenham, Edward Elgar 2016).

Substantive conclusions, when they are made at all, typically take the form of tautology: claims to the effect that some people will leave 'hotspots' and some will not;[41] that 'people are as likely to migrate *to* places of environmental vulnerability as *from* these places';[42] that 'environmental change is equally likely to make migration less possible as more probable';[43] that there is a continuum of forced to voluntary migration in the face of climate change;[44] and that immobility matters as much as mobility.[45] Such claims may all be true, but they are not useful. They are true only to the extent that they are tautological truths, covering all the possible options, without helping us decide which option – or projection – they entail in any particular case.

All this matters, of course, because – as has already been noted – if policy or law is to be written about migrants or displacees from climate change, it is first important to understand *who* such people are, or would be, as opposed to who they are not, or would not be. Indeed, Nash makes this case persuasively, writing how these problems of ambiguous knowledge 'make the nexus between migration and climate change difficult to pin down, making it in turn incredibly difficult to address precise but wide-reaching policies'.[46] This matters, she argues, because 'if policy making is to provide "solutions", a known phenomenon must be present to be solved'.[47] Indeed, she goes so far as to say that a 'recognition of a relation between migration and climate change is foundational for the construction of a policy-making discourse, for if no relation exists … why is a policy response called for?'[48]

There are many reasons as to why causality has eluded the best efforts of empirical research, and the most careful wordsmithery of those engaged in coining categories and honing definitions. Among those, four reasons are worth noting.[49]

First, 'global climate change' is something that is, by definition, aggregate and abstract. It is, as the name implies, a global average, and, in terms of the 'change' it is concerned with, it is meaningful only on a 30-year rolling average, as already noted.[50] Determining the causal linkage between an aggregate generalisation and particular societal circumstances, such as migration, is not impossible so much as

[41] Jon Barnard and Michael Webber, 'Migration as Adaptation: Opportunities and Limits', in McAdam (n 29) 37, 40.

[42] Foresight, 'Migration and Global Environmental Change: Final Project Report' (London, Government Office for Science 2011) 9.

[43] ibid.

[44] Graeme Hugo, 'Climate Change-Induced Mobility and the Existing Migration Regime in Asia and the Pacific', in McAdam (n 29) 9, 12.

[45] Boas and others (n 33).

[46] Nash (n 26) 4–5.

[47] ibid 9.

[48] ibid 6.

[49] The text of the next three paragraphs is reproduced with permission from the author's chapter in Benoit Mayer and Alexander Zahar (eds), *Debating Climate Law* (Cambridge, Cambridge University Press, 2021) 215.

[50] Cubasch and others (n 3).

a category mistake. The two simply do not exist on the same plane of reasoning, still less in a manner that may be subject to coherent causal articulation.

Second, the causality problem in the study of migration in general has long proven a bugbear to hardened migration scholars. One of the few theoretical conclusions of migration studies has been a negation: that linear causality – between any 'driver' and any migration outcome – is largely a myth.[51] 'Causality' – to the extent the word has meaning in the context of human decision-making, for we are animate beings with conscious minds – is always 'complex', which is often used simply as a euphemism for the less edifying admission that 'we do not know'. That migration studies have, through empirical testing, over and over again shown the paucity of any positive migration 'theory', betrays less a problem with the data, or even with the methodology per se – rather, it betrays the category mistake of assuming that the movement of people – let us call them terrestrial bodies – can be studied in the same way as an astronomer studies celestial ones. Causal determinism by definition leaves little room for free will, a point that will be returned to in section III.B.

Third, since the 1980s,[52] perhaps the single most profound and substantiated conclusion of disaster-risk-reduction scholarship is that 'there is no such thing as a natural disaster'. Rather, there are natural hazards, but any societal outcome is dependent on social, political, and economic conditions – so-called 'social root causes'.[53] The implication is that we cannot simply reason, in a linear, causal manner, from an environmental (let alone climatic) 'independent variable' to the effects on a dependent societal outcome – the thing that we wish to respond to with law.[54]

Fourth, simply to talk of 'migration' is not nearly as straightforward as might be presumed. There is, first, the basic 'Sorites Paradox'[55] problem of delineating between 'migrant' and 'non-migrant' (for the first concept logically cannot exist without its antithesis). After how many miles travelled and how many days away from their home is it correct to classify someone as a migrant? The answer, of course, is that there is no 'objective' answer to this question – it is entirely arbitrary. If and when a decision is made, it is not in relation to some objective change in

[51] See Gunvor Jónsson, '"Climate Migration"? Empirical Insights and Conceptual Cautions from Political Ecology and Migration Studies', ch 3 in this volume.

[52] Although, as with all good ideas, the insight about disasters being 'socially constructed' was hardly new. Voltaire famously argued something similar in his poem responding to the 1755 Lisbon Earthquake. See Voltaire, 'Poème sur le désastre de Lisbonne' (1756).

[53] Ben Wisner and others, *At Risk: Natural Hazards, People's Vulnerability and Disasters*, 2nd edn (Abingdon, Routledge 2003).

[54] This point is explored more in Ilan Kelman, 'Climate Change–Disaster–Migration: Manufacturing a Nexus', ch 2 in this volume.

[55] The Sorites Paradox, also known as the Paradox of the Heap, is a logical argument that challenges the concept of gradual change by posing the question of how many grains of sand make a heap; starting with a large number of grains and removing one grain at a time, it is hard to determine at what point it stops being a heap. This paradox illustrates the difficulties in establishing clear boundaries and definitions in certain concepts, particularly when dealing with vague or ambiguous terms. In this case, 'migrant' is the equivalent of 'heap'.

condition, but a change in the inherently subjective attitude of the classifying body, typically the nation-state. Crossing an international border, and remaining across it for a set period of time, may lead to the designation 'migrant'. Yet, this is an entirely *political* designation. To study migration as a 'distinct phenomena' is not, therefore, to study something that exists, ontologically, independent of the state. Rather it is to study people under, or in reaction to, a regime of classification that is itself an expression and manifestation of the state. To presume otherwise is to engage in what some scholars have termed 'methodological nationalism' whereby one assumes that 'the nation-state is the natural social and political form of the modern world'.[56]

The problem of understanding 'migration' is not, however, simply ontological, but also more profoundly metaphysical. Indeed, since at least the 1990s anthropologists have observed that common perceptions of migration tend to be underpinned by a 'metaphysics of sedentarism',[57] with one having argued that while it is often assumed that 'populations used to be immobile and have been uprooted by economic or environmental forces', in reality there is 'much evidence to challenge this sedentary bias' and that we should 'view population movement as the norm rather than the exception'.[58] Strip away the nation-state context in which we are now embedded, and it is perhaps true to say that 'the history of the world is unavoidably a history of mobility'[59] – and that, as such, 'if we think historically about the human condition it might seem that we should really have a stasis studies rather than a migration or mobilities studies'.[60]

These arguments have two main implications. First, we realise that what we mean by 'migration' is a social construct of the state, and thus one that denies any truly objective understanding of migration as one variable impacted by some other variables, climate not least. Second, and perhaps more importantly, we realise that the very interest we have to study migration at all – an interest that presumes it is a problem to be solved – reveals less about migration than it does about ourselves. It reveals that we have adopted wholesale the unnatural frame of reference of the nation-state, and in doing so, see in migration an aberration to be solved, rather than recognising that, perhaps, the aberration that needs explaining is precisely our own frame of reference, informed as it is by methodological nationalism.

[56] Andreas Wimmer and Nina G Schiller, 'Methodological Nationalism and Beyond: Nation-State Building, Migration and the Social Sciences' (2002) 2(4) *Global Networks* 301, available at doi.org/10.1111/1471-0374.00043.

[57] Akhil Gupta and James Ferguson (eds), *Anthropological Locations: Boundaries and Grounds of a Field Science* (Berkeley, University of California Press 1997) 6.

[58] Arjan de Haan, 'Livelihoods and Poverty: The Role of Migration – A Critical Review of the Migration Literature' (1999) 36(2) *Taylor & Francis Journals* 1, 7.

[59] Bridget Anderson, 'New Directions in Migration Studies: Towards Methodological De-Nationalism' (2019) 7(36) *Comparative Migration Studies* 1, 1, available at doi.org/10.1186/s40878-019-0140-8.

[60] Nina G Schiller and Noel B Salazar, 'Regimes of Mobility across the Globe' (2013) 39(2) *Journal of Ethnic and Migration Studies* 183, available at doi.org/10.1080/1369183X.2013.723253.

For all these reasons, among others, it is little surprise that the causal relation, which is essential to the 'climate migration' concept by dint of both its ontological content and normative context, has not been discovered. The problem is less a matter of data or definitions, or of metrics or methodologies, but, more profoundly, to do with our frames of reference; answers are not forthcoming because we are asking the wrong questions.

B. The Causal Compulsions

Given the widely acknowledged problems with causality, we might reasonably ask what the general, legal, and policy literature on 'climate migration' is saying, for it is clear the causal problem has not proven a roadblock to writing on the topic. Indeed, the literature only seems to proliferate.

As explored by this author in a number of other pieces,[61] in lieu of saying anything clearer about causality, the literature typically lapses into six tendencies that allow it to skirt the causal problem.

One has already been outlined in the previous section: the tendency to resort to logical tautologies. To the extent to which the literature has positive conclusions, it is this. However, as noted, and much like the tautology 'it is raining or it is not', while tautologies are necessarily true statements, they are not useful. To say 'it is raining or it is not' is little help if deciding whether I need an umbrella.

Another common tendency is, in a sense, the opposite of tautology. While tautology is a claim that must, logically, be true, contradiction must, logically, be false. Contradictions are rampant across the literature, if we care to see them. For instance, if a paper at one point states that 'there is no direct connection between climate change and human migration', but goes on to talk of 'the issue', 'this issue', 'this highly complex issue', 'such movements', 'the movement', 'people … deeply affected', 'those affected', 'the matter', and 'how this type of mobility unfolds', or if it states something like 'there is a governance gap to fill, even if the direct cause is disputable', then the paper is clearly caught in contradiction.[62] How can we at once

[61] Calum TM Nicholson, 'Climate Change and the Politics of Causal Reasoning: The Case of Climate Change and Migration' (2014) 180(2) *Geographical Journal* 151, available at doi.org/10.1111/geoj.12062; Calum TM Nicholson, '"Climate-Induced Migration": Ways Forward in the Face of an Intrinsically Equivocal Concept', in Benoit Mayer and Francois Crépeau (eds), *Research Handbook on Climate Change, Migration and the Law* (Cheltenham, Elgar Publishing 2017) 49; Calum TM Nicholson, 'A Due Diligence Approach to Buzzwords for Disaster Risk Reduction including Climate Change Adaptation', in Ilan Kelman, Jessica Mercer, and Jean-Christophe Gaillard (eds), *The Routledge Handbook of Disaster Risk Reduction Including Climate Change Adaptation* (Abingdon, Routledge 2017); Calum TM Nicholson, '"Climate Mobility" Is Not a Proper Subject of Research and Governance', in Mayer and Zahar (eds) (n 49) 215; Calum TM Nicholson, 'Review of Negotiating Migration in the Context of Climate Change: International Policy and Discourse' (2021) 34(4) *Journal of Refugee Studies* 4594, available at doi.org/10.1093/jrs/feab087.

[62] Ingrid Boas, '"Climate Mobility" is a Proper Subject of Research and Governance', in Mayer and Zahar (eds) (n 49) 206.

state that, as Gertrude Stein famously put it, 'there is no there there', and then also talk about 'it' as if there was, in fact, something there?

The third and fourth tendencies mirror each other, much as tautology and contradiction do. One is the temptation to lapse into arbitrariness. It is one thing to ask, in a given context, 'what are the causes of migration?', which is a question free from bias towards one cause or another. However, to ask, in the same context, 'what are the causes of climate migration?' is to put the cart before the horse, for it is to presume we know the cause. The results will likely be arbitrary, with little capacity to be generalised to other cases.[63] The other tendency is not to make arbitrarily specific claims, but claims that are so general that they might be applied to any case at all. To state, for instance, that 'there is a causal connection between climate change and population movement, but this is often not direct and is mediated by a range of factors, playing out in different ways',[64] is to say something so general that it might be applied to any and all cases of migration. In its sheer inclusiveness, it loses all analytical utility.

The fifth tendency is when, on encountering the causal problem, there is simply a call for 'more' or 'better' research. However, in their lack of detail as to what either would entail (how would more research overcome a patterned problem? What would be better research?), it would seem that such admonitions constitute less a guide to what we ought to have in the future, and more a comment on what we have not had to date; far from a blueprint for success, they are an admission that we have none.

The final tendency is precisely what was outlined in section II.B – the laundering of the causal problem through a proliferation of new terminology. As noted, the literature is a chaotic confusion of overlapping concepts. Looking longitudinally at the literature, it is quite clear that, over the years and decades, once one concept or label has worn out its welcome (due, of course, to the causal lacuna at its heart), the literature seems to have simply adopted a loose synonym. Thus, 1990s discussions of 'environmental refugees' gave way to 'environmental migration', which in turn shifted to 'climate migration' (a spectrum of more hedged versions such as 'climate-induced migration' or 'migration in the context of climate change'), and has been followed by, most recently, a strong turn to 'climate mobility'.

The latter – 'climate mobility' – warrants some more detailed consideration, as the way it is being used highlights the intensity of the illogic that the persistence of the causal problem is increasingly pushing the 'climate migration' literature into.

As already noted, the 2019 comment piece in *Nature Climate Change*, 'Climate Migration Myths', took as its premise that it is 'not empirically possible in most, if not all, circumstances' to identify 'climate migrants'.[65] It is particularly interesting, therefore, that the paper goes on to call for a new research agenda that 'moves

[63] See EACH-FOR project, 'Preliminary findings from the EACH-FOR project on Environmentally Induced Migration', Environmental Change and Forced Migration Scenarios Report (2008).
[64] ibid 208.
[65] Boas and others (n 33) 902.

beyond simplistic assumptions and more accurately advances knowledge of the nexus between human mobility and climate change'. In doing so, it proposes six priorities for research.

This list begins promisingly, calling for funding to support work that 'interrogates, rather than simply reinforces', the assumption that there is a discernible causal relationship between climate change and migration. It makes the important points – long established by migration scholars – that migration is always multicausal; that isolating the influence of climate on migration is always difficult; and that it is therefore, as noted above, not empirically possible in most, if not all, circumstances to identify 'climate migrants'. This is all in keeping with excellent analytical work done on the topic in the last two decades.[66]

But conceptual difficulties – which will be familiar in their structure to anyone who has worked on this topic – set in with the second priority, when the paper states that, in the face of the diversity of ways in which people 'do or do not become mobile in response to a changing climate', the term 'migration' should be avoided, and 'research should shift its attention from climate migration to climate mobilities'. As a *negatory* agenda, this does constitute a form of progress: we should indeed try to wean ourselves from phrases like 'climate migration' which are – in their reductive, simplistic, and causally mechanical framing – doctrinaire and technocratic abstractions, not to mention formulations that seem to beg the causal question.

But as a *positive* agenda, what in practice would fulfilling it entail, and to what end? The piece defines 'mobility' as encompassing short and long-term movement; near and long-distance movement; movement to and from a particular location; the impacts of such movement on places of origin, transit, and destination; the realities of multicausality; and immobility. That is, it avoids the ethical and epistemological pitfalls inherent in the specific, exclusive, and thus politically loaded concept of 'migration' by instead being so general and inclusive that it is *by definition* neutral. But if, *reductio ad absurdum*, everything is amplified, nothing is clarified. What 'signal' is being discerned if research views all the 'noise' with complete neutrality, thus assuming it is *all* signal? Who, ultimately, is such neutral research for? What can it hope to even reveal? What end does it serve, if it is not simply an end in itself – ie research for its own sake?

As the third priority, the piece states that 'research should focus on whether (and if so, how) climate change will alter existing interconnections and human mobility patterns under different scenarios of global warming and mitigation and adaptation policies, and how these are in turn shaped by existing mobilities'.[67] But given that the paper began, in its introduction, by rejecting the grand, totalising causal theories of 'climate displacees', 'climate migrants', and other 'climate

[66] Bettini (n 40); Betts (n 40); Betts and Pilath (n 40); Black (n 40); Castles (n 40); 'Migration and Global Environmental Change' (n 43); Gemenne and Baldwin (n 40); Hartmann (n 40); Kelman (n 40); James Morrissey, 'Rural-Urban Migration in Ethiopia' (2008) 31 *Forced Migration Review* 28; Mayer (n 40).

[67] Boas and others (n 33) 902.

refugees' as propounded by policy actors, one is left wondering what is meant by 'whether (and if so, how)' and, indeed, what is meant by 'alter'. Is the purpose of this to fulfil the interrogatory goal as outlined in the first? In which case, why it is separate? Or is it – as seems evident – proposing its own substantive, positivistic research agenda? If the latter, it seems to in fact imply an empirical project that is at least as ambitious and totalising as anything that has gone before, and one which will be just as fraught with causal conundrums as the research on 'climate migration' which it seeks to move beyond. How, after all, can we talk of the way in which climate change will 'alter' mobility patterns without returning to the problem of causation? There is a real risk here of the paper seeking – like a great deal of the literature on this topic – to *deny* the possibility of isolating a causal relationship between 'climate' and 'migration', while simultaneously talking in terms that *imply* this very possibility.

As its fourth priority, the paper then emphasises the need for 'research that better accounts for the non-linear complexity of mobility in the context of climate change and social change', to counteract the 'linear "crisis" and "mass" migration assumptions' – built on attempts to quantify and predict 'climate migration' – that are widespread in the news media and policy discourses.[68] But if the idea of 'climate migration' is indeed to be avoided, and if the intentionally general phrase 'context of climate change' is used to keep the causal relationship between 'climate change' and 'mobility' vague, it does raise the question of why the study of the climate's societal impact has been delimited to that on 'mobility'? Indeed, why have researchers privileged 'climate' as an influence on 'mobility'? Surely, by the inclusive logic of 'climate mobilities', climate affects everything, not just migration; and mobility (to the extent this refers to movement rather than just society in general) is affected by everything, not just climate? What, therefore, does the 'climate mobility' framework advance, in terms of a positive project for understanding the societal impacts of climate change? Again, what is gained and what is lost when we amplify everything?

These problems echo through the remaining two research priorities. The fifth seeks 'to better include affected populations in climate mobilities research'. Given the explicitly inclusive use of 'mobility', who does this involve? Or rather, who does it *not* involve? Who is excluded from a phrase as general as 'populations involved in mobility associated with climate change'?[69]

The final research priority states that 'research on climate mobilities needs to shift part of its focus from climate-sensitive sending areas to destination areas'.[70] It goes on to talk of 'such mobility'. First, what areas are not climate sensitive? Second, given that it was already established, in the first research priority, that it is not possible to isolate a 'climate migrant' from a 'non-climate migrant', what exactly does it mean to talk of 'such mobility'?

[68] ibid.
[69] ibid.
[70] ibid.

As a result, we can see that the concept of 'climate mobility' amounts to one of two things, neither of which can be said to constitute real progress. That is, it is either simply another synonym for 'climate migration', concerned – as all labels before it – with causality; or it is not strictly about climate as a cause, nor about migration as an effect at all, but about whatever arbitrary focus we may care to choose. If the latter, what purpose does it serve, and indeed, what relevance or relation does it have to the original concern with the effects of climate change on society, still less on migration?

C. Why the Compulsion to Think Causally?

To a great extent, the most interesting – and perhaps most pressing – challenge with the 'climate migration' literature is less to understand that the search for causality is a wild goose chase, but rather to understand why so many seasoned researchers, lawyers, and policy-makers find themselves pursuing it even when they tacitly acknowledge that what they are chasing is, in fact, a wild goose. What compels them, repeatedly, to do so?

Various theories have been offered to explain this.

One is what we might call the 'intellectual self-trading' critique, which holds that researchers, constantly in need of funding, and wishing to be able to present themselves as 'policy-relevant', are faced with perverse incentives to publish despite the recurring pattern of problems, leading them to gloss over the causal problem, or suggest it may simply be resolved by more research. As such, in 'creating knowledge [in response] to … calls they have had a hand in creating',[71] policy-relevant researchers may be said to constitute less an epistemic community than an epistemic ouroboros. By this argument, the continuing pursuit of 'climate migration' simply reflects professional, albeit cynical, self-interest – an argument that has been made by Benoit Mayer[72] and Sarah Nash,[73] among others.

A second theory is that the continuing interest in the topic reflects systems of structural racism, whether conscious or unconscious. Andrew Baldwin, in particular, has argued (both in this volume and elsewhere)[74] that the 'climate migration' concept operates as a racist and racialising category, serving the interests of hegemonic networks of power to maintain a Eurocentric world order.

[71] Nash (n 26) 180.

[72] Benoit Mayer, 'Who are "Climate Refugees"? An Inquiry into Post-Truth Academic Politics', in Simon Behrman and Avidan Kent (eds), *'Climate Refugees': Beyond the Legal Impasse?* (Abingdon, Routledge 2018) 89; Mayer (n 5).

[73] Sarah Louise Nash, 'Knowing Human Mobility in the Context of Climate Change: The Self-Perpetuating Circle of Research, Policy, and Knowledge Production' (2018) 4 *movements. Journal for Critical Migration and Border Regime Studies* 67.

[74] Andrew Baldwin, 'Race, Migration, and Climate Change: A Cautionary Note', ch 7 in this volume. See also, for example, Andrew Baldwin, 'Climate Change, Migration, and the Crisis of Humanism' (2017) 8(3) *Wiley Interdisciplinary Reviews: Climate Change* 1, available at doi.org/10.1002/wcc.460;

While it may be that either, or perhaps both, theories have some merit – at least in particular cases, or ranges of cases – neither can explain *all* cases. This is for the simple reason that many – likely most – researchers are neither cynical nor prejudiced (or an unwitting tool of prejudice) but operate carefully and entirely in good faith, and nevertheless find themselves deeply invested in the 'climate migration' theme.

Rather than the problem being scientific (ie problems of insufficient data and inadequate definition), or political-economic (ie a problem of the 'academic-institutional complex' and regimes of power), perhaps it is fundamentally a cultural one – of how we see the world and understand our relationship to it.

Specifically, perhaps it is a problem rooted in the organising metaphor that is implicit in the causal model of reasoning which informs how our institutions, in the age of the nation-state, understand the world that they wish – and we wish them – to act upon. In the case of the interest in 'climate migration', the implicit metaphor would seem to be a *classical mechanical* one, inclusive of assumptions that are essentially social scientific versions of Newton's three Laws of Motion: first, a sedentary assumption that a person will not migrate unless acted on by an external force (in this case, climate change); second, an assumption that the rate of migration will be directly proportional to the magnitude of that force; and, third, an assumption that any change in human migration patterns will be proportionately disruptive and thus unwelcome for the society that receives it.

While seemingly widespread, this mechanical metaphor has always been inappropriate for understanding migration, not only in its particulars but also in its general spirit. The general problem is precisely that it is spiritless: it is a dead model that assumes that people are simply terrestrial bodies that we may categorise, model, and predict as we do celestial ones; it is a monistic framework that assumes people are a unity – sharing a common outlook, compelled by the same desires and fears, and in receipt of the same facts – rather than a plurality with endlessly divergent mores, motives, and forms of meaning. As such, it is a metaphor founded not simply on a misunderstanding, but an exclusion, of everything that makes us human – the particular, the uncertain, the subjective, and the contradictory.

It would seem that to talk of migration in the context of climate change is always and inescapably to talk from within such a mechanical metaphor, for any such discussion always implies, in the end, and as has been argued, a concern for causality. Herein lies the paradox at the heart of literature on 'climate migration': to speak coherently on the subject requires one to adopt the metaphor; but to adopt the metaphor is to retreat into an abstract realm bearing little relation to the real world and the lives of real people.

For at least a decade, this paradox has been something of an unwelcome elephant in the corner of any conference room where 'climate migration' has been discussed. While many researchers seem to recognise its existence, few are willing to formally and publicly contemplate its full implications. Yet the paradox is no less conspicuous for being ignored, and constitutes perhaps the most profound and pressing issue facing research on the topic, regardless of whether that research is empirical or normative.[75]

Ironically, in the forlorn pursuit of this classical mechanical model of causal relationships between climate change and societal outcomes, and migration specifically, the literature exhibits reasoning far more analogous to *quantum mechanics*. Famously, in quantum mechanics, a system can be in two states simultaneously, known as a superposition. Similarly, in discussions of 'climate migration', researchers, lawyers, and policy-makers often find themselves trapped in 'superpositional' or 'quantum' reasoning, whereby they simultaneously embrace contradictory positions, such as those illustrated above in section III.B. Such 'superpositions', in being contradictions, reveal little about the world. However, once exposed, and given their ubiquity, they do perhaps reveal to us something about ourselves and how we think, that we may always be experiencing but rarely notice. Noticing them has some obvious implications, which will be explored in section IV.

IV. The Implications of Causal Paradox

Section II established the centrality of causality in any claim about 'climate migration' – not just in relation to its 'truth-content', but also its 'use-context'. Indeed, section II's argument implied that one cannot exist without the other: a discussion of the subject's content (the ontological preoccupation of empirical researchers) cannot meaningfully occur without a consideration of its contextual purpose; and for there to be a meaningful discussion of contextual purpose and use (the normative preoccupation of legal scholars and policy-makers), there must be some consideration of the issue's ontological status.

Section III then assessed how the search for the epistemic 'holy grail' of causality has gone. As explained, and by the field's own admission, it has not gone terribly well. Section III went on to argue that this was not simply an empirical or conceptual problem that may be solved by a higher quantity of data[76] or a higher quality

Andrew Baldwin, Christiane Fröhlich, and Delf Rothe, 'From Climate Migration to Anthropocene Mobilities: Shifting the Debate' (2019) 14(3) *Mobilities* 289, available at doi.org/10.1080/17450101.2019.1620510; Andrew Baldwin, *The Other of Climate Change: Racial Futurism, Migration, Humanism* (Lanham, Rowman & Littlefield 2022).

[75] The previous four paragraphs were first published in Calum TM Nicholson, 'Review of Negotiating Migration in the Context of Climate Change: International Policy and Discourse' (2021) 34(4) *Journal of Refugee Studies* 4594, available at doi.org/10.1093/jrs/feab087.

[76] It is worth noting that, in the 1990s and 2000s, the 'climate migration' debate was divided, according to some scholars (Astri Suhrke, 'A Crisis Diminished: Refugees in the Developing World' (1993) 48(2) *International Journal* 191, available at doi.org/10.1177/002070209304800202; Morrissey (n 11)), into a case of 'maximalists' versus 'minimalists'. This debate hinged not on whether 'climate migration' or 'environmental migration' was identifiable, but on the numbers of people who would be displaced by climate change. That is, both 'sides' assumed that causality was identifiable. As such, they arguably had more in common than they had apart, and this commonality was a presumption that the literature itself does not seem to bear out or sustain.

of definition, but rather a problem rooted in the 'classical mechanical' frame of reference that lies implicit in any discussion of 'climate migration', and which is not suitable for understanding human behaviour – migration not least.

In light of these arguments, we might reasonably – and rightly – ask what the implications are for law, policy, and research. The answer will be given on three levels, addressing the implications of the chapter's arguments for how we understand (i) human migration as a *specific effect* of climate change; (ii) climate change as a *general cause* of societal effects; and (iii) the preoccupation of nation-state institutions with such causes and effects.

A. Implications for Thinking about the Causes of Migration

As noted at the introduction of this chapter, the appeal of 'climate migration' lies, in no small part, in the presumption that it is presumed to be a more or less self-evident and straightforward consequence of climate change. In the face of the topic's intrinsic and therefore inescapable problems and paradoxes, scholars and practitioners tend to react in one of three ways.

The first is that they do not seem to notice that there are problems and paradoxes. This is more typically the case when writers are not specialists on migration, are encountering the issue only to the extent to which it intersects with their own primary themes of interest, and (from their citations) do not seem to have read much of the literature. For instance, in a recent book entitled *Climate Changed: Refugee Border Stories and the Business of Misery*, having cited a single[77] (and contested)[78] paper implicating climate change in Syria's 2007–10 drought, the author – a criminologist – immediately leaps to the conclusion that 'man-made climate change is therefore a prominent factor in people displacement, and this needs to be acknowledged'.[79] Later, referencing this earlier statement, he claims that in it he had shown 'that the mass exodus we are now witnessing from rural areas to urban areas is related to … climate change',[80] a claim about which, in the Syrian context, there is debate, and from which it would, at the very least, be bold to generalise. Furthermore, reviewing the book's approximately 400 citations, only one appears to relate in any way to the literature on 'climate migration'.

[77] Colin P Kelley and others, 'Climate Change in the Fertile Crescent and Implications of the Recent Syrian Drought' (2015) 112(11) *Earth, Atmospheric, and Planetary Sciences* 3241, available at doi.org/10.1073/pnas.1421533112.

[78] Jan Selby and others, 'Climate Change and the Syrian Civil War Revisited' (2017) 60 *Political Geography* 232–44.

[79] Daniel Briggs, *Climate Changed: Refugee Border Stories and the Business of Misery* (Abingdon, Routledge, 2021) 4.

[80] ibid 51.

His approach is not uncommon among academics,[81] and entirely common in media coverage of 'climate migration'.[82]

As Gregory White makes clear in this volume,[83] there is a danger in scholars, journalists, advocates, politicians, and creative artists engaging with the 'climate migration' concept in an uncritical manner which presumes that 'they' are a discrete and discernible category of people. As he argues, doing so can have many unintended consequences, not least provoking unfounded fear of phantasmagoric 'climate migrants', or worse, inciting prejudice against actual and ordinary migrants by assuming they are driven by climate.

The second response is that scholars and practitioners do recognise the problems and paradoxes of the literature, and quietly retreat from the topic entirely. In chapter five, David Durand-Delacre gives examples of this among policy-makers in France.[84]

The third response is that scholars and practitioners recognise the challenges intrinsic to the topic, yet continue to talk and write about it regardless. This necessarily immures them a sort of epistemic limbo, by which they are (as noted earlier) required to think in classical mechanical terms if they are to talk coherently about 'climate migration', and yet in doing so are no longer talking about something in the real world. Admittedly, some writers seem entirely unperturbed by this, and their consequential reliance on superpositional thinking, perhaps for reasons attributable to the intellectual self-trading critique outlined earlier, and a primary concern for professional positioning. Yet, for the less cynical, this epistemic limbo is surely a rather dispiriting place to be stuck.

Stated plainly, none of these reactions surely hold much appeal. Yet, there is perhaps an alternative. That is, rather than attempt to *solve* the question 'what is climate migration', we might instead try to *dissolve* it, by asking why we are lured into it.

This suggestion may appear to be of little utility, and perhaps even an unhealthily reflexive endeavour. It might well be if one's only goal has been to work on 'climate migration'. Yet, it is worth remembering that, although 'climate migration' may be the thematic focus, it is of interest precisely because it is held to speak to broader, contextual considerations of either the effects of climate or the causes of migration. Put another way, research on 'climate migration' is never an end in itself, but merely a means to one (or both) of those two broader ends.

To have concluded that we cannot render 'climate migration' a policy-operable category that may guide action in the real world does not itself constitute a real-world problem, nor a limit on our ability to deal with such problems. First, it is not

[81] See Thomas Nail, 'The Climate-Migration-Industrial Complex', *Public Seminar* (10 January 2020), available at perma.cc/A78L-MWHP.

[82] For a recent example, see Gaia Vince, 'Climate Migration is Coming', *Wired* (11 January 2023), available at www.wired.com/story/migration-climate-environment-refugees.

[83] Gregory White, 'The "Others" in John Lanchester's *The Wall*', ch 4 in this volume.

[84] David Durand-Delacre, 'Obstacles to Action on "Climate Migration": A Story of Persistent Analytical and Political Ambiguity', ch 5 in this volume.

a problem because the entire point of the above critique is that 'there is no there there': there *is* no problem we can construe *as* 'climate migration'. It is not a case that 'climate migrants' exist 'out there', and we have failed to find them. It is not an *empirical constituency* in search of being *seen* by the state as a *conceptual representation*, but a *conceptual construct* in search of an *empirical constituency*.

The problem has been that our metaphors and frames of reference have given rise to a concept that has bewitched us with what Jacques Derrida called a 'metaphysics of presence', in which we delude ourselves that our concepts must have some present, stable 'thing' or substance in the real world to which they refer. Second, and as a result of the first point, simply to say that we cannot speak usefully about 'climate migration' does not mean we cannot address real problems in the world. The only implication is that the concept of 'climate migration' was not aiding us in addressing them.

In research, there is a danger in thinking that the only imperative is to produce positive knowledge. Researchers, surely, also have a negatory role: tempering expectations, institutionalising doubt, and encouraging the humility to recognise the *limits* of our capacity to produce positive knowledge, and evidence that can inform law and policy. In the case of 'climate migration', fulfilling this negatory role matters, because, in fact, our limits are in plain view, and they are no less conspicuous for being ignored, and constitute the most profound challenge facing anyone who takes an interest – be it as a researcher, a policy-maker, a lawyer, or an advocate – in the impact of environmental or climate change on human migration or displacement.

B. Implications for Thinking about the Societal Effects of Climate Change

If the first implication of the preceding arguments is for how we view and engage with migration as a specific 'effect' of climate change, the second is with regard to how we understand climate change as a general cause of a societal outcome, be it 'mobility', 'immobility', and much else besides well beyond the theme of migration.

If the argument that we cannot hope to talk meaningfully about 'climate migration' is accepted, then it would seem to have a natural consequence for how we talk about climate change more broadly. As was noted in this book's Introduction, climate change is, of course, of such broad popular and political interest because there is a widespread assumption that it will lead to dramatic and negative societal changes. 'Climate migration' was widely assumed to be a relatively self-evident and straightforward example of such changes. Now that the causal logic of this has been questioned, this naturally should raise some questions about how we view climate change as a driver of societal change more generally and, thus, as a source of concern.

Famously, there has long been a tendency, in discussions of climate change, for the debate to polarise into two camps, often loosely termed the 'believers' and the 'deniers'. The former are given to declare that 'the science is a consensus', while the latter refute this. It is, however, arguable that both sides are wrong–and, in their way of being wrong, have more in common than they have apart and certainly than they care to admit.

Namely, both sides have always presumed that the question of climate change was a strictly scientific one and that, as such, the debate begins and ends with the hard science and facts and data about climate change. Yet one might instead argue that 'the science' is only half the discussion, and perhaps both the less consequential and less difficult half. The other half has to do not with the nature of the climate, but with the nature of society. On the latter, things are much more complicated, not least because everything – like the term migration itself – is inherently subjective and political.

In this, the discussion of climate change has much in common with the discussion of Covid-19. Both had a pathology – the virus for Covid, and excess carbon dioxide emissions for climate change. The official response for both then depended on modelling – epidemiological models for the virus and climate modelling for climate change. In the face of both phenomena, governments have made clear that they intend to be 'guided by the science'. Yet, in both cases this was a foolish statement at best, and a misleading one at worst, for the question of the appropriate policy response was not strictly a scientific question. With Covid, the question of the proportionality of 'lockdown' policies was not one that could be answered simply by looking at the science of the disease, but by weighing that science against the myriad other considerations of society.

Risk assessment involves trade-offs, and there are no 'objectively' correct answers to difficult but inevitable questions such as whether there is 'more to life than the avoidance of death?'[85] A worldwide 'zero covid' strategy *may* have been successful in slowing the spread of the disease, but at what societal cost? Similarly, a 'net zero' goal for climate change *may* slow climate change, but at what societal cost? These questions are not ones that natural science is equipped to answer, as they involve a consideration of highly subjective, and intrinsically political debates around culture and value. Science can inform our decisions, but it cannot tell us what we must do, for in making any decisions, we must consider much that lies beyond the science.

What the 'climate migration' case demonstrates for how we understand climate change is that it is never enough to simple talk of and refer to the content of 'the science' when we are considering its impact on society, and thus the role of law and policy. Policy responses require us to consider societal context, too, and society is never a blank slate, or a passive actor, still less a 'dependent variable' to be causally

[85] Jonathan Sumption, 'Locking Up the Elderly until Coronavirus Is Defeated is a Cruel Mockery of Basic Human Values', *The Daily Mail* (3 May 2020), available at www.dailymail.co.uk/debate/article-8281007/Former-Supreme-Court-judge-LORD-SUMPTION-gives-withering-critique-Governments-lockdown.html.

impacted by climate change. Far from revealing what our problems are, and how we ought to act, the literature on 'climate migration' reveals how little we know about either. The question that emerges about climate change from the discussion of 'climate migration' is not 'is climate change happening?' but something more subtle, and indeed profound, as it is as much about ourselves as about the climate. The question is: *what is gained, and what is lost, when we privilege climate change in our understanding of human affairs, and human problems in particular?*

This question is important not because climate does not matter, but precisely because it does. Rigour should trump sentiment, and to be rigorous does not simply imply an imperative to gain certainty in knowledge, but also – where necessary – to gain clarity by clearing away misunderstanding, unfounded assumption, and well-meaning but nevertheless meaningless conceptualisation.

C. Implications for Thinking about Ourselves and Our Institutions

The above discussion of migration as a specific effect of climate change and climate change as a general cause of (potentially negative) societal change implies a deeper set of questions. These questions have to do with the very context in which both issues are being discussed and with their potential (or at least perceived) utility: the nation-state system and its suite of international institutions through which collective action on common problems are – in principle at least – coordinated.

Much has been made, in recent years, of the fact that this global system is 'Eurocentric' in its model of thought and governance, as a consequence of having emerged from a western European society that was enriched by empire and having spread worldwide through colonialism. The truth of these claims may or may not be as simple as is often presented, but the crucial question of these critiques is a moral one: is the system fair, just, and ethical?

To a great extent, this question appears rather moot, as it is unclear what finding an answer would achieve. How could the removal of such a system – assuming it came to that, and indeed assuming it is even possible – be achieved with confidence that what would replace it would be any more fair, just, and ethical? History suggests that the imposition of any new ideology or societal structure is rarely an edifying experience for those subject to it, as post-communist states can now attest, having escaped the decades of violence that the pursuit of virtue brought upon them.

There is perhaps a more useful critique of the nation-state than an ethical one, and this is one that focuses purely on practicality – less on virtue than on fitness for purpose. As this chapter has argued, a 'classical mechanical' metaphor underlies much of the reasoning of institutions in the nation-state system. This metaphor, far from being a way to arrive at societal solutions, seems to be constitutive of the problems with how the nation-state relates to society and people, as it is based on not just a misunderstanding, but an exclusion, of much of what makes us human.

As a result, this metaphor leaves our best efforts at understanding mired in superpositional contradictions.

How might lawyers, policy-makers, and researchers, working and thinking within the broader framework of the nation-state system, go about their business in a way that does not simply replicate the paradoxes that appear to be 'genetic' to that system and the understanding of the world it holds implicit? What would it mean to escape 'classical mechanical' goals for understanding, and the absurd 'quantum mechanical' results?

Perhaps we could turn again to physics for a new way of seeing the world as we find it. Whereas classical mechanics assumed that space and time were a neutral, static context within which the material content of the universe was dynamic, Einstein's relative mechanics assumed that the context was not neutral and static, but implicated and dynamic in the play of the universe. Similarly, rather than seeing the nation-state – and ourselves who (in both senses) make them up – as neutral actors with (at least in principle) an Archimedean position by which we might survey phenomena like climate change and migration, instead researchers, lawyers, and policy-makers might begin by recognising that they and we are always implicated the analysis. We should not limit ourselves to understanding knowledge, law, and policy's relation to the world, but should also consider our own relationship to all three. For, in the end, these amount to the same thing, for when we speak of the world, we really mean ourselves, and when we talk of ourselves, we really mean the world.

***

Having discussed the need for a more relative and reflexive approach to knowledge, law, and policy, there is however one final caution that should be made, in relation to a new trend sweeping across research.

In as much as this chapter may have criticised 'the science', and indeed policy and the law, in those cases where practitioners of all three have assumed things are known that, in fact, are not, the purpose has never been to reject or dismiss science, policy-making, or law as such and in general.

Yet, this is precisely what is beginning to happen within the 'climate migration' discourse, as is outlined in the recent legal case of a Kiribati citizen named Ioane Teitiota who set a curious precedent by becoming the first person to self-identify as a 'climate refugee' in his attempt to claim refugee status in New Zealand.[86] That Mr Teitiota lost his case is beside the point. The significance of the case, as Carol Farbotko tells it in her chapter in this volume, is that his claim depended not on an appeal to either the science, or the law, but simply to his own 'lived experience' as a 'climate refugee'.

[86] This case is discussed by both Carol Farbotko, 'Identifying as a "Climate Migrant": Implications for Law, Policy, and Research', ch 8 in this volume and Giovanna Lauria, 'International Law, the Climate-Migration Nexus, and *Teitiota v New Zealand*', ch 9 in this volume.

Such a development is, of course, merely a climate-related example of what appears to otherwise be a broader and growing trend across the cultures of the historically protestant countries of the so-called 'Global North'. This trend is gradually seeing identified authorities on 'the truth' losing ground to self-identifying authors of 'my truth'.

The introduction of such a logic to the 'climate migration' discourse raises a range of interesting questions for law, policy, and research. Science and indeed the law do not, of course, exist or gain their authority in a vacuum. Both, ultimately, depend on a degree of consent for the weight they are given in society. People at some point agreed that the most reliable way to resolve technical problems was to adopt a set of methods that we have now come to call 'science'. In the face of subjective questions of norms and value – and two agreeable values can nevertheless be in conflict – people have also at some point agreed a social contract whereby we have laws that proscribe or prescribe certain behaviours, not necessarily because they are 'good' or 'bad', but because a choice is necessary when preferences and values are in conflict, for the conflict itself poses a greater threat than the choice itself.

The new trend of appealing to 'lived experience' is one that implies – *reductio ad absurdum* – a deposition of both science and the law, by substituting lived experience for both. The question of whether one believes this is a positive or negative development is beside the point. The point is that, if a critical mass of people begins to believe something – in this case, that lived experience as a climate refugee trumps the facts of climate's societal impact, or the law's position on this issue to date – then the trend becomes a social fact in itself that needs to be taken seriously as such. To simply argue that Mr Teitiota's claim – and those of others who follow his example – has no foundation in the science and is not in keeping with legal precedent is not sufficient. The potential implications of the trend need to be made apparent to ensure that there is a clear awareness that while in an exceptional case a successful appeal to lived experience may appear like justice, if this was applied to all cases, the system that has the power and integrity to make such exceptions would itself be at risk.

V. Conclusions

Climate change, in our era, is the most politically potent issue discussed by science, and migration is arguably the equivalent for social science. As such, it was perhaps inevitable that the two would become fused, by some technocratic alchemy, into a single relation. The emergent concern – 'climate migration' – represents a fusion of science and social science, of research and policy, and, not least, of formal knowledge (*episteme*) and popular belief (*doxa*). There are dangers in all three.

First, when *science and social science* are fused, there is a tendency for the differences between them to be elided in favour of the former. While the subject of science – things – is a unity best understood by generalisable rules, the subject of the social sciences – people – is a plurality, with each person an exception to the rule in their own way. As Oswald Spengler wrote, 'the means whereby to identify dead forms is Mathematical Law. The means whereby to understand living forms is Analogy.'[87] We forget this at our peril, and the discussion of 'climate migration' often does. One might say that the discussion of 'climate migration' (and of the societal consequences of climate change in general) is characterised less by its rich understanding of the climate and the science than by an impoverished understanding of people and society.

Second, the fusion of *research and policy* runs the risk of subjugating research to policy-making agendas. As migration scholar Oliver Bakewell has written:

> The search for policy relevance has encouraged researchers to take the categories, concepts and priorities of policy-makers and practitioners as their initial frame of reference for identifying their areas of study and formulating research questions. This privileges the worldview of the policy makers in constructing the research, constraining the questions asked, the objects of study and the methodologies and analysis adopted.[88]

If policy – and thus government and institutional action – may claim some form of moral legitimacy, it is that it is 'evidence-based'. But what if the people gathering the evidence are not marginalised from policy-making, but co-opted by it, becoming subject to the 'combined legitimacy' of institutions and advocacy actors who 'create [a] set of very dominant narratives on the migration and climate change nexus' leading to 'hegemonic closure'?[89] If this is occurring, what does it say about the foundations of law and policy and the legitimacy of the state and institutional actors who enact it?

Third, when *episteme* and *doxa* are intermixed, the quiet dispassion required to conduct careful and impartial analysis can easily be drowned out by the passionate clamour for action, regardless of what the analysis has, in fact, concluded. Due partly to the increasing popular momentum around climate change, there is a danger that this might occur, and indeed, a sense that this is happening already. What value, then, do we put on rigour and coherence, in both analysis and debate? Does a concern for rigour trump the emotiveness of the topic at hand? What, ultimately, would constitute a standard for a rigorous – and thus useful – conceptual claim, let alone the empirics that would connect it to the real world?

These questions are not ones that may be solved solely by an engagement with the science and social science. They are questions not about what is, or even what ought to be, but rather, and fundamentally, questions about ourselves – the people-who are interested in the former two questions. As such, they are questions rooted not in the facts, but in our culture and values.

This chapter opened with a quote from the great twentieth century philosopher and historian of ideas, Isaiah Berlin:

> We cannot confine our attention to the great impersonal forces, natural and man-made, which act upon us. The goals and motives that guide human action must be looked at

[87] Oswald Spengler, *Decline of the West, Volume 1: Form and Actuality* (Alfred A Knopf, 1932) 4.

[88] Oliver Bakewell, 'Research Beyond Categories: The Importance of Policy Irrelevant Research into Forced Migration' (2008) 21(4) *Journal of Refugee Studies* 432, 432.

[89] Nash (n 26) 82.

> in the light of all that we know and understand; their roots and growth, their essence, and above all their validity, must be critically examined with every intellectual resource that we have.[90]

Berlin's point is that any proper examination of a given topic requires not just data and some conceptual apparatus, but also a degree of reflexivity and, indeed, of humility. Given the pattern of problems that have stalked research on the topic since the beginning, both would seem necessary in any effort we make towards conceptualising 'climate migration'.

[90] Berlin (n 1) 2.

2

Climate Change–Disaster–Migration: Manufacturing a Nexus

ILAN KELMAN

I. Is Everything about Climate Change?

Climate change is a major topic in science, policy, practice, and communication. Widely disparate phenomena and ideas are linked to and often blamed on climate change, from tangible events such as tsunamis[1] (without any explanation of how tectonics are linked to climate change, despite some speculation)[2] to less tangible ones such as a loosely defined idea of injustice[3] (even when none of the concerns raised started with or is exclusive to climate change). Among the phenomena often assumed to be linked directly to climate change are disasters and migration. In this discourse, an understanding of the meaning of all these terms is frequently absent.

Starting from basic definitions, 'climate' is average weather.[4] Weather parameters such as precipitation, temperature, and wind speed are averaged over decades, typically thirty years, although this can vary. The resulting statistics are climate. Climate change is, as per the phrase, a change in the climate. It means that weather statistics are changing, again usually over thirty years but this timeframe is not fixed.

Climates change for many reasons, across both spatial and temporal scales. Many of these reasons have to do with natural phenomena. A forest's characteristics affect the ground-level and canopy microclimates in terms of temperature, moisture, and wind speed.[5] The formation or erosion of mountains impacts

[1] Ruth G Bell, 'What to do about Climate Change' (2006) 85 *Foreign Affairs* 105, 105.

[2] Bill McGuire, 'Potential for a Hazardous Geospheric Response to Projected Future Climate Changes' (2010) 368 *Philosophical Transactions of the Royal Society A: Mathematical, Physical and Engineering Sciences* 2317, available at doi.org/10.1098/rsta.2010.0080.

[3] Farhana Sultana, 'Climate Change, COVID-19, and the Co-Production of Injustices: A Feminist Reading of Overlapping Crises' (2021) 22(4) *Social & Cultural Geography* 447.

[4] IPCC Sixth Assessment Report, *Impacts, Adaptation and Vulnerability: Working Group II Contribution* (Cambridge, Cambridge University Press 2022) 2902.

[5] Jiaojun Zhu and others, 'Microclimate Regimes following Gap Formation in a Montane Secondary Forest of Eastern Liaoning Province, China' (2007) 18(3) *Journal of Forestry Research* 167, available at doi.org/10.1007/s11676-007-0035-7.

atmospheric circulation, and can encourage or inhibit precipitation and wind.[6] The Earth's orbit around the Sun varies, and the Earth's axis with respect to the Sun wobbles. Both affect the amount of incoming solar radiation, and are a major factor in starting and ending Ice Ages.[7] The Sun, of course, also varies its radiation output.[8] Global-scale hazards, such as a large meteorite strike, a significant volcanic eruption, or a flood basalt in which lava covers tens of thousands of square kilometres, all alter the climate. This natural climate change is as old as the Earth itself.

A major added factor today is human-caused climate change.[9] Many human activities release gases into the atmosphere that trap the Sun's heat and warm the planet. Most notable is the combustion of the fossil fuels of coal, oil, and gas to generate electricity and for transportation. Other examples are methane, released by livestock, and sulphur hexafluoride, used as an electrical insulator and to prevent electrical arcing that can start fires. In the meantime, other human activities reduce the uptake of these gases. For example, trees and swamps store large amounts of greenhouse gases, yet deforestation and paving over wetlands destroy these ecosystems, thereby substantially reducing their uptake of the gases.

This combination of human actions has pushed the atmospheric concentration of greenhouse gases to a higher level than at any time during the previous 800,000 years. Expectations along current trajectories are that the atmospheric greenhouse gas concentration could soon exceed the maximum seen during the Pliocene Epoch, which ran from 5.3 million until 2.6 million years ago.[10] There is no doubt that human activity is changing the climate and thus the planet rapidly and substantively, with many impacts clearly visible. In tandem, many local decisions such as forest management further influence local microclimates.[11] These statements do not mean that human-caused climate change is the dominant factor (or even a factor at all) in every observed change in environments and societies, nor do these statements mean that all impacts related to climate change are detrimental.

It is, in fact, unclear how human-caused climate change is affecting and will affect human migration and disasters – phenomena which are often attributed to climate change. This chapter outlines what is known and expected about human-caused climate change influencing or not influencing migration and disasters. The discussion demonstrates how the climate–disaster–migration nexus is artificially constructed and does not account for all scientific understandings.

[6] Gilles Ramstein and others, 'Effect of Orogeny, Plate Motion and Land-Sea Distribution on Eurasian Climate Change over the Past 30 Million Years' (1997) 386 *Nature* 788, available at doi.org/10.1038/386788a0.

[7] David A Hodell, 'The Smoking Gun of the Ice Ages' (2019) 354 *Science* 1235.

[8] Giuliana C Castagnoli and others, 'Solar Radiation Variability in the last 1400 Years Recorded in the Carbon Isotope Ratio of a Mediterranean Sea Core' (2002) 29(12) *Advances in Space Research* 1989.

[9] IPCC Sixth Assessment Report, *WGII* (n 4).

[10] IPCC Sixth Assessment Report, *The Physical Science Basis: Working Group I Contribution* (Cambridge, Cambridge University Press 2021) 44.

[11] Jiquan Chen, Jerry F Franklin, and Thomas A Spies, 'Contrasting Microclimates among Clearcut, Edge, and Interior of Old-Growth Douglas-Fir Forest' (1993) 63 *Agricultural and Forest Meteorology* 219.

II. Climigration?

On the presumption that 'climate migration' or 'climate change refugees' are important, the term 'climigration' is explained as being 'when a community is no longer sustainable exclusively because of climate-related events and permanent relocation is required to protect people'.[12] This definition in itself indicates a misapprehension. Since climate occurs over decades, 'climate-related events', strictly speaking, do not occur. Weather-related events, such as storms and floods, do occur, but climate is hard to confine in time through 'events'. The key in the definition of 'climigration', though, is the term 'exclusively'. It would be hard to eliminate all non-climate influences within an instance of 'a community [that] is no longer sustainable' and when considering 'permanent relocation'. After all, resources must be available in order to be sustainable and to migrate, hence availability of resources is an obvious factor in being 'sustainable' and in permitting 'permanent relocation'.

The availability of well-documented and well-accepted definitions,[13] extensive migration research,[14] and critiquing analyses of climigration[15] has not stopped grandiose statements about climigration. One description made claims about 'refugee camps and cities overwhelmed with migrants fleeing climate change and its impacts'.[16] *The Independent*, a British newspaper, published a headline '[c]limate change could force more than a billion people to flee their homes'[17] when reporting on one paper.[18] This paper actually detailed that

> climate change is the sole contributing factor for at least 4,400 people who are already being forced to migrate, worldwide. The total number of people vulnerable to migration might increase to 1 billion by the end of the century without significant further action on climate change.[19]

The caveat on the one billion figure was 'plus or minus' 50 per cent. Even the 4,400 figure was tenuous since one example given was the resettlement of populations

[12] Robin Bronen, 'Alaskan Communities' Rights and Resilience' (2008) 31 *Forced Migration Review* 30, 31.

[13] See IPCC Sixth Assessment Report, *WGII* (n 4), Annex II.

[14] Elena Fiddian-Qasmiyeh and others (eds), *The Oxford Handbook of Refugee and Forced Migration Studies* (New York, Oxford University Press 2016), available at doi.org/10.1093/oxfordhb/9780199652433.001.0001.

[15] Benoit Mayer, *The Concept of Climate Migration: Advocacy and its Prospects* (Cheltenham, Edward Elgar 2016); Calum TM Nicholson, 'Climate Change and the Politics of Causal Reasoning: The Case of Climate Change and Migration' (2014) 180(2) *The Geographical Journal* 151, available at doi.org/10.1111/geoj.12062.

[16] Andrew T Guzman, *Overheated: The Human Cost of Climate Change* (New York, Oxford University Press 2013) 181.

[17] Andrew Griffin, 'Climate Change Could Force More Than a Billion People to Flee Their Homes, Says Major Health Report' (*Independent*, 2017), available at perma.cc/C8GQ-S3UP.

[18] Nick Watts and others, 'The Lancet Countdown on Health and Climate Change: From 25 Years of Inaction to a Global Transformation for Public Health' (2018) 391(10120) *The Lancet* 581, available at doi.org/10.1016/S0140-6736(17)32464-9.

[19] ibid 593.

from the Carteret Islands in Papua New Guinea,[20] for which more robust investigation has suggested the need to downplay climate change as a factor in migration.[21]

The desire to blame climate change for forced migration, irrespective of evidence, might stem in part from a long-standing discourse assuming that migration, especially across international borders, must be unwanted and problematic.[22] Migration is often framed as a result of a failure to take effective action to arrest everything from eroding shorelines to declining economies. Yet plenty of work countervails this viewpoint, explaining how migration can be an active and desired choice in response to climate change's impacts among other factors.[23] In many instances (for instance, in Nicaragua),[24] even with discernible impacts from climate change on a particular location, migration is neither strictly a failure to adjust to climate change nor strictly an actual adjustment or response to climate change. Consequently, neither migration nor populations remaining in place (non-migration or immobility) can be immediately constructed as either a problem or as an opportunity, irrespective of the influence of climate change. Understanding is needed of people's available choices and their reasons for selecting a particular choice in a specific circumstance.

To presume that 'climigration' can (and even should) be isolated as a discrete phenomenon is to ignore fundamental and long-standing observations of and conclusions from migration studies.[25] People display many, diverse reasons for migrating and for not migrating, in addition to mobilities and migration theories leading to more self-reflection and reducing prejudices.[26] It is unclear why this knowledge and these lessons are not considered by so many scholars and policy-makers who choose to highlight climate change.

As a typical truism, context matters. As another truism, exploring how climate change might or might not affect migration and non-migration as problems or solutions should never start with the assumption of climigration or the absence of climigration. Nor should assumptions be made about people's interests.

[20] Sarah Strauss, 'Are Cultures Endangered by Climate Change? Yes, but …' (2012) 3(4) *Wiley Interdisciplinary Reviews Climate Change* 371, available at doi.org/10.1002/wcc.181.

[21] John Connell, 'Last Days in the Carteret Islands? Climate Change, Livelihoods and Migration on Coral Atolls' (2016) 57 *Asia Pacific Viewpoint* 3, available at doi.org/10.1111/apv.12118.

[22] Clifford J Jansen, 'Migration: A Sociological Problem' in Clifford Jansen (eds), *Readings in the Sociology of Migration* (Oxford, Pergamon Press 1970) 3, available at doi.org/10.1016/B978-0-08-006915-9.50006-1.

[23] Robert Stojanov and others, 'Migration as Adaptation? Population Dynamics in the Age of Climate Variability' (Global Change Research Centre 2014); Cecilia Tacoli, 'Crisis or Adaptation? Migration and Climate Change in Context of High Mobility' (2009) 21(2) *Environment and Urbanization* 513, available at doi.org/10.1177/0956247809342182.

[24] Claudia Radel and others, 'Toward a Political Ecology of Migration: Land, Labor Migration, and Climate Change in Northwestern Nicaragua' (2018) 108 *World Development* 263, available at doi.org/10.1016/j.worlddev.2017.04.023.

[25] Egon F Kunz, 'The Refugee in Flight: Kinetic Models and Forms of Displacement' (1973) 7(2) *International Migration Review* 125; William Petersen, 'A General Typology of Migration' (1958) 23(3) *American Sociological Review* 256, available at doi.org/10.2307/2089239.

[26] Elena Fiddian-Qasmiyeh (ed), *Refuge in a Moving World: Interdisciplinary Conversations* (London, UCL Press 2019); Elena Fiddian-Qasmiyeh (ed), *Refuge in a Moving World: Refugee and Migrant Journeys across Disciplines* (London, UCL Press 2020); Fiddian-Qasmiyeh and others (n 14).

Instead, evidence should be collected and examined – a tenet of science. Perhaps climate change does, or will sometimes, force migration. These migrants will include some people who are devastated at leaving and losing their home and everything they have ever known. Other people may be happy to seek new opportunities – never looking back to what they left. There will be further groups who would and could have moved, but decide not to, or are forced not to, due to climate change's impacts on their destination, rather than on their area of origin. Yet others might refuse to move, dying as a result, which is not uncommon for several forms of environmental changes including rapid-onset hazards.[27]

Destinations for migrants also tend to demonstrate a diversity of responses, further diluting the impacts of climate change on migrants and migration. People already living in a location where migrants settle may be variously welcoming, hostile, or apathetic, with many people combining or moving among these reactions.[28] When starting research, no assumptions should be made about why people migrate, where they will end up, and how they will be received. Instead, the starting point must be that migrants are first and foremost people. Why they do or do not migrate, and how they do or do not adjust to any new circumstances, relies more on societal and human factors than on climatic ones.

Yet scenarios exist in which human-caused climate change might dominate some migration decisions. Known cases are dealt with later in this chapter. Additionally, the possibility always remains that climate change turns out to be worse or better than current projections suggest[29] which could mean different influences on both migration and non-migration. Overall, it is unrealistic to either deny or presume that climate change and migration have strong links. Focusing primarily on climate change or trying to highlight it as the dominant factor in migration decisions is thus unrealistic and unhelpful for policy and practice.

Scientific work provides a rich understanding of population dynamics, covering human mobilities,[30] immobilities or 'trapped' populations,[31] and climate change placed in wider and broader contexts of disasters, development, and sustainability.[32] As a truism, human movement has always involved a range of

[27] See Jack Estes and Dennis Shaw, 'Popular Culture and Mt. St. Helens: A Study of a Response' (1985) 18(4) *The Journal of Popular Culture* 135, available at doi.org/10.1111/j.0022-3840.1985.00135.x; Ronald W Perry, 'Evacuation Decision-Making in Natural Disasters' (1979) 4 *Mass Emergencies* 25.

[28] Jody L McBrien, 'Refugees, Asylum Seekers and Education for Citizenship and Social Justice', in Andrew Peterson and others (eds), *The Palgrave International Handbook of Education for Citizenship and Social Justice* (London, Palgrave Macmillan 2016) 18, available at doi.org/10.1057/978-1-137-51507-0.

[29] IPCC Sixth Assessment Report, WGII (n 4).

[30] Stephen C Lubkemann, 'Involuntary Immobility: On a Theoretical Invisibility in Forced Migration Studies' (2008) 21(4) *Journal of Refugee Studies* 454, available at doi.org/10.1093/jrs/fen043.

[31] Sonja Ayeb-Karlsson, '"When We Were Children We Had Dreams, Then We Came to Dhaka to Survive": Urban Stories Connecting Loss of Wellbeing, Displacement and (Im)Mobility' (2021) 13 *Climate and Development* 348, available at doi.org/10.1080/17565529.2020.1777078.

[32] Jessica Mercer, 'Disaster Risk Reduction or Climate Change Adaptation: Are we Reinventing the Wheel?' (2010) 22(2) *Journal of International Development* 247, available at doi.org/10.1002/jid.1677; Jean-Christophe Gaillard, 'Vulnerability, Capacity, and Resilience: Perspectives for Climate and Disaster Risk Reduction' (2010) 22(2) *Journal of International Development* 218, available at doi.org/10.1002/jid.1675.

differently weighted factors, including a changing climate, which itself occurs for multiple reasons across multiple scales of time and space. Today's human-caused climate change does not affect this starting point. Climate change scenarios quite rightly look both several millennia into the future[33] and aeons into the past,[34] suggesting that much of human history and numerous possible futures ought to be considered when analysing the influences of climate change on people moving or staying.

III. Clidisasters?

The nuances, subtleties, contexts, and provisos that attend any discussion of 'climigration' apply equally to any discussion of climate change influencing disasters or so-called 'clidisasters'.

Nature has always produced and continues to produce weather-related phenomena and processes such as storms, tornadoes, floods, droughts, wildfires, avalanches, and mudslides – the pattern of which inevitably changes as the climate does. If, in the context of such phenomena, people have been injured and/or killed, infrastructure damaged, livelihoods disrupted, and/or people forced to leave an affected area, this means there has been a disaster. If, however, few negative impacts are seen, there has not been a disaster. Why does similar weather lead to vastly different outcomes, some disastrous and some not, sometimes with forced migration and sometimes without it?

The difference is due to the variability of people's abilities, skills, and mechanisms for dealing with weather. If people have the power, knowledge, and resources to avoid death, damage, and disruption, then water is just a potential flood hazard and wind is just a potential tornado hazard, without them becoming disasters. Having or not having all these possibilities for dealing or not dealing with weather refers to 'vulnerability'.[35] Long-term social actions such as corruption, resource misallocation, inequity, oppression, and marginalisation make people and places vulnerable. Thus, due to vulnerabilities, weather hazards become disasters.

Vulnerability, irrespective of nature's behaviour and no matter what the weather, could result from breaking planning regulations, not having or not obeying building codes, not being able to access or afford insurance or healthcare, poorly communicated warnings, inadequate education or people banned from receiving it, or the fear of crime while evacuating, when in a shelter, or when returning home.

[33] Peter U Clarke and others, 'Consequences of Twenty-First-Century Policy for Multi-Millennial Climate and Sea-Level Change' (2016) 6 *Nature Climate Change* 360.

[34] IPCC Sixth Assessment Report, WGII (n 4).

[35] Ken Hewitt (ed), *Interpretations of Calamity: From the Viewpoint of Human Ecology* (New York, George Allen & Unwin 1983); James Lewis, *Development in Disaster-prone Places: Studies of Vulnerability* (Intermediate Technology Publications 1999); Ben Wisner and others, *At Risk: Natural Hazards, People's Vulnerability and Disasters* 2nd edn (Routledge 2003).

People frequently experience marginalisation, oppression, or discrimination based on sex, sexuality, gender, religion, race, ethnicity, language, disability, or other personal factors. As a result, their choices about where and how they live, what livelihoods to pursue, or how they might get ready for and respond to weather, including typical phenomena such as storms or droughts, may be limited.

Hence, disasters happen not because of weather or changes to the weather, but because of people's choices, not least those of people in power. Vulnerable people and places lead to disasters, not because of nature's behaviour or the weather's behaviour, but because of society's behaviour. Consequently, disasters are not natural, which is why the phrase 'natural disaster' is best avoided. Instead, they are merely 'disasters'.

Since disasters are not natural and do not arise from the environment, weather does not cause disasters and disasters do not arise from weather. The consequence of this is that, by definition, a changing climate cannot be blamed for disasters. This point is evidenced when examining specific weather. For instance, tropical cyclones refer to hurricanes, typhoons, and cyclones; all three are the same type of storm with the label depending on the location of formation. Human-caused climate change is shown to be decreasing the frequency of tropical cyclones while augmenting their intensity.[36] In many places, regardless of whether a tropical cyclone forms, greater rainfall intensity is appearing which sometimes leads to worse flooding. Examples occurred in western Europe in July 2021 and Pakistan in September 2022. Yet the storms, rainfall, and floods do not themselves produce the disasters that ensue. Human-caused climate change influencing weather[37] does not mean that it must or will lead to disasters.

For a disaster to occur, vulnerability must first exist, and vulnerability can take many forms. People might not have access to information about floodplains, or forewarning about imminent rainfall, or about a tropical cyclone about to make landfall. Or they might have the information, but lack the resources or options to move out of flooding areas. They might have both, but nevertheless prefer to implement local measures to reduce their flood risk, yet in doing so discover they do not have the resources or power to do so. Meanwhile, corruption or an eagerness for quick profits can lead to dwellings being built in floodplains without providing flood risk and flood management information to residents, or implementing flood resistance measures. Floods then become disasters because human decisions created and perpetuated vulnerabilities.

As such, since most disasters cannot be attributed to climate change so much as they can be attributed to societal factors (with exceptions to be discussed later), both 'clidisaster' and 'climigration' are as much misnomers as 'natural disaster'. The migration is from disaster, and disasters result from socially constructed vulnerability to weather, not the presence of weather.

[36] Savin S Chand and others, 'Declining Tropical Cyclone Frequency under Global Warming' (2022) 12 *Nature Climate Change* 655, available at doi.org/10.1038/s41558-022-01388-4.

[37] Stephanie C Herring and others (eds), 'Explaining Extreme Events in 2020 from a Climate Perspective' (Bulletin of the American Meteorological Society 2021) S1–S17.

IV. Disaster Migration or Vulnerability Migration?

Vulnerability also explains the baseline for much forced migration. When people are in difficulty or are seeking opportunity for any reason, migration is one option that may be considered. Most migration requires some level of resources, even if it is just the ability to travel with few possessions. Studies of migration have demonstrated that, almost irrespective of whether it is from a disaster or a conflict, it is the people who have the resources who are typically the first to leave, especially if they can afford passports, travel tickets, and accommodation, while the poorest and most marginal are typically the last to do so.[38] Perhaps when the choice appears to be between definitely dying in place or possibly dying en route do the poorest people try to migrate, which leads to images of hungry children, people scrambling to cross borders, and families arriving at temporary camps set up for humanitarian relief. Yet despite noting that disasters are long-term processes emerging from vulnerability, it can nevertheless still be difficult to pinpoint how and when specific migration decisions are made.

Not that migration is necessarily a detrimental choice or an option of last resort. Migration and mobility studies have long explained (often with inherent biases and prejudices) that moving geographically is an activity common within many cultures, and indeed is part of the human condition.[39] One paper even states that '[w]e are all migrants' in its subtitle.[40] The decision to migrate (or not) is not always a purely voluntary choice, but one that can be forced – or, more commonly, results from – a combination of forced and voluntary aspects.[41]

Assessing the respective role of choice and constraint in migration decisions can be difficult, as perspectives are subjective, and the categories involved are ambiguous. People who migrate for jobs, education, and healthcare are making a voluntary choice, but might feel forced to do so because they believe that no other option exists due to a lack of services in their home area. When employers relocate or amalgamate offices, their employees might be told to relocate with the office or else they will lose their jobs. It is a choice to accept redundancy to avoid moving, yet many would feel forced to move in order to continue their career – or just to bring in an adequate income. Regarding non-migration or immobility, some people find themselves fixed in a location for personal reasons, such as staying close to family or wishing to remain within their culture. It is a choice to prioritise identity or family, but it constrains migration decisions.

[38] Fiddian-Qasmiyeh, *Refuge in a Moving World* (n 26); Fiddian-Qasmiyeh and others (n 14).

[39] Robert E Park, 'Human Migration and the Marginal Man' (1928) 33(6) *American Journal of Sociology* 881; George IJ Dixon, 'Land and Human Migrations' (1950) 9(2) *The American Journal of Economics and Sociology* 223.

[40] Jan N Pieterse, 'Globalization and Human Integration: We are all Migrants' (2000) 32(5) *Futures* 385, 385, available at doi.org/10.1016/S0016-3287(99)00082-8.

[41] Fiddian-Qasmiyeh, *Refuge in a Moving World* (n 26); Fiddian-Qasmiyeh and others (n 14).

Nonetheless, disasters can and do force migration decisions. Volcanic eruptions are a major example throughout human history, ranging from Mt Lamington, Papua New Guinea in 1951[42] to Tungurahua, Ecuador in 1999.[43] From the Pacific[44] to Kalaallit Nunaat (Greenland),[45] people have left their homes throughout past centuries due to wide-scale environmental changes.

Other forms of disastrous conditions can force people to leave or stay with little voluntariness. Many homes and settlements have been flooded to improve cargo transport such as along the St Lawrence Seaway between Canada and the United States,[46] and to build dams, such as in Finland[47] and China.[48] Expropriation has forced people out for reasons such as a road in Ethiopia[49] and an airport in Canada.[50] Facing the prospect of death, violent conflicts, or persecution can leave some individuals with no 'choice' but to migrate, in which case they will generally qualify for international protection as refugees.[51]

Indeed, the Refugee Convention states that someone should be given the option to remain in safety if they are unable to return to their country of origin 'owing to well-founded fear of being persecuted for reasons of race, religion, nationality, membership of a particular social group or political opinion'.[52] These latter instances could legitimately be designated 'disaster migration' since people are forced to migrate due to disastrous conditions, whether violent conflict or deliberate destruction of their home for building infrastructure. When an environmental phenomenon, such an earthquake or a flood, forces people to migrate, is it then also 'disaster migration'? Much depends on how a disaster is viewed, echoing the above discussion that challenged the assumption that disasters are 'natural'.

To avoid disasters, as well as forced migration from disasters, those with the power, resources, and opportunities would need to tackle the causes of vulnerabilities.

[42] Cyril Belshaw, 'Social Consequences of the Mount Lamington Eruption' (1951) 21(4) *Oceania* 241, available at doi.org/10.1002/j.1834-4461.1951.tb00175.x.

[43] Lucille R Lane, Graham A Tobin, and Linda M Whiteford, 'Volcanic Hazard or Economic Destitution: Hard Choices in Baños, Ecuador' (2003) 5 *Environmental Hazards* 23, available at doi.org/10.1016/j.hazards.2004.01.001.

[44] Patrick D Nunn and Mike Carson, 'Collapses of Island Societies from Environmental Forcing: Does History Hold Lessons for the Future?' (2015) 8 *Global Environment* 110.

[45] Andrew J Dugmore, Christian Keller, and Thomas H McGovern, 'Norse Greenland Settlement: Reflections on Climate Change, Trade, and the Contrasting Fates of Human Settlements in the North Atlantic Islands' (2007) 44 *Arctic Anthropology* 12.

[46] Heather M Cox and others, 'Drowning Voices and Drowning Shoreline: A Riverside View of the Social and Ecological Impacts of the St. Lawrence Seaway and Power Project' (1999) 10(2) *Rural History* 235.

[47] Fae L Korsmo, 'Swedish Policy and Saami Rights' (1993) 11 *Northern Review* 32.

[48] Hwang Sean-Shong and others, 'Anticipation of Migration and Psychological Stress and the Three Gorges Dam Project, China' (2007) 65 *Social Science & Medicine* 1012.

[49] Belachew Y Alemu, 'Expropriation, Valuation and Compensation Practice in Ethiopia: The Case of Bahir Dar City and Surrounding' (2013) 31(2) *Property Management* 132.

[50] Eric G Poulin, 'Mirabel Airport: In the Name of Development, Modernity, and Canadian Unity' (2022) *Economic Anthropology*, available at doi.org/10.1002/sea2.12252.

[51] Convention Relating to the Status of Refugees (adopted 28 July 1951, entered into force 22 April 1954) 189 UNTS 137 ('Refugee Convention').

[52] ibid art 1A(2).

For instance, for people with disabilities, everyone's needs could be met by ensuring that warnings are issued across multiple media and communication platforms, while evacuation routes and shelters could be made suitable for access irrespective of a person's physical, mental, and cognitive abilities. Stopping everyday sexism, everyday racism, and everyday homophobia means that everyone participates in teaching, learning, and acting to reduce vulnerability. Enacting and enforcing design, construction, and planning regulations that factor in nature's variety keeps infrastructure functioning and reduces livelihood disruption. Ensuring that all these amorphous societal processes combine to reduce vulnerability, and not to create or exacerbate it, gives people power, opportunities, and resources to make their own choices – including choices about migrating or not.

Conversely, settlements, structures, and societies that are vulnerable to environmental phenomena – for instance, developed in burnable ecosystems without considering fires[53] and on unstable slopes without considering landslides[54] – remove choices about migrating (or not). When businesses burns, homes collapse, or public transit ceases to function, people are not necessarily being forced to migrate – or forced into a position that their best choice is to migrate – due to the disaster per se. Rather, it is due to vulnerability. A term better than 'disaster migration' could therefore be 'vulnerability migration'.

The same argument applies when people wish to migrate due to a disaster but cannot afford to: the issue of trapped populations, non-migration, or immobility. It is not the disaster per se that forces them to stay when they would prefer to leave, but rather their long-term vulnerability conditions that have removed the power, resources, and options to make their own decisions about moving. 'Vulnerability non-migration' and 'vulnerability immobility' could be better terms than 'disaster non-migration' and 'disaster immobility'.

This focus on vulnerability and the attribution of consequences – such as migration, immobility, deaths, injuries, infrastructure damage, and disruption – to vulnerability means that the disaster (or the process of a disaster being generated) is effectively the vulnerability. This point again emphasises how disasters are not the result of hazards or hazard influencers, such as climate change. 'Clidisasters', 'climate disasters', and 'climate change disasters' are as much misnomers as 'climigration' and 'natural disaster'. Just as the nexus between climate change and migration is hard to identify, the nexus between climate change and disasters, and notably the nexus between climate change and vulnerability, is also hard to identify.

[53] Alexandra D Syphard, Teresa J Brennan, and Jon E Keeley, 'The Importance of Building Construction Materials Relative to Other Factors Affecting Structure Survival during Wildfire' (2017) 21 *International Journal of Disaster Risk Reduction* 140, available at doi.org/10.1016/j.ijdrr.2016.11.011.

[54] Bayes Ahmed, 'The Root Causes of Landslide Vulnerability in Bangladesh' (2021) 18 *Landslides* 1707, available at doi.org/10.1007/s10346-020-01606-0.

V. Possible Exceptions

Accompanying every rule are exceptions – a rule that itself has exceptions. In the context of climate change, disasters, and migration, the rule is that disasters and migration are strongly connected, with definite links to natural climate change, but with few links to human-caused climate change. There are, however, exceptions.

Currently, heat-humidity is the most significant exception since human-caused climate change is producing heat-humidity regimes well beyond millennial-scale averages and extremes. Locations are being pushed into heat-humidity realms that modern humanity has never experienced. There are physical limits on what heat-humidity combinations the human body can survive.[55] This weather is already being experienced with direct attribution to human-caused climate change.[56] Especially when it does not cool down sufficiently at night, the only option for survival is artificial cooling. Fans, too, have limitations, since eventually they just blow hot air onto people, dehydrating them faster. Aside from the high electricity use and pollution from artificial cooling, most people cannot afford to pay for it. For others, such as construction and agriculture workers who depend on being outside for their livelihood, access to artificial cooling is infeasible.[57]

For those, the choice tends to be limited to losing income, dying, or migrating. These cases may truly be 'clidisasters' leading to 'climigration'. Without stopping human-caused climate change, large tracts of land will be affected in this manner. As the heat-humidity begins to kill crops and livestock, major adverse impacts on the world's food supply will be witnessed, with expectations of this phenomenon becoming evident over the next decade or so, barring any concerted effort to tackle the problem.[58]

As the next decades unfold, changes to oceans might bring further prospects for 'clidisasters' producing 'climigration', most prominently ocean acidification[59] and sea-level rise.[60] As the seas absorb excess atmospheric carbon dioxide, this gas combines with water to produce carbonic acid, lowering the oceans' pH level. The possible impact on shorelines and ecosystems is not yet fully understood.

[55] Jonathan Chambers, 'Global and Cross-Country Analysis of Exposure of Vulnerable Populations to Heatwaves from 1980 to 2018' (2020) 163 *Climatic Change* 539, available at doi.org/10.1007/s10584-020-02884-2.

[56] Werner Marx, Robin Haunschild, and Lutz Bornmann, 'Heat Waves: A Hot Topic in Climate Change Research' (2021) 146 *Theoretical and Applied Climatology* 781, available at doi.org/10.1007/s00704-021-03758-y.

[57] Marina Romanello and others, 'The 2021 Report of the Lancet Countdown on Health and Climate Change' (2021) 398 *The Lancet* 1619, 1626, available at doi.org/10.1016/S0140-6736(21)01787-6.

[58] ibid 1631.

[59] Scott C Doney and others, 'The Impacts of Ocean Acidification on Marine Ecosystems and Reliant Human Communities' (2020) 45 *Annual Review of Environment and Resources* 83, available at doi.org/10.1146/annurev-environ-012320-083019.

[60] Anny Cazenave and Goneri Le Cozannet, 'Sea Level Rise and its Coastal Impacts' (2014) 2(2) *Earth's Future* 15, available at doi.org/10.1002/2013EF000188.

Depending on the rate and extent of acidifying oceans, especially in combination with rising sea surface temperatures as the oceans absorb atmospheric heat,[61] ecosystems might either adapt, change significantly, or be wiped out. Where people fish, grow coastal crops, or harvest other coastal and marine resources, they will need to adjust their livelihoods to the local environmental changes or else they could face calamity.

These experiences – potentially compelling people to migrate, particularly where they already have high vulnerability, constricting their options – could face the added complication of sea-level rise. At the moment, about half of sea-level rise is from melting ice, snow, and permafrost leading to freshwater runoff which has less land-based storage available due to urban development and ecosystem destruction, so more water goes into bodies of water. The other half of current sea-level rise occurs when water heats up above four degrees Celsius and becomes less dense, so it expands.[62] By 2100, these factors in combination are expected to raise sea levels by no more than two metres above 2000 levels.[63]

As this science is being developed, refined, and discussed, plenty of claims continue to be made about coastlines 'drowning' and coastline peoples, particularly islanders, fleeing their disappearing homes as climate change destroys them.[64] Thus far, attributing the changing profile of coastlines to sea-level rise has been difficult to prove, because empirical studies have shown that other factors are more significant than climate change's impacts. Examples are tectonic subsidence in Vanuatu[65] and building a sea wall that might exacerbate coastal erosion in Narikoso and Vunidogoloa, Fiji.[66] Other than constructing walls, causeways, levees, and other structures, local human actions that are rapidly morphing coastlines around the world include land reclamation, sand mining along beaches, and pollution killing local vegetation and leading to erosion.

Looking to the future, the largest contribution to sea-level rise is expected to be the melting of major ice sheets, namely in Kalaallit Nunaat (Greenland) and Antarctica. More than a quarter of a metre of sea-level rise from Kalaallit Nunaat's (Greenland's) ice sheet already appears to be inevitable, no matter how successfully human-caused climate change is mitigated.[67] Without efforts to

[61] Rui Ruela and others, 'Global and Regional Evolution of Sea Surface Temperature under Climate Change' (2020) 190 *Global and Planetary Change* 103190, available at doi.org/10.1016/j.gloplacha.2020.103190.

[62] Gregory C Johnson and John M Lyman, 'Warming Trends Increasingly Dominate Global Ocean' (2020) 10 *Nature Climate Change* 757, available at doi.org/10.1038/s41558-020-0822-0.

[63] IPCC Sixth Assessment Report, *WGI* (n 10), 21.

[64] Karen E McNamara and Helene JD Combes, 'Planning for Community Relocations due to Climate Change in Fiji' (2016) 6 *International Journal of Disaster Risk Science* 315, available at doi.org/10.1007/s13753-015-0065-2.

[65] Valérie Ballu and others, 'Comparing the Role of Absolute Sea-Level Rise and Vertical Tectonic Motions in Coastal Flooding, Torres Islands (Vanuatu)' (2011) 108(32) *PNAS* 13019, available at doi.org/10.1073/pnas.1102842108.

[66] Michael Green, 'Contested Territory' (2016) 6(9) *Nature Climate Change* 817, available at doi.org/10.1038/nclimate3112.

[67] Jason E Box and others, 'Greenland Ice Sheet Climate Disequilibrium and Committed Sea-Level Rise' (2022) 12 *Nature Climate Change* 808, 809, available at doi.org/10.1038/s41558-022-01441-2.

curtail human-caused climate change, both ice sheets could melt completely in the coming centuries, thereby raising sea levels by an average of over sixty metres, which would inundate dozens of current cities and thousands of other settlements (if they still exist).[68] If it happens, 'climigration' from this 'clidisaster' could occur. Direct and singular attribution of these impacts and decisions to human-caused climate change nonetheless has ambiguities. After all, with centuries to prepare, it would be preferable to plan to assist billions of people to migrate or live in situ rather than waiting for a crisis to unfold. Climate change does not influence the policy choice to prepare to assist people before they suffer, even if it requires planning decades into the future.

While it is potentially too late to avert the catastrophic impact of heat-humidity induced by human-caused climate change, as it is already with us, this is not the case on all fronts. There is plenty of time to prevent other potentially catastrophic impacts. The term 'potentially' is important here, for the outcome is determined by the choices we make now, and going forward.

VI. Manufacturing a Nexus

As is seen from the rule that 'climigration' and 'clidisasters' do not happen, and the exceptions to this rule, major challenges emerge when trying to attribute migration or non-migration to climate change, including through the intermediary of disasters. Certainly, the most straightforward demonstration of the difficulties emerges when attempting to quantify or tabulate people who are climate (change) migrants. The difficulties in counting climate (change) migrants diverges from the simplicity of counting climate (change) refugees. Given the definition of 'refugee',[69] the number of climate refugees, climate change refugees, and environmental refugees is known exactly. This number is zero, since no one can claim refugee status for environmental reasons. If the definition of 'refugee' changes, then the number will equal the number of people granted refugee status for climate, climate change, or environmental reasons.

Back to migrants, empirical evidence for people migrating due to climate change is tricky since it requires asking them to explain why they moved. There might be incentives to claim or not to claim climate change as the reason for moving. Perceptions can be recorded, but corroborating what people state could require undermining their own viewpoints or second-guessing their experiences.

[68] Andrew Zammit-Mangion and others, 'Resolving the Antarctic Contribution to Sea-Level Rise: A Hierarchical Modelling Framework' (2014) 25(4) *Environmetrics* 245, available at doi.org/10.1002/env.2247; Daniel P Lowry and others, 'The Influence of Emissions Scenarios on Future Antarctic Ice Loss is Unlikely to Emerge this Century' (2021) 2 *Communications Earth & Environment* 221, available at doi.org/10.1038/s43247-021-00289-2; Ralf Greve and Christopher Chambers, 'Mass Loss of the Greenland Ice Sheet until the Year 3000 under a Sustained Late-21st-century Climate' (2022) 68(269) *Journal of Glaciology* 618, available at doi.org/10.1017/jog.2022.9.

[69] Refugee Convention (n 51) art 1A(2).

Otherwise, estimates and predictions have been published without any confirmable information or even attempts to provide this material.

One 2005 document generated significant publicity with the statement that 'by 2010 the world will need to cope with as many as 50 million people escaping the effects of creeping environmental deterioration'.[70] No method was presented to monitor, tabulate, estimate, or otherwise track this figure. No way existed to refute or verify it, so when by 2010 no evidence for or against the statement had been found, the organisation removed most of the material available to the public and endured some ridicule for having presented it in the first place. No clear indication was ever provided by the organisation or by the document's authors for the reasoning behind the initial claim, or indeed its subsequent burial.

Not much later, another paper – perhaps riffing off the 2005 document without having read it properly – explained that '[t]he UN projects that there will be up to 50 million people escaping the effects of environmental deterioration by 2020',[71] without any evidence or citations to support this point. The lead author on this paper presented exactly the same statement the following year, and received significant media attention for it, again without providing any evidence or references.[72] 2020 arrived with no way of examining the claim in order to prove or disprove it. No retraction has ever been made.

Similarly, one letter to a journal referred to 'New Zealand's creation of the Pacific Access Category, in response to concerns about climate change'[73] without providing documentation to support this statement. The Pacific Access Category's own material has continually been updated, but to date no documentation or information from official sources has been found which either mentions or implies that climate change (or another environmental driver) is linked to this visa programme. This visa category is instead described as permitting some Pacific island citizens to migrate to New Zealand as long as they have a job offer and are skilled and healthy, among other criteria. It is puzzling why the letter[74] made the claim about the Pacific Access Category without evidence. In 2017, New Zealand suggested that it would consider a new visa category for people leaving the Pacific islands due to climate change.[75] No link was made to the Pacific Access Category, and the idea of this new visa category was soon dropped before it could be put into practice.

[70] United Nations University, 'As Ranks of "Environmental Refugees" Swell Worldwide, Calls Grow for Better Definition, Recognition, Support' (2005) MR/E29/05, 1.

[71] Cristina M Tirado and others, 'Climate Change and Food Safety: A Review' (2010) 43 *Food Research International* 1745, 1756.

[72] Cristina M Tirado, 'Global Climate and Environmental Change: Implications for Food Production and Safety Systems' (American Association for the Advancement of Science Annual Meeting, Washington Convention Center, 2011), available at perma.cc/3LX2-QXST.

[73] Neil W Adger and Jon Barnett, 'Compensation for Climate Change Must Meet Needs' (2005) 436 *Nature* 328, 328, available at doi.org/10.1038/436328c.

[74] ibid.

[75] Leandra Fiennes, 'New Zealand's Climate Refugee Visa, a Framework for Positive Change: Creating a Regional Framework of Protections for Climate Migrants from the Pacific' (LLB thesis, University of Otago 2019) 3, available at perma.cc/Q7K7-6NT9.

Such authors and governance regimes seem intent on producing policy and law on 'climigration' irrespective of evidence for or against climate change and migration connections. Any nexus (or lack thereof) for climate change, disasters, and migration should be determined by investigating the evidence, as well as what constitutes 'evidence', and using the evidence and gap analyses for drawing robust and verifiable conclusions. Instead, many simply seem to want to assume, independent of evidence, that climate change *is* the starting point for disasters and migration, an assumption that allows for the manufacturing of a climate change–disaster–migration nexus.

In the above arguments, the purpose is not to deny the possibility of cases in which people are forced to migrate due to disasters, due to climate change's impacts, or due to disasters that are directly linked to climate change's impacts. Rather, the purpose is to draw attention to the importance of beginning not from what we believe *ought* to be, but from what science tells us *is* the case. That is, articulating what is known about the influence of human-caused climate change on patterns of both disaster and migration (including non-migration). This approach as a priority is not always evident in the work and statements of those engaged in manufacturing the climate change–disaster–migration nexus.

3

'Climate Migration'? Empirical Insights and Conceptual Cautions from Political Ecology and Migration Studies

GUNVOR JÓNSSON*

I. Introduction

While international migration and climate change are each in their own right political issues of high priority, the potential combination of these processes in the form of 'climate-induced migration' has in recent years been receiving increased attention from the media, policy-makers, and practitioners who want to plan for future responses. Indeed, claims that climate change will shape the future of global migration are continuously being made in academia as well as in popular and policy circles. In brief, there is a widespread assumption that a changing climate could lead to an increase in international migration, particularly the displacement of people from the poorer parts of the world.

This chapter critically appraises and, indeed, questions the conceptual and empirical basis for the popular and policy concern for the causal nexus between migration and the environment (including climate change).

The chapter contains two initial conceptual sections. Section II outlines the context within which the 'climate–migration' causal nexus emerged in the 1980s and 1990s, and the trajectory of the discussion thereafter. Section III then addresses problems of terminology and definition. On this topic, the terminology is often confused, frequently conflating concepts such as environment and climate, or change and variability, which leads to confusion and misunderstanding with regard to discussions of both climate change and migration itself.

* This chapter is an abridged and lightly edited version of an International Migration Institute working paper that was published online in 2010. See Gunvor Jónsson, 'The Environmental Factor in Migration Dynamics: A Review of African Case Studies' (2010) International Migration Institute Paper No 21, available at perma.cc/8NF5-PU82. The author is grateful to Calum Nicholson for his careful editing of the chapter, reducing it in length while retaining the essential arguments of the piece.

The chapter then proceeds in three sections which introduce some key lessons for research on the climate–migration nexus, highlighting relevant empirical and theoretical insights which have tended to be overlooked by analysts, despite their importance.

First, section IV describes central empirical findings on 'environmentally induced' migration in the Sahel. The Sahel is chosen as it is a region characterised by high climate variability, including cycles of increasing and decreasing rainfall and recurring drought, which were particularly severe in the 1970s and 1980s. For some researchers, this environment therefore serves as an analogy for future climate change in Africa, where the Intergovernmental Panel on Climate Change (IPCC) predicts increased water stress and the compromising of agricultural production as a result of future climate variability and changes.[1] Inevitably, the Sahel is thus also often cited as a likely region of origin for future 'climate migrants'. However, the chapter will ultimately demonstrate that, far from serving as a guide to how we may understand the impact of climate change on migration, the case of the Sahel in fact serves to remind us of the limits on any such aspiration.

Second, drawing on insights from political ecology, section V unpacks the difficulties of separating, for analytical purposes, the 'environment' as an 'independent variable' that may be seen to influence migration as a 'dependent variable'.

Third, drawing on insights from migration studies, section VI criticises the use of static push–pull frameworks which suggest that migrants are being 'pushed out' of marginal and degraded environments, neglecting the intertwined environmental, political, economic and cultural factors.

The chapter concludes with a call for research to explore the complex interrelationship between environmental factors and mobility rather than starting from the assumption of a simplistic causal relationship.

II. Background on the Environment–Migration Nexus

For many years following its emergence in the late 1980s, research on the environment–migration nexus was often classified as either 'minimalist' or 'maximalist', following a distinction made by Astri Suhrke in 1994. According to Suhrke, the maximalist view posits environmental degradation as a direct cause of large-scale displacement of people. In contrast, in the minimalist view, environmental change is a contextual variable that can contribute to migration, but analytical difficulties and empirical shortcomings make it hazardous to draw firm conclusions.[2] In the literature, maximalism has often been used to denote studies that predict

[1] Martin L Larry and others, 'Summary for Policymakers', in IPCC, Fourth Assessment Report, *Climate Change 2007: Impacts, Adaptation and Vulnerability* (Cambridge, Cambridge University Press 2007).

[2] Astri Suhrke, 'Environmental Degradation and Population Flows' (1994) 47(2) *Journal of International Affairs* 473, 474, available at www.jstor.org/stable/24357292.

and quantify the flows of future 'climate migrants'. Minimalism has been used to refer to studies that highlight the complexity of causality, and to draw attention to the intervening social factors that contribute to migration.

By the late 1990s, as the debate on the environment–migration nexus became more entrenched, the dichotomy of approaches became increasingly rigid, with studies classified as either 'alarmist' or 'sceptic'. Alarmists estimated the number of current and future 'environmental refugees'[3] to be several million and considered environmental displacement as a worrying potential cause of conflict and environmental degradation in receiving areas. Sceptics, on the other hand, considered the term 'environmental refugee' as nonsensical, criticised the lack of any empirical justification for alarmism, and refuted claims of any direct causal links between environmental change and migration.[4]

In academia, this schism was epitomised in the works of Norman Myers[5] (on the alarmist side) and Richard Black[6] (on the sceptic side). Myers forecast future flows and hotspots of 'climate migration', which, he claimed, were fast-growing. His various studies estimate the current numbers of 'environmental refugees' at 25 million, with figures rising up to 200 million by 2050. In his report with Jennifer Kent, he argued that developed countries needed to pre-empt the problems of unsustainable (environmental) development in poor countries, in order to avoid having to 'import growing numbers of environmental refugees'.[7] Myers has later argued that, 'already there are sizeable numbers of environmental refugees who have made their way, usually illegally, into OSCE countries – and today's stream will surely come to be regarded as a trickle when compared with the floods that will 'ensue in [the] decades ahead'.[8]

Black, in turn, not only argued that such alarmist and 'environmental refugees' discourses played into and potentially reinforced xenophobic fears, but also questioned whether environmental refugees were a distinct group of migrants

[3] For an excellent review of the origins and development of the 'environmental refugee' construct, documenting its origins in the neo-Malthusian literature, see Patricia L Saunders 'Environmental Refugees: The Origins of a Construct' in Philip A Stott and Sian Sullivan (eds), *Political Ecology: Science, Myth and Power* (Oxford, Oxford University Press 2000) 218.

[4] James Morrissey, 'Environmental Change and Forced Migration: A State of the Art Review' Refugee Studies Centre Background Paper 2009, available at perma.cc/RS9Y-MMU7.

[5] See Norman Myers, 'Environmental Refugees in a Globally Warmed World' (1993) 43(11) *BioScience* 752, available at doi.org/10.2307/1312319; Norman Myers and Jennifer Kent, *Environmental Exodus: An Emergent Crisis in the Global Arena* (Washington, Climate Institute 1995); Norman Myers, 'Environmental Refugees' (1997) 19 *Population and Environment* 167, available at doi.org/10.1023/A:1024623431924; Norman Myers, 'Environmental Refugees: A Growing Phenomenon of the 21st Century' (2001) 357(1420) *Philosophical Transactions of the Royal Society* 609, available at doi.org/10.1098/rstb.2001.0953.

[6] See Richard Black, *Refugees, Environment and Development* (Abingdon, Routledge 1998); Richard Black, 'Environmental Refugees: Myth or Reality' (2001) UNHCR Paper No 34, available at perma.cc/2S3B-HLBC.

[7] Myers and Kent (n 5) 160.

[8] Norman Myers, 'Environmental Refugees: An Emergent Security Issue' (22 May 2005) *13th Economic Forum*, EF.NGO/4/05, 4–5, available at perma.cc/A36V-TWU6.

deserving the world's attention, and argued that the conceptualisation of environmental degradation as the primary cause of forced displacement is unhelpful and analytically unsound. His paper entitled 'Environmental Refugees: Myth or Reality?'[9] is often considered as one of the more radical early attempts to fundamentally undermine the environmental refugee thesis.[10] In the paper, Black cautioned that academic and policy writing on environmental refugees may have more to do with the bureaucratic agendas of international organisations and academics than any real theoretical or empirical insight.[11]

Since, many other scholars have questioned alarmist predictions, particularly the estimates of the numbers of environmental refugees, which do not appear to be based on any sound empirical evidence. As François Gemenne put it:

> When it comes to predictions, figures are usually based on the number of people living in regions at risk, and not on the number of people actually expected to migrate. Estimates do not account for adaptation strategies, different levels of vulnerability to change, or simply – though it might sound harsh – disaster-related casualties.[12]

While the distinction between minimalism and maximalism might be helpful for orientation in the broader debate on environmental change and migration, it is perhaps too crude for classifying most of the empirical case studies conducted by academic researchers. Maximalism does not refer to a particular theory or framework of analysis, and it can potentially be used to label and justify claims which may otherwise be considered 'unscientific' or uninformed statements about the environment–migration nexus. In fact, none of the case studies reviewed for this chapter are pure maximalist studies, because all of the authors acknowledge, to varying extents, the multiple causalities of migration. Furthermore, the association of maximalism with alarmism, and minimalism with scepticism, can be misleading.

For example, while Meze-Hausken's study addresses the complexity of causality, and therefore appears to fit the label of minimalism, the author is not particularly sceptical about the notion of 'climate migrants' – a phrase which she uses almost uncritically.[13] Minimalists, on the other hand, are – according to Suhrke[14] – primarily migration experts, who emphasise complexity and multi-causality, but typically do not produce new insights that can be generalised.

This chapter tries to move beyond the maximalism/minimalism binary, by asking more fundamental conceptual questions, such as: how do we *distinguish*

[9] Black, 'Environmental Refugees' (n 6).

[10] See, for example, Morrissey (n 4).

[11] Black, 'Environmental Refugees' (n 6) 14.

[12] Francois Gemenne, 'Environmental Changes and Migration Flows: Normative Frameworks and Policy Responses' (PhD thesis, Institut d'Etudes Politiques de Paris 2009) 159.

[13] Elisabeth Meze-Hausken, 'Migration Caused by Climate Change: How Vulnerable are People in Dryland Areas? A Case Study in Northern Ethiopia' (2000) 5(4) *Mitigation and Adaptation Strategies for Global Change* 379, available at doi.org/10.1023/A:1026570529614.

[14] Suhrke (n 2).

'climate' or 'the environment' from other factors and variables impacting on societal outcomes, migration not least? How do we understand what *determines* the decision to migrate? And how can we even begin such a discussion without first agreeing on the terminology? The latter will now be discussed, using illustrative examples drawn from relevant case studies on the Sahel.

III. Definitional Considerations

In order to generalise research findings and develop theory about environmental factors in migration dynamics, there is first a need to clarify the terms of the debate and the objects of study. However, definitions are a central point of confusion in this field regarding both elements of the supposed causal nexus, 'climate' and 'migration'. These two topics will now be addressed in turn.

First, there is a frequent confusion between terms such as *climate change* and *climate variability*, or between *climatic conditions* and *climatic events*. Bleibaum, for example, argues that environmental degradation in Senegal is caused by both climate variability and human actions.[15] She does not explain how climate variability has degraded the environment and confounds (natural) climate *variability* with (anthropogenic or natural) climate *change*.

Climate *variability* is natural, long-term, normal statistical fluctuation in climate that occurs without human interference. Climate variability per se cannot cause environmental degradation, but it may exacerbate already existing processes, such as land degradation.[16] By contrast, climate *change* entails unprecedented changes, which may well contribute to environmental degradation, because ecosystems are not geared to such conditions. This distinction is not drawn by Bleibaum, who uses the two terms interchangeably.

Similarly, Henry and colleagues found that more people migrated out of rural areas affected by land degradation than out of areas affected by poor climatic conditions. On this basis, they contended that 'migrations are likely to be more influenced by a slow-acting process such as land degradation than by episodic events such as droughts'.[17] This conclusion is confusing because the authors use the term 'climatic conditions' interchangeably with the term 'episodic events', which refers to events such as drought. Climatic conditions are not episodic *events*, but rather long-term *patterns*. A climate *event* would be something recurrent in that pattern, like the monsoon, or El Nino, or indeed, drought. While, as the authors

[15] Frauke Bleibaum, 'Senegal Case Study Reports', in 'Environmental Change and Forced Migration Scenarios' (EACH-FOR 2009) 44, available at perma.cc/J2LV-7BC6.

[16] See Piers Blaikie and Harold Brookfield (eds), *Land Degradation and Society* (Abingdon, Routledge 1991).

[17] Sabine Henry and others, 'Descriptive Analysis of the Individual Migratory Pathways According to Environmental Typologies' (2004) 25(45) *Population and Environment* 397, available at doi.org/10.1023/B:POEN.0000036929.19001.a4.

claim, drought may not influence migration, certainly the long-standing migration patterns in the Sahel are related to the difficult *climatic conditions* in the region, as well as the need to diversify income-earning opportunities.[18] Failure to clearly define the terms of analysis has the effect of further confusing our understanding of the nature of the relationship between environmental change and migration.

Apart from confusions in the 'climate migration' debate over what constitutes 'the environment', a second definitional problem relates to the lack of clarity about 'migration' itself. While some researchers refer to the analytical notion of refugees, others acknowledge the complex interplay of structure and agency which complicates the empirical distinction between forced and voluntary migrants. There is a long-standing debate on the distinction between forced (refugees) and voluntary migration. The analytical distinction between the categories of refugees and migrants is very blurred in practice, as most migration contains elements of force and volition.[19] As Richmond notes, human agency implies an element of choice, as a consequence of which some degree of uncertainty is always present, even when the choices in question are severely constrained by external conditions.[20]

Meanwhile, taking the binary distinction between refugees and migrants for granted, researchers tend to assume that environmental or climate change is merely related to *forced* movements.[21] Yet environmental factors often play a role in 'normal' migration decisions in the Sahel. While circumstances of life in the Sahel may be tough, particularly because of the vagaries and harshness of the climate, it would be wrong to assume that when people migrate it is always an involuntary response to crisis, reflecting a lack of agency. Migration in the Sahel is often a normal part of a person's livelihood and life-course. Movements witnessed during drought were often planned and initiated long before the onset of the drought and play into greater patterns of migratory dynamics that are shaped not only by environmental change, but also by political and socio-economic factors.

Apart from the refugee-migrant distinction, another that researchers on 'climate migration' often fail to make explicit is the distinction between short and long distance migration. The concept of migration tends to be applied to almost any kind of human movement, with authors rarely making explicit how they actually define migration. As this chapter's subsequent arguments will show, it is very unlikely that people affected by environmental change will migrate to the 'Global North', or even cross the border into a neighbouring country, since most of the observed movements are within countries, and occur over relatively short distances.

[18] Black, *Refugees, Environment and Development* (n 6) 28.

[19] Anthony H Richmond, 'Reactive Migration: Sociological Perspectives on Refugee Movements' (1993) 6 *Journal of Refugee Studies* 7, available at doi.org/10.1093/jrs/6.1.7; Hein de Haas, 'Mobility and Human Development' (2009) International Migration Institute Paper No 14, available at perma.cc/49QC-83WL.

[20] Richmond (n 19) 9.

[21] Gemenne (n 12).

This takes us to another pertinent debate, which is whether it is more appropriate to talk about mobility rather than migration in the context of environmental changes. In most cases, movements associated with environmental change were more subtle and gradual and therefore difficult to characterise as migrations. Perhaps such movements are better captured with the term mobility, although this term itself encounters its own problems, as Nicholson's chapter in this volume makes clear.[22]

Having discussed definitional issues to do with both 'climate' and 'migration', this chapter will now consider the difficulties that lawyers, policy-makers, and researchers face when attempting to isolate 'the environment', still less 'the climate', as a 'driver' of human migration. The first step is to outline the empirical insights to be gleaned by reviewing the literature on the Sahel.

IV. Empirical Insights

Case studies on the Sahel provide a number of empirical insights, which challenge key assumptions about migration in the context of environmental and climate change.

First, it appears that environmental stressors such as drought do not necessarily lead to migration. This is usually because migration – particularly long-distance and international migration – requires resources, and during drought resources are scarce. This was confirmed by studies in Ghana and Burkina Faso, where severe droughts limited people's ability to invest in migrations,[23] and in Mali, where migration during drought was limited to short-distance rather than international destinations.[24] Moreover, migration requires social networks outside the local area that the migrant can draw upon for support, and if a community has no previous history or tradition of migration, such facilitating networks will not be present to help people migrate during drought.[25]

Second, migration during drought tends to be within the borders of the migrants' country of residence. Findley, for instance, points out that it would be wrong to assume that drought-related migrants cross international borders.[26]

[22] Calum TM Nicholson, 'Conceptualising "Climate Migration"', ch 1 in this volume.

[23] Henry and others (n 17); Kees van der Geest, 'Migration and Natural Resources Scarcity in Ghana', in 'Environmental Change and Forced Migration Scenarios' (EACH-FOR 2009) 46, available at perma.cc/J2LV-7BC6.

[24] Sally E Findley, 'Does Drought Increase Migration? A Study of Migration from Rural Mali during the 1983–1985 Drought' (1994) 28(3) *International Migration Review* 539, available at doi.org/10.2307/2546820.

[25] Ralph H Faulkingham and Peter F Thorbahn, 'Population Dynamics and Drought: A Village in Niger' (1975) 29(3) *Population Studies* 463; Thomas J Bassett and Matthew D Turner, 'Sudden Shift or Migratory Drift? Fulbe Herd Movements to the Sudano-Guinean Region of West Africa' (2007) 35 *Human Ecology* 33, available at www.jstor.org/stable/27654168.

[26] Findley (n 24).

As mentioned, this is largely related to a lack of resources. Bleibaum shows that in two villages in the Peanut Basin, the village that had more resources had seen people emigrating to larger cities or Europe where they settled for a longer time, while the poorer village had seen seasonal migration to the cities.[27] Moreover, as Findley argues, it cannot be assumed that drought-related migrants leave their homes permanently.[28] Drought-related migrants may want to return once conditions improve, and it therefore makes sense if they only move a relatively short distance.

Third, when migration occurs during drought, there are other non-environmentally related factors that interact with drought to lead to migration. These other factors tend to be context-specific. For example, Ezra and Kiros observed that vulnerability of the studied community to food crisis had significant positive effect on out-migration, especially to assist elderly relatives in the destination and to send remittances to family in the place of origin.[29] Meze-Hausken, on the contrary, showed that there was no correlation between vulnerability and the time elapsed until migration, as the most vulnerable left after a similar number of months as the least vulnerable.[30]

Fourth, the assumption that drought 'causes' people to flee suddenly is challenged by several of the case studies. Population movements in the Sahel under conditions of environmental change appear to be progressive rather than sudden. Mounkaila writes about Niger that permanent abandonment of the rural territory is an exceptional form of migration and a strategy of last recourse.[31] However, he adds, if the food deficit becomes chronic, as the trend over the last decades is indicating, it is likely that migration will progressively result in complete abandonment of this area.

Fifth, many of the case studies show that the choice of destination for drought-related migrants is not random but depends on various conditions at the destination. One factor, alluded to above, is the presence of social networks and a sense of familiarity in terms of cultural practices, language, and religion.[32] Environmental conditions at the destination can be important too.[33] Political-economic factors also play an important role: Basset and Turner found that pro-pastoralist policies in Cameroon and Cote d'Ivoire attracted Fulbe pastoralists.[34]

[27] Bleibaum (n 15).
[28] Findley (n 24).
[29] Markos Ezra and Gebre-Egziabher Kiros, 'Rural Out-Migration in the Drought Prone Areas of Ethiopia: A Multilevel Analysis' (2001) 35(3) *International Migration Review* 749, available at doi.org/10.1111/j.1747-7379.2001.tb00039.x.
[30] Meze-Hausken (n 13).
[31] Harouna Mounkaila, 'De la migration circulaire à l'abandon du territoire local dans le Zarmaganda (Niger)' (2002) 18(2) *Revue européene des migrations internationales* 161, available at doi.org/10.4000/remi.1662.
[32] See ibid; Van der Geest (n 23).
[33] Henry and others (n 17).
[34] Bassett and Turner (n 25).

Sixth, a community of people affected by the same environmental changes does not necessarily react to such change as one homogenous group. Hence, it is not necessarily the entire affected community that leaves during drought, and structural conditions such as marriage practices and gender inequality may be decisive in who gets to move and who stays behind. In Mali, Findley noted that an increase in the short-distance migration of women and children could be observed during drought.[35] Meanwhile, Afifi's study in Niger showed that women were usually left behind by their emigrated husbands.[36] And in the case of Ghana presented by Carr, younger men would emigrate relatively quickly, while older men would stay put for as long as possible in an attempt to maintain their position of local and household authorities.[37] Related to this is the observation that environmental change may be associated with a variety of migratory patterns. As de Bruijn and van Dijk showed, some of the Fulbe who moved south settled outside established villages, others were continuously moving between various villages, and yet others established their own settlements.[38]

Seventh, the studies also show that adaptation and non-migratory responses to environmental change also need to be taken into account. It is worth noting that life in the Sahel generally tends to be under difficult conditions, at the margin of subsistence. For example, Mounkaila writes that food insecurity is a constant factor in the economic history of his study area in Niger.[39] Under such circumstances, people have developed many adaptation mechanisms and they might adapt to environmental and climate change through other mechanisms than migration.[40] This point is borne out in the papers on various responses to environmental change. Mounkaila's paper on Niger explicates the numerous non-migratory strategies that a community employs to cope with food insecurity, including reduction of food consumption, receipt of humanitarian food aid, mutual support, eating wild crops, and secondary commercial activities.[41] Faulkingham and Thorbahn's study in Niger showed that migration was not a useful response to drought; instead, the communities kept the demand on food down through endogamous and patrilineal marriage practices, which limited population increase from immigration.[42]

[35] Findley (n 24).

[36] Tamer Afifi, 'Niger Case Study Report', in 'Environmental Change and Forced Migration Scenarios' (EACH-FOR 2009) 42, available at perma.cc/J2LV-7BC6.

[37] Edward R Carr, 'Placing the Environment in Migration: Environment, Economy, and Power in Ghana's Central Region' (2005) 37(5) *Environment and Planning* 925, available at doi.org/10.1068/a3754.

[38] Mirjam de Bruijn and Han van Dijk, 'Changing Population Mobility in West Africa: Fulbe Pastoralists in Central and South Mali' (2003) 102(407) *African Affairs* 285, available at www.jstor.org/stable/3518680.

[39] Mounkaila (n 31).

[40] See Meze-Hausken (n 13).

[41] Mounkaila (n 31).

[42] Faulkingham and Thorbahn (n 25). See also Jon Pedersen, 'Drought, Migration and Population Growth in the Sahel: The Case of the Malian Gourma: 1900–1991' (1995) 49 *Population Studies* 111, available at www.jstor.org/stable/2175324.

Finally, many of the studies point out that migration is not merely or necessarily a response to crisis or change, such as drought. Often migration is a *normal* part of an individual's life-course and part of a household strategy for economic improvement, to diversify income, release pressure on resources, and spread risk.[43] Mounkaila, for example, writes about Niger that migration persists even when agriculture is sufficient to cover villagers' food requirements.[44] De Bruijn and van Dijk observe that, for the Fulbe, mobility has always been part of the cultural repertoire for responding to varying and often insecure and risky environmental conditions, and this prerogative has become part of their self-definition as a wandering people.[45] In fact, it could be argued that climate change in the Sahel is problematic because it *undermines* migratory livelihoods and patterns of migration.[46]

V. Cautions from Political Ecology

On close inspection, there are at least five challenges that attend any attempt to isolate 'the environment' (still less, climate) as an independent variable that can be said to drive societal (still less, migratory) outcomes.

First, what counts as an environmental problem is relative. As Meze-Hausken writes, an Irish farmer would probably consider a month without rainfall as a drought, whereas people in Ethiopia might have quite different views about such weather phenomena.[47] *Perceptions* of environmental change, and not merely environmental change per se, might be an important factor explaining migration decisions.

An illustrative case is a study by Carr on migration in Ghana. While residents claimed that environmental changes, such as declining rainfall and land degradation, were taking place, Carr comments that such claims could not be scientifically proven. Considering this lack of scientific evidence of environmental changes, Carr might have considered analysing villagers' *perceptions* of their local environment: he explains that the demise of logging and ensuing unemployment deprived villagers of sources of income they had come to rely upon as part of their household income; perhaps then, high levels of consumption during decades of prosperity in the village meant that, after the demise of logging, villagers' expectations from local crop production to meet their high demands did not match the capacities of the local environment.[48]

[43] Ezra and Kiros (n 29); Mounkaila (n 31); Bleibaum (n 15); van der Geest (n 23).
[44] Mounkaila (n 31).
[45] De Bruijn and Van Dijk (n 38).
[46] See Morrissey (n 4).
[47] Meze-Hausken (n 13) 389.
[48] Carr (n 37).

Bleibaum similarly highlights the importance of considering subjective understandings of environmental change. Bleibaum writes that in the Senegal River Valley, where access to land and irrigation is difficult for local residents, many households depend on migration; yet, the region also experiences the *in-migration* of people who come to work there in irrigated agriculture.[49] Clearly, local residents' and in-migrants' perceptions and experiences of the environment in the Senegal River Valley diverge.

Second, changes in the environment cannot always simply be blamed on changes in the climate. Socio-political factors such as misguided development strategies, unequal distribution of power and resources, conflict, and lack of rights are part of the explanation for why people have been victims of drought and famine. Climate is only one aspect of the environment. The concept of 'the environment' includes natural, built, and social surroundings. Humans directly experience their environments, and, through their agency, they modify their environments. The natural, built, and social aspects of the environment are intricately linked, and this complicates the task of separating 'natural' causes of migration from social ones. The idea of an environment lacking any effects of human activity is largely an analytical construct; humans have always affected the ecosystem of the area which they inhabit.[50]

Third, it is often in fact unclear what precisely is meant by the concept of 'the environment', as distinct from 'political economy'. In a case study of the Sahel, van der Geest construed resource scarcity as an environmental problem and as such an 'environmental cause' of migration.[51] Conversely, in another Sahelian case study, Ezra and Kiros considered drought as an economic problem and an economic reason for migration.[52]

Understandings of 'environmental change' itself also vary across the literature. Some authors seem to believe that the causes of environmental change are natural (climate variability is the typical example in the reviewed studies), while others acknowledge the dynamic interplay of ecological, political, economic, and other social causes of environmental change. These analytical discrepancies are related to contrasting conceptualisations of human–nature relationships.

It is here perhaps helpful to clarify the different academic traditions that conceptualise the relationship between humans and nature, in particular the different theories of carrying capacity. Black distinguishes between neo-Malthusian, technological, and institutional/political approaches to carrying capacity.[53]

A *neo-Malthusian* approach considers the relationship between people and resources to be related in a deterministic manner with the independent variable

[49] Bleibaum (n 15).
[50] See Blaikie and Brookfield (n 16).
[51] Van der Geest (n 23).
[52] Ezra and Kiros (n 29) 758.
[53] Black, *Refugees, Environment and Development* (n 6).

being population pressure, that is the demand of a growing population on a finite amount of natural resources. Humans are therefore seen as standing outside the environment, posing as consumers or degraders of the environment, particularly when their numbers rise with increasing fertility rates or immigration.

By contrast, a *technological* approach argues that carrying capacity is constantly changing as technological advances increase the productivity of natural and other resources. This is related to Esther Boserup's argument that population pressure provides social and economic imperatives to innovate and develop new technologies.[54]

Finally, what Black refers to as the *institutional* or *political* approach to carrying capacity argues that the adequacy of resources to meet human needs is determined by the distribution of resources rather than the ratio between population and resources.[55] This is related to Amartya Sen's entitlement approach, which he applied to the causes of famine – demonstrating that famine does not necessarily occur as a consequence of an absolute lack of food, but rather due to unequal food distribution.[56]

Case studies of 'environmentally induced' migration in the Sahel generally fall into one of two camps: they rely either on neo-Malthusian type of reasoning when considering environmental change, or instead, they reflect a political ecology approach (ie echoing Black's institutional or political approach). Malthus' principal hypothesis was that a lack of equilibrium in the relationship between population and natural resources is followed by some kind of negative response from either side. Hence, crises including famine are responses resulting from a lack of balance between resources and population, so-called 'population pressure'.[57] Neo-Malthusianism applies these notions to environmental sustainability, linking environmental degradation to population pressure.

One of the key problems with neo-Malthusian theory, however, is that it assumes the environment to be a finite source that sets absolute limits for human action, a framing that suggests that famine and starvation are 'natural' and inevitable.[58] This deterministic approach, and particularly the notion of population pressure on resources, ignores the significance of socio-economic change and technological input, such as the introduction of new crops.[59] Karl Marx was one of the earliest critics of Malthusian theory, arguing that progress in science and technology would allow for indefinite exponential population growth. Even in extremely

[54] Ester Boserup, *The Conditions of Agricultural Growth: The Economics of Agrarian Change under Population Pressure* (Abingdon, Routledge 1965).

[55] Black, *Refugees, Environment and Development* (n 6).

[56] Amartya K Sen, *Poverty and Famines: An Essay on Entitlement and Deprivation* (New York, Oxford University Press 1981). See also Markos Ezra, 'Demographic Responses to Environmental Stress in the Drought- and Famine-Prone Areas of Northern Ethiopia' (2001) 7(4) *International Journal of Population Geography* 259, available at doi.org/10.1002/ijpg.226.

[57] Ezra (n 56).

[58] Paul Robbins, *Political Ecology: A Critical Introduction* (Cornwall, Blackwell Publishing 2004).

[59] Blaikie and Brookfield (n 16).

poor countries, out-migration and the receipt of food aid relax the constraints imposed by a country's carrying capacity.[60] Moreover, as Blaikie and Brookfield argue, it should not be assumed that population pressure leads inevitably to land degradation: high population pressure provides abundant labour with which to do intensive management, and, where land is abundant, the need to conserve it may not be apparent.[61]

Yet, in spite of such critiques, much of the work on the environmental change and migration nexus in recent decades has been informed by neo-Malthusianism, 'apolitical' ecology. For example, Meze-Hausken uses the term 'climate migrants' to denote migrants who moved during the droughts in Ethiopia in the 1970s and 1980s, which coincided with civil war.[62] This term reduces the complex causes of drought to purely climatic factors; it does not address the issue of entitlements identified by Sen, which explain why droughts lead to famine and, in this case, eventually to migration.

Meze-Hausken argues that migration is a 'second-order climate impact', rooted in the processes directly affected by climate change and which determine food and livelihood security.[63] But since food and livelihood security never simply depend on the climate, the notion of 'climate migrants' does not seem to make much sense. Meze-Hausken adds that, while not being the reason for migration, the coinciding civil war essentially influenced coping strategies: many people were disturbed in carrying out off-farm activities and trading, and food aid did not reach the villages due to political conflicts.[64] This seems to suggest that what she terms 'climate migration' could, in fact, be termed a 'second-order civil war impact'.

Another example is van der Geest's analysis of interviews with migrants in Ghana, which reduces the causes of migration to environmental factors, thus downplaying the complexity of the matter.[65] His interviewees mentioned land as the key factor causing their migrations: most had left because farming conditions were better in the destination than at home. Yet, the interviews made no reference to unreliable rainfall patterns, droughts, or floods. The second most important reason for migrating was financial. However, the author claims that the cause of these factors, including poverty, hunger, and food scarcity, is partly environmental because, prior to migrating, the interviewees were farmers depending on the natural resource base for their livelihood. Hence, he concludes that the most mentioned causes of migration were 'either directly or indirectly environmental'.[66]

[60] See Eric Neumayer, 'An Empirical Test of a Neo-Malthusian Theory of Fertility Change' (2006) 27(4) *Population and Environment* 327, available at www.jstor.org/stable/27503966.

[61] Blaikie and Brookfield (n 16).

[62] Meze-Hausken (n 13). By contrast, this problematic analytical tendency has been repeated in the context of the Syrian Civil War. See Daniel Briggs, *Climate Changed: Refugee Border Stories and the Business of Misery* (Abingdon, Routledge 2021).

[63] Meze-Hausken (n 13).

[64] ibid.

[65] Kees van der Geest, 'Ghana: Case Study Report: Migration and Natural Resources Scarcity in Ghana' (2008) EACH-FOR Paper No 044468, available at perma.cc/C7TJ-4VME.

[66] ibid 24.

Yet it seems just as valid to argue that the causes were either directly or indirectly *economic*, depending on how one distinguishes between environmental and economic factors. Also, the author assumes that the societies under study are productively and technologically constant and entirely agrarian, and therefore that these people's livelihoods depend entirely on the natural resource base. This is a common stereotype of rural African societies that has been refuted by numerous studies, including classical studies of colonialism and rural-urban labour migration.[67] Rural households in Africa and elsewhere tend to diversify the risks related to agriculture by relying on various other income sources, including various trades and income generated by migrants.[68]

A contrasting approach, that focuses explicitly on politics, the role of states, and human agency is *political ecology*.[69] Political ecology is an interdisciplinary area which connects politics and economy to problems such as environmental change, thus questioning strict separations between society and environment, and paying particular attention to the social construction of the environment. The guiding objective of political ecology is understanding the complex relations between nature and society through analysing the forms of access and control over resources.[70]

Political ecologists emphasise historical and structural factors as mediators in the relationship between population and environment. They question the normative and conservationist assumptions of the population pressure debate, according to which any change, including migration, is bad. Depending on the political economic context, 'environmental stress' can coincide with innovation and livelihood improvement or, alternatively, with productivity decrease and impoverishment.[71]

Informed by such understanding, researchers have argued that misguided developments in agricultural practices and policies were the main reason why drought turned into famine in the 1970s in the Sahel. Brooks explains that exceptional decades of high rainfall in the Sahel during the 1950s and 1960s encouraged optimistic and recently de-colonised African nations to rapidly expand agriculture northward, into areas where pastoral nomads traditionally herded their cattle. This pushed the herders into the Sahara, while these populations were further marginalised by policies that restricted their access to pastures. As a result, herders

[67] The Manchester school of anthropology, founded by Max Gluckman, dealt particularly with these issues.

[68] Kate Hampshire and Sara Randall, 'Seasonal Labour Migration Strategies: Coping with Poverty or Optimising Security?' (1999) 5(5) *International Journal of Population Geography* 367; Frank Ellis, 'A Livelihoods Approach to Migration and Poverty Reduction' (2003) *Department for International Development*, available at perma.cc/V65G-XXKE.

[69] Raymond L Bryant, 'Political Ecology: An Emerging Research Agenda in Third-World Studies' (1992) 11 *Political Geography* 12, available at doi.org/10.1016/0962-6298(92)90017-N.

[70] Robbins (n 58); Julian Bloomer, 'Using a Political Ecology Framework to examine Extra-Legal Livelihood Strategies: A Lesotho-Based Case Study of Cultivation of and Trade in Cannabis' (2009) 16 *Journal of Political Ecology* 49.

[71] Blaikie and Brookfield (n 16).

became more vulnerable to drought and, when rainfall conditions in the Sahel returned to lower levels in the 1970s, these marginalised pastoralists were starving and forced to move south.[72]

The political ecology approach is often evident in studies which suggest that there are multi-level and contextual 'drivers' of migration. For example, de Bruijn and van Dijk argue that the specific cultural responses and characteristics of the Fulbe nomads are not merely the functional consequences of environmental instability. Rather, they are the result of a historical development, in which environmental instability, economic fluctuations, and political and military turmoil provided the background against which people had to secure their existence. The authors claim that, historically, the impetus for mobility patterns has changed: previously, the reasons were the agricultural seasons and political developments, whereas presently the Fulbe were fully exposed to the vagaries of the Sahelian climate and resulting economic fluctuations in the form of oscillating food prices.[73] It is important to note that this does not necessarily mean that the climate is driving contemporary migration but rather, that the changing political economy has made the Fulbe more vulnerable to drought. As the authors emphasise, mobility and the vagaries of the climate are nothing new to the Sahel.

Similarly, a study by Carr is explicitly based on political ecology. Carr shifts the focus from conditions that drive migration toward the local power/knowledge in which environment, ecology, and politics are understood. The ways migrants negotiate and transform their context and the objectives behind such negotiation and transformation are the condition and result of this understanding.[74] Carr's study shows how the environment, economy, and society are linked in migration decisions. He argues that the Ghanaian migrations show how environmental change becomes inseparable from local perceptions of economy and local politics through local manifestations of power. In this study, the environment always impacts on migration decisions, because it is a key element of any local power/knowledge. Hence, according to Carr, all migrants from that community are environmental migrants in some form or other.

Fourth, the debate on environmental change and migration is often biased by a framing expectation that, in general, people live under stable climatic conditions. As a consequence, arguments and research are often guided by the assumption that a stable, predictable, and conducive environment is the (historical) norm, and that environmental change and extreme climatic variability is exceptional and disruptive. Yet, to some people, environmental change, stress, and degradation are not necessarily experienced as a deviation from the norm, but as a constant factor in life.

This is particularly the case in the Sahel, where change and crisis tend to be regular features. Several of the authors even refer to what is called '*la condition*

[72] Nick Brooks, 'Climate Change, Drought and Pastoralism in the Sahel' (World Initiative on Sustainable Pastoralism 2006), available at perma.cc/C5N6-SJ2H.
[73] De Bruijn and van Dijk (n 38).
[74] Carr (n 37).

sahélienne' to denote this peculiar normativity, whereby change and disruption, including unstable climatic circumstances, irregular rainfall patterns, and periods of drought, are often described as pervasive factors in the Sahel.[75] In their study of Niger, Faulkingham and Thorbahn write that drought is a recurrent phenomenon and societies have adapted culturally to respond to the resulting high mortality, by being 'pro-natalist'.[76]

In another study of Niger, Mounkaila describes food insecurity as a *constant* fact in the economic history of that area.[77] Similarly, Meze-Hausken writes that '[s]o-called "normal" rainfall in the semiarid tropics is perhaps fictional. For subsistence farmers with rain-fed agriculture variability is the current norm'.[78] De Bruijn and van Dijk argue that in the context of *la condition sahélienne* (the Sahelian condition), mobility plays a central role in livelihood strategies.[79] Their study is based on fieldwork over a period of fifteen years and focuses on the processes underlying the rural–rural migration from the north to the south of Mali, which has been occurring since the 1960s. The authors argue that, for the Fulbe, mobility has always been part of the cultural repertoire for responding to varying and often insecure and risky environmental conditions, and that this prerogative has become part of their self-definition as a wandering people.

Fifth and finally, literature on 'climate migration' is often subject to another implicit bias, namely that (environmental) change is necessarily negative. Indeed, most Sahelian case studies on the link between environmental change and migration seem to build on an assumption that migration is related to environmental *stress*, such as drought and land degradation. However, the relationship between *improvements* in environmental conditions and migration is just as relevant for understanding the nexus.

As mentioned in the introduction to this chapter, the debate on environmental change and migration is often driven by concerns over climate change. Yet, not all climatic changes are threatening lives or livelihoods; there are also movements related to environmental factors that are entirely unrelated to climate change.[80] For example, the great Indian Ocean tsunami in 2004 caused mass displacements, but was entirely unrelated to climate change. Moreover, droughts, for example as witnessed in the Sahel, are not necessarily related to climate change, but may be part of a long-term climate pattern which includes episodes of very low rainfall.[81]

The confusion over the types of environmental changes is a major difficulty in understanding the driving forces behind the 'environment–migration' or indeed the 'climate–migration' nexus.[82] It is not at all clear exactly which environmental

[75] De Bruijn and van Dijk (n 38).
[76] Faulkingham and Thorbahn (n 25) 476.
[77] Mounkaila (n 31).
[78] Meze-Hausken (n 13) 386.
[79] De Bruijn and van Dijk (n 38).
[80] Dominic Kniveton and others, 'Climate Change and Migration: Improving Methodologies to Estimate Flows' (International Organization for Migration 2008), available at perma.cc/D3SU-UDT5.
[81] Black, 'Environmental Refugees' (n 6).
[82] Gemenne (n 12) 161.

factors qualify to be addressed under this debate. Should research only focus on climate change, or also the weather, natural disasters, and socially engineered development projects? Where do we draw the line? And ought it to be drawn by lawyers, policy-makers, or researchers? Whichever the case, the act of defining an environmental problem is inevitably a matter and expression of politics and power. Authorities may have a different opinion than migrants about what constitutes an environmental problem, just as policy-makers may have a different interest in examining the environment–migration nexus than academic researchers.

Having here discussed the challenges facing any effort to isolate 'environmental' from 'societal' drivers of migration, this chapter will now draw on insights from migration scholarship to highlight the complementary difficulty that may be faced when talking about the 'causes' or 'drivers' of migration itself.

VI. Caveats from Migration Studies

A central problem with much of the 'climate migration' literature is its failure to account for the advances made in the general field of migration studies. This is of consequence, as modern migration theory has long since evolved past neo-Malthusian assumptions about simplistic 'push' factors of migration; as such, this body of theory can help improve the analysis of the relationship between environmental change and migration. Simplistic 'stimulus–response' models of migration, generally known as 'push–pull' frameworks, have been criticised by migrations scholars for several reasons.

Push–pull frameworks have tended to dominate the debate on the 'environment–migration' nexus. Typically, environmental change in poor countries has been linked to population pressure on resources and unsustainable exploitation of land beyond its carrying capacity, with resulting impoverishment and, consequently, migration. More recently, a common argument is that extreme climate variability and, potentially, climate change are threatening poor people's lives and depriving them of a livelihood, which in turn forces them to migrate to more stable environments, possibly in the 'Global North'. Based on the assumption that environmental (and climate) change has a straightforward and inevitable impact on populations, these analyses are informed to varying degrees by neo-Malthusianism – but rarely do they explicitly mention this, nor do they reflect on the criticism of this approach.

A fundamental problem with the 'push–pull' type of studies is a relative lack of consideration for the empirical and theoretical insights developed in the general field of migration studies. For example, both Henry and colleagues and van der Geest find it surprising that migration decreased during the severe drought years in the 1970s and 1980s.[83] Meanwhile, a well-established observation in contemporary

[83] Henry and others (n 17); van der Geest (n 23).

migration studies is that migration requires resources and, as a consequence, that it is generally not the poorest people who migrate long distances. As such, a study by Meze-Hausken[84] lacks a historical and livelihoods perspective on migration dynamics in the study region and fails to apply newer migration theory. This leaves one wondering why the Ethiopian farmers that the author labels as 'climate migrants' had not migrated before famine set in, and why circular migration and migrant remittances did not feature as attempts to help out the drought-stricken villagers.

Secondly, studies that emphasise 'push factors' of migration focus mainly on macro-level structural factors derived from quantitative and secondary data. For example, a study by Henry and colleagues[85] did not include data from first-hand contact with the migrants themselves and does not produce much in-depth insight into the complex motivations for migration (except for ruling out a few possibilities). Their analysis thereby overlooks the significance of migrants' subjective experiences in determining their motivations, and also fails to distinguish between the migration of farmers and that of herders. Push–pull frameworks have generally been criticised for disregarding the agency of migrants and their households, and for not taking multi-causality into account, including networks and the cultural, historical, existential, and political factors that tend to be part and parcel of migration decisions.

Thirdly, push–pull theories disregard the complex interactions between migration and structural change and cannot explain the phenomenon of cumulative causation,[86] where migratory movements, once started, become self-sustaining social processes.[87] In this light, a notion of 'environmental push and pull', proposed by van der Geest,[88] does not seem theoretically progressive. Such an approach overemphasises the significance of environmental causes of migration. Most of the case studies on the Sahel show that it is problematic to single out the environment as an independent driver of migration and, as Gemenne writes, one can legitimately ask whether isolating environmental drivers is even possible or makes conceptual sense.[89]

Fourth, a major weakness of push–pull frameworks is their failure to explain non-migration. Afifi, for example, analyses coping mechanisms against environmental problems, mainly focusing on women left behind by husbands who have emigrated.[90] However, it is not clear why these women themselves do not migrate.

[84] Meze-Hausken (n 13).
[85] Henry and others (n 17).
[86] Douglas S Massey, 'Social Structure, Household Strategies, and the Cumulative Causation of Migration' (1990) 56 *Population Index* 3, available at doi.org/10.2307/3644186.
[87] Steven Castles and Mark J Miller, *The Age of Migration: International Population Movements in the Modern World* 4th edn (Palgrave Macmillan 2009).
[88] Van der Geest (n 23).
[89] Gemenne (n 12) 147.
[90] Afifi (n 36).

In particular, the author does not elucidate the power relations that determine who gets to migrate and who does not. Moreover, the author mentions respondents who were *not* willing to migrate, because they were attached to their regions or had adapted to the environmental problems. Yet, he does not analyse how and why these peoples' situation differs from those who have decided to migrate. Hence, it is not clear what causes people to stay in an environmentally degraded place rather than emigrating.

Faulkingham and Thorbahn refer to the 'cultural ecology' of Hausa communities to explain non-migration during drought.[91] They argue that migration is deterred by cultural factors: because of patri-local and endogamous marriage practices in the community, residents felt that they would have no place to go if they were to emigrate, as they had no relatives or social networks outside the village. This explanation builds on a rather static and essentialising notion of culture that disregards the reality of social conflict and change, which may result in, for example, migration. If poor people acted as the rational *homo economicus* presumed by neo-classical theories, one would expect them to move to the places where their chances of making a living are optimal, that is, prosperous countries in the 'Global North'. From a Eurocentric point of view, it seems easy to identify a long list of reasons why migrants from the South would want to enter the 'El Dorado' of the European welfare states. Yet, only about 3 per cent of the world's population are international migrants. This raises a paradox: why have not many more people left the poor South? To explain this, researchers need to account for the barriers to migration.[92]

A fifth critique of the (environmental) push-factor approach to migration dynamics is that it not only tends to ignore or downplay the social causes of migration, but also tends to reduce the complex causes of environmental change to climatic variables, like levels of precipitation. However, environmental changes such as land degradation and drought are often caused by interactions between humans and nature. Such environmental changes are therefore not naturally occurring phenomena.[93] At worst, the push-factor approach de-politicises and de-contextualises the causes of migration, downplaying the importance of factors like wealth and welfare gaps or political conflict, and portraying history, culture, identity, networks, household, and livelihoods as rather insignificant factors in migration decisions.

[91] Faulkingham and Thorbahn (n 25).

[92] Tomas Hammar and Kristof Tamas, 'Why do People Go or Stay?', in Tomas Hammar and others (eds), *International Migration, Immobility and Development: Multidisciplinary Perspectives* (Oxford, Berg Publishers 1997); Gunnar Malmberg 'Time and Space in International Migration', in Hammar and others (eds) (ibid); Gunvor Jónsson, 'Migration Aspirations and Immobility in a Malian Soninke Village' (2008) International Migration Institute Paper No 10, available at perma.cc/HH8H-RBJ6.

[93] Blaikie and Brookfield (n 16); Robbins (n 58).

VII. Conclusion

There is a popular assumption that there *is* a significant relationship between migration and environmental change which can be documented and analysed. Meanwhile, we may well question whether there is in fact such a direct link.

While climate science strongly suggests that climatic conditions will in future fundamentally change in many African countries, often for the worse, it is simply not clear *how* this will affect human mobility. The simplistic and alarmist views of several millions of displaced people moving across borders are based on very little evidence and take little account of the wide variation in responses to environmental stress that have been observed in different contexts. The empirical evidence reviewed in this chapter reveals that it would be presumptive to assume that environmental change automatically leads to long distance, let alone international, migration. It might affect human mobility in various ways, such as triggering more movements of short distances, but this observation in itself is not particularly useful for understanding the complex relationship between change and movement. Instead, we need to focus on understanding the details of how environmental change impacts on people's lives and livelihoods, how they cope with it, and what role migration plays in such livelihood and coping strategies.

Having engaged with the literature on 'climate migration' in the Sahel, two caveats are worth observing. First, migration is not a phenomenon that is particular to the Sahel, various migration patterns criss-cross the entire continent and, indeed, the world.[94] Second, other environmental factors besides drought deserve closer attention, to enable us to generalise findings about the role of environmental factors in migration dynamics.

With these caveats having been noted, it is worth reiterating the key point from the literature. That is, whether and how migration is associated with environmental change depends upon the wider context, and the entire set of factors affecting migration. It is therefore unlikely that a general theory will emerge which can predict people's movements in response to environmental change. In the Sahel, it seems that whether and how people migrate in response to environmental change depends largely upon the role that mobility already plays in their lives and livelihoods: are they pastoral nomads, are they involved in seasonal migration to towns and cities or rural plantations, or are they averse to migrating and favour a more sedentary lifestyle? Whether and how drought-stricken people in the Sahel choose to move also depends on whether they have access to other income sources; their resilience and adaptive capacities; and whether migration complements other coping and adaptation strategies.[95] This diversity of contextual factors entails a diversity of possible responses to environmental change, which may or may not include migration.

[94] Hein de Haas, 'The Myth of Invasion: Irregular Migration from West Africa to the Maghreb and the European Union' (International Migration Institute 2007), available at perma.cc/2JVN-5DSV.

[95] Hampshire and Randall (n 68); Morrissey (n 4).

It is often claimed that there is a lack of data on the relationship between the environment, or the climate, and patterns or instances of human migration, and that this ought to be lamented. However, it is clear that this is not strictly true. There *is* in fact a body of empirical studies available, and there *is* also a well-established debate on the relation between population and environment among geographers and demographers. The problem is that lawyers, policy-makers, and even researchers often fail to consider, or are unaware of, this literature.

Even when they are, they often still fail to recognise the limited predictive value of case studies. The case studies show that migration dynamics are context specific and findings are very hard to generalise; moreover, migration cannot be explained in a deterministic linear way, as its causes are complex and dynamic. As such, it is an error to think that the barrier to establishing the exact nature of the causality between environmental change and migration is simply a dearth of data. The problem is more ontological and epistemological – to do with the unwitting use (and sometimes conscious abuse) of simplistic or antiquated understandings of both 'migration' and 'the environment'.

Indeed, many of the case studies reviewed in this chapter draw on quite simplistic frameworks to explain migration, largely ignoring wider theoretical debates on the relation between population and environment. A viable starting point for future research would be to largely abandon concepts such as population pressure and push–pull frameworks and, instead, to consider environmental factors in a manner that does not presume them to be deterministic of migration. There is a need for more critical attitudes towards rather obsolete migration theories.

There is also a need to develop more critical perspectives on what we mean by 'the environment', or indeed 'climate change', in the context of a concern for human or societal outcomes. It is very complex, if not to say impossible, to isolate the effects of environmental change from other processes of (social, cultural, economic, political) change affecting migration. Most ecosystems on the planet are socially modified and the distinction between the natural and the socially engineered and constructed environment is by no means clear-cut. Most natural processes are intertwined with social processes.

Looking to the future of law, policy, and research on the topic, it would also be helpful to broaden the debate by not considering the relationship between environmental change and migration in a deterministic manner. For example, few have attempted to synthesise the findings from several case studies, in order to establish a broader overview of past and current dynamics and develop empirically founded conceptualisations of the environment–migration nexus.

Furthermore, our insights into this issue can only improve if scientific research sufficiently detaches itself from policy in order to scrutinise the issue from a more neutral perspective. Therefore, a policy-driven quest for numbers and predictions should not be steering the intellectual research on environment and migration.

Some years ago, reflecting on conceptual frameworks in current migration studies, Stephen Castles lamented that, '[a] key problem is the attempt to see migration as something distinct from broader social relationships and change processes'.[96] Castles argued that scholars can make significant progress by re-embedding migration research in a more general understanding of contemporary society. By highlighting the agency of migrants, future research may be able to challenge the stimulus–response model of 'climate migration' and show that causes of migration are complex and cannot and should not be reduced to one single factor.

[96] Stephen Castles, 'Understanding Global Migration: A Social Transformation Perspective' (Conference on Theories of Migration and Social Change, Oxford, 2008) 1, available at perma.cc/J6FA-MLZY.

PART II

Context

4

The 'Others' in John Lanchester's *The Wall*

GREGORY WHITE*

I. Introduction

John Lanchester's *The Wall* was released in 2019 to great acclaim.[1] Reviews invariably praised the quality of Lanchester's writing and his imaginative prowess, especially concerning the climate crisis. One review claimed, '[t]his novel is necessary reading for citizens of the new normal'.[2] Another added, '*The Wall* is a harrowing but beautifully written novel that speaks not only to the uncertainties of life in the Anthropocene but also to recent discourses surrounding racial and economic divisions, nationalism, and immigration'.[3] A third called it a 'topical and deftly satirical novel'.[4] Michael Lewis' back cover blurb proclaimed the novel as a '*1984* for our times'. Other book jacket praise put Lanchester on par with prominent climate fiction (or 'cli-fi') writers such as Margaret Atwood and Kim Stanley Robinson.[5] *The Wall* was longlisted for the UK's prestigious Booker Prize and shortlisted for the 2020 Orwell Prize.

The Wall is a dystopian novel set in the near future. In the aftermath of a climate event known as 'the Change', a massive wall has been constructed around a fictional island country. While the countryside inside the 'National Coastal Defence Structure' is depicted as quaint and bucolic, beaches have been obliterated to build a 16-foot-high concrete structure. National conscription requires every citizen to spend two years of their life as a 'Defender' – patrolling the concrete battlement and defending against the seaborne onslaughts of desperate 'Others'.

* The author gratefully acknowledges the critical comments of the editors as well as Malcolm Sen, Ally Tutay, and Sydney White.

[1] John Lanchester, *The Wall* (London, Faber & Faber 2019).

[2] Nick Pyenson, Book Review of *The Wall* (2021) *Harvard Review*, available at perma.cc/B5KR-3MBF.

[3] Amy Brady, 'In "*The Wall*," Climate Change Pushes us Further Apart' (2019) *Chicago Review of Books*, available at perma.cc/3SZK-SZ8J.

[4] Anna Mundow, '"*The Wall*" Review: We Shall Defend our Island' (*The Wall Street Journal*, 1 March 2019), available at perma.cc/T2D3-LH58.

[5] Margaret Atwood, *MaddAddam* (Canada, McClelland & Stewart 2013); Kim S Robinson, *Ministry for the Future* (London, Orbit 2020).

The Others arrive by boat and are cunning; there are even rumours of disloyal Defenders who collaborate with the threatening outsiders. The Wall, for its part, is cold and grim. Time passes achingly slow. But a Defender has to be alert. The punishment for failure is banishment and exile to the water as an Other, almost a certain death sentence. The state is depicted as a surveillance behemoth, too, with biochips implanted in citizens to monitor their movements. The ultimate goal is to sustain security against the broken, watery world beyond the Wall – a world filled with desperate hordes of 'climate refugees and migrants'.

The protagonist and first-person narrator is a young man named Kavanagh beginning his two-year service. He quickly becomes involved with a woman in his battalion, Hifa, and wonders about the prospect of becoming a 'Breeder' with her. Since the population is so low, some members are matched into couples and obligated to procreate to replenish society. In addition, Defenders and Breeders also rely on 'Help'. The Help are Others who made it across the Wall, but were apprehended and sentenced to provide labour to support the system.

While Kavanagh's overriding ambition is to become a member of the protected elite, in the novel's third and final act – after a group of Others succeed in breeching the Wall against his battalion – he is put to sea in a boat with Hifa, along with a traitor from their Defender ranks and an elite politician. They then have to fight for their survival.

***

This chapter endeavours to examine this work of climate fiction as an act of political imagination. Above all, the main goal is to highlight the ways in which the novel imagines – or, rather, profoundly *under-imagines* – the 'climate migrants' known as 'Others', who have been shut out of society since the Change. Although the Others are invoked repeatedly and are central to the novel, as entities they are largely blank and empty. Should the reader sympathise with them? How many are there? How are they racialised? Where are they from? Moreover, throughout the novel the Wall is strangely *not* besieged. Serving on the Wall as a Defender is portrayed as agonising monotony; the Others are a threat who, in fact, do not appear very often at all. And when Joseph and Hifa are banished in the novel's final act, they do not encounter hordes of Others over the horizon – only relatively few. So, what purpose is the Wall really serving?

This chapter argues that *The Wall* merits engagement for several reasons. First, there are few cli-fi books that imagine 'climate migration' to any great extent. Typically, in the now voluminous genre of cli-fi, 'climate migration' is a background theme or a mood setter. 'Climate migration' is, perhaps, invoked as a sign of turmoil, chaos, and disorder. By contrast, Lanchester's *The Wall* is one of the few cli-fi works that positions 'climate migration' as a central theme.[6]

[6] Another novel that engages with 'climate migration', set in the far distant and deeply fantastic future, is Sam J Miller, *Blackfish City* (New York, Harper Collins 2018).

Second, although the work is set in the future, it has a very '2019' feel to it. In that year Donald Trump was still in the White House, having been elected in 2016 as President of the United States with the explicit promise to 'build a wall' on the border with Mexico. For its part, the UK was struggling to implement its 2016 decision to exit the European Union (EU) in a manner that did not harden the land border between Northern Ireland and the Republic of Ireland – an action feared for its potential to reignite the Troubles. Lanchester is British, and the analogies in the novel are abundantly clear. The cruel irony is that the fictional island in *The Wall* would be analogous to Great Britain, and thus would include England, Wales, and Scotland – but exclude Northern Ireland. In other words, a wall around Great Britain would be far more harmful to Northern Ireland's status in the UK than the customs border in the Irish Sea put in place by the Northern Ireland Protocol as part of Brexit. As examined more fully below, in *The Wall* there is simply no intimation of a nearby landmass. In its world, the island of Ireland does not exist. Europe certainly does not.

An additional point with respect to the novel's year of publication is that the Covid-19 pandemic had not yet been experienced. In retrospect the novel possesses a quaintness; citizens within the rustic countryside are certainly not besieged by a pandemic virus. It is hard to know for sure, but if *The Wall* were written after 2020 it would likely have incorporated epidemiological concerns. The bottom line is that *The Wall* was released in a broader political and social milieu that was highly praising of the work for its political and social importance. Perhaps the book may hold up for the reader a decade after its publication, but it is hard to know.

Most of all, beyond the centrality of 'climate migration' and the 2019 publication, the novel's treatment of 'climate migration' is oddly apolitical. On the one hand, *The Wall* is a quick read suitable for the beach and probably easily adaptable as a film or TV series. On the other hand, its view of 'climate migration' is also dreamlike and esoteric. It operates at a level of surreality that attenuates its political and emotional impact. The 'future imprecise tense' seems to undermine any clear insights into 'climate migration' as a potential phenomenon. 'Climate migration' is a harbinger: the threat that will come (even though, as discussed below, it does not really do so in the novel).

In this regard, it mirrors the many problems associated with so much of the 'climate migration' discourse. Using the 'climate' adjective to modify the 'migration' noun is a deeply depoliticising move. It not only simplifies power, but shortens the analysis of the complicated factors that push migratory movements and refugee flows. The anxiety and fear 'climate migration' engenders, along with the enormity of the looming spectre of multitudes of desperate peoples, more often undermines political or policy action. The focus in the novel is on the 2019 aspect of 'The Wall', within the context of Trump's demagogic proposal to build a wall or the Brexiteers scoring an 'own goal' on themselves in breaking up the UK. But it is not really about 'climate migration' or the Others themselves.

To deepen the argumentative point, *The Wall* illuminates something that has been the case for several decades now: not only has the 'climate migration' discourse largely failed, but so have critics of the concept, too. The discourse itself has a number of failings. Warnings about 'climate migration' have long been introduced with a kind of breathlessness – as if the reader or listener had never thought about the prospect before.[7] Such warnings are invoked with the direct suggestion that there is a new, looming or threat that has not yet been considered as climate change continues to worsen. It is often introduced as the 'new normal', as one reviewer puts it.[8] Yet, since the 'climate migration' discourse's emergence in the 1980s, it has *not* galvanised actors on the 'green Left' to leap to action to 'take climate change seriously'. Nor does it really prompt the fear and anxiety that actors on the 'security Right' wish to nurture. At least not yet, although this remains a growing concern, with hard-right populist parties such as the Alternative for Germany (AfD), the Freedom Party of Austria, and the Sweden Democrats pointing to 'climate migration' as a concern.[9] Across the political spectrum, 'climate migration' is invoked as a harbinger of a monster yet to come and a reason to be concerned about climate change and borders.

In response to the 'climate migration' discourse, scholars of migration and environmental studies – who pursue a more nuanced approach to the impact of climatic change on human populations – have also been unsuccessful. Countless efforts in the empirical literature have acknowledged that climate change and environmental stress certainly affect human society and contribute to complicated migration patterns. Yet the vast bulk of that impact is within national borders or at a subregional level. The literature has also pointed to a lack of precision and the fundamental fact that environmental change (both gradual onset and sudden events) does *not* induce major cross-border migration. Human migration is much knottier than the phrases 'climate migration' or 'climate refugees' suggest.[10]

Whether it be the challenges of conveying scientific understanding to a wider audience, or the fact that the audience may not be receptive to nuance, the bottom line is that criticisms do not seem to have gained traction. The 'climate migration' premise remains persistently evergreen and infatuating. Despite the findings of scientific studies – which are clear that climate change is neither (and will not likely become) the primary driver of displacement, nor does it displace people great distances – there remains the chronic seduction of the topic's logic.

An alarm bell keeps getting rung. It is demonstrated that the alarm is false, misguided, and even counterproductive. Yet it still keeps getting rung.

[7] Gregory White, '"Climate Refugees": A Useful Concept?' (2019) 19(4) *Global Environmental Politics* 133, available at doi.org/10.1162/glep_a_00530.

[8] Pyenson (n 2).

[9] Kate Aronoff, 'The European Far Right's Environmental Turn' (*Dissent*, 31 May 2019), available at perma.cc/JX34-H8TM; Sam Moore and Alex Roberts, 'The Threat of Ecofascism' (*Ecologist*, 25 June 2021), available at perma.cc/UX4Z-KZ4E.

[10] See, for example, Ingrid Boas and others, 'Climate Migration Myths' (2019) 9 *Nature Climate Change* 898, available at doi.org/10.1038/s41558-019-0633-3; Sonja Ayeb-Karlsson, Andrew W Baldwin, and Dominic Kniveton, 'Who Is the Climate-Induced Trapped Figure' (2022) 13(6) *Wiley Interdisciplinary Reviews Climate Change* 1, available at doi.org/10.1002/wcc.803.

In *The Wall*, for its part, the threat of the Others does not fully materialise. Once Kavanagh and Hifa are at sea, on the watery side of the wall, they and their companions do not meet with large numbers of people after all. So why did Lanchester feel a need to write such a novel? Why did he not engage more carefully with (or know about) the natural and social scientific literature that would provide a more nuanced understanding of 'climate migration'? Perhaps he did, and the relative lack of Others on the outside is part of his point. But if that is the case, he certainly did not make that central or clear. Why not?

To explore these matters, this chapter is structured as follows: section II details the novel's plot and its key themes. Section III then offers a more detailed appraisal, focusing on the striking and curious lack of Others on the far side of The Wall. Finally, section IV considers, in light of the critical praise the novel received, not so much what the novel could have been, but rather how a climate fiction novel would have to be different in order to avoid using 'climate migration' as a convenient foil or scapegoat. Specifically, it suggests the need for a novel that would not be grounded in the cruel premise of structural violence: a wall around an entire country designed to keep 'Others' out.

II. Race, Simplistic Classes, Generational Thinking, and a Concrete Wall

The Wall has three sections or acts, with Kavanagh as the first-person narrator. The plot is also largely linear, although at the very end there is a crucial loop back to the beginning of the novel. In the first act, Kavanagh is assigned to defend the Wall against the Others. At the end of the second act, he and his battalion fail and, as a result, are exiled to sea to become Others themselves. The third act details their survival; ultimately Kavanagh and Hifa are stranded on an abandoned oil rig. The novel concludes with Kavanagh beginning to tell the story of his assignment to defend the Wall.

The opening chapter begins with Kavanagh on his first day as a Defender. Kavanagh is resigned to his duty. Hardly looking forward to his mandatory two-year conscription, he quickly comes to term with the bad food, the bone-chilling coastal air, and the boring 12-hour shifts. He also dreads the prospect of an attack by the Others. A Defender's job is to shoot to kill. Failure is not an option.

As is often the case with dystopian stories – by Orwell, Huxley, Atwood – the worst has already happened.[11] In *The Wall*, the 'Change' happened in the recent past. Not only was it cataclysmic, but Kavanagh's generation holds his parents' cohort responsible. Interestingly, however, not much detail is given about the Change. It is left vague and uncertain; it is ambiguous about whether it was

[11] Mundow (n 4).

precipitous or gradual or even whether it was really that devastating for people on the island. There is no intimation of the trauma of mass casualties, nor do citizens appear to suffer any climatic or environmental hardship in their day-to-day lives. They ride bicycles, the food is fresh, and the countryside is lovely. It is a surreal cataclysm: dreadful, yes, and yet not really *that* bad.

On the Wall, Kavanagh becomes acquainted with other Defenders, most notably Hifa and the Captain. Unfortunately, Hifa's character is rather underwritten, receiving little development throughout the story. Nevertheless, she and Kavanagh quickly become an intimate couple, even as they try to be discrete within their battalion.

The Captain's character is initially mysterious, but Kavanagh quickly learns his extraordinary backstory. A secondary character named Sarge provides the explanation while on a nighttime shift:

> 'I'll tell you something about the Captain. It's not a secret, but it's something he prefers to tell people for himself. When he does tell you, do me a favor and act like it's a surprise.' [Sarge] looked around, as if he was worried about eavesdroppers, and he lowered his voice so that I could barely hear him over the wind. 'The Captain was an Other. He got here ten years ago, before the laws changed. That why he's so hardcore. That's why he's so strict. He knows what it's like out there. He knows he's not going back. He's done four turns on the wall because he's obsessed with keeping them out and proving he is worth being allowed to stay.' He let it sink in then hissed: 'The captain was an Other!'[12]

Kavanagh uses the revelation of the Captain's past as an Other to provide further narrative exposition.

Until about ten years previously, Others who showed they had valuable skills could stay, at the cost of exchanging places with the Defenders who had failed to keep them out. The law was changed because this fact became known to Others and started to act as a 'pull factor' – a reason they came to the island. Now, today, Others who get over the Wall have to choose between being euthanised, becoming Help, or being put back to sea.[13]

It is further revealed that, with the introduction of implanted microchips within the last ten years, there is no way that Others could avoid detection if they were to get over the Wall.

There is so much to unpack here about the Captain and the Others, not least the suggestion that Others had previously engaged in a micro-level rational calculation (ie a premeditated decision to respond to a 'pull' factor). But what is especially intriguing about the Captain is that he appears to be the only main character who is Black. It is true, when we meet Hifa's mother in the second act, she is described as having 'the same caramel skin tone as Hifa' and is wearing a 'turban wrapped complicatedly around her head'.[14] 'Complicatedly' is an exoticising adverb, and Hifa is a name common in Urdu, Arabic, Hebrew, and Swahili. But Hifa's character

[12] Lanchester (n 1) 44.
[13] ibid 45.
[14] ibid 137.

is not explicitly racialised. For the Captain, by contrast, there is repeated reference to 'tribal scars on his face' and, of course, his origin from beyond the Wall.

This is the first key theme to highlight in *The Wall*: race and the racialisation of characters on this and the other side of the Wall. Racial difference and non-whiteness is most often associated with Others, or with Help who are former Others. Perhaps it helps to exoticise and make the categories different and stark.

To add to this bluntness, the Help (and the Captain, too) are nameless. In chapter nine (still in the first act), Kavanagh, Hifa and a few comrades from their battalion go on a camping trip during a leave from service on the Wall. The group takes two Help to carry equipment and prepare the campground. Leisure camping. With servants! Kavanagh muses that the Help are 'a couple I think, from their familiarity with each other and the way they hardly spoke. I didn't ask them their story and they didn't have to tell it, which is perfect too. He did the cooking and she did everything else.'[15] At the end of the chapter, the reader still does not know the couple's names. And Kavanagh admits that something is bothering him.

> I'd never really thought about Help before, either having it or being it, and the linked questions of what their lives had been like before and after the Change, and the journeys they had made to get here, and how they had got over the Wall, and what it had been like to be among the Others and now to be Help.[16]

He then adds an odd musing:

> I can just about imagine burning sand, a huge yellow sun close overhead, salt water stinging in cuts, the weak being left behind, the bitter tastes of exile and loss, the longing for safety, the incandescent desperation and grief driving you onwards … no, I couldn't really imagine. And yet here they were.[17]

This seems peculiar because it has a certain naiveté to it. Rather than a civil society inundated with images and accounts of 'climate migration' – in order to depict their desperate situation and intent to overwhelm the security provided by the Wall – Kavanagh confesses that he had never really thought about them before. People are apparently largely oblivious to the Others? Once again, there is not much thought put into 'climate migration' discourses. They seem to be accepted uncritically – a means to express urgency about climate change without offering any detail or requiring any action to mitigate climate change's causes, adapt to its effects, or even repair its damage.

With further respect to processes of racialisation, the camping trip concludes with Kavanagh turning to the Help and asking the man:

> 'What happened to the world; we here have a name for it, we call it the Change. But what I've been wondering is what other people call it, if there's a word for the same thing, or if

[15] ibid 68.
[16] ibid 77.
[17] ibid.

> it's just something that happened. I hope you don't mind me asking, but is there a word for the Change, what we call the Change, in your language?'[18]

The clear implication, of course, is that English is not the man's first language. The man abruptly responds, 'Coo-ee-shee-a', and walks away without saying goodbye. Kavanagh looks the word up on his smart phone, but initially does not tell the reader what he finds. But a few pages later the chapter ends with the sentence: '*Kuishia* is a Swahili word. It means "the ending"'.[19] That is it. There is no exposition about the realisation that the two Help are likely from somewhere in East Africa – from a former British colony such as Kenya, Tanzania, or Uganda. Only that Swahili is their language.

All of the above matters, again, because a common factor in 'climate migration' discourse is its racial dimension.[20] Whether ostensible 'climate migrants' themselves are portrayed as victims (the 'human face of climate change') or security threats, the vast bulk of images conveyed in photos, websites, and documentary films display people of colour.[21] Andrew Baldwin has persuasively demonstrated that such racialised representations in 'climate migration' discourse are part of a North Atlantic construction of 'whiteness' – a projection onto the non-white world of difference and otherisation in order to augment an ideological effort to craft a white ethnonational space.[22]

In addition to race, a second major theme in the novel is the role of classes. As in Plato's *Republic*, people are sorted into starkly different classes according to their capacities and virtues.[23] In the *Republic* Socrates imagines a perfectly-ordered society (or *kallipolis*) that is filled with classes that align with the 'myth of the metals'. Philosopher kings are of gold; warriors and artisans have silver and bronze qualities, respectively. Socrates also uses these classes to illuminate the importance of respective virtues in the body politic. The philosopher kings possess reason and wisdom. Warriors have spirited qualities (or *thumos*) such as courage. Artisans (and other labourers and farmers) have appetites and desires that, of course, must be moderated. For Socrates, justice is achieved when the classes in the *kallipolis* – and the virtues in individual's souls – are in balance.

[18] ibid 78.

[19] ibid 79.

[20] See, for example, Neel Ahuja, *Planetary Specters: Race, Migration and Climate Change in the Twenty-First Century* (Chapel Hill, University of North Carolina Press 2021); Andrew Baldwin, *The Other of Climate Change: Racial Futurism, Migration, and Humanism* (Lanham, Rowman & Littlefield 2022). See also Reece Jones, *White Borders: The History of Race and Immigration in the United States from Chinese Exclusion to the Border Wall* (Boston, Beacon Press 2021).

[21] For documentary films see, for example, Michael Nash, 'Climate Refugees: The Global Human Impact of Climate Change' (*The Video Project*, 29 January 2010), available at perma.cc/SH43-2264; Jared P Scott, 'Age of Consequences' (*The Environmental Film Festival in the Nation's Capital*, 2016), available at perma.cc/CS3C-RWXK.

[22] Baldwin (n 20); Andrew Baldwin, 'Racialisation and the Figure of the Climate-Change Migrant' (2013) 45(6) *Environment and Planning A: Economy and Space* 1474, available at doi:10.1068/a45388.

[23] Plato, *The Republic* (Benjamin Jowett trans, Arcturus Publishing 2018). For an example from young adult literature with a similar dystopic conceit of sorting a population by capacities, see Veronica Roth, *Divergent* (New York, Katherine Tegan Books 2014).

In *The Wall*, the Defenders, the Breeders, and the Help provide crucial roles that strike a balance within the walled-in society. In this instance, however, there is no analogy to philosopher kings. Indeed, politicians in *The Wall* are held in low regard, and society does not seem to be particularly well-governed – perhaps reflecting the novel's distinct allusion to Brexit. Moreover, defenders like Kavanagh are not especially preoccupied with justice: they just want to get through their service, even if it means having to shoot Others. In the end, unlike Socrates' classic thought experiment, the classes in *The Wall* are blunt and feel 'off' in their presentation.

A third theme, as noted above, is the prevalence of deeply-clichéd generational thinking: Kavanagh sharply resents his parents' generation. Here the story does not assign responsibility for the Change in a nuanced fashion. There is no class-analysis, sectoral-analysis, or country-specific attribution for the causes of climate change. In other words, there is no effort to hold affluent classes responsible for their outsized contribution to the emissions that cause climate change. Nor are the fossil fuel, automotive, transportation, or agriculture industries held to account. Nor are the richest countries in the Global North acknowledged as emitters of the vast bulk of greenhouse gases. Instead, Kavanagh's younger generation is wholesale in a blunt, simplistic condemnation of their parents' entire generation – and not prior generations. Perhaps it stands to reason, in part, because the Change is implied to be a precise moment. It may have built over time as a process, it is suggested.[24] But it still happened recently and seems to be over. Kavanagh narrates:

> None of us can talk to our parents. By 'us' I mean my generation, people born after the change. You know that thing where you break up with someone and say, *It's not you it's me?* This is the opposite. It's not us, it's them. Everyone knows what the problem is. The diagnosis isn't hard – the diagnosis isn't even controversial. It's guilt: mass guilt, generational guilt. The olds feel they irretrievably fucked up the world, then allowed us to be born into it. You know what? It's true. That's exactly what they did. They know it, we know it. Everybody knows it.[25]

This also affects the younger generation's burden. Kavanagh adds:

> To make things worse, the olds didn't do time on the Wall, because there was no Wall, because there had been no Change so the Wall wasn't needed. This means that the single most important formative experience in the lives of my generation – the big thing we all have in common – is something about which the olds have exactly no clue. The life advice, them knowing better, the back-in-our-day wisdom which, according to books and films, was a big part of the whole-deal between parents and children, just doesn't work. Want to put me straight about what I'm doing wrong in my life, Granddad? No thanks. Why don't you just travel back in time and un-fuckup the world and then travel back here and maybe then we can talk.[26]

[24] Lanchester (n 1) 104–05.
[25] ibid 53.
[26] ibid 54.

As the 'okay, boomer' Internet meme suggests, such generational 'analysis' is all-too common. It feels intuitively appealing. To be sure, as Stephen Gardiner persuasively argued, intergenerational justice is obviously a crucial piece of moral reasoning in the context of climate change.[27]

Nevertheless, despite the ubiquity of artificial categories such as 'baby boomers' or 'generation X', there is no denying that the distinctions are clunky and lack analytical precision. In *The Wall*, too, there is an awkward and totalising categorisation of generations. How can an entire 'generation' be held responsible for something when not all members of a purported generation are equally culpable? And where should the line be drawn between generations? Is a generation twenty years in length? Twenty-five? Where and how do they overlap? When does one start, apart from an empirical event such as the end of a war or the turn of a decade or century? Above all, were not the ecological forces that led to the Change the product of decades (and even a century or more) of dynamism? The end result in *The Wall* and too often in climate change discourse in general is the ubiquitous and apolitical notions of '*we* are all to blame' or 'what are *we* doing that will affect *our* children and grandchildren?' or 'why didn't (or don't) *we* do more?'[28] The fact is that some individuals and entities are far more culpable than others, and articulations of collectivised responsibility are false.

Put differently, there is no denying that young people may feel resentment toward older generation(s) for the world they have inherited. But the wisest of young people also understand that they might not have acted differently were they alive earlier. Above all, culpability is simply not equally spread among 'the ancestors'. And *The Wall* fails to capture this nuance.

Before turning to the fourth and final theme – the Wall itself – the character of the elite politician merits mention, as it also ties into the roughshod generational categories. The politician is Kavanagh's age and described as a 'short shiny young man with a mop of blond hair'.[29] It is easy to imagine an opportunistic, dissembling Boris Johnson fresh out of Eton College. We ultimately learn that the politician's name is James, and he first appears at a daily briefing to the Defenders where he expounds insincerely. Kavanagh describes the eye-rolling and the utter contempt that Defenders feel toward politicians.

> He was a baby politician, an infant member of the elite. He still had his training wheels. I may have been sleep deprived, I might possibly still have been a bit drunk, but I fell for a moment into a reverie, a kind of guided dream, in which I imagine baby members of the elite being born from chrysalises, already wearing their shiny suits, their ties

[27] Stephen M Gardiner, *A Perfect Moral Storm: Climate Change, Intergenerational Ethics and the Global Environmental Tragedy* (Oxford, Oxford University Press 2011).

[28] For a vivid example of this totalisation of responsibility for climate change – a thoroughgoing first-person-plural examination of the 1980s and how 'we' (all of us!) did not act, rather than fossil fuel corporations or the US government or affluent classes – see Nathaniel Rich, 'Losing Earth: The Decade we Almost Stopped Climate Change' (*New York Times*, 1 August 1 2018), available at perma.cc/9HNL-RRU7.

[29] Lanchester (n 1) 103.

pre-knotted, their first clichés already on their lips, being wiped down of cocoon matter and pushed towards a podium, ready to make their first speech, spout their first platitude, lose their virginity at lying. They'd be made to do that before they were given any food or drink or comfort, just to make sure it was the thing they knew first and best, the thing which came most naturally. They tell us that everyone goes to the Wall, no exceptions. Somehow, though, when I saw the baby politician, I knew for the first time that couldn't be true. This man had clearly never been on the Wall. He had never been a Defender. You could smell it on him.[30]

Once again, Kavanagh seems to be noticing things for the first time. He has not encountered members of the political class in his life before? Not on TV? Perhaps Kavanagh's insight is borne of the time that he has now spent in service as a Defender, but it seems late and clueless.

In his speech to the Defenders, James provides three crucial pieces of exposition. First, he simplistically emphasises the culpability of the entire older generation: 'There was our parents' world, and now there is our world'.[31] Second, although the interior of the island appears to be just fine, the politician quickly emphasises that it is getting profoundly worse on the outside. And more Others will come!

'In many hotter places of the world, in particular, the Change is still continuing, still reshaping landscapes, still impacting people's lives. Men and women fled from it, fled from its consequences, tried to make new lives for themselves, to scramble for new shelter, to climb to higher ground, to find a ledge, cave, well, an oasis, a place where they could find safety for them and their families. But,' he said, his tone changing again, and now he really did sound like a member of the elite, a man used to giving orders and breaking bad news, 'the Change did not stop. The shelter blew away, the waters rose to the higher ground, the ground baked, the crops died, the ledge crumbled, the well dried up. The safety was an illusion. So the unfortunates must flee again and they have begun, again, in numbers, like the numbers from many years ago when the Change first struck. Big numbers, dangerous numbers. So that is the first thing I'm here to tell you. The Others are coming. We have had years of relative peace and calm, but the time is now over. You will be busy.'[32]

Here we see a dynamic common in so much of the 'climate migration' and border security discourse: the invocation by state security/defence actors of the looming threat of enormous (and imprecise) numbers of desperate 'climate migrants'. As James menaces, '[b]ig numbers, dangerous numbers'. Estimates from venerable international organisations and NGOs are often similarly enormous and rounded. As the Nobel prize-winning Polish poet Wisława Szymborska wrote: 'History counts its skeletons in round numbers. A thousand and one remains a thousand, as though the one had never existed'.[33] Such 'round numbers' are ever common in 'climate migration' discourse.

[30] ibid.
[31] ibid 104.
[32] ibid 105.
[33] Wisława Szymborska, 'Hunger Camp at Jaslo' (Grazyna Drabik and Austin Flint trans, *Poetry nook*, 13 January 2003), available at perma.cc/MDT7-A58T.

Curiously, too, the novel never seems to suggest that the climate is worsening on the island; again, the environment seems perfectly fine within the Wall. It is only on the outside that the climate is horrible. And Others will come.

This ties into the third piece of the young politician's discourse: there is a security threat not only from the Others but more worryingly from people on the *inside* of the Wall who are either sympathetic to the plight of 'climate migrants' or, worse, collaborating and helping them.

> 'They are taking the side, not of the ordinary decent people of this country, the people you Defenders guard and protect, the people for whom you spend your long nights and days on the Wall, the people whose security is the meaning and purpose of what you do – no, they don't take their side.' He was getting into it now. He dropped his voice to a loud, histrionic whisper. 'They take the side of the Others!'[34]

A discourse of securitisation typically has an external dimension. Entrepreneurial and demagogic actors such as politicians or media personalities accentuate that there is an external threat. One must beware of communists, immigrants, Muslims, terrorists. Even zombies are a threat![35] Such outsiders are coming to take jobs, terrorise society, and threaten cultural identity. But the *real* threat, especially with ethnonationalism, is when an external regard is turned inward and the polity questions itself: 'Are you loyal? Are you really part of us? Are you undermining the nation from within?' And this quickly devolves into a question of authenticity: 'Are you white enough? Man enough? Christian enough? Straight enough?' Once citizens within a securitised polity are made aware of an external threat (and they are reminded repeatedly) they need to be loyal and be watchful for those who might be abetting the threat – which is far worse.

This raises the fourth and final theme to explicate: the Wall itself. It is a character in the novel in its own right, one borne of an emphasis on security – inward and outward. It is inanimate: cold, concrete, and monolithic. It is at once impossible to imagine *and* yet also plausible. How could a wall be built on an undulating and uneven coastline? Rocky cliffs? Sandy beaches? Estuaries? No way that could be done! And yet, before long, the reader and, apparently, citizens on the fictional island succumb to the conceit. It becomes possible to imagine that a barrier might entirely wall off an island citizenry from the outside.

Relatedly, the Wall possesses an external dimension at the same time that it offers an interiority. Citizens internalise its attributes; they acquiesce to and reinforce its presence. It is an artifice *and* deeply real. And citizens embrace it, in significant part, because of the threat of outside Others. As Pink Floyd sang, we are just bricks in the wall.[36]

The Wall also has an implacability and immutability as a character. There are intimations that it needs maintenance and reconstruction as it has been built over

[34] Lanchester (n 1) 106.
[35] Daniel W Drezner, *Theories of International Politics and Zombies* (Princeton, Princeton University Press, 2014).
[36] Pink Floyd, 'Another Brick in the Wall' (Harvest and Columbia, 1979).

time, especially with respect to the mouths of rivers. Nevertheless, it is not going anywhere. Its solidity imprisons Kavanagh and other characters within the novel. Erected to protect and provide security, the Wall quickly becomes a sentence that chokes people's humanity. It gives them the illusion of protection, but it also isolates and makes them even more miserable.

It is hard to know how the author, Lanchester, really imagined the character of the Wall in the novel – whether it was an analogy to Trump's infamous pledge to build a wall and make Mexico pay for it, or if Lanchester intended the story to align with the fact that there has been a proliferation of security barriers put into place around the world in the last several decades.[37] What is striking, of course, is that such walls are often crafted against an external counterpart, usually a neighbouring country or two. For example, in a real-world maritime context relevant to the novel's watery setting, Spain's Integrated System for Vigilance of the Strait of Gibraltar (Sistema Integrado de Vigilancia del Exterior, or SIVE) is arrayed against Morocco and Algeria. The EU's border agency Frontex's implementation of the European Border Surveillance system (EUROSUR) in Italian or Greek waters is similarly arrayed against Tunisia, Libya, and Turkey. In other words, in those instances, surveillance mechanisms such as radar, sonar, and satellite technologies are constructed *against* migrants from nearby sovereign powers.

In *The Wall*, by contrast, there is no sovereign nation-state identified *against which* the island conducts relations. 'Climate migration' discourses often have the tendency of nationalising an issue that is inherently global in nature. In *The Wall* there is no intimation of diplomacy. No sovereign counterpart. The country in *The Wall* is an *island* that seems utterly alone. There are no adjacent or nearby 'transit states' to cajole and/or browbeat into cooperation. International relations do not exist.

In the referendum held in 2016, Northern Ireland voted for the UK to remain in the EU by a majority of 56 per cent.[38] The Northern Irish majority vote (along with Scotland's) could not overcome the majorities in England and Wales that voted to leave. The point is that the Brexiteers in Northern Ireland's minority – those who wanted to leave the EU but of course remain in the UK – would likely read Lanchester's thought experiment as a wholesale negation of their country's very existence. For that matter, as noted at the outset, the entire island of Ireland seems to be completely effaced in the novel's imagination. There are also no sovereign entities with which to collaborate, perhaps, on the 'externalisation' of border security – à la US policy-makers enjoining Mexico to stop migration on its borders with Guatemala and Belize, or EU officials providing financial 'assistance' to Morocco or Turkey in exchange for draconian efforts to keep migrants out the EU.

[37] The Data Team, 'More Neighbours Make More Fences: Boundary Fences Worldwide' (*The Economist*, 7 January 2016), available at perma.cc/LE4V-43PK.

[38] 'EU Referendum: Northern Ireland Votes to Remain' (*BBC News*, 24 June 2016), available at perma.cc/NB8J-W677.

The bottom line is that The Wall in *The Wall* is not a wall of state sovereignty. There are no other nations against which to construct a norm of conventional international sovereignty. Instead, it is a wall entirely *against* 'climate migration'.

III. Exile, the Realisation that there are Very Few 'Others', and Violent Imaginaries

At the end of the second act, a small group of Others attack while Kavanagh and Hifa are on a shift. Initially, the Captain appears to be mortally wounded in the assault. But when Kavanagh, Hifa, James the politician, and a comrade Hughes are banished to sea as punishment for the failure to stop the invaders, they find the Captain semiconscious in the small boat and recovering from his wounds.

What is striking about the exile at sea is that Kavanagh and his boat actually encounter few Others. At night they see a boat in the distance with lights, but it becomes apparent before long that it is a pirate ship. In time, too, they join a small group of Others, a flotilla of rafts and boats tied up together off of an uninhabited island. But the flotilla only has eight boats and two rafts – and only a few dozen migrants. After a brief period of gentle cooperation with the other boats in the flotilla, the pirate ship suddenly reappears and attacks. After a dramatic escape, Kavanagh and Hifa move off on their own and eventually find an oil rig that has one catatonic occupant. Again, there is the intimation that there are Others in far-off lands. But they are never encountered.

This raises again the central paradox of the novel. The island nation has constructed the Wall against an external threat that never fully materialises. Yes, there are assaults on the Wall. And Kavanagh and his group are banished because one occurs while they were on a shift on the battlement. But the Wall seems to be constructed against a threat that does not exist. One might argue that the threat does not materialise often because of the Wall's intimidation; Others are not endeavouring to approach the island because they know its defences are robust. But it also seems to suggest that the Wall itself may not really be justified.

So much of the cli-fi genre is situated around the imagining of a profoundly violent, dystopian future.[39] In this case, it is an implacable concrete barrier that is, by definition, at the heart of systemic and structural violence. A fortified wall is essential for border control, incarceration, and gated communities. Johannes Galtung's seminal work in the late 1960s examines how structural violence is different than individual or personal violence.[40] As Benner and others observe in

[39] See Daniel Kramb, *From Here* (London, Lonely Coot 2012); Atwood (n 5); Marcel Theroux, *Far North* (New York, Farrar, Straus and Giroux 2009); Emmi Itäranta, *Memory of Water* (New York, Harper Voyager 2014); Paolo Bacigalupi, *The Water Knife* (New York, Vintage Books 2015).

[40] Johan Galtung, 'Violence, Peace, and Peace Research' (1969) 6(3) *Journal of Peace Research* 167.

their superb report, *Violent Climate Imaginaries: Science-Fiction-Politics*, Galtung's structural violence is, by definition:

> An impersonal form of violence that results from unequal power relations and structural injustices … In fact, an increasing number of scholars are now discussing climate change – present and future – as a form of structural violence … Considering that the exposure to environmental risks is highly unequally distributed and depends on the race, gender, class, and geographic location of affected populations, a structural notion of violence directly links up with questions of inequality and climate justice.[41]

The point is that Galtung's insights into a structuralist analysis were crafted in the late 1960s – well before climate change became a profound concern. It pertained more to Cold War politics, colonial legacies, and/or unjust economic systems. More to the point, his framework also lacked a treatment of individual agency. Perpetrators were not fully held accountable as individuals since they are situated in a macro-structural class or national-level analyses. The victims of violence, for their part, are passive receptors. There is no overt struggle.

The point is that if novelists and social science analysts craft future climate imaginaries as violent – and cast 'climate migrants' as desperate, faceless hordes – then the apocalyptic framing can foment and nurture an ideological acquiescence to current (and future) violence. Such 'anticipatory regimes' offer a future vision that seems imminent and therefore demanding a posture.[42] The emergency has already happened – in the future's past – so the present requires an acceptance of violent action. Surely, there are going to be Others who will want to invade an isolated island nation. And surely building a coastal barrier makes great sense!

Here the Captain's anger and lack of remorse becomes central. In chapter nineteen (early in the third act), the exiled group in the boat confronts the Captain for his betrayal. It is revealed that he had abetted the group of Others on the night of the attack. (It turns out that James the politician was right in his frenzied concern about collaborators within the Wall.) For his part, the Captain not only refuses to apologise, but he criticises a 'lifeboat ethics' mentality redolent of Garrett Hardin's gallingly influential work. In the aftermath of his seminal 1968 'Tragedy of the Commons' article, Hardin further deepened his white ethnonationalist (and ecofascist) arguments in the early 1970s.[43] Specifically, Hardin argued for the importance for rich countries to save themselves from immigration – even at the

[41] Ann-Kathrin Benner and others, *Violent Climate Imaginaries: Science-Fiction-Politics* (Institute for Peace Research and Security Policy at the University of Hamburg 2019) 9, available at perma.cc/6ZGJ-VU2K.

[42] Vincanne Adams, Michelle Murphy, and Adele E Clarke, 'Anticipation: Technoscience, Life, Affect, Temporality' (2009) 28 *Subjectivity* 246, available at doi.org/10.1057/sub.2009.18.

[43] For a critique of Hardin's seminal essay, as well as the damage the ubiquitous metaphor has done, see Matto Mildenberger 'The Tragedy of the Tragedy of the Commons' (*Scientific American*, 23 April 2019), available at perma.cc/6LVD-94XB. See also Garrett Hardin, 'The Tragedy of the Commons' (1968) 162(3859) *Science* 1243, available at www.jstor.org/stable/1724745.

expense of poorer countries.[44] The Captain (rightly) rejects this kind of immoral thinking in pointing to society's hypocrisy in building a Wall around itself.

> 'The thing we most despised about you, you people, is your hypocrisy. You push children off a life raft and wish to feel good about yourselves for doing it. OK, fine, if that's what you want to do, but you can't expect the people you push off the side of the raft to think the same. To admire your virtue and principal while we drown. So, no, I'm not going to be like you. I'm not going to lie, I'm not going to be a hypocrite, and I'm not going to say I'm sorry.'[45]

In turn, the Captain makes a persuasive case that they should 'head south'. Lanchester does not capitalise 'south' in the novel, although it is used as a vague, totalising category.

> [The Captain] said there were islands and stretches of coast where we could find somewhere to stay. He said we would never be able to get back over the wall but there are other places to live. He said he was the only one among us to have made a long journey in a boat and he knew how to do it and he could do it again. He said that because we came from an island we thought the whole world had a Wall around it, but that wasn't true and there were places, not many but some, where we could get to safety.[46]

Kavanagh wants to kill the Captain out of his own anger at the betrayal. James the politician does, too. But upon reflection they decide to let the Captain live. More than that, they even decide to follow his leadership. The Captain's argument that there are safe places beyond the Wall to the South seems to blow the minds of the group. To a considerable extent, actually, it should blow the mind of the reader, too. Wait, there are safe places out there?

Importantly, in both *The Wall* and Miller's *Blackfish City* – two cli-fi novels that feature 'climate migration' directly – 'the South' takes on a distinctly Conradian vibe, a 'heart of darkness' locale where disorder and mayhem reign, and from where migrants come.[47] Antonio Gramsci famously wrote about 'the Southern question' within the context of an analysis of the regional differences in Italy's class struggle.[48] At the global scale, there is a similar spatiality to the North versus the South. The South features prominently in the recurrent 'uninhabitable' trope in analyses of the future impact of climate change on entire regions of the world.[49]

[44] Garrett Hardin, 'Lifeboat Ethics: The Case Against Helping the Poor' (1974) 5 *The Hastings Center* 4, available at doi.org/10.2307/3560937.

[45] Lanchester (n 1) 178.

[46] ibid 179.

[47] Miller (n 6); Joseph Conrad, *Heart of Darkness* (London, Penguin Books 2012).

[48] Antonio Gramsci, *The Southern Question* (Pasquale Verdicchio trans, Bordighera Press 1995).

[49] See Gaia Vince, 'Where We'll End up Living as the Planet Burns' (*Time*, 31 August 2022), available at perma.cc/PFN7-LXJ6; David Wallace-Wells, *The Uninhabitable Earth: Life after Warming* (New York, Tim Duggan Books 2019). See also Andrew Jeong, 'Extreme Heat Could Make Parts of Asia, Africa Uninhabitable in Decades' (*The Washington Post*, 11 October 2022), available at perma.cc/P355-E4VC. To its credit, the *Washington Post* article does not slip into the simplistic assumption that extreme heat would prompt people to migrate long distances. Wallace-Wells' book does, as he writes that people will be 'turned outward to wander through hostile territories in search of a new one', at page 9.

It also factors into a crafting of the South as a (or perhaps *the*) source of environmental insecurity.[50]

A reader of *The Wall* could plausibly conclude that Kavanagh's failure as a Defender and exile as an Other might make the deeper point that 'we are all Others'. Perhaps. One might also find themselves in sympathy with the Captain and his moral authority.

But there may be something else at work here. The novel has an innovative ending. As suggested earlier, the plot is linear, but at the end it does circle back to the beginning. In the final paragraph, Hifa asks Kavanagh to tell her a story. To pass the time. To relieve boredom. To come to grips with their new exile on the desolate oil rig. Kavanagh complies, recognising the importance of 'storytelling'. Kavanagh muses:

> I said this to myself over and over again, that's what a story is, something that turns out all right, and then it came to me, and what I said out loud began like this: 'It's cold on the Wall'.[51]

The last sentence of the novel – '[i]t's cold on the Wall' – is the same as the novel's first sentence. Of course, it is not clear whether the author, Lanchester, is seeking to point to the circularity of the Wall's existence. Are citizens on the island – are we readers – caught in an inevitable time loop, trapped behind a Wall, with life seemingly same as it ever was? Is there a futility to trying to write a different story, a different narrative of the past, a different imagining of what could be in an alternative future? Is being marooned with one's lover on a soulless and abandoned oil rig in a wrecked world a story that 'turns out all right'!

But there is a deeper problem at work and that needs to be plumbed. Again, for decades now there have been alarmist threats (and social imaginaries) of a world overrun with enormous numbers of 'climate migrants and refugees'.[52] Warnings since the 1980s have suggested that there will be millions, hundreds of millions, and even a billion people pushed to move because of climate change. We are told it will occur soon, or within a matter of a few decades, or by mid-century, or by the end of the century. Climate change will work as a threat multiplier (for the security-minded) or a 'vulnerability multiplier' (for the more sympathetic).

Such predications have been sharply challenged and questioned by scholars and analysts. Predictions have been put to empirical tests, with an attention to the complicated interplay of climate change, demography, and migration. Researchers have challenged the imprecision of the estimates and their tendency to be inflated; no one wants to underestimate a potential concern, so circular citations and

[50] Harry Verhoeven, 'Gardens of Eden or Hearts of Darkness? The Genealogy of Discourses on Environmental Insecurity and Climate Wars in Africa' (2014) 19(4) *Geopolitics* 784, available at doi.org/10.1080/14650045.2014.896794.

[51] Lanchester (n 1) 254.

[52] See Gregory White, *Climate Change and Migration: Security and Borders in a Warming World* (New York, Oxford University Press 2011).

repetition of ranges of estimates leads to inflation.[53] The agendas of speakers have also been challenged, too. Not only are the xenophobic, racist, and anti-immigrant agendas noted (as done above with respect to Garrett Hardin) – or simplistic acceptance of neo-Malthusian assumptions challenged[54] – but even those who acknowledge that while climate change may not induce enormous migration and refugee flows it is still a good way to mobilise support for mitigation, adaptation, and even reparation.[55]

More than 'merely' criticising the 'climate migration' discourse others have pointed to the *material* interests inherent in such alarmism, too.[56] This is not to minimise the power of discursive fields, but only to point to the dialectical interactions between such ideological frameworks and material interests. For example, the EU's Frontex has used the threat of 'climate migration' as a pretence to justify the purchase and deployment of expensive remote-sensing technologies. In its *2022 Strategic Risk Analysis*, Frontex offers language that is striking in its use of neo-Malthusian assumptions as a justification for Europe's robust spending on border security.

> Climate change is the megatrend that will possibly have the greatest effects on border security in the future. Climate change will affect other megatrends in varied degrees, exerting socioeconomic pressures – especially on low-income countries and the most vulnerable and deprived communities – and deepening structural inequalities around the world. The increasing frequency of extreme weather phenomena and the resultant environmental degradation, resource scarcity and lack of access to basic goods such as food and water will have a great impact upon health, economies, security, migration and competition over limited resources.[57]

The Frontex report is a sustained call for enhanced expenditures not only for border control – the agency's *raison d'être* – but also for the use of remote-sensing satellite technology, Sentinel 2 (S2), ostensibly to gather data on migration

[53] For an analogous take on the innumeracy associated with human trafficking data, see David A Feingold, 'Trafficking in Numbers: The Social Construction of Human Trafficking Data' in Peter Andreas and Kelly M Greenhill (eds), *Sex, Drugs, and Body Counts: The Politics of Numbers in Global Crime and Conflict* (New York, Cornell University Press 2011) 46.

[54] See Larry Lohmann, 'Malthusianism and the Terror of Scarcity' in Betsy Hartmann, Ranu Subramanium, and Charles Zerner (eds), *Making Threats: Biofears and Environmental Anxieties* (Lanham, Rowman & Littlefield 2005) 81; Betsy Hartmann, 'Converging on Disaster: Climate Security and the Malthusian Anticipatory Regime for Africa' (2014) 19(4) *Geopolitics* 757.

[55] See François Gemenne, 'One Good Reason to Speak of "Climate Refugees"' (2015) 49 *Forced Migration Review* 70, available at www.fmreview.org/climatechange-disasters/gemenne; Benoit Mayer, 'Who are "Climate Refugees"? Academic Engagement in the Post-Truth Era' in Simon Behrman and Avidan Kent (eds), *'Climate Refugees': Beyond the Legal Impasse?* (Abingdon, Routledge 2018) 89.

[56] See Elizabeth Vallet and Charles-Philippe David, 'Walls of Money: Securitization of Border Discourse and Militarization of Markets' in Elizabeth Vallet (ed), *Borders, Fences and Walls: State of Insecurity*? (Ashgate Publishing 2014) 143; Martin Lemberg-Pedersen, 'Private Security Companies and the European Borderscapes' in Thomas Gammeltoft-Hansen and Ninna N Sorensen (eds), *The Migration Industry and the Commercialization of International Migration* (Abingdon, Routledge 2013) 152.

[57] The European Border and Coast Guard Agency, *Strategic Risk Analysis 2022* (SAMD/RAU/SFALEM/7782/2022, 2022) 9, available at perma.cc/43Z9-U96G.

movements associated with environmental change. The S2 fleet of satellites is part of the EU Commission's Copernicus programme, which is a collaboration between the European Space Agency and the private sector.[58] The takeaway is that there are mixed public–private interests that are profiting from such expenditures; they almost certainly will seek to continue to do so. And they almost certainly will continue to emphasise the threat of rampant 'climate migration'.

IV. Critical Praise and What *The Wall* Could (Should?) Have Been

Given the empirical, conceptual, and ideological challenges to the concept of 'climate migration', why then does it continue to persist? Why would a novel like *The Wall* deploy 'climate migration' as a central conceit? Is it because cli-fi novelists are unfamiliar with the social and natural science evidence? Is it because scholars and experts have been unpersuasive in their criticisms? Or is it because violent imaginaries of a climate change future with rampant 'climate migration' are so compelling and fearful? The 'world-making' of a novel such as *The Wall* is enthralling to readers and critics, perhaps, because it coincides with the real-world dynamics of Trump's wall against Mexico, or Brexit's 'middle finger' to the EU.

This is not to put an author like Lanchester on the hot seat and unduly criticise him for sliding into comfortable assumptions that do not accurately reflect the realities of 'climate migration' or that accept the structural violence of the Wall as fundamentally legitimate. Well, actually, maybe it is. Amitav Ghosh has contended that there is a crisis of imagination in climate change discourses: *The Great Derangement* argued that fiction authors have fundamentally evaded the responsibility about writing about climate change and called for more.[59]

But what are we to do with the failure to convey the complexities of 'climate migration'? Or the usage of blunt class categories, simplistic generational thinking, and (at best, clumsy) racialisation? Are we to be more critical of authors? What are we to do when they seem oblivious to the long-demonstrated problems with 'climate migration' as an 'overwhelming horde' thesis? Why would Lanchester not 'do his homework' and get the social and natural scientific knowledge pertaining to 'climate migration' correct?

Novelists often bone up on a subject to deepen the veracity of their writing and to convey nuance. Consider recently published novels. Geraldine Brooks'

[58] Kathrin M Walter, 'Migration as a Security Threat in our Warming World? Frontex and the Securitisation of Climate Change-Induced Migration through Practices and Speech Acts' (LLM thesis, King's College London 2022).

[59] Amitav Ghosh, *The Great Derangement: Climate Change and the Unthinkable* (Chicago, University of Chicago Press 2017); Aaron Matz, 'Flaubert's Planet: Do Novelists, and their Readers, Bear Some Responsibility for the Climate Crisis?' (*The New York Review*, 21 July 2022) available at perma.cc/7QTC-XC4Z.

Horse is replete with compelling historical detail about horse racing in Kentucky in the 1850s and the complicated interplay with slavery: horses, grooms, and jockeys were all owned by white slave masters.[60] Although her characterisations of the novel's main figures are somewhat clichéd and certainly criticisable, the book nevertheless displays a clear attention to the historical record. It has a multipage afterword that acknowledges the resources and people she engaged with as she wrote about horseracing in the context of the antebellum South. David Santos Donaldson's *Greenland* also carefully plumbs history – with a plotline pertaining to EM Forster's pre-World War I relationship with his young, Egyptian lover, Mohammed El Adl.[61] For an example from cli-fi, Kim Stanley Robinson's magisterial *Ministry for the Future* is replete with careful, deeply-informed research about Earth science, public policy, and political sociology.[62]

For his part, by contrast, Lanchester clearly (and unfortunately) eschewed such careful preparation. Nevertheless, as stated at the outset, *The Wall* was praised in reviews and marketing. Laila Lalami is a marvellous fiction and non-fiction author who has written extensively about immigration and othering.[63] She offered praise for *The Wall*, for 'telling a story of climate change and migration in the speculative mode at a time when reality itself can seem like a dystopia'.[64] She appeared to praise the novel above all because of its focus on migration. Lalami writes:

> In 2018, for example the Trump administration announced a zero-tolerance policy on undocumented immigration. Almost immediately, US Customs and Border Protection began separating migrant and asylum-seeking children from their parents, placing them in detention facilities or in foster care, without the necessary paperwork to keep track of them. We may not yet have the Wall as Lanchester (or Trump) has imagined it, but new horrors are revealed every day: a five-year-old child persuaded to sign papers forgoing her right to a bond hearing, a two-year-old girl forced to appear in federal immigration court alone, detained siblings being told they are not permitted to hug each other. And yet we all seem to carry on as if this were acceptable.[65]

This political contextualisation of Lanchester's novel is perfectly reasonable given the Trump Administration's family separation policy. But Lalami's praise seems off. After all, how does *The Wall* really reveal anything insightful about Trump's border policies? Forcibly separating children from their parents is one of the most chilling and pernicious displays of sovereign power imaginable – certainly on par with the 'extraordinary rendition' of individuals to Central Intelligence Agency (CIA) 'black sites'. But Lanchester's *The Wall* does not really come close to depicting this kind

[60] Geraldine Brooks, *Horse* (New York, Viking 2022).

[61] David S Donaldson, *Greenland* (New York, Amistad 2022).

[62] Robinson (n 5).

[63] See especially Laila Lalami, *Hope and Other Dangerous Pursuits* (New York, Algonquin Books of Chapel Hill 2005); Laila Lalami, *The Other Americans* (New York, Pantheon Books 2019). For non-fiction, see Laila Lalami, *Conditional Citizens: On Belonging in America* (New York, Pantheon 2020).

[64] Laila Lalami, 'Walled Off: John Lanchester's Speculative New Novel about our Not-So-Distant Future' (*The Nation*, 3 June 2019), available at perma.cc/Y2H6-XVQ3.

[65] ibid.

of structural violence. Not at all. Lalami's praise, in fact, suggests that Lanchester does an act of worldbuilding in *The Wall* that downplays the actual violence of a real-world wall. It is too preoccupied with 'climate migration', even as its treatment of it is so flawed.

Put differently, as Benner and colleagues observe, there is a tendency for cli-fi to be violent and catastrophist, to pit humanity against nature, to embrace violent narratives, and to implement anticipatory frameworks that imagine collapse and apocalypse.[66] If fiction writers are imagining a future that is ferocious and bordered, one overrun by 'climate migration' – even when we know that the 'climate migration' discourse is so flawed – then we can criticise it as unproductively dystopian. A constructive or useful imagining of a dystopia, by contrast, would be the kind that offers a cautionary tale. It might offer a 'recipe', perhaps, for *avoiding* getting to that state. But if fiction writers are falling into cliché and acquiescing to an imagined violent and bordered world, then they should not be praised.

Put differently, why didn't Lanchester write a novel about the Change that did not have the threat of overwhelming 'climate migration'? If he is seeking to make a political commentary, then shouldn't he be criticised for the message of the novel? As Granjou, Walker, and Salazer observe:

> Anticipation has become a common, lived affect-state of daily life, shaping regimes of self, health, spirituality, but also our relations and technological entanglement with non-human nature. In other words, anticipation takes on epistemic and normative value as a politics of temporality and affect; 'a virtue emerging through actuarial saturation as science of the actual are displaced by speculative forecast'.[67]

Science and knowledge of the actual – what is really happening and observable – is being displaced by a fearful 'speculative forecast'. The fear of 'climate migration' far outstrips the actual empirics. It informs policy decisions, public imaginaries, and, in this case, a deeply British novel.

The problem with such a misrepresentation of present and future 'climate migration' is clear: the assumption that 'climate migration' will be an expected outgrowth of future climate change already crafts present stances towards refugees and migrants. Jacket blurbs for *The Wall* pronounced the novel as 'brilliant', 'relevant', 'chillingly real', 'all too real', and 'essential reading for anyone who cares about the planet's future'. It quotes *Washington Post* reviewer, Stephen Dyson: 'It's not clear what it will take to finally convince us that it's time to panic about climate change, but works of fiction such as *The Wall* have an important role to play'.

Dyson and others are wrong. The goal should not be to persuade 'us' that 'it's time to panic'. When it comes to this kind of depiction of 'climate migration', works of fiction do *not* have an important role to play if they are going to do so in a slipshod and counterproductive manner.

[66] Benner and others (n 41).

[67] Celine Granjou, Jeremy Walker, and Juan F Salazar, 'The Politics of Anticipation: On Knowing and Governing Environmental Futures' (2017) 92 *Futures* 5, available at doi.org/10.1016/j.futures.2017.05.007.

V. Conclusion

Imagine a cli-fi novel that would tell a story that is not violent. That would tell a future in which adaptation, mitigation, and justice go hand in hand. That would not fall into unreflective and simplistic neo-Malthusianism. Imagine, instead, a novel that would point to the essential importance of equitable, nonviolent, and sustainable use of resources and emissions. That would envision policies by local, provincial, national, and international-level policy-makers that would move in a constructive direction. Imagine, too, a novel that would treat creatively the need for small-'r' reparations – not money transfers to individuals, but systematic projects that would address and alleviate past injustices.[68]

Imagine a cli-fi novel that would also get at the complicated interaction of climate change on humans and Earth's ecosystems in a manner consistent with natural and social scientific knowledge. Above all, imagine a novel that would not use 'climate migration' as a scare tactic. That would not imagine 'Others' as an affective strategy to implicate the reader in the story and suggest that 'it's time to panic about climate change'.

Fundamentally, how do scholars and experts who are keen on studying 'climate migration' – for a variety of political and normative reasons – convey the complexity of the topic? How can we nurture a productive appreciation in the humanities and natural and social sciences, such that others who step into the knowledge domain do so and evade the clichés and hackneyed assumptions that are so fraught?

The ultimate frustration with *The Wall* is that if there were a dreadful political conflagration over the horizon, or people fleeing broken economies or authoritarian regimes and seeking to gain refuge, it would be easy, perhaps, to imagine a dystopian island nation building a wall and saying: 'not my problem' or 'sorry not sorry'. And if the island has a deep imperial history and the conflagrations on the horizon are closely tied to that imperial legacy – as is certainly the case with the UK (including Northern Ireland) – then one could imagine a process of accountability and responsibility for that country.

But still, there is a sense that Lanchester (and so many cli-fi authors, as well as journalists and critics) are *using* climate change – the 'Change' – as a hook on which to hang their analyses of walls and border security. Ultimately, it is a deeply cynical amalgamation of policy and a *misunderstanding* of the actual impact of climate change on human migration.

The Wall may not be read widely enough to seep into full public consciousness, but it is nonetheless reflective of the ongoing construction of 'climate migration' and 'climate refugees' as phenomena that require a society to respond, if they are

[68] Olúfémi O Táíwò, *Reconsidering Reparations* (New York, Oxford University Press 2022).

to be kept out. As such, we must hope that we are spared an adaptation of *The Wall* for the big or indeed the small screen – either would only further normalise the assumptions at the heart of the story. But in the event it is adapted, there will be all the more reason for the story to be met with a deep critical appreciation of its fundamental flaws.

5

Obstacles to Action on 'Climate Migration': A Story of Persistent Analytical and Political Ambiguity

DAVID DURAND-DELACRE

I. Introduction

The academic literature on 'climate migration' often assumes that its subject is an issue of widespread interest and concern. As one recent editorial puts it: 'There is no question that climate change will impact human migration'.[1] Somewhat more carefully, McLeman and colleagues note that 'there is general agreement that migration is one of a range of outcomes that may emerge as households and communities cope with and adapt to climatic risks and hazards'.[2] Furthermore, scholars note that some policy-makers – particularly at international organisations like the International Organization for Migration (IOM) and United Nations High Commissioner for Refugees (UNHCR), and involved in the United Nations Framework Convention on Climate Change (UNFCCC) negotiations[3] – are expressing concern about the potential emergence of new migratory patterns raised in such assessments. These same policy-makers also seek to develop and disseminate expert guidance on how to respond to 'climate migration' as a distinct phenomenon. More broadly, Desai and colleagues identify 'a rapidly growing demand for comprehensive risk assessments that include displacement and its associated costs to inform humanitarian

[1] 'From Migration to Mobility' (2019) 9 *Nature Climate Change* 895, available at doi.org/10.1038/s41558-019-0657-8.

[2] Robert McLeman and others, 'Conceptual Framing to Link Climate Risk Assessments and Climate-Migration Scholarship' (2021) 165 *Climatic Change* 24, available at doi.org/10.1007/s10584-021-03056-6.

[3] See Sarah Louise Nash, 'Knowing Human Mobility in the Context of Climate Change' (2018) 4 *movements. Journal for Critical Migration and Border Regime Studies*, available at movements-journal.org/issues/06.wissen/04.nash--knowing-human-mobility-in-the-context-of-climate-change-the-self-perpetuating-circle-of-research-policy-and-knowledge-production.html; Marine Denis, 'IOM and UNHCR Beyond Their Mandates: Legal and Administrative Functions in the Protection of Environmentally Displaced People' (2018) 16 *Medzinarodne Vztahy* (Journal of International Relations) 68.

response and national planning and coordination',[4] while Naser argues that 'the foundations of a global consensus on climate-related mobility have been built'[5] and that 'a slow-moving but dynamic, step-by-step process of international policy development on climate-related mobility'[6] is ongoing.

Regardless of whether these claims are well founded or not, it is arguable that they nevertheless pass over cases where policy stakeholders have engaged in 'climate migration' debates only to subsequently withdraw. In this chapter, I re-evaluate the apparent obviousness and self-evidence of 'climate migration', pointing to the many instances where it has been discussed, debated, or studied without this leading to any concrete action. My analysis is rooted in the perspectives of French stakeholders who have attempted to develop policies and projects to tackle 'climate migration'. I find that, by and large, interviewees have failed to 'operationalise' the concept.

Furthermore, I argue that these failures are commonplace. Indeed, one of this chapter's main contributions is to highlight the many places where the 'climate migration' concept and its analogues have not found purchase. The cases I recount from the French context illustrate the real-world workings of well known, persistent, and perhaps insurmountable analytical and political ambiguities that thus appear as inherent features of 'climate migration' debates. Ultimately, this chapter raises the question of what *use* these debates serve once their limitations are acknowledged. I therefore conclude by examining one promising 'use' of the ambiguous 'climate migration' concept. Using France as a case study, I show its potential to serve as an entry point for deeper conversations about who can and should be held responsible for the negative consequences of both climate change and migration, while noting obstacles that need to be overcome for these conversations to happen.

II. Methods and Perspectives

The analysis in this chapter is based on interviews with French stakeholders, triangulated with document analysis and a corpus-driven analysis of 'climate migration' media coverage (1,660 articles from a wide range of French national and regional newspapers spanning the years 1986–2020). Between September 2019 and January 2021, I interviewed fifty stakeholders, spanning a range of stakeholder groups. The first major group was civil servants, primarily within the Agence Française de Développement (AFD). The second major group was NGO representatives, many of whom were participants in an NGO network called Des Ponts

[4] Bina Desai and others, 'Addressing the Human Cost in a Changing Climate' (2021) 372(6548) *Science* 1284, available at doi.org/10.1126/science.abh4283.

[5] Mostafa M Naser, *The Emerging Global Consensus on Climate Change and Human Mobility* (Abingdon, Routledge 2022) 2.

[6] ibid 86.

Pas des Murs (DPPDM, meaning 'Bridges, not Walls') that held working group discussions on the subject of 'environmental migrations' between 2019 and 2022. In addition, I also interviewed small samples of politicians, journalists, and researchers.[7]

This choice of a national level study was motivated by the need to understand how 'climate migration' debates are contextualised and situated in a setting different from the international expert negotiations usually studied. In an article concerned with 'some of the mechanisms by which [discourse on human mobility] has emerged and is being perpetuated', Nash describes a 'self-perpetuating circle of research, policy, and knowledge production'[8] that dominates academic and policy discussions. The typical perspectives on 'climate migration' within this 'UN bubble', are, she adds, often so self-referential as to deserve the diagnosis of 'knowledge narcissism'.[9] In this context, it seems worthwhile to explore how 'climate migration' is discussed by other stakeholders. Given that international negotiations have yet to produce any international agreement or initiative for the protection of people displaced specifically by climate change, it also seems worthwhile to ask what potential role there is for stakeholders outside the UN bubble that currently dominates discussions.

The perspectives related in this chapter are therefore those of stakeholders with a potential role to play in primarily French 'climate migration' discourses, projects, and policies: as development practitioners, civil society actors for local and international solidarity, and knowledge producers. For the most part, these stakeholders are outside the UN bubble, though some engage with it in passing. What this chapter does not provide, however, are perspectives from communities and individuals with direct experiential knowledge of why people decide to migrate and what it might mean to be a 'climate migrant'. This may be because they themselves are migrants, or have decided not to migrate, and can therefore speak to their own decision, its causes, and its consequences. This may also be because they have been individually or collectively designated as actual or potential 'climate migrants' by actors in international 'climate migration' discourses – a designation they may embrace or reject.[10] Some stakeholders, NGO representatives in

[7] The analysis proposed here is based on work carried out in the context of my PhD thesis: David Durand-Delacre, 'Epistemic Mobilities of Climate Migration: A French Case Study' (Doctoral thesis, Cambridge University 2022), available at doi.org/10.17863/CAM.93511.

[8] Nash (n 3) 69.

[9] ibid 75.

[10] See, for example, Carol Farbotko, 'Identifying as a "Climate Migrant": Implications for Law, Policy, and Research', ch 8 in this volume; Alex Arnall and Uma Kothari, 'Challenging Climate Change and Migration Discourse: Different Understandings of Timescale and Temporality in the Maldives' (2015) 31 *Global Environmental Change* 199, available at doi.org/10/f7ffbz; Papa Faye, Jesse Ribot, and Matthew Turner, 'Climate change is not the Cause, Migration is not the Problem: Local Representation and Precarious Young Farmers Leaving Senegal' (2019) *Swedish International Centre for Local Democracy Research Report No* 14, available at perma.cc/MZM9-AYYN; Celia McMichael and others, 'Rising Seas, Immobilities, and Translocality in Small Island States: Case Studies from Fiji and Tuvalu' (2021) 43 *Population and Environment* 82, available at doi.org/10.1007/s11111-021-00378-6.

particular, do refer to exchanges they have had with international partners and project beneficiaries. I highlight these wherever possible, but these are second-hand accounts at best. The perspectives relayed in this chapter should therefore be understood to reflect the points of view of French elite professionals working in a specific set of NGOs, international development administrations, and parts of academia and print media.

III. Confronting the Cacophonous Proliferation and Categorical Emptiness of 'Climate Migration' Terminologies

'The field of climate migration', Nicholson points out, 'is most notable for the cacophony of terms and labels, and the essential nebulousness of both its subject and purpose'.[11] The list of available terms is long and varied. Newcomers to 'climate migration' debates need to choose at least two terms: one referring to the causal driver (eg climate) and another to describe the resulting movement of people (eg migration). The options on both sides of this equation – cause and effect – are many, and the combinations exponentially greater. For example, Nicholson counts seventeen different terms in a single edited book on the subject,[12] which for him is the sign of 'a semantic uncertainty that suggests a field ill at ease with itself'.[13] This diversity suggests that terms remain contentious, never consensual. What's more, this terminological proliferation is compounded by a second challenge. Terms like 'climate migration', 'environmental displacement', or 'eco-refugees' are often used in vague and interchangeable ways. In many cases, they lack a precise definition. This is a well-established problem, diagnosed for example by Venturini and colleagues in their study of a corpus of web pages gathered via Google searches. They found that terms like 'climate refugee' or 'environmental migrant' were often used synonymously, emptying them of their technical meanings. They called this phenomenon 'categorical emptiness'.[14]

Faced with the proliferation of terms and vagueness of definitions, some academics argue for developing common, consensual definitions for terms and typologies as a necessary condition for 'climate migration' policy development. Indeed, there is a strong case for (social) scientists to clarify the analytical

[11] Calum TM Nicholson, 'Climate Change and the Politics of Causal Reasoning: The Case of Climate Change and Migration' (2014) 180(2) *The Geographical Journal* 151, available at doi.org/10.1111/geoj.12062.

[12] Calum TM Nicholson, Review of 'Climate Change and Displacement: Multidisciplinary Perspectives', edited by Jane McAdam (2012) 25(4) *Journal of Refugee Studies* 584.

[13] Nicholson (n 11) 154.

[14] Tommaso Venturini, François Gemenne, and Marta Severo, 'Des migrants et des mots: Une analyse numérique des débats médiatiques sur les migrations et l'environnement' (2012) 88 *Cultures & conflits* 133, available at doi.org/10.4000/conflits.18594.

definitions they use, so that their work can be properly evaluated, compared, and generalised.[15] In this vein, Venturini and others deplore 'the absence of a clearly defined typology' because it 'considerably hinders the search for a definition' from which to 'establish quantified estimations and develop adequate public policies'.[16] What's more, as Blake and colleagues argue: 'defining climate migration can be a challenging task but is necessary for policymakers'.[17] The proliferation of terms and the resulting ambiguities are not just obstacles to academic knowledge creation, but also hinder any project or policy development that could rely on such knowledge. Who, for instance, is the target population? What, indeed, should interventions focus on? Ferris also encapsulates this view when she argues that 'it is still too early to deal with the terminology issue … but the sooner a consensus emerges, the better'[18] for 'climate migration' policy development and project design.

Against this, French stakeholders' perspectives reveal that precise definitions and a consensus on terms are neither likely nor, perhaps, even desirable. Most stakeholders, when first encountering 'climate migration' as a concept, attempt to define the 'right' terms. One NGO representative first decided to join the DPPDM's discussions on 'environmental migration' because 'the words we were using were very vague, it wasn't very clear between climatic, environmental, migrants, refugees, displaced persons, all of that'.[19] They wondered which terms to use. AFD interviewees shared a similar intention. One interviewee in the migration unit was planning a meeting of representatives from several AFD departments, together with other government administrations, academics, and journalists. Their objective was to see if it was possible to overcome 'the cacophony of messages'[20] on 'climate migration' and achieve some minimal degree of coordination around the language in use. Ultimately, neither the DPPDM nor the AFD succeeded in overcoming these problems of cacophony and vagueness. As the remainder of this section demonstrates, they were frustrated in their attempts at clarity and consensus because any term chosen will be deeply entangled with legal, ethical, and political considerations. Not only does this lead to significant disagreements between stakeholders about the 'right term', but which term is deemed most appropriate by any stakeholder is also, by extension, liable to vary across contexts and over time, depending on shifting political objectives, ethical values, and communication strategies.

[15] Lori M Hunter, Jessie K Luna, and Rachel M Norton, 'Environmental Dimensions of Migration' (2015) 41 *Annual Review of Sociology* 377, 390–91, available at doi.org/10.1146/annurev-soc-073014-112223.

[16] Venturini, Gemenne, and Severo (n 14) 151.

[17] Jonathan Blake, Aaron Clark-Ginsberg, and Jay Balagna, *Addressing Climate Migration: A Review of National Policy Approaches* (RAND Corporation 2021) 5, available at doi.org/10.7249/PEA1085-1.

[18] Elizabeth Ferris, 'Research on Climate Change and Migration Where Are We and Where Are We Going?' (2020) 8(4) *Migration Studies* 612, 619, available at doi.org/10.1093/migration/mnaa028.

[19] Interview, solidarity NGO representative (Bizi!), phone, February 2020.

[20] Interview, civil servant (AFD migration), Paris, January 2020.

A. Example 1: 'Climate' or 'Environment'?

One good example of this concerns the term designating the cause of migration, which is often posed as a choice between 'climate' and 'environment'.[21] Over the past three decades, French stakeholders have adopted one or the other for a variety of reasons. When the topic of 'climate migration' first took hold in the late 1990s and early 2000s, the preferred terminology tended to be 'environmental refugees' or 'ecological refugees'.[22] Though climate change sometimes featured in academic discussions, it was then treated as just one factor among others, including natural disasters, deforestation, pollution, industrial accidents, or displacement caused by large infrastructure developments, such as dams. In the press, the term 'ecological refugees' recurred with reference to the Chernobyl catastrophe. It was in the middle to the end of the first decade of this century that 'climate' became the preferred causal term. At the time, Donatien Garnier, the co-author of *Réfugiés Climatiques*,[23] thought that 'environmental refugees … was too broad, we needed something that was more cutting'.[24] Thus the focus on 'climate' provided a more focused narrative, in tune with rising and contested concern about climate change at the time. Today, the pendulum is swinging back. If there is one terminological point NGO members of the DPPDM network agree on, it is that 'to think only in terms of climate change is maybe a bit reductive'.[25] Meeting in late 2019 to discuss 'environmental migrations', they collectively concluded that identifying environmental change as the causal factor was preferable.[26] This is because it allows the DPPDM to touch on causes of migration that do not neatly fit under 'climate change' but which are of central concern to the DPPDM: problems like pollution, extractivism, and global economic inequalities.[27]

B. Example 2: 'Refugee', 'Migrant', or 'Displaced Person'?

A second useful example is that of 'climate refugee' (*réfugié climatique*). Though much used in the press and by NGOs from the mid-2000s, the term is now widely

[21] See, for example, Des Ponts Pas des Murs, 'Les migrations environnementales pour les nul.le.s: Etat des lieux des réflexions sur les migrations environnementales du point de vue de la solidarité internationale' (Des Ponts Pas des Murs 2019) 7, available at perma.cc/CY9Z-58JA.

[22] Christel Cournil, 'Les réfugiés écologiques: quelle(s) protection(s), quel(s) statut(s)?' (2006) 4 *Revue du droit public et de la science politique* 1035; Patrick Gonin and Véronique Lassailly-Jacob, 'Les réfugiés de l'environnement: Une nouvelle catégorie de migrants forcés?' (2002) 18(2) *Revue européenne des migrations internationales* 139, available at doi.org/10/fj2cnv.

[23] Jean Jouzel and others, *Réfugiés climatiques* (Paris, Infolio 2007).

[24] Interview, journalist (Donatien Garnier), Skype, October 2019.

[25] Interview, migration NGO representative (La Cimade), Skype, April 2020.

[26] Interview, DPPDM network coordinator, Paris, January 2020.

[27] Elizabeth Lunstrum, Pablo Bose, and Anna Zalik, 'Environmental Displacement: The Common Ground of Climate Change, Extraction and Conservation' (2015) 48(2) *Area* 130, available at doi.org/10/gfgnzs.

considered a legal and political impossibility. The reason for this is encapsulated in a refrain, heard in many stakeholder interviews but also in parliamentary debates and auditions: that the Geneva Convention excludes environmental pressures and climate change from the list of valid reasons to seek asylum. Based on this, stakeholders tend to exclude the possibility of officially recognising a status for 'climate refugees'. Some stakeholders note a similar absence of the environment from the criteria for obtaining subsidiary protection (the other main option for obtaining international protection in France). However, calls for including environmental criteria to either status tend to be dismissed or ignored. Many stakeholders worry that attempts to renegotiate the Geneva Convention and other existing protection mechanisms would be counterproductive. They argue it is already hard enough to guarantee the rights of asylum seekers as it is. Opening existing protections for debate only risks creating opportunities for governments to further weaken these protections. The priority, stakeholders repeatedly said, is 'to preserve what has been achieved, because even that isn't straightforward'.[28]

It is also important to remember that any talk of 'climate migration' is taking place in an already tense, crowded discursive field. French stakeholders have systematically pointed out that they operate in a political context hostile to migrants in general. What's more, this hostility draws on and continually reinforces a ubiquitous distinction between (somewhat welcome) political refugees on the one hand, and (decidedly unwelcome) economic migrants on the other.[29] As a result, many hesitate to use the term 'migrant' because of its negative connotations. One NGO interviewee explained that they have entirely 'proscribed' the word 'migration' from their funding pitches because 'it brings up too many things that are fantasised in the collective unconscious'.[30] Similarly, Marie Verdier explains how she 'avoids the term "migrant", which has become pejorative and anonymising, to designate an amorphous mass of individuals we can mistreat' even though 'it is a generic term that is hard to do without'.[31] So while some stakeholders elect to speak of 'environmental migration' or 'climate migration', they often see it as an imperfect solution.

Another alternative, 'displacement', is often considered. However, it is generally used to designate people moving within their own country and not to France. The *Secours Catholique*, for example, draws an explicit distinction between 'environmental migrants', who cross borders, and 'the internal environmentally-displaced',

[28] Interview, civil servant (Expertise France), phone, January 2020.

[29] cf Karen Akoka, 'Réfugiés ou migrants? Les enjeux politiques d'une distinction juridique' (2018) 1(25) *Nouvelle revue de psychosociologie* 15; Laura Calabrese, 'Faut-il dire migrant ou réfugié? Débat lexico-sémantique autour d'un problème public' (2018) 210(2) *Langages* 105.

[30] Interview, environmental NGO representative (Fondation pour la Nature et l'Homme), Skype, July 2020.

[31] Marie Verdier, 'Sur les migrations, on n'avance ni politiquement ni médiatiquement' in Barbara Joannon and others (eds), *Les migrations dans l'œil des médias: Infox, influence et opinion* (Paris, De facto 2022) 27.

who do not.[32] For this reason, the term 'displacement' is only potentially appealing or useful to stakeholders whose work has an international aid or development component. NGOs working with asylum seekers already in France see little value in it where their day-to-day activities are concerned. While stakeholders tend to agree, in line with the academic literature,[33] that most human movement associated with climate change will be within countries, this conclusion leads to a spatial distancing effect, making it *less* relevant to French migration policy.[34]

One consequence of all this is the continued use of 'climate refugee' terminology. The term still dominates in the French press today because journalists seem to consider it clearer and more attention-grabbing than the alternatives (migration, displacement).[35] Some scholars, once critical of 'climate refugee' terminology, are reconsidering their position. François Gemenne, for example, has argued that 'contrary to what I might have thought (and written) in the past, and despite the legal difficulties, I think this is a very strong reason to use the term again: because it recognises that these migrations are first and foremost the result of a persecution that we are inflicting on the most vulnerable'.[36] In a similar vein, a report by the *Conseil Économique, Social et Environnemental* recently recommended that France propose a new status for 'climate refugees' at COP22.[37] This despite experts making the case against the term in hearings leading to the report.[38] The documentary filmmaker Michael P Nash, interviewed for another project,[39] persisted in calling his film *Climate Refugees* (2009)[40] even in the face of criticism. He told me: 'you know, I'm not writing policy, I'm actually making a film, I want to bring this to people's attention'. The point is that stakeholders have conscious, valid reasons to use the term 'climate refugees', despite everything. That they persist in using it is not simply a matter of not knowing that the term 'climate migration' comes with a raft of complications. The examples above show that consensus on

[32] Secours Catholique, 'Migrations environnementales: Note d'analyse et de positionnement' (Caritas France 2020) 4.

[33] See, for example, Roman Hoffmann, Barbora Sedova, and Kira Vinke, 'Improving the Evidence Base: A Methodological Review of the Quantitative Climate Migration Literature' (2021) 71 *Global Environmental Change* 4, available at doi.org/10.1016/j.gloenvcha.2021.102367; Ingrid Boas and others, 'Climate Migration Myths' (2019) 9 *Nature Climate Change* 901, available at doi.org/10.1038/s41558-019-0633-3.

[34] Durand-Delacre (n 7) 147–50.

[35] ibid at 114 (Figure 9). There is similar evidence for the Anglophone press in the special issue introduced by Katherine Russo and Ruth Wodak, 'Introduction: The Representation of "Exceptional Migrants" in Media Discourse: The Case of Climate-Induced Migration' (2019) 21(2) *Anglistica*, available at doi.org/10/gg8qvj.

[36] François Gemenne, 'One Good Reason to Speak of "Climate Refugees"' (2015) 49 *Forced Migration Review* 70, 71.

[37] Jean Jouzel and Agnès Michelot, 'La justice climatique: Enjeux et perspectives pour la france' (Conseil Economique, Social et Environnemental 2016), available at perma.cc/DY6S-W25Y.

[38] ibid.

[39] David Durand-Delacre, '(Mis)Representing Climate Mobilities: Lessons from Documentary Filmmaking' (2022) 48(14) *Journal of Ethnic and Migration Studies* 3397, available at doi.org/10.1080/1369183X.2022.2066260.

[40] Michael Nash, 'Climate Refugees: The Global Human Impact of Climate Change' (*The Video Project*, 29 January 2010), available at perma.cc/SH43-2264.

'climate migration' terminology will always remain elusive because context matters hugely for stakeholders' choice of words. The cacophonous proliferation of terms, and the inherent ambiguity of their definitions, thus appear as inherent features of 'climate migration' debates that stakeholders must contend with if they wish to instrumentalise the concept.

IV. Rejecting the Terminological Debate Altogether

So far, I have reviewed arguments put forward under the assumption that establishing the cause of migration is important and, more generally, that identifying clear terms to designate people on the move is desirable. But to stop the analysis here would be to miss a key consideration of the 'climate migration' debates in France: the causal question is regarded by many stakeholders as practically unnecessary, politically regressive, and morally untenable, and is thus rejected on that basis.

These stakeholders – who tend to have expertise on migration as researchers or practitioners in academia, NGOs, or the AFD – reject the causal question so central to 'climate migration' debates first on practical grounds. They argue that to act on migration, it is unnecessary to disentangle its causes. This argument always begins with a recognition of migration's multi-causality. One AFD civil servant summarised it thus: 'If we start with a logic of analysing the drivers, the factors of migration, well we'd be hard put – everyone recognises this – to dissociate economic, political, cultural or social factors'.[41] Knowing this, stakeholders who work with (potential) migrants, whether in their countries of origin or in France, tend to focus on their needs first. The job is to deliver assistance: food, shelter, physical and mental healthcare, language lessons, job opportunities. To do this, many stakeholders insisted, one does not really need to ask why people are where they are.

In practice, of course, Western governments constantly sort migrants into categories, only some of which are granted special rights – for example, to work, settle, or be joined by their families – as well as financial assistance. In some cases, the process of categorising migrants is used as a tool to deny migrants' basic rights, such as the right to asylum guaranteed by the Geneva Convention (itself founded on the fundamental principle of non-refoulement). Stakeholders note how xenophobic, anti-immigration actors categorise people who cross the French border as unwelcome *economic* migrants to justify illegal turn-backs at the border, arbitrary detainment and deportation practices, and the criminalisation of irregular migration.[42]

[41] Interview, civil servant (AFD Migrations), Paris, January 2020.

[42] Eg Jérôme Valluy, 'De l'asile aux répulsions: La radicalisation des frontières' (2012) *Le sujet dans la cité* 84, available at doi.org/10.3917/lsdlc.hs01.0084; Mary Bosworth and Marion Vannier, 'Blurred Lines: Detaining Asylum Seekers in Britain and France' 56 *Journal of Sociology* 53, available at doi.org/10.1177/1440783319882534; Pauline Doyen, Annaëlle Piva, and Oriane Sebillotte, 'Les oubliés

Stakeholders who report witnessing the negative impacts on migrants' lives of such practices also reject the debate about 'climate migration' terminology for ethical reasons. They assert that categorising migrants according to the cause of their migration creates fertile ground for arbitrary discrimination, and that focusing on climate change or the environment changes little to this point. As one journalist specialising on migration contended, 'for now, climate refugees are [considered] economic migrants. And they will be discredited as such'.[43] Others argued more broadly that, even if this was not the case, 'from the moment you emphasise *climate* refugee or *climate* migrant, even more than environmental, well what you're saying is "this person has the right, the greater legitimacy to migrate, to come here, than this other person", thereby creating a distinction that is "a little dangerous" and therefore best avoided'.[44]

This rejection of categorisation among French migrant solidarity NGOs echoes a widespread concern among critical migration scholars. Crawley and Skleparis, for instance, are sceptical of dominant categories like 'refugee' or 'migrant' because they have come to be associated with oversimplified causal explanations ('political persecution' or 'economic reasons' as the two possible and distinct drivers of migration) and so 'fail to capture adequately the complex relationship between political, social and economic drivers of migration, or their shifting significance for individuals'.[45] Moreover, such categories have contextual meanings that shift over time and space, and they are often used to actively discriminate against the very people whom they were or could be intended to protect.[46] Categories like 'climate migrant' or 'climate refugee' are not exempt from these problems.[47]

The rejection of the causal question ('why do people migrate?') for practical and moral reasons is significant because it means that conversations starting from an ostensibly straightforward question about the causal role of climate change ('should we speak of climate or the environment as a driver of migration?') often reach a point where participants must contend with the fact that categorising people might be counter-productive. This realisation undermines the very basis

du droit d'asile: Enquête sur les conditions de vie et d'accès aux droits des exilés fréquentant 5 structures d'accueil à Paris' (2021), available at perma.cc/744B-NS28; Matilde Rosina, 'France: Instrumentalisation, Courts, and Marginalisation' in Matilde Rosina (ed), *The Criminalisation of Irregular Migration in Europe: Globalisation, Deterrence, and Vicious Cycles* (Basel, Springer 2022), available at doi.org/10.1007/978-3-030-90347-3_5.

[43] Interview, journalist (Politis), Skype, October 2020.

[44] Interview, solidarity NGO representative (Bizi!), phone, February 2020.

[45] Heaven Crawley and Dimitris Skleparis, 'Refugees, Migrants, Neither, Both: Categorical Fetishism and the Politics of Bounding in Europe's "Migration Crisis"' (2018) 44 *Journal of Ethnic and Migration Studies* 48, available at doi.org/10/gfkcrm.

[46] Tazreena Sajjad, 'What's in a Name? "Refugees", "Migrants" and the Politics of Labelling' (2018) 60(2) *Race & Class* 40, available at doi.org/10.1177/0306396818793582; Karen Akoka, *L'asile et l'exil: Une histoire de la distinction réfugiés-migrants* (Paris, La Découverte 2020); Karin Scherschel, 'Who Is a Refugee? Reflections on Social Classifications and Individual Consequences' (2011) 8 *Migration Letters* 67.

[47] Augustine Yelfaanibe and Roger Zetter, 'Policies and Labels for Negotiating Rights Protection for the Environmentally Displaced in Ghana: The Dagara Farmer in Perspective' (2017) 37(2) *African Geographical Review* 83, available at doi.org/10.1080/19376812.2017.1350988.

of the initial conversation; the cause of migration ceases to matter as a guide to action. In some cases, it even led to a breakdown in discussions among stakeholders. One interviewee reported that making environmental migration a central subject of discussion 'cost DPPDM the participation of several organisations that assist migrants … because they didn't agree with categorising migrations' and because even talking about 'international environmental migrations implies that there are some migrations that are more legitimate than others' – a position many migrant-solidarity NGOs reject.

Again, when one steps back from efforts to find the 'right' way to speak about 'climate migration', it rapidly becomes clear that there is no such thing. The appropriate term will only ever be appropriate for a specific context, to achieve specific objectives, when facing a specific audience. This leads to an inherent ambiguity in 'climate migration' debates because stakeholders often operate in several different contexts. They have diverse objectives, and multiple audiences to cater to. Sometimes, this means the subject is simply deemed too complicated or confusing to develop a communication strategy, project, or policy around.

Some stakeholders, discouraged, just stop talking about 'climate migration' altogether. The NGO coordinating the DPPDM network, for instance, dropped the theme of environmental migrations after two years of debates. Their latest multi-annual strategy makes no mention of it.[48] In November 2021, my AFD interlocutors reported no change since our interviews in late 2019/early 2020. Stakeholders explained this by contrasting the 'climate migration' concept – so ambiguous and vague – to other pressing issues that they felt could more easily be resolved. Many added that when working with limited financial and human resources, it was inevitable that a subject as complex and time-consuming to discuss as 'climate migration' would lose traction or be abandoned altogether.

V. 'Climate Migration' is Not an Operational Concept

Ultimately, French stakeholders emerge from 'climate migration' debates with a largely inoperative set of concepts; 'climate migration' and its analogues are not terms they can use to articulate clear policies or projects. Stakeholders can talk about 'climate migration', but do not know what to do about it. Perhaps the most striking illustration of this is the case of the NGO named *Care*. It stands out because many of its employees have, over the years, been involved in various research projects about 'climate migration'.[49] Yet, project managers at *Care* struggle

[48] Centre de Recherche et d'Information pour le Développement, 'CRID: Orientations pluriannuelles 2021–2024: validées à l'AGE 29 mars 2021' (CRID, 2021).

[49] Koko Warner and others, 'In Search of Shelter: Mapping the Effects of Climate Change on Human Migration and Displacement' (United Nations University 2009); Center for International Earth Science Information Network at the Earth Institute (Columbia University, 2009); Samantha Boardley, 'Where the Rain Falls Phase III' (2020) CARE France Final Evaluation Report, available at perma.cc/8VQ3-JUM5.

to apply lessons learned from this work. They still wonder: 'these research results, how do we transcribe them into our adaptation projects?'[50] Their participation in research projects has had no operational implications.

This seems to be typical of a much broader pattern of 'climate migration' research failing to find clear applications. A recent review of projects in the AidDATA database (pulled out with the search 'climate AND migration') found, for instance, that 'the majority of the projects are research related, designed to generate knowledge on the links between climate and migration in regions thought to be particularly susceptible to climate change impacts'.[51] Although 'climate migration' is a subject that lends itself well to research, it rarely seems to translate to practical projects. It is possible to object to this assessment, pointing to relocation projects around the world[52] or initiatives for labour migration targeted at people designated as potential 'climate migrants'.[53] However, the criticism stands because, in each case, one finds significant disagreement about the actual cause of migration, what shape 'it' might take, and how desirable it is. It remains exceedingly hard to claim with any confidence what is meant by 'climate migration' when considering any of these projects.

Stakeholders working directly with communities abroad report that the 'climate migration' concept is of little practical relevance for their adaptation and resilience projects. A *Care* employee, for instance, reported that as 'our mandate as an international solidarity NGO … is really to work as closely as possible with vulnerable populations and to give them the most decent living conditions possible. We don't judge the fact that people move or not'.[54] Their priority is to help and empower communities to overcome the vulnerabilities they face, so they added that they 'haven't prioritised this question [of causality] because it's not all that important to us, in the end'.[55] They were not alone in adopting this stance. Other NGO representatives and AFD employees involved with projects outside France similarly concluded that whether 'climate migration' can be said to occur is irrelevant to the success of climate adaptation projects. With all these tensions running through 'climate migration' debates, it could be tempting to write the 'climate migration' concept off as irredeemably flawed and intractable – an interesting object of inquiry with no practical applications. However, the fact is the debate is unlikely to end, nor will attempts to make the concept useful. For all their scepticism, each

[50] Interview, international solidarity NGO representative (Care), Skype, September 2020.

[51] Robert Stojanov and others, 'Climate Mobility and Development Cooperation' (2021) 43(2) *Population and Environment* 209, 218, available at doi.org/10.1007/s11111-021-00387-5.

[52] Erica Bower and Sanjula Weerasinghe, 'Leaving Place, Restoring Home: Enhancing the Evidence Base on Planned Relocation Cases in the Context of Hazards, Disasters, and Climate Change' (2021) Platform on Disaster Displacement, available at perma.cc/T2C5-ZR3T.

[53] Carol Farbotko and others, 'A Climate Justice Perspective on International Labour Migration and Climate Change Adaptation among Tuvaluan Workers' (2022) 2 *Oxford Open Climate Change* 1, available at doi.org/10.1093/oxfclm/kgac002.

[54] ibid.

[55] ibid.

and every interviewee noted that 'everybody seems to be speaking about it' and 'it is hard to miss' – even if they themselves had concluded they can do nothing about it, and had thus withdrawn from the arena. We are stuck, for better or worse, with 'climate migration' as a category that one interviewee strikingly described as 'here without being here'.

VI. Learning to Live with the Inherent Conceptual Ambiguity of 'Climate Migration'

Ultimately, stakeholders experience terminological uncertainty and ambiguity as an inherent feature of 'climate migration' debates. If a consensus on definitions is out of the picture, perhaps the only option left is to accept these ambiguities as inevitable and learn to live with them. What accepting this might mean, however, depends on who is speaking. For some civil servants, an acceptable solution might simply be to keep the conversation superficial: 'I would say, in a pragmatic sense, that we simply have to accommodate the ambiguity', one said, adding: 'this political category, [the 'climate migrant'], everybody has an interest in it remaining vague, at least for now'.[56] Why? Simply because to create the category would be to entertain the possibility of creating a new set of protective measures which could give more migrants the right to enter and remain in France. This is a political non-starter that was not, for them, worth confronting.

But such 'pragmatic' resignation is unacceptable to most interviewees. Another approach prevails among NGO representatives in particular. The *Secours Catholique*, for instance, offers a two-pronged strategy. On the one hand, they make an explicit case for developing new legal categories and 'specific measures to address the situation of environmental migrants'.[57] This case, expressed in a position statement targeted at international policy-makers, was developed largely as part of their lobbying efforts to influence the formulation of the Global Compact on Migration.[58] On the other hand, the *Secours Catholique* representative also acknowledged a 'paradox' because they 'don't want to fall into over-categorisation of people … we need to look at, instead of categories, the needs of people, and not applying yet another label, which is a fiction because migrations are multi-causal'.[59] In such cases, my interlocutors attempt to make the ambiguity inherent to 'climate migration' productive. It allows them to pursue two contradictory strategies, at two different scales (international and national), with different audiences.

[56] Interview, civil servant, Skype, June 2020.
[57] Secours Catholique (n 32) 20.
[58] Interview, international solidarity NGO representative (Secours Catholique), Paris, January 2020.
[59] ibid.

Among French stakeholders, a third attitude to ambiguity is evident. It is the approach that would have the ambiguities and definitional trouble that surrounds the topic of 'climate migration' serve as an entry point for the dissemination of more nuanced, sophisticated knowledge about climate change, migration, and their intersection in all its context-dependent complexity. As argued above, the reality of 'climate migration' discussions is that stakeholders deploy different terms in different contexts, depending on what aspects of the issue they want to underline in the moment. Different terms carry different political messages and can therefore be directed at different audiences. One NGO interviewee, who had spent a long time thinking about these issues, had exactly this attitude. They hoped that 'by introducing several words [like displacement], you can complexify the person's thinking' since it would allow them to show that '[climate] migration isn't just one thing'.[60]

The hope here is that discussing 'climate migration' can still be useful, not in spite of but perhaps *because* of its ambiguous nature. In this view, the concept's inherent ambiguity is used as an educational tool, steering the audience – other NGOs, policy-makers, passers-by at the local fair – away from the usual interrogations ('how many 'climate migrants'?') towards more complex and necessary questions. The diversity of terms available, and their debated definitions, serve as so many entry points for more extensive, nuanced conversations about the multi-causality of migration, the complex patterns of human movement, and the appropriate moral and political responses to migrants' plights. In contrast, focusing on clearing up ambiguity and pursuing a single terminology poses the risk of oversimplification, thus constraining policy options to a narrow set of often problematic and likely counterproductive measures.[61]

VII. 'Climate Migration' for 'Climate Justice'? A Difficult Convergence

The third attitude to ambiguity described above opens the door to a more political understanding of the 'climate migration' concept's potential usefulness. The hope harboured by French stakeholders who persist in discussing 'climate migration' was that it could help draw attention to questions of justice and responsibility in climate action. In this, they share in a hope cautiously expressed by many academics and activists who call for a climate justice approach to 'climate migration'. For example, Klepp and Herbeck argue that 'the inclusion of post-colonial perspectives in the debates on environmental migration can render visible the political

[60] Interview, volunteer in NGO project on environmental migrations (Youth on the Move), Paris, October 2019.

[61] See James Morrissey, 'How Should we Talk about Climate Change and Migration?' (2021) 9 *Migration Studies* 150, available at doi.org/10.1093/migration/mnaa031.

nature of climate adaptation choices and reconnect global negotiations to questions of fair burden sharing in adaptation'.[62] This concluding section explores how French migrant-solidarity NGOs have attempted to do this in practice, and the obstacles they face.

To illustrate the difficulty of using the 'climate migration' concept to support calls for climate justice, it is worth returning to the case of the DPPDM, starting with the network members' initial motivations for discussing environmental migrations. Employees in French migrant-solidarity and international-solidarity NGOs, of which the network is largely composed, increasingly feel marginalised from mainstream political discourse. Migration experts, whether academics or practitioners, report that they are forced to argue about the most basic facts of migration. Things that are well established in migration research and practice – the dangers of securitising and criminalising migration, the ineffectiveness of European detention-for-deportation regimes, the availability of excellent migration statistics[63] – are constantly, exhaustingly challenged if not outright ignored by politicians, on social networks, and in the media. The case for solidarity with migrants appears, in this context, as far from given.

By contrast, migrant-solidarity NGOs perceive 'the climate movement' as relatively powerful and well accepted.[64] At least, the basic facts of climate change – that it is anthropogenic, and that mitigation and adaptation measures are required – do not appear to be greatly contested by French policy-makers and the general public. Evidence of this varies widely from study to study and depends on the exact survey question considered. While studies are consistent in finding that 80 to 90 per cent of the surveyed population acknowledges that climate change is happening, beliefs regarding its anthropogenic nature and the scale of the required response appear harder to assess, with some reporting levels of climate scepticism as low as 2.5 per cent,[65] while others find only 57 per cent of respondents agree that climate

[62] Silja Klepp and Johannes Herbeck, 'The Politics of Environmental Migration and Climate Justice in the Pacific Region' (2016) 7 *Journal of Human Rights and the Environment* 54, available at doi.org/10/gf4j4q. See also Giovanni Bettini, Sarah L Nash, and Giovanna Gioli, 'One Step Forward, Two Steps Back? The Fading Contours of (In)Justice in Competing Discourses on Climate Migration' (2017) 183(4) *The Geographical Journal* 348, available at doi.org/10/gckb89; Rebecca Buxton, 'Reparative Justice for Climate Refugees' (2019) 94(2) *Philosophy* 193, available at doi.org/10/gf88nj; Kyle Whyte, Jared L Talley, and Julia D Gibson, 'Indigenous Mobility Traditions, Colonialism, and the Anthropocene' (2019) 14(3) *Mobilities* 319, available at doi.org/10.1080/17450101.2019.1611015; Farbotko and others (n 53).

[63] See François Héran, 'La recherche produit des données de qualité sur les migrations et les migrants: Utilisons-les pour un débat réellement informé!' in François Héran (ed), *Chiffrer les migrations: À quelles fins?* (De Facto 2020) 20, available at perma.cc/K3RN-LY6D; Barak Kalir and Céline Cantat, 'Fund but Disregard: The EU's Relationship to Academic Research on Mobility' (*Crisis Magazine*, 9 May 2020) available at perma.cc/XH3V-3QC3.

[64] At the AFD, the migration department felt this contrast keenly too, telling me: 'We have a climate department that is extremely strong, that intervenes in a lot of areas'. Interview, civil servant (AFD Migration), Paris, January 2020.

[65] Zakaria Babutsidze and Lionel Nesta, 'Le changement climatique en France: Croyances, comportements, responsabilites' (*Sciences Po*, 10 December 2018) 43 OFCE Policy Brief, available at perma.cc/8B5C-Y7LS.

change is anthropogenic.[66] Additionally, denialist viewpoints circulate primarily online and in right-wing conservative media outlets seeking controversy[67] and are given little to no space in other outlets.[68] What is certain, however, is that the French government has committed – in words if not in deeds – to climate action.

With this in mind, DPPDM network members felt they needed to 'go looking for allies in the cause of migrants among climate activists'[69] and 'to give migration questions a place in the climate movement'.[70] These interviewees expressed the hope that since 'speaking about migration only, about the right to asylum, about the refugee status, its application, its protection … dialogue can become a little tense', perhaps 'speaking about climate migration could be another entry to speak about migration once again'.[71] Perhaps they could 'legitimise the fight for migration by connecting to the climate question'[72] and make migrant solidarity a feature of climate action in the process. In short: their intention was to at once benefit by association from the climate movement's relative prominence, acceptability, and authority in public/political debates – a strategy known as 'climate bandwagoning'[73] – while centring principles of justice in climate action, including migrant justice *in general.*

Some migrant solidarity NGOs, however, are sceptical of bandwagoning. They fear that any discussion of 'climate migration' within the climate movement would inevitably fall back on familiar expedients: once again recasting 'climate migration' as a threat to the stability of western Nations.[74] My interlocutors often justified these concerns by pointing to the climate movement's reliance on emergency rhetoric: 'You just can't speak about migration as a crisis.' Nor can you speak, by extension, about a 'climate migration' crisis. Even as some interviewees took tentative steps towards the climate movement, others held back for fear of being led down a dangerous path, either antithetical to (migrant) justice, or undermining important relationships with other and more sceptical migrant solidarity organisations.

All the environment/climate NGO representatives spoken to were well aware of the need to avoid alarmist claims about 'climate migration'. They had no desire to repeat problematic 'climate refugee' narratives. Moreover, many called 'climate justice' their priority. Nonetheless, they hesitated to engage in 'climate migration' debates for several reasons. First, many felt ill-equipped to speak about migration

[66] Antoine Dechezleprêtre and others, 'Fighting Climate Change: International Attitudes toward Climate Policies' (*VOX EU*, 14 October 2022), available at doi.org/10.1787/3406f29a-en.

[67] Such as CNews, Le Point, and Valeurs Actuelles.

[68] Renaud Hourcade and Albin Wagener, 'Le climatoscepticisme: Une approche interdiscursive' (2021) 127 *Mots: Les langages du politique* 9.

[69] Interview, international solidarity NGO representative (Ritimo), Skype, October 2020.

[70] Interview, DPPDM network coordinator (CRID), Paris, January 2020.

[71] Interview, international solidarity NGO representative (Secours Catholique), Paris, January 2020.

[72] Interview, international solidarity NGO representative (Ritimo), Skype, October 2020.

[73] Sikina Jinnah, 'Climate Change Bandwagoning: The Impacts of Strategic Linkages on Regime Design, Maintenance, and Death' (2011) 11(3) *Global Environmental Politics*, available at doi.org/10.1162/GLEP_a_00065.

[74] The problems with this are well established, cf Boas and others (n 33).

in a sufficiently informed manner. Second, they feared that the hyper-politicised topic of migration is too polarising. So much so that they fear raising the topic is to run the risk of their message being drowned in a hostile public debate about migration, or to see their voices dismissed by government politicians and mainstream news editors if they espouse so-called 'pro-migrant' views. One of them explained that the mere mention of migration unleashed negative comments on their organisation's social media – to a degree they did not experience with any other topic. Another was reluctant to embrace the 'climate migration' concept, feeling it was too risky a strategy that could lose them funding from governmental and corporate sources: 'we don't have a discourse on migration … I've taken everything out because it creates division'.[75] And third, the two previous reasons combined to place migrants among the most difficult climate-vulnerable populations to defend. Commenting on the work of *Notre Affaire à Tous* (an organisation suing the French State for climate inaction) and on climate litigation in general, one interviewee explained that 'the migrant is quote-unquote "competing" with other forms of vulnerability in litigation'.[76] Many of the conventional litigation strategies focused on 'demanding justice, holding to account, etc, *that* helps the climate justice narrative move forward, whereas litigation around migration? There's no possibility of developing *that*'.[77] Thus, for many in the climate movement today, the concept of 'climate migration' appears of little help in pursuing climate justice.

In short, while (some) French migrant solidarity NGOs hope to legitimise their cause by association with the climate movement, (many) environmental NGOs fear it might delegitimise their own cause, ultimately diminishing their access and influence. Having accepted that past discourses on 'climate refugees' were problematic, many environmental NGOs now prefer not to speak about migration at all. This problem is not new, of course. There is a precedent from 2009, during COP15, when environmental and humanitarian NGOs rallied around the concept of 'climate refugee' to call for climate action.[78] But as Sylvie Ollitrault noted then, their alliance was short-lived.[79] Despite the obvious value of an alliance, NGOs felt it was 'at the risk of diluting in part their specificities' and 'being confined to a role of agitators … without influencing state positions' on climate change.[80] This is a major challenge for anyone seeking a convergence between 'climate migration' and

[75] Interview, environmental NGO representative (Fondation pour la Nature et l'Homme), Skype, July 2020.

[76] Interview, academic researcher, Paris, December 2019.

[77] ibid.

[78] See WWF France and others, 'L'ultimatum Climatique, l'appel Pour La Conférence de Copenhague', 29 May 2009, available at web.archive.org/web/20090529194554/http://copenhague-2009.com:80/appel.

[79] Sylvie Ollitrault, 'De la sauvegarde de la planète à celle des réfugiés climatiques: L'activisme des ONG' (2010) 4 *Revue Tiers Monde* 19, available at doi.org/10.3917/rtm.204.0019.

[80] ibid (page 33, my translation).

'climate justice' discourses, a challenge which has no obvious resolution. It is clear, however, that the challenge needs to be acknowledged and addressed if the 'climate migration' concept is ever to strengthen 'climate justice' agendas in this context.

VIII. Conclusion

In this chapter, I have shown that the development of policies and projects to address 'climate migration' face some major obstacles which far too often go unremarked. Identifying these obstacles require 'climate migration' to be treated as an issue that is neither obvious, self-evident, or even natural. Such a stance allows for a more refined analysis of exactly how and why the concept fails to translate to policy and practice. The perspectives of French policy stakeholders suggest efforts to design policies and projects specifically targeting 'climate migrants' appear inherently flawed. In the French context at least, potential stakeholders find the concept inherently ambiguous. Any attempt to define terms and typologies is always contested, because the 'right' term to use is highly context-dependent and liable to vary over time depending on stakeholders' shifting political objectives, ethical values, and communication strategies. Consequently, French stakeholders find the 'climate migration' concept and its analogues to be too unstable to operationalise. That is, the subject is not clear-cut and operable enough to expend the time, money, and effort necessary to develop policies and projects around it.

These insights are valuable because they go against much received wisdom behind calls for better 'climate migration' policies. One of the admonitions of this chapter is that calls for more and better data on 'climate migration' – while of obvious value to further academic research aims – fail to address fundamental obstacles to 'climate migration' policy-making and project development. Developing 'climate migration' policies and projects is less about acquiring new knowledge, and more about accounting for the context-dependent political, moral, and pragmatic considerations of stakeholders involved in these processes.

The 'climate migration' concept's inherent ambiguity and apparent inoperability does not mean, however, that all stakeholders have entirely given up on it – although many have – not least because the concept is 'continuously returning to the scene'.[81] Indeed, 'climate migration' debates constantly attract newcomers seeking to understand the relationship between climate change and migration. Acknowledging this, many stakeholders are seeking ways to live with the concept's ambiguities and practical limitations. In line with trends in critical 'climate migration' scholarship, many hope that any new discussions about 'climate migration' can be made to focus less on turning the concept into a tool for project development,

[81] Giovanni Bettini, 'And yet it Moves! (Climate) Migration as a Symptom in the Anthropocene' (2019) 14(3) *Mobilities* 336, 339, available at doi.org/10/gf7fbx.

and more on introducing new stakeholders to the political and moral issues raised by both climate change and migration, especially as they relate to questions of responsibility. In this way, they hope that newcomers in debates about the 'climate migration' concept can be introduced to climate justice agendas. However, as the example of the *Des Ponts pas des Murs* NGO network shows, there remain significant obstacles to any such convergence.

6

The View from the Fortress: European Governance Perspectives on Climate Change and Migration

SARAH LOUISE NASH*

I. Introduction

To date, the scholarship on climate change and migration as two linked phenomena[1] has overwhelmingly been focused on people moving (or not moving, or even just potentially moving) within the Global South, or between it and the Global North. This focus implies a corollary failure to explore how politics and policy on climate change and migration is developing within the Global North.[2] At the same time, those carrying out this research are overwhelmingly from, and funded by research agencies in, the Global North,[3] which suggests power imbalances in how the debate around climate change and migration is unfolding. This chapter is interested in how policy actors in the Global North, particularly in Europe, approach the relation between climate change and migration.

One important actor in knowledge creation has been the European Union (EU). In a 2022 EU Commission staff working document, the role of the EU in knowledge creation on climate change and migration was sketched as follows:

> The EU has positioned itself as a major actor in the quest to advance knowledge on disaster and climate-related displacement and migration over the past years. Research

* This research has received funding from the European Union's Horizon 2020 research and innovation programme under the Marie Skłodowska-Curie grant agreement No 840661.

[1] This chapter refers to climate change and migration, or the links between climate change and migration throughout. This stands in contrast to much of the scholarship that employs distinct terminology referring to climate change and migration as a phenomenon in its own right (for example 'climate migration'). This decision reflects the varying degrees to which climate change and migration are linked with each other in the discourse explored in this chapter, which does not always have the recognition of a distinct phenomenon at its centre.

[2] For a notable exception, see Gregory White, *Climate Change and Migration: Security and Borders in a Warming World* (Oxford, Oxford University Press 2011).

[3] Etienne Piguet, Raoul Kaenzig, and Jérémie Guélat, 'The Uneven Geography of Research on "Environmental Migration"' (2018) 39(4) *Population and Environment* 357.

> in this area is an important pillar of the Commission's work towards a new policy framework on climate change and migration.[4]

This tells us that European policy-makers, in particular the EU Commission, are thinking about climate change and migration. The Commission is contributing to the problematisation of climate change and migration, who the affected people are, and what role the EU could and should be playing. However, very little scholarly attention is being placed on how European policy-makers are thinking about climate change and migration and what governmental alternatives are emerging. Furthermore, while the EU is an important player and is active in shaping the European as well as international discourse, it would be remiss to focus on EU politics and policy without considering the positions of its Member States.

A focus on EU Member States is vital for understanding the policy-making of the EU on climate change and migration and the EU's climate diplomacy in this area moving forward. Since the so-called 'European migration crisis' in 2015–16, the controversial nature of every contour of European migration policy has become even clearer, and consensus among Member States on policy change even rarer. For instance, reforms to take pressure off those Member States that are points of entry for migrants have failed to materialise; only nineteen of the then twenty-eight Member States voted in favour of the Global Compact for Safe, Orderly and Regular Migration at its adoption at the UN General Assembly in 2018;[5] and Austria has vetoed recent attempts to extend the Schengen free movement area to include the EU Member States Romania and Bulgaria, citing fears about border control and current high numbers of asylum applications.[6] Any EU policy and legislation on climate change and migration would also need an agreement among Member States, which cannot be taken as given.

This chapter explores the perspectives of European national policy communities on climate change and migration, with a particular interest in what these perspectives mean for the European climate change and migration regime. It does so by drawing on research in four EU Member States: Austria, Germany, Denmark, and Sweden.

These cases were chosen for two reasons. First, the selected Member States share borders with each other and, as was particularly visible in 2015–16, often constitute the last stage of the migration route for people moving north after entering the EU, allowing differences and similarities between direct neighbours

[4] EU Commission, 'Commission Staff Working Document: Addressing Displacement and Migration Related to Disasters, Climate Change and Environmental Degradation' (2022) SWD(2022) 201 Final, 17, available at perma.cc/R9QK-D4R7.

[5] Lena Kainz and Camille Le Coz, 'The Winding Road to Marrakech: Lessons from the European Negotiations of the Global Compact for Migration' (Migration Policy Institute 2022), available at perma.cc/B2PY-SCWM.

[6] Parlament Österreich [Parliament of Austria] Gesetzgebungsperiode [GP] XXVII, 'IV-17 der Beilagen zu den stenographischen Protokollen des Nationalrates XXVII: GP Beratungen des Hauptausschusses in Angelegenheiten der Europäischen Union' (12 December 2022), available at perma.cc/T83N-DHX7.

to come into focus. Second, in Germany and Sweden, the case selection includes two Member States that are renowned for their openness towards new arrivals, in particular during 2015–16. In 2016, these two countries granted asylum status to more individuals than any other EU Member State, both in absolute numbers and in proportion to their population.[7] The other two countries selected, Austria and Denmark, are known for their more restrictive approaches to migration, and for their strong, right-wing populist political parties. At the time this project was conceptualised in 2018–19, Austria's coalition government included just such a party.

The analysis draws on empirical data gathered in the project 'Climate Diplomacy and Uneven Policy Responses on Climate Change and Human Mobilities'. It is a product of extensive document analysis, and a series of thirty-four semi-structured interviews conducted between September 2020 and April 2022 with stakeholders from government agencies, political parties, and civil society.[8] The majority of documents analysed were published in German, Danish, or Swedish. As few translations were available, they were analysed in the original languages. Interviews were conducted in either English or German. The translations of the quotes in this chapter are my own.

In examining the perspectives of national policy communities in Austria, Germany, Denmark, and Sweden on climate change and migration, the focus will be not only on the *content* of relevant legal and policy frameworks or proposals, but also on the discursive *context* in which these frameworks are situated. Specifically, this means also examining how the links between climate change and migration are produced as a problem to be addressed by politics and in policy, and how this impacts political debates and policies adopted. The following analysis uses the concept of the migration regime, broken down into the categories of *framing*, *management* and *regulation*, to examine how the links between climate change and migration are being made governable, before considering the resulting *modes of governing*.

II. The Climate Change and Migration Regime

In this analysis, I draw on the concept of a 'migration regime', which has become common usage in migration studies in general.[9] This concept recognises the

[7] Eurostat, 'Asylum Decisions in the EU: EU Member States Granted Protection to More than 700 000 Asylum Seekers in 2016' (news release, 26 April 2017), available at perma.cc/XTU9-MZ2M.

[8] The interviews are anonymised. They are cited according to the nation-state they refer to, and are numbered (for instance, Interview Austria 1). While most of the interviews were conducted with individuals living and working in the nation-state they were interviewed about, this was not always the case. Two interviews were conducted with individuals who are experts in two of the cases analysed (one interview on Austria and Germany and one interview on Denmark and Sweden respectively).

[9] Andreas Pott, Christoph Rass, and Frank Wolff (eds), *Was ist ein Migrationsregime? What is a Migration Regime?* (Osnabrück, Springer 2018).

complex combination of norms, rules, constructions, knowledge and actions of institutional actors that influence migration in various ways.[10] I follow Oltmer's definition of a migration regime as an 'integrated sphere of organisation and action of institutional actors that are focused on particular aspects of migration, channel migration movements, and categorise the (potential) migrants'.[11] Each migration regime is different, with its own institutional actors, problematisations, ways of planning and acting, specific rules, norms and procedures, and expectations regarding the creation, appraisal, and communication of knowledge.[12] In one of the most cited definitions of a migration regime, Sciortino describes the 'mix of implicit conceptual frames, generations of turf wars among bureaucracies and waves after waves of "quick fix" to emergencies, triggered by changing political constellations of actors'.[13] This definition highlights that a migration regime not only consists of planned components, but is also reactive. Furthermore, in order to understand it, it has to be situated in its historical, political, and social context.

At the international level, scholarship on the emergence of climate change and migration as a problem in need of policy solutions is already fairly advanced,[14] with great attention having been paid to the climate change negotiations of the United Nations Framework Convention on Climate Change (UNFCCC),[15] the United Nations High Commission for Refugees (UNHCR)[16] and the International Organization for Migration (IOM).[17] Previous contributions that draw on the concept of a 'climate migration' regime to analyse these developments, including by Carsten Felgentreff, have pointed to the performativity of climate politics, producing the figure of the climate migrant and making the phenomenon of 'climate migration' governable.[18]

[10] Jochen Oltmer, 'Das Aushandeln von Migration: Historische und historiographische Perspektiven' (2016) 14(3) *ZSE Zeitschrift für Staats- und Europawissenschaften* 333, 343, available at doi.org/10.5771/1610-7780-2016-3.

[11] ibid 344 (author's translation).

[12] ibid.

[13] Giuseppe Sciortino, 'Between Phantoms and Necessary Evils: Some Critical Points in the Study of Irregular Migrations to Western Europe' in Anita Böcker, Betty de Hart, and Ines Michalowski (eds), *Migration and the Regulation of Social Integration* (IMIS-Beiträge 2004) 17.

[14] Sarah Louise Nash, *Negotiating Migration in the Context of Climate Change: International Policy and Discourse* (Bristol, Bristol University Press 2019).

[15] Sarah Louise Nash, 'From Cancun to Paris: An Era of Policy Making on Climate Change and Migration' (2018) 9 *Global Policy* 53, available at doi.org/10.1111/1758-5899.12502; Andrea C Simonelli, *Governing Climate Induced Migration and Displacement: IGO Expansion and Global Policy Implications* (London, Palgrave Macmillan 2015); Benoit Mayer, 'Migration in the UNFCCC Workstream on "Loss and Damage": An Assessment of Alternative Framings and Conceivable Responses' (2017) 6 *Transnational Environmental Law* 107, available at doi.org/10.1017/S2047102516000078.

[16] Nina Hall, *Displacement, Development, and Climate Change: International Organizations Moving beyond their Mandates* (Abingdon, Routledge 2016).

[17] Simonelli (n 15).

[18] Carsten Felgentreff, 'Migration durch Klimapolitik: Die globale Produktion von Klimamigrantinnen und Klimamigranten' in Andreas Pott, Christoph Rass, and Frank Wolff (eds), *Was ist ein Migrationsregime? What Is a Migration Regime?* (Osnabrück, Springer 2018) 139.

In a recent contribution to the literature that sets out a research agenda on 'climate mobilities',[19] Boas and colleagues have defined climate mobilities regimes as 'interconnected sets of socio-economic and political relations consisting of different types of actors, that frame, manage, and regulate the nexus between mobilities and climate change in a particular manner, resulting in particular modes of governing of climate mobilities'.[20] This definition inspires the following analysis, which is also structured along the lines of framing, management, regulation, and modes of governing.

I contend that the European 'climate migration' regime that I begin to explore in this chapter is both part of Felgentreff's 'climate migration' regime and Boas and colleagues' climate mobilities regimes, as well as overlapping with the EU's migration regime more broadly. I argue that this European 'climate migration' regime constitutes a distinct migration regime in its own right, with a specific set of actors, institutions, norms, procedures, problematisations of migration and knowledge, which shape how climate change and migration are becoming governable in Europe.

With this in mind, the following sections will consider three aspects of this regime, namely the framing, management and regulation of climate change and migration. They will do so through the cases of four European nation-states, namely Austria, Germany, Denmark, and Sweden. The intention is to outline the regime in a European political context, including the interlinkages between framing, management and regulation, before extrapolating what this regime implies for modes of governing, and what this all might mean for the politics of climate change and migration more broadly.

III. Framing

I understand frames as 'strong and generic narratives that guide both analysis and action in practical situations'.[21] Rein and Schön further note that '[s]uch narratives are diagnostic/prescriptive stories that tell, within a given issue terrain, what needs fixing and how it might be fixed'.[22] Fram*ing*, therefore, 'offers a way to describe

[19] The climate mobilities paradigm can be seen as a reaction to conceptual critiques of climate change and migration research. See Ingrid Boas and others, 'Climate Migration Myths' (2019) 9 *Nature Climate Change* 901, available at doi.org/10.1038/s41558-019-0633-3. In sketching their intention with the concept of climate mobilities, Boas and colleagues state that it 'pays attention to the multiplicity of climate change-related human mobility (involving immobility, relocation, circular mobility, etc.), its embedding in ongoing patterns and histories of movement, and the material and political conditions under which it takes place'. See Ingrid Boas and others, 'Climate Mobilities: Migration, Im/Mobilities and Mobility Regimes in a Changing Climate' (2022) *Journal of Ethnic and Migration Studies* 1, 2, available at doi.org/10.1080/1369183X.2022.2066264.

[20] Boas and others, 'Climate Mobilities' (n 19) 7.

[21] Martin Rein and Donald Schön, 'Frame-Critical Policy Analysis and Frame-Reflective Policy Practice' (1996) 9 *Knowledge and Policy* 85, 89, available at doi.org/10.1007/BF02832235.

[22] ibid.

the power of a communicating text' and involves 'select[ing] some aspects of a perceived reality and mak[ing] them more salient in a communicating text, in such a way as to promote a particular problem definition, causal interpretation, moral evaluation, and/or treatment recommendation'.[23] Frames are not fixed but rather contingent, as they are continuously being modified, contested, and renegotiated. The frames identified here are understood as outputs of a process of framing situated in a particular moment in time.

Although the links between climate change and migration have 'played a central role neither in the political answers to climate nor in migration politics'[24] in the four nation-states in question, these links do 'pop up regularly'.[25] When they do, the dominant framing is one of impending or potential future-oriented displacement.[26] Displacement linked to climate change is then framed in two distinct ways: as a humanitarian issue, by which displaced people are perceived as the victims of climate change caused by the Global North's emissions; or as an ever-increasing, future-oriented security threat. In the Danish context, one interviewee summed up the climate displacement framing as such:

> I believe that … more and more Danes are concerned about displacement issues, for two separate reasons. One part of the population [recognise that] we need to help the poor people in the South to adapt and to be able to live where they are because it's not fair. It's 'climate injustice': we can call it that when the poorest people in the South are paying … the biggest price for the emissions that are driven by rich countries. … And then there's another part of the population who are more concerned with what … climate change mean[s] regarding asylum seekers and migration towards Europe and Denmark.[27]

These two different interpretations of climate displacement are not new, and have been previously identified in the broader international discourse on climate change and human mobilities.[28] However, when the European nation-state framing is looked at more closely, nuances that are not so obvious in the more technocratic discourses of international policy become more visible.

Specifically, the securitised interpretation of 'climate displacement' is even more prevalent at the European nation-state level than studies of international

[23] Robert M Entman, 'Framing: Toward Clarification of a Fractured Paradigm' (2006) 43(4) *Journal of Communication* 51, 52, available at doi.org/10.1111/j.1460-2466.1993.tb01304.x.

[24] Interview Austria 5.

[25] ibid.

[26] A word frequently to describe these movements translates to 'escape' or 'flight' in English, but is frequently used in German (*Flucht*), Danish (*flugt*) and Swedish (*flykt*) to describe non-voluntary, presumably rather chaotic movements of people. In all three languages, this word is related to the word 'refugee' (Flüchtling, flygtning, and flykting, respectively).

[27] Interview Denmark 2.

[28] Giovanni Bettini, 'Climates Barbarians at the Gate? A Critique of Apocalyptic Narratives on Climate Refugees' (2013) 45 *Geoforum* 63, available at doi.org/10.1016/j.geoforum.2012.09.009; Giovanni Bettini, Sarah Louise Nash and Giovanna Gioli, 'One Step Forward, Two Steps Back? The Fading Contours of (In)Justice in Competing Discourses on Climate Migration' (2017) 183 *The Geographical Journal* 348, available at doi.org/10.1111/geoj.12192.

governance suggest, as is the sole focus on migration occurring in the Global South at the expense of also considering, for example, intra-European migration. Furthermore, possible framings are very dependent on the dominant national migration politics, which, in many European nation-states, has reached dystopian levels of restrictiveness. The securitised debate on climate change and displacement often resurges with the release of new estimates for the number of people who will be displaced due to climate change. Although many of the older (yet remarkably persistent) estimates have been subject to methodological critique,[29] and although scholars continue to warn of the securitising and dehumanising effects of inaccurate, off-the-charts estimates,[30] new estimates continue to create 'peaks in the debate' (ie points in time where climate change and migration are discussed more intensively).[31]

In the words of one interviewee, it is 'these kind of numbers' that give 'the debate more or less momentum, but it's not like then there is a disaster in Bangladesh and then we talk about the displaced people'.[32] The spectre of large numbers of displaced people is therefore one of the most important elements in the discussion on climate change and migration, even in abstract terms: 'because we know that climate change will change the living conditions of hundreds of millions of people'.[33]

A frequently suggested corollary to the large estimates is the (sometimes tacit) 'dystopic assumption' that the people displaced due to climate change will be coming to Europe: 'that they are going to come here'[34] and officials are most interested in 'how many climate refugees will come to this particular town in Sweden in, like, ten years'.[35]

These factors, when combined, lead to the 'more dystopic and often racialised narration of ... impending mobility doom as seen from a [Global] Northern perspective'.[36] A Swedish interviewee notes that 'the discussion is about the security of the Swedish people when it comes to preparing for migrant flows'.[37] At the same time, civil society actors continue to emphasise the scale of the (future-oriented) problem of immigration due to climate change:

> when it comes to climate-induced migration, ... I don't think the majority of common people have understood the magnitude of the issue – and what it might mean for the

[29] François Gemenne, 'Why the Numbers Don't Add up: A Review of Estimates and Predictions of People Displaced by Environmental Changes' (2011) 21 *Global Environmental Change* 41, available at doi.org/10.1016/j.gloenvcha.2011.09.005.

[30] David Durand-Delacre and others, 'Climate Migration Is about People, not Numbers' in Steffen Böhm and Sian Sullivan (eds), *Negotiating Climate Change in Crisis* (Cambridge, Open Book Publishers 2021) 63.

[31] Interview Denmark 4.

[32] ibid.

[33] Interview Austria 6.

[34] Interview Denmark 1.

[35] Interview Sweden 4.

[36] Interview Denmark 1.

[37] Interview Sweden 2.

> European Union as a community, as an economic community, what it might mean for Sweden and Swedish societies or communities, the communes that need to take their own responsibility in taking in people. I don't think people have realised what's ahead of us.[38]

Europe will also face climate change impacts that may alter migration patterns, for example sea-level rise or increased flooding risk. However, migration within European nation-states is generally couched in very different terminology: as planned retreat rather than flight. The issues are being thought about on a very local level, 'but then it's not really called … climate-induced migration'.[39]

For example, mid-July 2021, during my empirical research for this project, extreme flooding in the German states of Rhineland-Palatinate and North Rhine-Westphalia killed 183 people and destroyed many homes.[40] The link between the flooding and climate change is being routinely made, with Germany's President Frank-Walter Steinmeier declaring on the first anniversary of the disaster that 'climate change has reached us now'.[41] Although the climate component of the disaster and therefore the potential for similar events to increase in frequency are routinely being pointed out, the decisions made by inhabitants as to whether to rebuild their homes or move to other towns are rarely articulated in terms of displacement or migration. An exception could be found in the German newspaper *Die Zeit*. In an article titled 'Germany's Climate Refugees', one inhabitant who had moved to a more elevated town nearby was asked what he thought of the term 'climate refugee' (*Klimaflüchtling*), to which he answered: 'I am one as well, no?'[42]

The almost exclusive focus on displacement as incoming to the EU from the Global South is a trope that research is complicit in (re)producing, with prime examples delivered by recent studies that survey attitudes to 'climate migrants' in the respective nation-states. For example, in a Danish study that surveys the willingness of the Danish population to grant residency to 'climate migrants' compared to other categories of migrants, survey participants were informed that the survey

> will be about how the rules on immigration should be in the future, with respect to immigration from countries outside the EU. In the context of this survey, an immigrant is a person who has been born in a country outside the EU, whose parents have also been born outside the EU.[43]

The justification for this limitation is 'because potential climate migrants would likely arrive from countries outside the EU'.[44]

[38] Interview Sweden 2.

[39] Interview Sweden 4.

[40] ibid.

[41] Frank-Walter Steinmeier, quoted in Jahrestag der Flut, 'Der Klimawandel hat uns erreicht' (*Tagesschau*, 14 July 2022), available at perma.cc/DZ8C-5DV7.

[42] Frida Thurm and Julia Sellmann, 'Deutschlands Klimaflüchtlinge' (*Die Zeit Online*, 11 July 2022), available at perma.cc/9KT3-U9YV.

[43] Troels F Hedegaard, 'Attitudes to Climate Migrants: Results from a Conjoint Survey Experiment in Denmark' (2022) 45 *Scandinavian Political Studies* 25, 33, available at doi.org/10.1111/1467-9477.12213.

[44] ibid.

In a similar study conducted in Germany, respondents were asked to respond to cases of fictitious migrants who want to immigrate to Germany, with two of these options being migrants whose 'entire home country is becoming uninhabitable due to soaring droughts' and whose 'entire home country is becoming uninhabitable due to sea level rises'.[45] An Austrian study, conducted with university students, uses the story of a 'fictitious person from Chad who plans to move to Austria',[46] while the reasons for moving varied, including the two environmental drivers of 'environmental degradation due to global climate change' or 'due to local resource overuse'.[47]

The focus on migration from outside of the EU has partly been attributed to the shift from considering 'environment' to 'climate', which also locates the issue in the international rather than the national realm. As one interviewee explained, if the focus is on '[e]nvironment, then [we talk about] Sweden, … because we are good at it, but [if] climate is the discourse then it's somewhere else [that is] the problem'.[48] Many civil society actors, in particular, frame climate change and migration as a climate adaptation issue, and climate financing was a policy avenue that interviewees frequently mentioned as one they would want their respective nation-state to explore.

However, this framing of adaptation is very much linked to the central narrative of national self-interest. As an interviewee put it, climate-induced displacement would also be bad for the Global North, and climate adaptation is 'a good investment if you want to create stability and reduce the pressure of migration'.[49]

> Our main message, or what we try to say to [the] media, it was a little bit more constructive instead of just shouting that the wolf is coming or that the problem is coming, we want to show that we can do something about this, we can hinder all this displacement, we can reduce the pressure on migration if we invest in adaptation. If we help local communities to adapt and to live with the effects of climate change, then the risk for conflicts will be reduced.[50]

In particular, this framing has been a strategic tool utilised by civil society in the face of the rising popularity of far-right political parties, 'to kind of tap into that kind of fear of the unknown, that it might be the easy way in to raise attention to this issue',[51] or 'to say that, okay, if you are really this afraid of having immigrants coming to Denmark …, it should be in your own interest to deal with the climate crisis'.[52] Thus, advocacy activities on climate change and migration have

[45] Marc Helbling, 'Attitudes towards Climate Change Migrants' (2020) 160 *Climatic Change* 89, 92, available at doi.org/10.1007/s10584-020-02697-3.

[46] Karla Henning, Ivo Steimanis, and Björn Vollan, '(Climate) Migrants Welcome? Evidence from a Survey Experiment in Austria' (2022) 22 *Regional Environmental Change* 108, 2, available at doi.org/10.1007/s10113-022-01955-7.

[47] ibid.

[48] Interview Sweden 6.

[49] Interview Denmark 5.

[50] ibid.

[51] Interview Sweden 2.

[52] Interview Denmark 4.

been carried out 'to get more support for climate protection measures but also … to increase Austria's financial contributions'.[53] This ethically questionable advocacy tactic leads to one area of policy convergence, namely in countering the root causes of migration or displacement: 'if we want to stop migration we need to somehow … attack its root causes and one of the root causes is climate change'.[54]

It is these framings that drown out more cautious organisations that 'wouldn't peddle the spectre' of 'huge waves of migration' due to feared 'very negative impacts'.[55] Among these organisations, the consensus seems to be that 'the migration debate is rather toxic' and they therefore 'don't want to derive the necessity of good climate politics from the argument that a migration wave otherwise threatens us'.[56] Such a narrative 'only fuels the right and right-wing extremist narratives',[57] including 'the answer of controlling borders so that nobody gets through, which the AfD [Alternative for Germany, a far-right political party] will immediately come up with'.[58]

Throughout the conversations with interviewees it was clear that the current state of the migration-policy debate in Europe was heavily influencing their lack of engagement with climate change and migration, 'because migration is such a heavily politicised issue it's so difficult to have a normal conversation'.[59] In particular, social democratic politicians have come into government after 'overbidding' right-wing parties on the restrictiveness of their migration policies in order to appeal to voters of far-right populist parties[60] and entrenching anti-migrant sentiment to an extent that it was no longer a point of contention in mainstream political debate. This character of the migration debate is perceived by some civil society actors as a stumbling block to developing any coherent policy on climate change and migration: 'in today's world I don't think we will see, in the near future at least, … any rational approach to the whole idea of migration'.[61]

IV. Management

In analysing the European 'climate migration' regime, I understand the concept of management along the lines of the critical migration management literature, which locates migration management as 'the technocratic vision of a comprehensive management of human mobility "for the good for all"'.[62] The concept sits on

[53] Interview Austria 5.
[54] Interview Sweden 3.
[55] Interview Austria 6.
[56] ibid.
[57] ibid.
[58] Interview Germany 5/Austria 7.
[59] Interview Sweden 5.
[60] Interview Denmark 1.
[61] Interview Sweden 5.
[62] Fabian Georgi, 'Kritik des Migrationsmanagement: Historische Einordnung eines politischen Projekts', in Miriam Höppner and others (eds), *Kritische Migrationsforschung? Da kann ja jeder kommen* (Institut für Sozialwissenschaften 2012) 153, 161.

the dual pillars of economic utility and the logics of the neoliberal nation-state. As such, this concept tends to prioritise neoliberal ideas over the 'individual rights, the interests and wishes of refugees and migrants'.[63] These ideas have also long been charted in climate change and migration policy at the international level.[64]

Thus, the focus of this section is on the strategies, recommendations, and other attempts to manage climate change and migration that stem from this tradition. Key components of the management of the relation between climate change and migration from the perspective of European nation-states have been the externalisation of any migration considered problematic, as well as the outsourcing of responsibility to other political arenas. However, at the same time there is a focus on drawing migration policy even closer under the control of the nation-state. This creates the paradoxical situation of simultaneously pushing away while also reining in policy action.

Turning first to the externalising components of climate and migration management, much of this is achieved by anchoring climate and migration within development policy. As one interviewee explained, 'it's always a problem out there … in the Global South. Because it's always a problem there, it's … climate issues there and … of course there will be internal migration, there will be displacement and … so then it becomes like a development issue'.[65] Furthermore, interviewees reflect a sense that development cooperation finance is utilised in ways that seek to prevent migration: 'If you look at how Danish development aid is allocated it's to a growing extent allocated in a way to prevent migration. … There is a political will to reduce migration to Europe and therefore investments in those countries where people [migrate] are very important'.[66]

This has turned migration prevention (with climate change considered a potential driver of migration) into an important pillar of development strategies.[67] A connection is also frequently established in politics between development finance and 'the willingness to take back rejected asylum seekers', showing 'extortionary tendencies'.[68] Climate adaptation finance has thus been promoted as attractive to any European leader wanting 'to get rid of refugees and migrants'.[69]

On the other hand, the increased climate focus of development policy has been criticised for the financial shuffling that has taken place between development assistance and climate adaptation, leading funders to look for 'what one is doing

[63] ibid.

[64] Sarah Louise Nash, 'Towards an "Environmental Migration Management" Discourse: A Discursive Turn in Environmental Migration Advocacy?' in Kerstin Rosenow-Williams and François Gemenne (eds), *Organizational Perspectives on Environmental Migration* (Abingdon, Routledge 2016) 198.

[65] Interview Sweden 6.

[66] Interview Denmark 5.

[67] Danida, *The World We Share: Denmark's Strategy for Development Cooperation* (Ministry of Foreign Affairs of Denmark 2021), available at perma.cc/C3AU-FCTE; Bundesministerium Europäische und Internationale Angelegenheiten, 'Dreijahresprogramm der österreichischen Entwicklungspolitik 2022 bis 2024' (2022), available at perma.cc/9RNP-DC7U.

[68] Interview Austria 3.

[69] Interview Denmark 4.

in other areas that one could count' as climate adaptation.[70] As one interviewee summarised it, 'you can say they made the poor pay for climate finance because they take the money from the aid budget and use it on climate financing'.[71]

Germany, in particular, has been increasing its climate diplomacy profile in official partnerships with affected nation-states in the Global South on projects on climate change and human (im)mobilities. The Global Programme on Sustainable Management of Human Mobility in the Context of Climate Change conducted by the German Society for International Development (GIZ) and financed by the Federal Ministry for Economic Cooperation and Development (BMZ) even recognises this management approach in the programme title, which refers to the 'sustainable management' of human mobility.[72]

The programme was set up in the lead-up to the climate negotiations of the UNFCCC in 2017, which were chaired by Fiji but hosted in Germany, and is an answer to a concrete request for assistance on climate change and migration.[73] However, the programme is also seen to be in Germany's interests, projecting an image of how Germany wishes to be perceived on climate action, 'showing that Germany takes it [the implementation of the Paris Agreement] seriously and sees the needs of those states affected by the phenomenon of climate change and wants to take those seriously'.[74] Germany has been the 'most important funder' of the Platform on Disaster Displacement, with which German ministries have 'close coordination' including 'regular, standardised formats for exchange' and supporting 'the implementation of the Platform on Disaster Displacement work plan with financial and human resources'.[75]

Despite these development-based programmes and strategies, much of the focus from the perspective of European nation-states is still very much on reducing or eradicating the 'drivers' of migration. The German Federal Government's Expert Commission on the Causes of Flight, an independent body commissioned by the German government, had the mission to 'look at irregular migration as well as displacement, to identify the fundamental causes of both and develop approaches for effective reduction'.[76] A substantial section of the Commission's report focuses on climate change as a reason for people moving.[77] However, the Commission's understanding of the causes of 'flight' has been criticised as narrow and Eurocentric: 'what people understand under causes of flight is those things that move people to come to Europe over the Mediterranean'.[78]

[70] Interview Austria 5.
[71] Interview Denmark 2.
[72] ibid.
[73] Interview Germany 2.
[74] ibid.
[75] ibid.
[76] Fachkommission Fluchtursachen der Bundesregierung, 'Krisen vorbeugen, Perspektiven schaffen, Menschen schützen' (Fachkommission Fluchtursachen 2021) 14.
[77] ibid 48–50; 105–18.
[78] Interview Germany 5/Austria 7.

A different dynamic of externalising responsibility for climate and migration is through the delegation of responsibilities to another political level, namely, the EU. One interviewee reports that Swedish officials are seeing a stronger role for the EU than for the individual Member States: 'but we are part of the EU, these are issues that the EU and we as part of the EU should push for'.[79] Indeed, any meaningful discussion on policy change should recognise that many Member States have passed laws that are 'basically on the rock bottom of what is allowed in the EU'.[80]

While striving for common EU approaches to migration may be a noble intention, the current contentions among EU Member States on migration policy means that this is a strategy unlikely to come to fruition in the near future, and that it could even be viewed as a delaying tactic. Some commentators have called for the establishment of 'coalitions of the willing' in EU migration politics more broadly in order to overcome the stagnation of migration politics as a result of Member State disagreements.[81] At the same time as responsibility and policy responses are being held at arm's length, European nation-states are however reining in control within their migration frameworks, 'so it's becoming more sort of cherry picking rather than looking at how many people could we actually help'.[82]

Increasing control over migration policy by nation-states has also cut off migration policy from other (often intertwined) policy areas. For example, the former Danish Minister for Integration, Mattias Tesfaye, who was in post from June 2019 until May 2022 while this research was taking place, was quoted as saying that he was not interested in climate change.[83] This trend was also concretely implemented with the creation of the position of a Migration Ambassador.[84] Whereas an ambassador in a third country usually has a broad remit covering a number of policy areas, a Migration Ambassador role 'abstracts migration from all of those other contexts in which migration is actually caused, influences, is influenced by, and keeps it as a remit of its own'.[85]

This is not just the case in Denmark. The Swedish Minister for Migration, at the time, Anders Ygeman, reportedly also viewed migration 'quite excluded from many of the underlying causes [of] migration'.[86] One interviewee thought that the Ministry 'just deal[s] with it [migration] when it happens more'.[87] Climate change and migration are most commonly thought together by institutions working on

[79] Interview Sweden 1.
[80] Interview Sweden 3.
[81] Gerald Knaus, *Welche Grenzen brauchen wir? Zwischen Empathie und Angst: Flucht, Migration und die Zukunft von Asyl* (Munich, Piper 2020).
[82] Interview Denmark 3.
[83] Morten Skærbæk and Jesper Houborg, 'Udlændingepolitik er ikke det vigtigste for tesfaye, og han interesserer sig hverken for klimaeller identitetspolitik' (*Politiken*, 28 March 2021), available at perma.cc/8D26-B6YS.
[84] 'Ny ambassadør skal åbne døre for modtagecenter uden for EU' (*Jyllands-Posten*, 10 September 2020), available at perma.cc/6JBQ-3EJT.
[85] Interview Denmark 1.
[86] Interview Sweden 7.
[87] ibid.

climate change impacts. In the words of one interviewee, the reticence of other governmental bodies to actively think about climate change and migration is perhaps 'a kind of diplomacy avoidance. Maybe our government authorities are not yet ready to ask that question' (ie about the links between climate change and migration).[88] Practically across the board, it was argued that, if migration patterns were to change in such a way as to affect European nation-states in any significant manner, this would tip the scale and insert the relation between climate change and migration into policy agendas.[89]

V. Regulation

In order to distinguish regulation from the concept of management discussed in the previous section, I draw on a restrictive definition of regulation as 'a specified set of legal commands'.[90] This definition is taken to be narrow as 'it does not include, for example, those regulatory measures that have no backing in "law" (such as self-regulation). It also is unable to accommodate the fact that formal rules and provisions are set within a system of informal understandings'.[91] The strict focus on legal commands – or proposals for such commands – allows a focused analysis of the (potential) role of the nation-state, as opposed to other actors that play active roles in the broader discourses on the relations between climate change and migration in the respective nation-states.

Given that a whole section of this chapter is devoted to regulation, it is perhaps counter-intuitive to open by acknowledging that there is a dearth of regulation of climate change and migration by European nation-states. However regulation 'is not currently really in the focus of political interests'.[92] This partly comes down to the well-documented difficulties with actually pinning down the populations whom the regulation would target.[93] The difficulty of identifying rights-holders also hampers rights-based approaches to protection at the intersection of climate change and migration.[94] According to civil society representatives, 'in the Danish context it is a bit difficult [to identify populations in need of protection], it is very hypothetical and maybe in some distant future some millions of people'.[95]

[88] Interview Sweden 5.

[89] Interview Sweden 4.

[90] Martin Lodge and Kai Wegrich, *Managing Regulation: Regulatory Analysis, Politics and Policy* (London, Red Globe Press 2012) 15.

[91] ibid 16.

[92] Interview Germany 1.

[93] Andrew Baldwin, 'Resilience and Race, or Climate Change and the Uninsurable Migrant: Towards an Anthroporacial Reading of "Race"' (2017) 5(2) *Resilience* 129, available at doi.org/10.1080/21693293.2016.1241473.

[94] Sarah Louise Nash, 'Between Rights and Resilience: Struggles over Understanding Climate Change and Human Mobility' in Melissa Labonte and Kurt Mills (eds), *Human Rights and Justice: Philosophical, Economic, and Social Perspectives* (Abingdon, Routledge 2018) 123.

[95] Interview Denmark 4.

As a result, while many organisations want to work on climate change and migration, they struggle to know where or how to begin:

> we have such a difficult time properly taking up the topic of migration and often end up stuck on buzzwords: 'climate refugees'. What is a climate refugee, exactly? And where are legal actors that can be taken to court? Who is that?[96]

Therefore, while some political parties, such as the Swedish Green Party have 'tried to lift it up as an issue',[97] no specific legal frameworks or policies have been passed.

This has not prevented calls for international frameworks, and suggestions that European nation-states should contribute to their development. Civil society representatives would like to see nation-states calling for 'a better framework for dealing' with climate and migration and displacement[98] and helping to 'create the international legal framework that we need'.[99] Frequent proposals are for the 'legal rights [of refugees] to be broadened' to include climate change as a qualifying factor for a protective status[100] and for a legal recognition 'that people might be seeking asylum' due to climate change.[101]

In Sweden, one interviewee reported that the former Minister of Development, Per Ohlsson Fridh, had discussions with the UNHCR on 'new global frameworks for the protection of forced climate displacement'.[102] However, the interviewee noted that nothing has come from this interaction.[103] Another interviewee reported that the former Minister believed that 'Swedish legislation should start to look at climate change and migration and incorporate that in some way'.[104]

However, support for legislation is not universal. While the calls for adapting national or international legislation are well known, many interviewees are 'not sure [they] would agree with that, at least not immediately'.[105] The crux of the argument against legislation is that it is unknown what benefit it would concretely bring to the status quo and, more specifically, what protection outcomes would ensue for affected people.

In two of the European nation-states examined, there have been attempts at regulation. On the one hand, the German Green Party submitted a parliamentary motion calling for the introduction of a so-called 'climate passport' that would allow people displaced due to climate change, or at risk of displacement due to climate change, to migrate to Germany.[106] The motion was resolutely rejected

[96] Interview Germany 3.
[97] Interview Sweden 2.
[98] Interview Denmark 5.
[99] Interview Denmark 4.
[100] Interview Denmark 3.
[101] Interview Sweden 2.
[102] Interview Sweden 1.
[103] ibid.
[104] Interview Sweden 4.
[105] Interview Sweden 3.
[106] Deutscher Bundestag, 'Antrag klimabedingte Migration, Flucht und Vertreibung: Eine Frage globaler Gerechtigkeit', 10 December 2019, BT 19/15775.

by the German Parliament, but not before being debated in a parliamentary session[107] and widely reported in the German media.[108] It has been described as 'a very interesting test balloon that really made waves'.[109] Nonetheless, most interviewees could not imagine new protection-related regulation being adopted, due in particular to the 'tendency that we currently see [which] is more in the direction of isolation'.[110]

This observation fits well with the other specific example of regulation, which comes from Sweden and is actually an example of back-pedalling on provisions relating to climate and migration. Sweden 'used to have' relevant regulation,[111] which was suspended in 2016 in response to the large number of arrivals in Sweden in the previous year, and then fully struck down in 2021. The legislation in question opened up the possibility of granting 'protection if you could not return to your country of origin because of an environmental catastrophe'.[112] However, this provision has never actually resulted in international protection being granted,[113] giving the impression that the paragraph was not 'very important from a practical point of view'.[114] The core of the statutory reform concerned other provisions. Interviewees acknowledged that the removed provision on environmental migration was not perceived 'as an important regulation because it wasn't used'.[115]

A final category of regulation is that which requires the government or governmental actors to take climate and environment into account in other policy areas, which some civil society actors have cited as potential regulative routes for increasing awareness of climate change and migration. In particular, in Sweden, there are 'policies when it comes to development aid that climate and environment should be perspectives considered'.[116] It is hoped that, with development being the main sector through which climate change and migration are currently addressed in the Swedish context, this regulation will boost climate change and migration concerns, at least on the development policy agenda.

107 Deutscher Bundestag, 'Stenografischer Bericht', 13 December 2019, BT 19/135 16866.

108 Ulrich Ladurner, 'Klimapass? Eine verrückte Idee' (*Zeit*, 21 November 2018), available at perma.cc/4YBA-C58M; 'Roth fordert "Klimapass" für Flüchtlinge wegen der Erderwärmung' (*Die Welt*, 13 December 2019), available at perma.cc/7PQH-QKCG; 'Außenminister maas erteilt "Klimapass" für Flüchtlinge eine Absage' (*Die Welt*, 17 December 2019), available at perma.cc/6RGK-GUR3.

109 Interview Germany 4.

110 Interview Germany 1.

111 Interview Sweden 2.

112 Interview Sweden 4; Sveriges Riksdag, *Utlänningslag*, 2005, 4 (2a-§2).

113 Matthew Scott and Russell Garner, 'Nordic Norms, Natural Disasters, and International Protection: Swedish and Finnish Practice in European Perspective' (2022) 91 *Nordic Journal of International Law* 101.

114 Interview Sweden 3.

115 ibid.

116 Interview Sweden 1.

VI. Conclusion: The Modes of Governing Climate Change and Migration in Europe

The modes of governing climate change and migration in the four European nation-states explored in this chapter are impossible to separate from the migration policy playbooks of Fortress Europe. The securitised, 'othering' framing that depicts climate and migration as a threatening 'phenomenon' playing out beyond Europe's borders, but with the possibility of penetrating them in the foreseeable future, underlies the entire area of policy and dictates how climate and migration can be thought about from a governmental perspective. The overarching politics of climate and migration was thus aptly summed up by one interviewee: 'Let's make sure to build a wall now because otherwise all of these people will come running'.[117] Or, drawing on White's analysis of securitisation of climate and migration: 'Fences make good politics'.[118]

The central mode of governing climate and migration in Europe is therefore as migration prevention, or better said prevention of migration *to* Europe. This leads to the deeply cynical combination of disavowing the relevance of climate change and migration for European nation-states until people actually begin to enter their territory, while at the same time actively constructing a migration regime that prevents migration linked to climate change, or contains it elsewhere, thus ensuring its continued irrelevance.

The mode of governance in question is extremely technocratic, based on managing mobilities through strategies and soft interventions, such as the provision of finance for climate adaptation, rather than through hard-law responses granting a protective status to affected people. Indeed, two of the case studies above have shown a reticence for regulatory responses. In the German case, attempts at introducing a so-called 'climate passport' were unsuccessful after the proposal predictably failed to gain parliamentary support. In the Swedish case, an existing statutory provision was removed in sweeping amendments tightening up Sweden's migration law. These two examples confirm a lack of political appetite for protection by regulation.

Despite the securitised logics that underlie the various attempts to manage climate change and migration, the strategies employed do not fit the stereotypical mould of securitised responses as militarised responses. Nevertheless, the securitised logics that provide a foundation for the policy responses from externalisation of asylum decision procedures, to climate adaptation finance, and international development cooperation linked to migration prevention benchmarks make these responses equally disconcerting.

[117] Interview Denmark 3.
[118] White (n 2) 11.

While in the best-case scenario, these policies are indeed promoting additional funding towards climate adaptation in affected areas of the Global South, in many cases, they merely result in a rebranding of existing projects, or in the diversion of funding from other projects equally beneficial to the Global South. Furthermore, when the fundamental goal of a policy is not necessarily the protection of the people most affected by the impacts of climate change but instead the prevention of migration into the EU, there is no guarantee that management strategies are going to maintain their humanitarian note if migration across Europe's borders increases.

The European modes of governing thus all sit upon an increasingly entrenched restrictiveness and xenophobia-driven migration policy in nation-states, with political parties converging around populist anti-migration policy stances in order to appeal to their electorates,[119] combined with a very Eurocentric perspective on migration that disregards European culpability for many drivers of (forced) migration.

If (meaningful) agreements on climate change and migration are to be reached at the international level, then European nation-states will likely be lively discussion partners, despite the consistent acknowledgement at the EU and Member-State level that migration to Europe in the context of climate change is not being seen at a large scale. However, there is a danger that, given the background political and policy discourse, productive negotiations will only be possible when the minimisation of migration to Europe is part of the agenda and that, even then, Member States will be hard pressed to reach consensus.

International migration policy already delivers ample examples of Global North nation-states pursuing these agendas. The Austrian government has repeatedly emphasised their rejection of the Global Compact on Safe, Orderly and Regular Migration,[120] and both Austria and Denmark have been actively pursuing 'asylum dumping'[121] in third countries outside of the EU.[122] As this analysis has shown, any future attempts to govern climate change and migration will not be immune to these dynamics.

In research that tries to disentangle the politics and policy of climate change and migration, it will be increasingly important to focus on the migration regimes of European nation-states and how they cope with the increasing understanding of climate change as a (potential) driver of migration. The research project 'Climate Diplomacy and Uneven Policy Responses on Climate Change and Human Mobilities', on which this chapter is based, has been a first attempt to understand

[119] Interview Denmark 4.

[120] 'Ministerrat lehnt Beitritt zu UN-Migrationspakt ab' (*Bundeskanzleramt Österreich*, 31 October 2018), available at perma.cc/B59G-BQWC.

[121] Interview Austria 6.

[122] Interview Austria 3; Austria 6; Denmark 1; Denmark 4.

what climate change and migration means for the policy communities of European nation-states, and what this means for the European climate and migration regime. Nevertheless, there will be a need to cast the analytical net wider and gather more diverse perspectives from across the Union, to gain a more complete picture of the EU as a whole.

7

Race, Migration, and Climate Change: A Cautionary Note

ANDREW BALDWIN

I. Introduction

This chapter sounds a cautionary note to researchers and practitioners engaging with the theme of climate change and migration. 'Climate-induced migration' is a standard feature of the political and legal discourse on climate change. Yet, as many chapters in this volume attest, it is one which rests on some rather shaky epistemic foundations. The chapter expands on this scepticism by cautioning that a complicated politics of race and racism organises the scientific and policy discourse on climate-induced migration in ways the climate change science and policy community can scarcely afford to ignore.[1]

The first section outlines how the discourse on climate change and human migration functions as a system of racial meaning. The argument here is not the simplistic claim that climate change will disproportionately displace the world's Black and brown majority world. Nor is it that, if left unabated, climate change will drive millions of so-called 'climate migrants' or 'climate refugees' from the Global South to Europe or America. Instead, the chapter cautions those engaging in discussions about climate change and human migration that the corresponding scientific and policy *discourse* acts as a proxy for the adaptation of structural racism. By structural racism, I mean a racism written into the language, assumptions, institutional structures, and cultural frames of reference that organise the discourse, as opposed to a more vulgar racism expressed in terms of elimination, hatred, or border fortification. My use of the term 'discourse' follows that of Stuart Hall for whom discourse 'should be understood as that which gives human

[1] The arguments in this chapter are an abridged version of those I make in Andrew Baldwin, *The Other of Climate Change: Racial Futurism, Migration, Humanism* (Lanham, Rowman & Littlefield 2022). Throughout the chapter, I take 'race' to be a system of meaning. By this reading, 'race' should be understood not merely as a social construction but a system of discourses and practices that has very real material effects in the world.

practice and institutions meaning'.[2] In this sense, the discourse on climate change and migration makes climate change meaningful in a very distinctive way. It is, as I clarify below, a discourse that *means* race. Or more precisely, it is a 'system of meaning' that makes climate change meaningful by bringing the figure of the 'climate migrant/refugee' into being as an historically specific racial other. To talk then about governing so-called 'climate-induced migration' or 'climate refugees' is to talk about governing this racial other. Much of my argument in this section is that the discourse is principally concerned with constructing this racial other as a means of shoring up Euro-western humanism in a turbulent planetary context in which the presumed stability of political or cultural identity can no longer be guaranteed. As we will see, science plays an important role in grounding the discourse, as a system of racial meaning, in nature.

The second section develops this idea in relation to a nascent policy discussion about 'climate change, migration and urbanism'. At COP26 in Glasgow, C40 and the Mayors' Migration Council launched the Global Mayors' Task Force on Climate and Migration. They would soon be followed by the US National League of Cities (NLC), based in Washington, DC, which released its own landmark report on the same theme in early 2022. Together these major new urban initiatives represent the first time the relationship between climate change and human migration would find its way onto the global urban policy agenda in any concerted way. Their aim is to equip cities with the expertise and planning needed to manage shifting patterns of migration to and from cities in a context of global climate change. How cities around the world respond to the challenges posed by so-called 'climate-induced' in- and out-migration will obviously depend on the unique circumstances of each city. We can, however, generalise by suggesting that the legal concept of property is a common denominator. At the heart of the urbanisation of climate change and migration discourse are a set of dilemmas concerning land and property, not least: where and on whose property will so-called 'climate migrants' live? And: what will their presence do to property values, particularly in high-rent neighbourhoods? These are not incidental questions, especially in contexts such as North America and the UK where their home is now most people's most valuable asset.[3] But they have wider application too, given how the promise of property ownership drives capitalist expansion in cities around the world.[4] In this second section, I turn to Cheryl Harris' landmark reading of 'whiteness as property' to consider how 'race' can be understood to structure these urban dilemmas.

[2] Stuart Hall, *The Fateful Triangle: Race, Ethnicity, Nation* (Cambridge, Massachusetts, Harvard University Press 2017).

[3] Melinda Cooper, *Family Value: Between Neoliberalism and the New Social Conservatism* (Princeton, Zone Books 2017).

[4] One could generalise here by arguing that land is most people's most valuable asset anywhere in the world, either as private property or as shared rights on common lands. However, for the sake of simplicity, I confine my argument to just urban property ownership.

One of the challenges I face in making these arguments about climate change, migration, and race is that both race and racism are poorly understood within the wider science and policy context of climate change. There is, for example, no real discussion about what these terms mean within the wider context of climate change political debate.[5] At best, race and racism are associated with calls for 'climate justice' where the prevailing idea is that climate change is a racial injustice, as it is expected to affect people of colour disproportionately. And while this way of viewing climate change is not without merit, it assumes a lot about race and racism. At worst, climate change is understood strictly as an environmental crisis, rectifiable by emissions reductions and new technology, while having nothing whatsoever to do with race and racism. This challenge is further compounded, however, given that we live today in what sociologists of race often describe as the condition of the 'postracial'.[6] Sometimes called 'racism without racists',[7] the postracial is the condition in which 'race' operates as an invisible system of meaning whereby racial meanings are codified in language in ways that make no explicit reference to race. The condition of the postracial is what allows racism to flourish through, for example, dog whistle racism, but also, paradoxically, through its explicit denial.[8] And finally, the challenge I am describing is compounded by the quality of innocence that surrounds climate change discourse. Mitigating and adapting to climate change are typically conceived as moral imperatives associated with bettering planetary humanity, whereas the denial of climate change science is often associated with those on the political right unwilling to relinquish fossil fuel dependency. This latter position is often, rightly or wrongly, associated with racism, white supremacy, and ethnonationalism.[9] The problem, however, is that narrowly associating racism with climate denialism leaves little scope for a more reflexive understanding of the way race works as a system of meaning within the context of climate change science and policy. My hope is that this chapter will add meaningfully to an expanding discussion concerning the way 'race' operates as a key term of reference within the discursive context of climate change.

[5] This is starting to change, however, as race is made increasingly more visible within wider debates about climate change and the Anthropocene. See, for example, Neel Ahuja, *Planetary Specters: Race, Migration and Climate Change in the Twenty-First Century* (Chapel Hill, University of North Carolina Press 2021); Andrew Baldwin and Bruce Erikson, 'Introduction: Whiteness, Coloniality, and the Anthropocene' (2020) 38 *Environment and Planning D: Society and Space* 3, available at doi.org/10.1177/0263775820904485; Carmen G Gonzalez, 'Racial Capitalism, Climate Justice, and Climate Displacement' (2021) 11 *Oñati Socio-Legal Series* 108, available at doi.org/10.35295/osls.iisl/0000-0000-0000-1137; Lisa Tilley and others, 'Race and Climate Change: Towards Anti-Racist Ecologies' (2022) *Politics*, available at doi.org/10.1177/02633957221127166.

[6] David T Goldberg, *Are We All Postracial Yet?* (London, Polity 2015).

[7] Eduardo Bonilla-Silva, *Racism without Racists: Colour-Blind Racism and the Persistence of Racial Inequality in America*, 5th edn (Lanham, Rowman & Littlefield 2017).

[8] Alana Lentin, 'Beyond Denial: "Not Racism" as Racist Violence' (2018) 32(4) *Continuum* 400, available at doi.org/10.1080/10304312.2018.1480309; Alana Lentin, *Why Race Still Matters* (Cambridge, Polity 2020).

[9] Andreas Malm and others, *White Skin, Black Fuel: On the Danger of Fossil Fascism* (London, Verso 2021).

II. 'Climate Change and Migration' Discourse: A New Structural Racism?

How does the discourse on 'climate migration' function racially? How does it work as a proxy for the adaptation of structural racism? Answering these questions requires that we first understand how the discourse produces its own unique racial other: the figure of the 'climate migrant/refugee'.[10] This means understanding not only how this figure is constructed racially – how it signifies, or means, 'race' – but also how this meaning helps to shore up humanism. At the heart of this explanation is the idea that the 'figure of the climate migrant/refugee' does not pre-exist its construction by empiricist 'science', but that empiricism actively calls the figure into being. This may seem counter-intuitive, given how contemporary media bombard us with the message that climate change stands to bring about new migration.[11] Such messaging is so relentless it seems almost irrefutable. Yet, as many of the chapters in this volume have shown, migration is not reducible to climate change alone. This means that there is no inherent relationship between climate change and human migration. Which, in turn, raises the question: then why invent a discourse that presumes there is?[12] My answer to this question is that the discourse serves the purpose of shoring up European humanism amid the existential crisis of climate change.[13]

This brings us squarely into discussion with Stuart Hall's important thesis that race is a sliding signifier.[14] What Hall means by this is that 'race is a discourse' whose 'signifiers reference not genetically established facts but the systems of meaning that have come to be fixed in the classifications of culture'.[15] On this reading, race has no underlying foundation in nature, nor any inherent meaning. It does, however, operate as a key term of reference in the realm of culture. Whatever meaning might be inscribed onto those said to be racially different is not a function of some innate, group characteristic, but is instead a mark of power. To construct Black people as threats or victims is not to read these terms off the

[10] Baldwin (n 1).

[11] For recent examples, see Abrahm Lustgarten, 'The Great Climate Migration Has Begun' (*The New York Times*, 23 July 2020), available at perma.cc/W9MY-5V2Z; Abrahm Lustgarten, 'How Climate Change Will Reshape America' (*The New York Times*, 15 September 2020), available at perma.cc/RH2Y-8MR9; Abrahm Lustgarten, 'How Russia Wins the Climate Crisis' (*The New York Times*, 16 December 2020), available at perma.cc/R34M-3TW6; Hanna Hett, 'As the Planet Warms, Canada Faces an Influx of Climate Refugees' (*Wired Magazine*, 10 September 2022), available at perma.cc/58HF-DL38; Parag Khanna, 'Migration Will Soon be the Biggest Climate Challenge of our Time' (*Financial Times*, 3 October 2021), available at perma.cc/U3X7-MVZT.

[12] Calum TM Nicholson, 'Climate Change and Politics of Causal Reasoning: The Case of the Climate Change and Migration' (2014) 180(2) *The Geographical Journal* 151, available at doi.org/10.1111/geoj.12062.

[13] Baldwin (n 1).

[14] Hall (n 2).

[15] ibid 45.

body, but to inscribe these values onto those who look a certain way.[16] In this way, values like 'threat' and 'victim' are not references to genetic difference, but instead reference a system of racial meaning in which both are signifiers of Blackness. If concepts like 'threat' or 'victim' signify Blackness, then within this system of meaning, concepts like 'innocence' and 'rescuer' signify a corresponding form of racialised identity, most notably Euro-western humanism. Thus, Blackness can be understood to secure the meaning of humanism.[17]

And yet for 'race' to work as a system of meaning that marks people as different (ie as threats or victims), it must also acquire the *appearance* of being natural. Because race thinking is ultimately about distinguishing Europeans from non-Europeans in a spatial hierarchy that seeks to valorise the former morally, politically, and above all, economically, it must always strive to make this system appear natural.[18] Doing so gives the system the appearance of timelessness, something outside the realms of history and political contestation, as opposed to one invented for the purpose of domination. Thus, for Hall, visible signs of difference may serve as 'markers of racial difference at the level of appearances', but these are really just 'signifiers of an invisible code' – an imagined, timeless code whose apparent location in nature is said to be accessible only to science.[19] And yet, paradoxically, a code that cannot ultimately be proved: hence the routine failures of racial and genetic science to prove once and for all the apparently natural foundations of race.[20]

We can read the discourse on climate change and migration in much the same way. As a system of racial meaning, it is made to rest on a naturalist footing, although not one founded on biology or genetics, but on what Paul Gilroy calls 'racial nomos'.[21] This is a sort of imagined spatial law of race that underpins all manner of racist fantasies, from the desire for global domination all the way down to urban racial segregation.[22] Racial nomos is the assumption that people are assigned their place (and value) in the world according to a natural global geography of race – Indians in India; Europeans in Europe (but also in settler colonial states like Canada, the United States, Australia, and New Zealand); Black people in Africa, the ghettos or banlieues and so on.[23] Assumptions about racial

[16] For a detailed account of the way race works first and foremost as a scopic regime, see Kalpana Seshadri-Crooks, *Desiring Whiteness: A Lacanian Analysis of Race* (Abingdon, Routledge 2000).
[17] Frank B Wilderson, *Afropessimism* (New York, Liveright 2020); Sylvia Wynter, 'Unsettling the Coloniality of Being/Power/Truth/Freedom: Towards the Human, After Man, its Overrepresentation – an Argument' (2003) 3(3) *CR: The New Centennial Review* 257, available at www.jstor.org/stable/41949874.
[18] Lentin, *Why Race Still Matters* (n 8).
[19] Hall (n 2) 63.
[20] On this point, Hall is very clear. He is not suggesting that science cannot distinguish between groups, but that science cannot fix the meaning of difference.
[21] Paul Gilroy, *Postcolonial Melancholia* (New York, Columbia University Press 2005) 39.
[22] ibid.
[23] These questions of moral geography are taken up in David Livingston, *The Geographical Tradition: Episodes in the History of a Contested Enterprise* (Oxford, Blackwell Publishing 1992).

nomos are precisely the reason some people are said to be 'out of place' at certain times and places.[24]

On this reading, climate change threatens to destabilise racial nomos, which we should understand as a set of assumptions that anchor people to place. In this way, we can think of the discourse on climate change and migration as a metonym for the undoing of a foundational racist fantasy that is always striving to anchor the system of racial meaning in nature. Pull up the anchor, undermine the fantasy, and the system of meaning starts to slip away from its assumed foundation in nature. Although we do not usually think of climate change this way, it poses precisely this kind of threat. Not only is climate change said to pose a physical danger to the Earth system, but for those who worry that climate change will catalyse migration, climate change threatens to undermine what is for them an important system of meaning that anchors modern conceptions of the human.[25] Climate change will move people to and fro; order will collapse into disorder; the certainties of racial nomos will give way to a profound uncertainty about how to place people geographically, and thus morally and culturally. To meliorate this anxiety, those who derive meaning from racial discourse must therefore find a way to re-anchor racial discourse to nature. And here, I would suggest, is where the figure of the 'climate migrant/refugee' enters the picture. It stands as a new kind of naturalised (ie climatised) other – one that is used to fix or secure the system of racial meaning that climate change threatens to overwhelm, thereby guaranteeing the discourse on 'race'. The figure may not be an actually existing thing in the world. But when climate change is imagined to pose a fundamental threat to what is assumed to be the very natural order of 'race' – when it threatens to undo the fantasy of racial nomos – the figure of the 'climate migrant/refugee', paradoxically, emerges as the racial other that will prevent the system of racial meaning from unravelling. In this way, this figure can be understood to occupy an important location within the symbolic order of climate change, as one of the key others that makes the science and policy discourse on climate change meaningful. Indeed, among the most powerful justifications for mitigating climate change is the claim that 'business-as-usual' will force millions from their homes, thus catalysing violence, crisis, and strife.[26] This, I would suggest, is what explains the relentless persistence of the discourse on climate change and migration even while it has been shown to be so problematic. It provides meaning to those who worry that the climate change crisis threatens to undermine our ability to find meaning in the world.

But we can take this analysis even further. If, as many assume, climate change threatens to redistribute people across the surface of Earth, the figure of the 'climate

[24] Audrey Kobayashi and Linda Peake, 'Racism out of Place: Thoughts on Whiteness and an Antiracist Geography in the New Millennium' (2000) 90(2) *Annals of the Association of American Geographers* 392, available at www.jstor.org/stable/1515242.

[25] Wynter (n 17).

[26] The Prime Minister of The Bahamas, Philip Davis, made this claim recently at COP27. See Hamish Cardwell, 'COP27: Cut Emissions or Face Tens of Millions of Climate Refugees: Bahamas PM' (*Radio New Zealand News*, 10 November 2022), available at perma.cc/746V-EWAT.

migrant/refugee' is a racial other constructed to shore up European humanism. Elsewhere I have sought to demonstrate how humanism undertakes to redefine itself by attempting to govern this other, either militarily, or through apparently benign logics, such as humanitarianism or the market.[27] Here we should remember that humanism is never just a form of identity but is primarily a genre of power that works by constructing the racial other outside the category of the human.[28] By this account, humanism imagines the climatic redistribution of people around the world not solely in terms of the loss of its own identity, but as the loss of its assumed power, or more precisely as the inability to guarantee the system of racial meaning from which it draws sustenance. And so, consequently, humanism strives to shore up its perceived loss of power.

How does humanism attempt to restore its imaginary lost power? Ironically, not by restoring racial nomos, not by forcibly keeping the 'climate other' in its place, and not by obsessively policing the border. It does so, first and foremost, I would suggest, through an appeal to science. It calls on science to recategorise or differentiate people – namely, 'climate migrants/refugees' – according to the geophysical impacts of climate change. Or in slightly different terms, science is used to re-codify human difference in the language of climate change, which is nature's new proxy. Thus, science is used to affirm that certain people either pose a threat to an existing order or will soon be victimised by climate change. By appealing to a new (climate) science of human difference, a line is drawn that distinguishes the human from the racial other, newly categorised as 'climate migrants' and 'climate refugees'. Here, the power of science lies in the way it naturalises this line; the way it seeks to delimit the racial other as an objective, inevitable consequence of climate change.

To better understand the role science plays in securing this system of racial meaning, consider how the figure of the 'climate migrant/refugee' is constructed racially, how it references the system of meaning of 'race', a system always striving to anchor difference to nature. Elsewhere, I document at length how this meaning derives from a series of intersecting racial tropes – naturalisation, recognition, the loss of political status, ambiguity, and excess.[29] Together these tropes construct the figure outside the category of the human. What makes the discourse so powerful is that it seeks to explain migration, one of the most contentious dimensions of contemporary political life – contentious *because* of its racial significance – in terms of climate and climatic variation. If 'race' is to find its ultimate guarantee outside the realms of history and politics, climate and climatic variation are used as naturalist metaphors to anchor race. Never mind that anthropogenic climate

[27] Baldwin (n 1).

[28] Wynter (n 17); Wilderson (n 17); Alexander G Weheliye, *Habeas Viscus: Racializing Assemblages, Biopolitics, and Black Feminist Theories of the Human* (Durham, Duke University Press 2014); Christina Sharpe, *In the Wake: On Blackness and Being* (Durham, Duke University Press 2016).

[29] This argument is developed in full in Andrew Baldwin, 'Racialisation and the Figure of the Climate-Change Migrant' (2013) 45(6) *Environment and Planning A: Economy and Space* 1474, available at doi.org/10.1068/a45388; Baldwin (n 1).

change is itself a product of modern history.[30] What matters is that climate change is routinely reduced to a set of geophysical impacts shorn of historical substance which are then used to explain migration. By this reading, complicated political phenomena like migration and security are reduced to nature, in this case the geophysical impacts of climate change.[31]

But if climate and climatic variation are the nature metaphors that serve to anchor race within the discourse on climate change and migration, it is the *promise of science* that seeks to provide race with its ultimate guarantee. Hence, the emphasis international institutions such as the World Bank and the Intergovernmental Panel on Climate Change (IPCC) seem to place on understanding the relationship between climate change and migration *scientifically*.[32] Their hope is that with enough empirical evidence linking climate change to migration, researchers will eventually establish the 'nature' of this relationship, thus allowing lawmakers to differentiate people according to the geophysical impacts of climate change. The presumption here is that only by knowing the other scientifically can policy-makers reasonably seek to govern it. And yet this hope is itself a fantasy, given that migration is always multicausal. What matters then is not whether science can find the missing link between climate change and migration, as no such link is there to be found. Instead, in order for science to guarantee race in the discourse on climate change and migration, science must be continuously re-invested with the *promise* that it can locate the missing link despite this being a logical impossibility. Here, it is not so much the truth of science that guarantees race, but the *belief* that science can establish a truth about the relationship between climate change and migration. If this sounds like an irrational belief, it is worth remembering that racism is itself fundamentally irrational. There is no scientific basis to race, just the habitual investment in systems of knowledge that seek to secure racial meaning. For those invested in systems of racial meaning, ensuring these persist, especially when such systems appear threatened, is therefore of the utmost importance, else one's sense of meaning may start to unravel. Investing in the belief that science can explain human difference provides this guarantee. The same holds for the discourse on climate change and migration. There is no science that will prove the link between

[30] Ian Baucom, *History 4° Celsius: Search for a Method in the Age of Anthropocene* (Durham, Duke University Press 2020); Jason W Moore (ed), *Anthropocene or Capitalocene? Nature, History and the Crisis of Capitalism* (Dexter, PM Press 2016); Andreas Malm, *Fossil Capital: The Rise of Steam Power and the Roots of Global Warming* (London, Verso 2016).

[31] Jan Selby, Gabrielle Daoust, and Clemens Hoffmann, *Divided Environments: The International Political Ecology of Climate Change, Water and Security* (Cambridge, Cambridge University Press 2022). This book offers an empirically grounded account of the way climate reductionism works in relation to climate security discourse.

[32] ibid; Sarah Louise Nash, *Negotiating Migration in the Context of Climate Change: International Policy and Discourse* (Bristol, Bristol University Press 2019). In making this claim, I am not for a moment suggesting that international institutions consciously seek to sustain racism through an appeal to science. I would, however, suggest that the ease with which science is used to differentiate people on the basis of climate change should alert us to the power that systems of racial meaning have today, namely, the power to organise political discourse without anyone even realising it.

climate change and migration once and for all. Only an investment in a system of racial meaning which, it is hoped, science will find a way to guarantee. The promise here is that the figure of the 'climate migrant/refugee', a signifier of race, can ultimately be known using the methods of science. Science will, of course, always fail to know the figure in its entirety. But this is irrelevant if what matters is ensuring the continuity of structural racism amid instabilities of climate change.

But what kind of science? How exactly is the figure of the 'climate migrant/refugee' known scientifically? Some further clarification is needed here. In fact, not surprisingly there is no agreed method for determining who or what is a 'climate migrant/refugee'. Even the IPCC has argued that 'the use of the term climate refugee is scientifically and legally problematic'.[33] Still, there is no shortage of efforts underway attempting to define the figure scientifically.

Two such efforts are noteworthy. The first is the practice of gravity modelling used recently by the World Bank, the results of which are cited by the IPCC's most recent assessment report.[34] The World Bank infers the existence of 'internal climate migrants' by combining socio-economic and climatic data sets into 'gravity models' and running these models multiple times.[35] These are sophisticated models, which, while potentially useful for helping decision makers plan for future eventualities, are not objective so much as they are constructivist models that call into being what the World Bank calls 'internal climate migrants'.[36] What makes these models so powerful, however, is that by conjuring up a number (for instance, 143 million 'internal climate migrants' by 2050),[37] they acquire the *appearance* of scientific objectivity and, thus, neutrality. It should therefore come as no surprise that the number this model generates now circulates as an established truth within the wider discursive context of climate change.

The second is the model encapsulated in the IPCC Sixth Assessment Report, in which 'climate-related migration' is conceptualised in a diagrammatic schema of risk.[38] The model is less concerned with quantifying 'climate migrants/refugees' than with devising a truth regime that, at least in principle, can be used to locate objectively those *at risk* of migration due to climate change. The power of this model lies not so much in its capacity to naturalise climate risk, as in the way

[33] W Neil Adger and others, 'Human Security', in IPCC Fifth Assessment Report, *Impacts, Adaptation and Vulnerability: Working Group II Contribution* (Cambridge, Cambridge University Press 2014) 755, 771.

[34] IPCC Sixth Assessment Report, *Impacts, Adaptation and Vulnerability: Working Group II Contribution* (Cambridge, Cambridge University Press 2022).

[35] Kanta K Rigaud and others, 'Groundswell: Preparing for Internal Climate Migration' (World Bank Group 2018); Viviane Clement and others, 'Groundswell Part 2: Acting on Internal Climate Migration' (World Bank Group 2021).

[36] On the question of performativity, see Derek Gregory, *The Colonial Present: Afghanistan, Palestine, Iraq* (Oxford, Blackwell Publishing 2004); Judith Butler, *Gender Trouble: Feminism and the Subversion of Identity* (Abingdon, Routledge 1990).

[37] Rigaud and others (n 35).

[38] Guéladio Cissé and others, 'Health, Wellbeing and the Changing Structure of Communities', in IPCC Sixth Assessment Report (n 34) 1041, 1081.

it constructs climate change as a set of measurable geophysical impacts separate from what it calls 'non-climate factors', which presumably include the history of capitalism. Here, climate change is made to appear as though it has no history, even while we know the history of climate change is intimately bound up with the history of fossil fuels, imperialism, and the US dollar.[39]

What these two approaches share is that both have the *appearance* of offering an 'objective' way to predict the future, rather than simply being imagined futures conjured using inherently subjective scenario modelling. Both appear invested in the belief that science can establish the truth about the figure of the 'climate migrant/refugee'. Inasmuch as the discourse on climate change and migration is a system of racial meaning, it needs to appear as though it were anchored in nature. My contention is that these scientific readings of 'climate change and migration' do this important anchoring work. By attempting to isolate the figure of the 'climate migrant/refugee', and by providing evidence that because some people appear to be at risk of migration, they threaten to destabilise the social conditions in which they are embedded, these models guarantee the discourse on climate change and migration and, thereby, secure it as a system of racial meaning. To be clear, I am not suggesting that those who have designed these models are themselves racists or consciously seek to sustain structural racism. My point is simply that whether they realise it or not, they are mobilising science to authorise a distinctive form of human difference rooted in one of nature's most powerful contemporary metaphors: climate and climatic variation.

III. Climate Change, Migration, Race, and the City

Let us turn now to consider how this system of racial meaning can be understood to work at the scale of the urban. Cheryl Harris' notion of 'whiteness as property' is indispensable here.[40] Not only does it provide important context for what follows, but 'whiteness as property' also offers a useful framework from which to question how the discourse on climate change and migration relates to urban politics in the contemporary American context. Questioning the discourse from this perspective is additionally significant not only given the history of racial segregation in American cities, but also because of what a growing number of voices now calls a 'climate apartheid'.[41] UN Special Rapporteur on extreme poverty and

[39] Timothy Mitchell, *Carbon Democracy: Political Power in the Age of Oil* (London, Verso 2011); Ahuja (n 5).

[40] Cheryl L Harris, 'Whiteness as Property' (1993) 106(8) *Harvard Law Review* 1707, available at www.jstor.org/stable/1341787.

[41] UN Human Rights Council, Forty-first session 24 June – 12 July 2019 'Report of the Special Rapporteur on extreme poverty and human rights' (17 July 2019) UN Doc A/HRC/41/39 at 12; Nancy Tuana, 'Climate Apartheid: The Forgetting of Race in the Anthropocene' (2019) 7 *Critical Philosophy of Race* 1, available at doi.org/10.5325/critphilrace.7.1.0001; Jennifer L Rice, Joshua Long, and

human rights, Philip Alston, described climate apartheid as a scenario in which the 'wealthy pay to escape overheating, hunger and conflict, while the rest of the world is left to suffer'.[42] Climate apartheid is itself potentially useful for conceptualising a new mode of segregation taking shape in response to climate change. Whiteness as property can help us grasp the racial contours of 'climate apartheid' in urban contexts that are expected to be destinations of choice for so-called 'climate migrants' and 'climate refugees'.

A. Whiteness as Property

According to C40, climate-related migration will reshape the geography and demography of cities in the coming decades, and cities around the world need to start preparing for this. The NLC makes a similar set of claims but goes one step further by making a direct appeal to city managers. It asks them to identity how 'climate-related migration' will affect their cities and to plan accordingly. The NLC invites city managers to consider, for example, whether their city is a vulnerable city (ie prone to climate-related out-migration), a recipient city (ie prone to climate-related in-migration, but spatially constrained), or a climate destination (ie typically those in the northeast with lower than usual population densities, for instance, in the former rust belt). Both C40 and the NLC offer useful openings for reimagining the political, economic, and cultural futures of cities worldwide. My intention here is not to condemn these efforts. Nor is it to trivialise in any way the geophysical impacts of climate change. Instead, in keeping with the cautionary nature of this chapter, my point here is simply that it would be disingenuous to stage this public discussion without also considering the history of racial segregation in American cities and the way whiteness in America is invariably bound up with property ownership and, as we will see momentarily, is itself a form of property protected by law. It is not a foregone conclusion that cities will respond nefariously to this new urban agenda by securing the property interest in whiteness. Still, researchers and practitioners, and, indeed, urban residents, are badly served if the emerging discourse on climate change, migration, and cities remains blind to this history. Later I speculate as to how this insight is potentially applicable to cities beyond the US context, including those in the 'Global South'.

Central to my analysis is Harris' landmark idea that whiteness has evolved into a form of property, the value of which is now protected by law.[43] On this reading, whiteness is not a form of identity equal to all other forms of identity

Anthony Levenda, 'Against Climate Apartheid: Confronting the Persistent Legacies of Expendability for Climate Justice' (2021) 5(2) *Environment and Planning E: Nature and Space* 1, available at doi.org/10.1177/2514848621999286; Gonzalez (n 5).

[42] UNHRC (n 41) 12.

[43] Harris (n 40).

but is best conceived as a specific form of property interest.[44] Her analysis begins with the idea that the 'origins of property rights in the United States are rooted in racial domination'.[45] The forced removal of Native Americans from their territory, alongside a policy of Native elimination, was accompanied by the concomitant establishment of property rights for whites. By the late seventeenth century, the slave codes would establish differential rights based on 'race', such that it would become illegal for Blacks to own property, travel without permits, or assemble publicly. The result was that 'Black' would mark those 'subject to enslavement'[46] objectified *as* property, while 'white' became a marker of freedom and, thus, a criterion for owning property. Thus, for Harris, 'the racial line between white and Black was extremely critical; it became a line of protection and demarcation from the potential threat of commodification'.[47] Whiteness would henceforth be a sign of 'privilege and protection', while its 'absence meant being the object of property'.[48] In this way, 'whiteness [would become] the characteristic, the attribute, the property of free human beings'.[49]

Harris then goes on to show that as property became encoded in American law, it would encode not just a legal right, but an historically constituted social relation. In this way, property law would simply encode the cultural value of property (ie the whiteness of property) as a benchmark in law. But the cultural value of property would not refer simply to the ownership or possession of a tangible object – it would also designate a set of rights and interests. The right to property would thus extend well beyond simple ownership and encompass, as Harris points out, a suite of related attributes, including 'jobs, entitlements, occupational licenses, contracts, subsidies, and indeed a whole host of intangibles that are the products of labor, time and creativity, such as intellectual property, business goodwill, and enhanced earning potential from graduate degrees'.[50] For our purposes, though, two such attributes matter most. Property would come to imply a set of settled expectations, which 'became tantamount to property that could not permissibly be intruded upon without consent'.[51] The expected future value of property was not to be infringed upon. It would also include the right to exclude.

Harris' innovation is to trace how whiteness in America would acquire the attributes of property. She illustrates this through two landmark cases in US law:

[44] Here it is worth recalling some of the political techniques that have been used to secure this privilege. As Mike Davis shows, the use of neighbourhood covenants was key to preventing non-white homeownership in the suburbs of Los Angeles. See Mike Davis, *City of Quartz: Excavating the Future in Los Angeles* (New York, Verso 2006).
Charles L Nier, 'Perpetuation of Segregation: Toward a New Historical and Legal Interpretation of Redlining Under the Fair Housing Act' (1999) 32(3) *John Marshall Law Review* 617.

[45] Harris (n 40) 1716.

[46] ibid 1718.

[47] ibid 1721.

[48] ibid.

[49] ibid.

[50] ibid 1728.

[51] ibid 1731.

Plessy v Ferguson[52] and *Brown v Board of Education*.[53] In the former, which justified racial segregation, the US Supreme Court protected the 'property right in whiteness' by 'acknowledging that whites could protect their reputation of being white through suits for damages and by determining that Plessy would be subject to rules that continued white privilege'.[54] While in the latter, famous for *reversing* educational segregation, the US Supreme Court upheld the assumption of whiteness as property by reworking it in relation to the ambiguity that surrounded the definition of equality in the case.[55] The result was that racial inequality would become a baseline norm in American society, regardless of the fact that such inequality was an artefact of a deliberately segregationist law, which the Court in *Brown v Board of Education* would itself overturn. Further, this would set in motion the settled expectation that being white in America entailed ongoing economic privilege. The ruling might have put America on a path towards desegregation but not one that would undermine the economic value of whiteness. Fast forward to the present, and here we find a context in which whiteness continues to be a valued social identity – not one reducible to skin or phenotype but one that confers elevated social status and opens up economic opportunities. One simply needs to look at the racial distribution of housing wealth to grasp this basic point.[56] But whiteness is also a fluid social category, which means it is available to just about anyone. Anyone, or any particular group, can acquire the status conferred by whiteness.[57]

But Harris draws out one additional element to her legal concept of 'whiteness as property'. Subsumed within this property right is the 'exclusive right to determine rules', and 'that against a framework of racial dominance and unequal power, fairness can result from a property rule, or indeed any other rule, that imposes an entirely externally constituted definition of group identity'.[58] In order words, 'whiteness as property' entails the right to determine group definition alongside when and how these definitions can be applied. Harris arrives at this

[52] *Plessy v Ferguson*, 163 US 537 (1896).

[53] *Brown v Board of Education*, 347 US 483 (1954).

[54] Harris (n 40) 1750.

[55] As Harris puts it, the Court held the view that segregation occurred in a context of 'substantive equality' and that 'Black schools and white schools either had been equalized or were being equalized'. See Harris (n 40) 1750. But she also notes that 'it is unclear what definition of equality was articulated by Brown I, and in this ambiguity, the property interest in whiteness continued to reside'. See Harris (n 40) 1751.

[56] Sanjaya DeSilva and Yuval Elmelech, 'Housing Inequality in the United States: Explaining the White-Minority Disparities in Homeownership' (2012) 27 *Housing Studies* 1, available at doi.org/10.1080/02673037.2012.628641; Aleatra P Williams, 'Lending Discrimination, the Foreclosure Crisis, and the Perpetuation of Racial and Ethnic Disparities in Homeownership in the U.S.' (2015) 6(2) *William and Mary Business Law Review* 601.

[57] Alexandra Filindra and Melanie Kolbe, 'Latinx Identification with Whiteness: What Drives it, and What Effects Does it Have on Political Preference?' (2022) 103(6) *Social Science Quarterly* 1424, available at doi.org/10.1111/ssqu.13210; Noel Ignatiev, *How the Irish Became White* (Abingdon, Routledge 1995); Linda M Alcoff, *The Future of Whiteness* (Cambridge, Polity 2015), especially at 20–29.

[58] Harris (n 40) 1766.

insight through a reading of *Mashpee Tribe v Town of Mashpee*,[59] in which the US District Court for the District of Massachusetts determined that Mashpee Tribe had forfeited its claim as collective tribal entity because, over time, it had included numerous outsiders into the tribal community.[60] What this determination overlooks, of course, is that Mashpee tribal identity was not based on genetics but on a distinctive relationship to Mashpee land. Whereas the Court would define tribal identity in terms of historical continuity, the Mashpee would define it as adherence to a law situated in land. By assigning the state the authority to determine collective identity, the Court would establish yet another important means of extending the property investment in whiteness. Whiteness would retain its enduring power so long as the state retained the power to determine the parameters of non-white group identity. As Harris puts it,

> the law holds to the basic premise that definition from above can be fair to those below, that beneficiaries of racially conferred privilege have the right to establish norms for those who have historically been oppressed pursuant to those norms, and that race is not historically contingent.[61]

She then goes on to say that 'what persists is the expectation of white-controlled institutions in the continued right to determine meaning – the reified privilege of power – that reconstitutes the property interest in whiteness in contemporary form'.[62] In other words, the law would recognise the illegality of racial discrimination but whiteness as property would persist by preventing collective redress against structural racism by controlling how race and racism are defined. Discrimination directed at racial minorities would be illegal, but the settled expectations of white privilege would not be disadvantaged through programmes that sought to reverse racial inequality, such as affirmation action. It was on this basis that the US Supreme Court would deem unconstitutional 'race-conscious remedial measures', such as certain forms of race-based affirmative action programmes.[63]

In summary, at the core of Harris' idea is that whiteness is a social category that confers advantages onto those who claim it. It is, in this way, a meaningful social category even though race is routinely said to be a social construction. Protecting the meaning and thus the social, political, cultural, and economic value of whiteness is what Harris means when she says whiteness is a form of property. But what, if anything, does Harris' notion of 'whiteness as property' have to do with the discourse on climate change and migration? Quite a lot it would seem.

[59] *Mashpee Tribe v Town of Mashpee*, 447 F.Supp. 940 (D. Mass. 1978).
[60] Harris (n 40) 1764–65.
[61] ibid 1762.
[62] ibid.
[63] ibid 1767.

B. Questioning Climate Change and Migration Discourse in the City

Many will consider migration a welcome addition to the urban climate change agenda – especially if it means cities become more attuned to the complicated relationship between climate change and migration and thus better equipped to respond to the related challenges. In a context in which cities are now understood to play a key part in climate change governance,[64] migration adds a potential new layer of political and legal authority for cities. How that authority materialises, how it is exercised, by whom, and to what effect, are questions it is still too early to answer, at least in the US context. Still, Harris' notion of whiteness as property provides a framework for raising questions about this new urban agenda, for speculating about how this authority might be exercised, and for interrogating the conditions that bring it into being.

On the basis of Harris' 'whiteness as property' and Hall's idea that race is a sliding signifier, it is not unreasonable to assume that as the discourse on climate change and migration articulates with questions about the city and urbanism, it will do so in a way that secures the property interest in whiteness. Indeed, as I sought to show earlier, not only does the discourse on climate change and migration mean 'race' (ie it references a system of racial meaning), it also signifies the undoing of a perceived form power associated with European humanism. It is easy to imagine how this discourse might translate in urban contexts, such as those in the US, physically structured along lines of race in ways that reflect the history of racial segregation.[65] As a racial discourse, it announces a future in which climate change can be understood to threaten the settled expectations of whiteness, which, in turn, suggests that, for those who have a property interest in whiteness, the discourse may be mobilised to reinforce such expectations or to consolidate the logics of whiteness as property. How exactly this plays out, if indeed it does, remains an open question. My point is simply that researchers and practitioners, not least planners, activists, and legal experts, working in urban contexts where 'climate change and migration' is gaining policy traction, would be well advised to approach the topic with a healthy dose of caution.

[64] Harriet Bulkeley and others, 'Climate Justice and Global Cities: Mapping the Emerging Discourses' (2013) 23(5) *Global Environmental Change* 914, available at doi.org/10.1016/j.gloenvcha.2013.05.010; Vanesa C Broto and Enora Robin, 'Climate Urbanism as Critical Urban Theory' (2021) 42(6) *Urban Geography* 715, available at doi.org/10.1080/02723638.2020.1850617.

[65] Anna Brand, 'The Sedimentation of Whiteness as Landscape' (2022) 40(2) *Environment and Planning D: Society and Space* 276, available at doi.org/10.1177/02637758211031565; Laura Pulido, 'Rethinking Environmental Racism: White Privilege and Urban Development in Southern California' (2000) 90 *Annals of the Association of American Geographers* 12, available at www.jstor.org/stable/1515377; Lisa SH Park and David Pellow, *The Slums of Aspen: Immigrants vs the Environment in America's Eden* (New York, New York University Press 2011).

Take the city of Orlando as a case example.[66] Famous for Walt Disney World and numerous other tourist attractions, Orlando is also a city, like so many in the US, beset by significant housing inequality.[67] It was also recently identified by modellers as one of the most desirable destinations for coastal Floridians who stand to be displaced by sea-level rise.[68] The model suggests that with a 1.8 m sea-level rise, over half a million people will migrate to Orlando between now and 2100, which, in turn, raises important questions about where these people might end up living and what they will do when they arrive. But the accuracy of this model is actually secondary. In fact, a 1.8 m sea-level rise is not even within the range of likely scenarios identified by the IPCC.[69] Nor is it accurate to imply, as the model does, that climate change will be the main factor determining Orlando's population over the next 80 years. What really matters, instead, is what the model signifies: a significant influx of so-called 'climate migrants', who, unless plans are put in place to manage them, stand to transform the political, cultural, and economic landscape of Orlando.

Indeed, this is precisely how the model has been taken up in contemporary media.[70] It has been used to foster a sense that Orlando will be a destination of choice for climate migrants, who are mediated as both threats and victims. For many, Hurricane Maria in 2017 was a wake-up call for what Orlando can expect under conditions of future climate change, as large numbers of people displaced by the hurricane, many from Puerto Rico, wound up in Orlando. The model in this sense simply affirms what many Orlando planners, residents, aid workers, and city officials already fear: that unless adequately managed, climate change will drive more and more poor people to Orlando, putting pressure on its already precarious housing situation, altering the appearance of the city, and changing the structure of its labour market. But if we take seriously the way that the discourse on climate change and migration works as a system of racial meaning, we can approach the model differently. Rather than simply a neutral political device for anticipating the future, the model can be understood as a tool that references a system of racial meaning in which terms like 'threat' and 'victim' are signifiers of Blackness, that those who pose the greatest challenge to Orlando are not just poor, but Black or brown as well. The model not only signifies the undoing of racial nomos at the scale of the East Central Florida region, but also guarantees this system of racial meaning by anchoring it to climate and climatic variation – two very powerful

[66] Carolyn Gramling, 'What Data do Cities like Orlando Need to Prepare for Climate Migrants?' (*Science News*, 12 May 2020), available at perma.cc/Q6JH-3BD9.

[67] Andrew Ross, *Sunbelt Blues: The Failure of American Housing* (New York, Metropolitan Books 2021).

[68] Mathew E Hauer, 'Migration Induced by Sea-Level Rise Could Reshape the US Population Landscape' (2017) 7 *Nature Climate Change* 321, available at doi.org/10.1038/nclimate3271.

[69] The latest report (AR6) estimates that sea-level rise will most likely be less than 1m by 2100 (compared with 1900) in a business-as-usual emission scenario; possibly just above 0.5m with deep emission reductions. See Richard P Allan, 'Summary for Policymakers', in IPCC Sixth Assessment Report, *The Physical Science Basis: Working Group I Contribution* (Cambridge, Cambridge University Press 2021) 3, 22.

[70] Gramling (n 66).

contemporary metaphors of nature. In this way, the model substantiates whatever fears Orlando residents, planners, and officials may have about climate change by constructing Orlando as being on the verge of inundation by those racial others who are seen either as a threat to the stability of Orlando's housing and labour market or as part of a pending humanitarian crisis and in need of assistance. Again, the veracity of the model is secondary. What matters here is the work the model does in fixing the meanings attributed to the other of climate change.

The model also casts climate change as a potential threat to the settled expectations of Orlando's property owners, whether 'white' suburban residents or hotel operators servicing Orlando's sprawling tourism sector. No doubt a key question that planners in East Central Florida are now contemplating is how best to accommodate the anticipated influx of new residents. But insofar as the discourse on climate change and migration is a system of racial meaning whose primary aim is to shore up humanism amid the uncertainties of climate change, researchers in the region would do well to be asking themselves how 'white' residents in the Orlando urban conurbation are responding. If whiteness as property combines the settled expectations of economic privilege with the right to exclude, it would hardly be a stretch to suggest that any such anticipatory governance would be designed to secure whiteness as property. Speculating about how precisely this might work lies beyond the scope of this chapter, but it would no doubt involve a complex mix of urban policy: everything from zoning, housing, education, and infrastructural planning.

We can also expect that Orlando's response will involve significant private sector investment, which brings us to the heart of what many are nowadays calling a 'climate apartheid'.[71] The question we need to ask of places like Orlando is whether and how scenarios of future 'climate' in-migration, such as those produced by the model discussed above, might be used to reinforce existing patterns of exclusion. Might poor Black and brown migrants wind up in under-serviced parts of the city, while more asset-rich 'white' migrants take advantage of real estate developments built in anticipation of their arrival? In fact, we might expect that the scenarios being developed in cities like Orlando are being undertaken with precisely this purpose in mind. After all, increasing numbers of Republican voters in Florida now recognise that climate change is a real problem, while Florida's Republican governor, Ron DeSantis, has also recently acknowledged the importance of investing in climate change adaptation.[72] Property insurers are also keenly aware of the risks that climate change poses to Florida's real estate market and are increasing premiums accordingly.[73] No doubt 'climate-migration models' will also be used to

[71] Tuana (n 41); Rice, Long, and Levenda (n 41); Gonzalez (n 5). See also UNHRC (n 41).

[72] Justin Worland, 'Ron DeSantis is at the Forefront of New Republican Climate Politics' (*Time Magazine*, 4 October 2022), available at perma.cc/7WFM-KZEW.

[73] Zac J Taylor and Manuel B Aalbers, 'Climate Gentrification: Risk, Rent and Restructuring in Greater Miami' (2022) 112(6) *Annals of the American Association of Geographers* 1685, available at doi.org/10.1080/24694452.2021.2000358; Stephen Collier and Savanah Cox, 'Governing Urban Resilience: Insurance and the Problematization of Climate Change' (2021) 50(2) *Economy and Society* 275, available at doi.org/10.1080/03085147.2021.1904621.

assess the future profitability of real estate in the state and to restructure state-wide real estate markets to capture new sources of value, issues that are both intimately bound up with the property interest in whiteness.

But this is Orlando. What about other cities around the world? How readily can 'whiteness as property' be used as a framework for evaluating how the discourse on climate change and migration operates as a racial signifier in places where there is no history of race, or at least not one like that which emerged in the US? Here it is worth remembering that the discourse is a system of racial meaning. In this way, wherever we find the discourse – whether it's Dhaka, Lagos, Rio de Janiero, Orlando, Malé, Houston, Freetown, or Milan – the effect is same. Vast numbers of people, often the poorest and most vulnerable, are simply re-codified in a way that explains their difference in terms of climate. They come to represent a potentially immense surplus populations that is said to pose a significant and immanent threat to established ways of urban life for those with settled expectations of privilege and the right to exclude. In this way, 'whiteness as property' is not about skin or other outward forms of difference, but the preservation of a unique form of power that allows certain groups to put in place measures designed to protect the economic value stored in their property.

IV. Conclusion

Researchers, activists, and policy-makers should be mindful that at stake in the discourse on climate change and migration is a complex politics of race and racism with potentially profound ramifications for law and policy. The purpose of this chapter has been to persuade readers that the science and policy discourse on climate change and migration is a proxy for the adaptation of structural racism. That the discourse makes no direct reference to race or whiteness does not mean that neither are present. It simply means that the discourse signifies race and racism; that both terms are embedded within the discourse, albeit invisibly. And it is precisely for this reason that the discourse warrants critical scrutiny.

But I have also sought to make the case that Cheryl Harris' notion of 'whiteness as property' offers a framework for further developing such critical scrutiny in urban contexts worldwide. Harris reminds us that whiteness operates through 'the right to prohibit the infringement on settled expectations'. How this right manifests will differ from place to place. My contention, however, is that where the issue of 'climate change and migration' does start to shape urban contexts in the US, but potentially elsewhere too, the property interest in whiteness follows close behind. Those whose privilege is defined in terms of property will go to great lengths to ensure that so-called 'climate migrants' do not infringe upon this right. My contention is that without holding urban authorities accountable to the intersections of whiteness and property in wider policy discussions about climate change and migration discourse, such authorities run the risk of fostering climate apartheid by putting in place policies that segregate urban politics racially along lines of climate privilege and precarity.

PART III

Implications for Research, Policy, and Law

8

Identifying as a 'Climate Migrant': Implications for Law, Policy, and Research

CAROL FARBOTKO*

I. Introduction

Many cases of human mobility are now reported on and discussed as a consequence of climate change, regardless of whether climate change has, technically, caused the mobility in question. Headlines such as '[c]limate disasters "caused more internal displacement than war" in 2020'[1] and '"[i]ntolerable tide" of people displaced by climate change'[2] are commonplace. Beyond the issue of contested accuracy underscored by lack of scientific causality establishing 'climate mobility' as an empirically observable phenomenon is another important issue: that 'climate mobilities' (particularly the more politically charged and publicly discussed variants 'climate migration' and 'climate refugee') exist as socially significant concepts – ideas that have general currency and circulate in and across public policy, in news media, and in science itself.

Regardless of whether it is scientifically correct to report on and discuss 'climate mobility' as an empirical reality,[3] narratives and uses of the idea of climate mobility are now prevalent, and the very real associated socio-politics of climate mobility requires research attention in its own right. If a social lens is applied, the social category of climate mobility is observable as having empirical effects. These include new visas being tabled for populations identified as vulnerable to climate

* Thanks to Elfriede Hermann, Benoit Mayer, and Calum Nicholson for helpful input into this chapter.

[1] Saeed K Dehghan, 'Climate Disasters "Caused More Internal Displacement than War" in 2020' (*The Guardian*, 20 May 2021), available at perma.cc/8CL2-NDNL.

[2] '"Intolerable Tide" of People Displaced by Climate Change: UN Expert' (UNHRC, 23 June 2022), available at perma.cc/33GM-664G.

[3] Calum TM Nicholson, 'Climate Change and the Politics of Causal Reasoning: The Case of Climate Change and Migration' (2014) 180(2) *The Geographical Journal* 151, available at doi.org/10.1111/geoj.12062.

displacement and relocation programmes being developed as a part of emergent climate mobility policies.[4]

Various scholars now use the term 'climate mobilities' as a tool to analyse the multiple ways in which human mobility is associated with climate change, including its embedding in ongoing patterns and histories of movement, and the material and political conditions under which it takes place.[5] From this perspective, climate change and human movement are both experienced and scripted, and indeed it may not be the bio-physical dynamics of climate that are most important in a particular context but rather their representation: people may just as well move (or not move) because of particular kinds of policy or communication about climate change impacts – such as adaptation strategies by government that could promote greater mobility (or facilitate staying put).[6] Therefore, it is not enough to understand only how climate mobilities occur, who is involved and how it is experienced; one may also need to link these to the representation of climate mobilities in arenas such as research, policies, activism, documentaries, and media reports, which seek to make climate mobilities visible and knowable.[7]

The mobilisation and circulation of ideas about climate mobilities, and the social effects of these ideas, is an emergent area of focus within the new climate mobilities approach. One specific way in which climate mobilities can be usefully identified and analysed as a social phenomenon is through praxiography.[8] In praxiography, objects are seen not as pre-given, defined entities but rather as emergent and inseparable from the practices in which they are enacted, with attention being paid to the techniques that make things visible, tangible, or knowable.[9] Objects of study, such as 'climate migrants', are not singular entities in praxiography but are always in a situated state of becoming, with multiple enactments. Praxiography, furthermore, includes as part of its field the practices of what are otherwise often assumed to be rather fixed, unquestionable institutions such as science and law – positioning instead scientific and legal practices as emergent, social phenomenon.[10]

[4] Carol Farbotko, 'The Spectre of Mass Migration Across International Borders: Dismantling an Unscientific Expectation' (2022) 5(8) *One Earth* 841, available at doi.org/10.1016/j.oneear.2022.07.009.

[5] See, for example, Ingrid Boas and others, 'Climate Mobilities: Migration, Im/Mobilities and Mobility Regimes in a Changing Climate' (2022) 48(14) *Journal of Ethnic and Migration Studies* 1, available at doi.org/10.1080/1369183X.2022.2066264; Laurie Parsons, 'Structuring the Emotional Landscape of Climate Change Migration: Towards Climate Mobilities in Geography' (2018) 43(4) *Progress in Human Geography* 670, available at doi.org/10.1177/0309132518781011; Hanne Wiegel, Ingrid Boas, and Jeroen Warner, 'A Mobilities Perspective on Migration in the Context of Environmental Change' (2019) 10(6) *Wiley Interdisciplinary Reviews: Climate Change* 451, available at doi.org/10.1002/wcc.610.

[6] Ingrid Boas, Carol Farbotko, and Kaderi N Bukari, 'Climate Change, Mobility and Borders' *Mobilities* (forthcoming).

[7] ibid.

[8] Carol Farbotko, 'Representation and Misrepresentation of Climate Migrants', in Benoit Mayer and François Crépeau (eds), *Research Handbook on Climate Change, Migration and the Law* (Cheltenham, Edward Elgar 2017) 67.

[9] Annemarie Mol, *The Body Multiple: Ontology in Medical Practice* (Durham, Duke University Press 2002).

[10] ibid; Michel Callon and Vololona Rabeharisoa, 'Research "in the Wild" and the Shaping of New Social Identities' (2003) 25(2) *Technology in Society* 193, available at doi.org/10.1016/S0160-791X(03)00021-6;

This means that praxiographic research does not assume that a particular institution or object has fixed characteristics, or what kind of boundaries it has: the social and material are everywhere related but never static. Praxiographic research considers how practices, such as the institutionalisation and communication of 'climate migration', become coherent, ordered, and accepted.[11] Thus, institutional practices such as debate on causality between climate and migration are seen as contributing to the enactment of, rather than existing objectively outside, the phenomena they seek to know and/or decide upon.[12] Praxiographic analysis of 'climate migration' therefore does not prioritise establishing scientific or legal causality between climate change and human mobility, but rather pays attention to the ways in which 'climate migrant' as a particular object of knowledge is relational, situated, and enacted and re-enacted, partly through scientific debate itself. 'Climate migrant', in praxiography, is never closed into itself or objectively knowable in a way separate from the world, but rather a product of ongoing practices that continually shapes and refines what is a 'climate migrant', through adjustment, coordination, contestation, and reorientation in and across and between arenas such as courts of law, scientific studies, and the media. Social identity specifically is viewed in praxiography not in terms of bounded characteristics of an individual, but as related to and inseparable to the world, its objects, people and institutions, all of which are equally undergoing adjustment, coordination, contestation and reorientation.

Thus, in a praxiographic climate mobilities research agenda, research into issues such as causality or identity sees these phenomena as themselves in part constitutive of, not separate to, the material, political, and emotional relations enabled and influenced by ideas about climate mobilities, and the practices such as photography, journalism, research interviews, philosophy, policy-making, or self-description that contribute to ongoing, multiple practices that shape or contest what a 'climate migrant' is, can, or should be. Praxiographic research, in sum, can elucidate the communicative and performative acts through which climate change and human mobility become both understood and used in particular ways. Indeed, once an issue such as causal reasoning is understood as a social process in its own right,[13] focus can turn to often overlooked issues, such as how a *lack* of evidence of causality between climate change and human mobility has, counter-intuitively perhaps, become the basis for policy;[14] how causality can be put to use to make

Eben Kirksey, 'Species: A Praxiographic Study' (2015) 21(4) *Journal of the Royal Anthropological Institute* 758, available at www.jstor.org/stable/43907902.

[11] Christian Bueger, 'Conducting "Field Research" When There is No "Field"', in Sarah Biecker and Klaus Schlichte (eds), *The Political Anthropology of Internationalized Politics* (Lanham, Roman and Littlefield 2021) 29.

[12] Mol (n 9).

[13] Fabien Cottier and others, 'Framing the Frame: Cause and Effect in Climate-Related Migration' (2022) 158 *World Development* 1, available at doi.org/10.1016/j.worlddev.2022.106016.

[14] Alexander Betts and Angela Pilath, 'The Politics of Causal Claims: The Case of Environmental Migration' (2017) 20 *Journal of International Relations and Development* 782, available at doi.org/10.1057/s41268-016-0003-y.

different conclusions about climate mobility, depending on how it is framed environmentally or socially;[15] or how a causal connection to climate change can help certain actors deny responsibility for mobility challenges.[16]

This chapter specifically uses the idea of climate mobility as a social phenomenon that is being enacted in various arenas to explore the implications for knowledge and public policy of a particular set of practices – personal, scientific, legal, and journalistic – that together enabled social identification of a single individual, Ioane Teitiota, as a 'climate migrant'. Ioane Teitiota was an international migrant from Kiribati, who had moved to New Zealand but was unsuccessful in his legal quest to remain in New Zealand, despite his reported fear of climate change impacts in his home country. It will be argued that Ioane Teitiota is the first member of a new social category of self-identifying 'climate migrants', and that Ioane Teitiota's identification as a 'climate migrant' was made possible not through objectively establishing a causal relationship between his international migration journey and climate change, but through the institutionalisation and communication of 'climate migration', which created the conditions for a particular individual to have his self-identification as a 'climate migrant' taken seriously. Ioane Teitiota's reported personal experience of both climate change and migration became a basis for testing legal mechanisms because of the research and policy processes that have, whether accurately or not, predicted people like him would exist, as well as the social practices in which he and others, such as journalists, interpreted his lived experience in a climate-impacted country and his move abroad as an issue of 'climate migration'.

The chapter proceeds as follows. In section II, I expand on the idea of climate mobility as a social concept. In section III, I describe how, through Ioane Teitiota's experience in the legal system, it became possible for him to become identified socially, if not scientifically or legally, as a 'climate migrant'. Finally, in section IV, I consider why Ioane Teitiota's identification as a 'climate migrant' is a turning point for climate mobility knowledge and I suggest a need to advance social studies of climate mobility that examine the social life of 'climate migration' simultaneously as an idea and as part of the lived experience of those who see themselves as 'climate migrants'.

II. The Social Life of Climate Mobility

While acknowledging that climate mobility might remain a contested theoretical proposition within science, climate mobility can also usefully be apprehended as a new social category in part untethered from that science, with a social life of its

[15] Cottier (n 13).

[16] Benoit Mayer, 'Climate Migration and the Politics of Causal Attribution: A Case Study in Mongolia' (2016) 5(2) *Migration and Development* 234, available at doi.org/10.1080/21632324.2015.1022971.

own in policy, law, the media, and other areas of public discourse. From this praxiographic perspective, climate mobility is not a self-evident phenomenon, nor a technical undertaking solely for experts, but an emergent and contested idea in a range of arenas, with real-world effects.

Praxiographic questions might include what processes are actively producing the existence of climate mobility, and do researchers bring climate mobility into existence on their own or are multiple agents involved?[17] Praxiography is useful because it can help build knowledge of the ways in which climate mobility is socialised, partly through the practices of science itself, but also those of other institutions, as authority is claimed over the concept of climate mobility, and as it is put to use in different ways with varying social results, such as new policy.[18] For example, with its own journal recently established – *Frontiers in Climate: Climate Mobility* – the idea of climate mobility as a field of research is becoming better defined and more visible.

If climate mobility is made social through ongoing practices of particular actors in particular institutions, including science, praxiography also recognises the mobility, security, humanitarian, and news regimes that include climate mobility within their remit. Both within and beyond science, climate mobility has a social circulation that reflects a rising interest in climate mobility in scientific activity, as well as in public policy and other arenas outside science. The media, for instance, sometimes reports on climate mobility as if it had an established causal empirical reality, sometimes without reference to science at all.[19]

From a praxiographic perspective, the point is not to simply identify cases of failed science communication, but to analyse how media and science actors might narrate and enact different versions of climate mobility in different ways, sometimes with reference to each other and sometimes not. For example, an observation of the media's role in producing a particular type of idea about climate change mobility was reported in the most recent of the synthesis reports of the Intergovernmental Panel on Climate Change, one of the scientific organisations claiming to represent an authoritative source of climate change and mobility knowledge, as follows:

> media reports and other studies in recent years suggest that climate change has driven large numbers of migrants to the US from Central America and to Europe from the Middle East and Africa, but empirical studies were not identified.[20]

[17] Kirksey (n 10).

[18] Caitlin Sturridge and Kerrie Holloway, 'Climate Change, Conflict and Displacement: Five Key Misconceptions' (Humanitarian Policy Group Briefing Note, September 2022), available at perma.cc/B45P-3TW4; Farbotko (n 4).

[19] Etienne Piguet, 'Linking Climate Change, Environmental Degradation, and Migration: An Update After 10 Years' (2021) 13 *Wiley Interdisciplinary Reviews: Climate Change* 1, available at doi.org/10.1002/wcc.746; Farbotko (n 4).

[20] Guéladio Cissé and others, 'Health, Wellbeing and the Changing Structure of Communities', in *IPCC Sixth Assessment Report, Climate Change 2022: Impacts, Adaptation and Vulnerability* (Cambridge, Cambridge University Press 2022) 1041, 1084.

It is of interest to social research on climate mobility that the media is tasking itself with reporting on climate mobility without reference to scientific studies of the phenomenon, producing particular versions of climate mobility that science does not, and yet in turn contributing to the very real social life of ideas about climate mobility. Other organisations, such as thinktank ODI, have commented on a durable 'echo chamber' of misconceptions about the specific nexus of climate change, displacement and conflict playing out in 'headlines, press releases and funding campaigns' despite scientific advances that speak directly to the misconceptions.[21]

In a review of the research on climate mobility between 2010 and 2020, it was noted that quantification of future climate mobility is no longer considered credible science, but neither attempts to quantify nor media interest in quantification have waned:

> Even though this quest for quantitative estimates was in vain – due to the impossibility of identifying clear-cut quantifiable categories in a context of multicausality of displacement and mixed migrations, aggregate numbers appeared regularly and attracted media attention.[22]

Similarly, an expectation of mass 'climate migration' across international borders continues to circulate widely in policy arenas even though sensationally large predictions of millions of 'climate migrants' across borders have been discredited.[23] It has been argued that misconceptions about mass international 'climate migration' have more influence than the science, given their persistence[24] and that the 'political currency' of climate mobilities research has 'long outstripped its analytic integrity'.[25] Within science on the other hand, claims are made about the ongoing policy relevance of debunked climate mobility models, suggesting that some scientists are prepared to invert the otherwise well-accepted principle of evidence-informed policy.[26]

There is also intense speculation about climate mobility within science, with research titled, for example, 'Climate Refugees: Why Measuring the Immeasurable Makes Sense Beyond Measure'[27] and 'An Interview with the Editors Which Never Took Place' in a volume on 'Climate Refugees: Global, Local and Critical

[21] Sturridge and Holloway (n 18) 4. See also Ingrid Boas and others, 'Climate Migration Myths' (2019) 9 *Nature Climate Change* 901, available at doi.org/10.1038/s41558-019-0633-3; David Durand-Declare and others, 'Climate Migration is About People, not Numbers', in Steffen Böhm and Sian Sullivan (eds), *Negotiating Climate Change in Crisis* (Cambridge, Open Book Publishers 2021) 63.

[22] Piguet (n 19) 1.

[23] Farbotko (n 4).

[24] ibid.

[25] Nicholson (n 3) 151.

[26] Farbotko (n 4).

[27] Johannes M Luetz, 'Climate Refugees: Why Measuring the Immeasurable Makes Sense Beyond Measure', in Leal Filho and others (eds), *Climate Action: Encyclopedia of the UN Sustainable Development Goals* (Basel, Springer 2019) 1.

Approaches'.[28] Meanwhile, the term 'climate refugee' has, after much debate, been rejected in some contexts but accepted in others. The UN High Commissioner for Refugees (UNHCR), for instance, states that 'the term "climate refugee" is not endorsed by UNHCR, and it is more accurate to refer to "persons displaced in the context of disasters and climate change"'.[29]

However, the recently appointed Special Rapporteur on Human Rights and Climate Change has placed climate refugees as one of his mandate's six highest priorities.[30] The term climate refugee also lives on in the narratives of organisations as diverse as Climate Refugees,[31] Zurich Insurance Group,[32] and Reuters.[33] Both used and contested regularly, the idea of the climate refugee contributes to the effects of ideas about climate mobility mentioned above, which appears to have real and not necessarily positive outcomes for the subjects of the narratives, ie those identified as at being at high risk of climate-related displacement.[34]

Thus, it is clear that climate mobility has a lively social existence: multiple ideas about climate mobility circulate and climate mobilities continue to be present in various forms across science, the media and policy. In the process of science considering whether and how climate mobility is scientifically intelligible, climate mobility has also become compelling – 'the stuff of fantasy and desire, power and subjugation'[35] – with social, policy, and political value, at times highly divorced from any foundation in credible science. Indeed, given the oft-recognised sensationalism and politicisation through which the issue of climate mobility is interpreted, it is not particularly surprising that the social concept of climate mobility exists and persists beyond and at times in defiance of scientific knowledge of climate change and human mobility.

Clearly, the ways in which the science and the sensationalism intertwine need to be unravelled. Praxiography helps us see that there is no predetermined fault line – with science and perhaps policy on one side and news and other arenas on another – along which it is possible to trace misconceptions or inaccuracies about climate mobility. Praxiography also helps us see how certain ideas about climate mobility can become part of the lived experience of real migrants, as the next section explores.

[28] Avidan Kent and Simon Behrman, 'An Alternative Introduction: An Interview with the Editors, Which Never Took Place', in Simon Behrman and Avidan Kent (eds), *Climate Refugees: Global, Local and Critical Approaches* (Cambridge, Cambridge University Press 2022) 1.

[29] 'Climate Change and Disaster Displacement' (*UNCHR: The UN Refugee Agency*, 2023), available at perma.cc/754L-HWLA.

[30] UNHCR, '"Intolerable Tide" of People Displaced by Climate Change: UN Expert' (*UNHCR*, 23 June 2022), available at perma.cc/4JZ9-S5NH.

[31] 'Climate Refugees' (*Climate Refugees*, 2023), available at perma.cc/3LN9-B26S.

[32] 'There Could be 1.2 Billion Climate Refugees by 2050: Here's What You Need to Know' (*Zurich Insurance Group*, 13 January 2023), available at perma.cc/BP7T-45VH.

[33] Swati Pandey, 'Hot and Dry Australia Could Join the Ranks of "Climate Refugees"' (*Reuters*, 15 January 2020), available at perma.cc/7EKW-BVAX.

[34] Farbotko (n 4).

[35] Hannah Appel, 'Toward an Ethnography of the National Economy' (2017) 32(2) *Cultural Anthropology* 294, 295, available at doi.org/10.14506/ca32.2.09.

III. 'Climate Migrant' as a Social Identity

Given the wide-ranging and contested attempts to identify, report on, and make policy about populations who are moving as a result of climate change, in the context of significant contestation about the extent to which climate change causes human mobility, what can be learned from Ioane Teitiota? In 2013, he brought a case in the court system of New Zealand against his deportation on the ground that he was a 'climate migrant'. His case was rejected by national courts and Mr Teitiota communicated it to the United Nations Human Rights Committee, whose deliberations focused on whether Ioane Teitiota's fear of climate change impacts in his home country should prevent his deportation from New Zealand.

Ioane Teitiota's narrative, reported in his case, concerning his migration from Kiribati to New Zealand was almost exactly what many science, policy, and media accounts of climate refugees expected: he came from one of the world's most vulnerable areas in terms of sea-level rise, a low-lying atoll nation. He remembered impacts such as coastal erosion and saltwater flooding making his life in Kiribati difficult. The legal record, read here as a social text rather than for its legal consequences, stated that:

> the effects of climate change and sea level rise forced him to migrate from the island of Tarawa in the Republic of Kiribati to New Zealand. The situation in Tarawa has become increasingly unstable and precarious due to sea level rise caused by global warming. Fresh water has become scarce because of saltwater contamination and overcrowding on Tarawa. Attempts to combat sea level rise have largely been ineffective. Inhabitable land on Tarawa has eroded, resulting in a housing crisis and land disputes that have caused numerous fatalities. Kiribati has thus become an untenable and violent environment for the author and his family.[36]

Ioane Teitiota was willing, following his move to New Zealand and subsequent legal case, to remember his experience as one of forced migration due to climate change. Along the process of his legal hearings, Ioane Teitiota was widely reported upon in the global news media as the world's first climate refugee.[37] Indeed, the BBC described him as 'The Man Who Would be the First Climate Refugee' in an article in which Ioane Teitiota himself was quoted as stating 'I'm the same as people who are fleeing war. Those who are afraid of dying, it's the same as me … I think being a refugee is the best way of protecting myself. Especially if something happens to Kiribati'.[38] It is plausible that Ioane Teitiota gained his information

[36] UNHRC, Communication No 2728/2016, *Ioane Teitiota v New Zealand*, UN Doc CCPR/C/127/D/2728/2016, para 2.1.

[37] See, for example, Tim McDonald, 'The Man Who Would be the First Climate Refugee' (*BBC News*, 5 November 2015), available at perma.cc/Y33L-NW79; 'New Zealand Deports Kiribati "Climate Change Refugee" After a Four-Year Battle' (*ABC News*, 23 September 2015), available at perma.cc/VDS4-V5XE.

[38] McDonald, 'The Man Who Would be the First Climate Refugee' (n 37).

about the impacts of climate change to Kiribati from the media, combined with his own memories of his life in Kiribati: 'Teitiota's case may have been born out of that sensational storytelling narrative … Teitiota and his lawyer were driven and inspired by what they heard, read and saw on the news about Kiribati'.[39]

Ioane Teitiota's identification as a 'climate migrant' diverged from expectations about international 'climate migration' in one crucial aspect. He and his wife were a lone pair. Two people were hardly the widely expected (albeit incorrectly predicted) masses crossing borders from the Global South to the Global North. Ioane Teitiota's initial case was heard when the idea of Migration with Dignity was prominent. Migration with Dignity, introduced by Kiribati's president at the time, Anote Tong, identified international migration, especially labour migration that enhanced skills and education for Kiribati people, as key to its climate change adaptation strategy.[40] It is not unreasonable to posit that Ioane Teitiota may have had some expectations about the Migration with Dignity idea shaping his reception in New Zealand, although when the case was heard in New Zealand the court did not explicitly refer to it.[41] There were others migrating to New Zealand from Kiribati around the same time, under the Pacific Access Category scheme, and also, likely, some who were overstayers like Ioane Teitiota. With the exception of Ioane Teitiota, however, none of them publicly identified as 'climate migrants' in a legal setting, even if some of them may have identified as such in their personal lives.[42]

The statements of Ioane Teitiota, combined with the writings of journalists, judges and researchers, each contributed to the cementing of an idea of a legally active 'climate migrant', possibly as a 'climate refugee', as the case unfolded, and as media and scholarly analysis abounded. Ioane Teitiota experienced intense scrutiny of his case, not faced by many others across the world facing deportation, likely because of the ways in which climate and mobility have captured the imaginations of scholars, policy-makers and publics.

Yet, Ioane Teitiota's legal team had no success in establishing his legal identity as a 'climate migrant' – neither before the national courts, nor then before the Human Rights Committee – on the ground that he did not provide sufficient factual evidence that the impacts of climate change were an immediate threat to his core human rights in Kiribati.[43] Although he did not legally become recognised as a 'climate refugee', he was arguably successful in achieving what a field

[39] Taberannang Korauaba, 'The Returning Son of a Disappearing Nation' (*Islands Business*, 11 October 2015), available at perma.cc/2DXA-3DCW.

[40] Carol Farbotko, Elaine Stratford, and Heather Lazrus, 'Climate Migrants and New Identities? The Geopolitics of Embracing or Rejecting Mobility' (2016) 17(4) *Social and Cultural Geography* 533, available at doi.org/10.1080/14649365.2015.1089589.

[41] ibid.

[42] Olivia E Yates and others, '"There's so Much More to That Sinking Island!": Restorying Migration from Kiribati and Tuvalu to Aotearoa New Zealand' (2022) *Journal of Community Psychology* 1, available at doi.org/10.1002/jcop.22928.

[43] UNHRC (n 36) para 9.12.

of scientific study as well as a legal system could not: establishing for a global public that 'climate migrants' can be self-identifying people, not merely abstracted subjects of statistical models or legal reasoning. Ioane Teitiota is, very possibly, the first person to self-identify as a 'climate migrant'.

Although unsuccessful in his personal bid to remain in New Zealand, Ioane Teitiota's self-identification as a 'climate migrant' contributed to a significant opportunity for the development of international law, as Teitiota's case has been written about extensively, even possibly excessively, by scholars interested in how it influences the development climate mobility law and policy.[44] This included increased pressure on states to develop 'climate refugee' policy. The Human Rights Committee in the case commented upon an expected role of New Zealand in advancing 'climate refugee' policy. The Committee reported that New Zealand's acceptance of the Fifth Assessment Report of the Intergovernmental Panel on Climate Change may have 'opened the door to accepting the legal concept of a climate change refugee in cases where an individual faces a risk of serious harm'.[45]

Despite being fruitful for law and policy debate globally, personally for Ioane Teitiota the case had an unfavourable outcome. The legal process resulted in Ioane Teitiota and his family being deported back to Kiribati, where he continues to live. While assessments of his case often position him as a victim of an as-yet failed promise of climate mobility justice,[46] his identity as a 'climate migrant' has also had negative impacts socially. Not only was his desire to live abroad legally thwarted, but some in Kiribati also did not see his court case favourably:

> Back home … the court case by the diaspora countryman has been viewed with mixed feelings. Some … feared that worst-case scenarios of sea level rise might be coming true if a countryman who surely loved his homeland saw his and his family's lives threatened … and didn't want to return. A few others felt that the diaspora man had brought shame on [them], as their beloved country would now seem to be a place no longer inhabitable in the eyes of the international community. Hurt in their national pride they shamed him in turn as a 'traitor' who had humiliated their young nation.[47]

However, the news about Ioane Teitiota's case also led some I-Kiribati in his home country to imagine migration to a piece of land the Kiribati government had bought in Fiji.[48] And the views of other I-Kiribati people are important

[44] Rouven Diekjobst, 'Book review: Climate Refugees: Global, Local and Critical Approaches' (2022) *South African Journal of International Affairs* 394, available at doi.org/10.1080/10220461.2022.2122549.

[45] UNHRC (n 36) para 7.1.

[46] See, for example, Andreas Neef and Lucy Benge, 'Shifting Responsibility and Denying Justice: New Zealand's Contentious Approach to Pacific Climate Mobilities' (2022) 22(3) *Regional Environmental Change* 1, available at doi.org/10.1007/s10113-022-01951-x.

[47] Carol Farbotko and others, 'Climate Mobilities, Rights and Justice: Complexities and Particularities' (2022) *Frontiers in Climate Mobility* citing Korauaba (n 39).

[48] Elfriede Hermann and Wolfgang Kempf, 'Climate Change and the Imagining of Migration: Emerging Discourses on Kiribati's Land Purchase in Fiji' (2017) 29(2) *The Contemporary Pacific* 231, available at doi:10.1353/cp.2017.0030.

for another reason. While Ioane Teitiota and his family wanted to stay in New Zealand, exactly as the 'climate refugee' discourse expected, it should also be noted that Ioane Teitiota's self-identification was important also because it was exceptional. There are no reported masses of people self-identifying as 'climate refugees' or 'climate migrants' in legal or other contexts.

Indeed, in other arenas, including the policy of the national government, many in Kiribati were quite active in articulating a desire to stay in their country, to build climate resilience, and to adapt in place.[49] In Kiribati, there was a governmental distancing from the Migration with Dignity policy when a new government was elected in 2016. Neither have similar cases from Kiribati or elsewhere been brought since. Thus, Ioane Teitiota's case is of social significance in part because his decision to attempt to legally identify as a 'climate migrant' was rare.[50]

IV. The 'Democratisation' of Climate Mobility Knowledge?

That Ioane Teitiota was the first citizen of Kiribati, and indeed globally, to publicly identify as a 'climate refugee', is an important and indeed pivotal event for a social understanding of climate mobility. This self-identification, by a person from the Global South and one of its most climate-vulnerable places, has put a human face to a previously theoretical and abstract concern, with potential implications for how the issue is discussed by lawyers, researchers, policy-makers, and journalists.

Ioane Teitiota's case provided an opportunity for emerging ideas about climate mobility to be debated differently, not only in legal arenas, but also in the media, research, and policy. His self-identification as a 'climate migrant' poses both a challenge and an impulse to the still prevailing common sense about faceless masses of 'climate refugees'. Once one person has self-identified as a 'climate migrant', it sets a precedent for others to do so; yet equally, Ioane Teitiota remains – for now – the only person to have done so. Few are following in his footsteps and publicly self-identifying as 'climate migrants' or bringing legal action, although it should be noted that this tells us little about how vulnerable people such as undocumented migrants might be considering their identity privately. Teitiota's case showed that courts are willing to debate the concept of 'climate refugees', but not to legally categorise a particular individual as such. While in legal research the 'test case'

[49] Farbotko and others, 'Climate Mobilities, Rights and Justice: Complexities and Particularities' (2022) *Frontiers in Climate Mobility* citing Korauaba (n 39); Elfriede Hermann and Wolfgang Kempf, 'Adaptation and the Question of Migration: Directions in Dealing with Climate Change in Kiribati', in Carola Klöck and Michael Fink (eds), *Dealing with Climate Change on Small Islands: Towards Effective and Sustainable Adaptation?* (Göttingen, Göttingen University Press 2017) 231.

[50] 'Pacific Islanders Reject "Climate Refugee" Status, want to "Migrate with Dignity"' (*ABC News*, 5 September 2014), available at perma.cc/3XNP-7TJU.

decision is what remains important, in sociology and other social sciences, Ioane Teitiota's self-identification is, in and of itself, an interesting sociological fact, with societal implications and effects, all of which are deserving of analysis.

Applying praxiography, Ioane Teitiota's identification as a 'climate migrant' does not speak to the empirical question of causality between climate change and migration that has vexed science and law, but rather draws our attention to the fact that, regardless of the science or the law, if people begin to identify in a particular way, this can lead to new social practices, which can in turn affect how science is received, and how the law is shaped. Ioane Teitiota's self-identification as a 'climate migrant' was made possible not through establishing a causal relationship between his international migration journey and climate change, but within the practice of institutions – science, law, and the media – that increasingly identify 'climate migration' as a theoretical possibility. He had a role in adding a new consideration to the debate about 'climate migrants' in terms of being one of the few people statistically at risk of climate displacement who has (thus far) chosen to personally identify as a 'climate migrant'.

Ioane Teitiota's personal experience of both climate change and migration became a basis for legal action because of the research and policy processes that have, whether accurately or not, predicted that people like him *would* exist, as well as the social and communicative mechanisms through which he and others, including journalists, have interpreted his lived experience in a climate-impacted country and his move abroad as an issue of 'climate migration'. Ioane Teitiota's attempts to access migration justice did not cement his legal identity as a (legally protected) 'climate refugee' as he was deported to his country of origin, but it did cement his personal identity as a (failed) 'climate migrant'. Teitiota's self-identification as a 'climate migrant' has, ultimately, had the sociological effect of in fact producing the possibility of others also identifying as 'climate migrants', which will continue to have effects, not necessarily personally for Teitiota, but for those who may seek or resist an identity as 'climate migrants' in the future.

Ioane Teitiota's self-identification as a 'climate migrant' therefore raises important questions about the status of knowledge on 'climate migration', and about the place of self-identification in the formulation of social categories, well beyond questions of legal status. Ioane Teitiota's self-identification was arguably a significant moment for 'climate migration' knowledge, as it means it needs to be asked what, precisely, *counts as* climate mobility knowledge. Should lived experience, and the voices of those who self-identify, be taken into account? Should climate mobility knowledge be 'democratised' in this way, bringing in subjective, lived experience, and self-identification? What advantages would accrue from doing so? Would such inclusion in fact lead to more just or equitable outcomes for those who self-identify in the way Ioane Teitiota did? After all, given his legal case was lost, and that he is now back in his home country, viewed as a victim of failed climate mobility justice, his self-identification as a 'climate migrant' has not gained him any particular advantage. The democratisation of knowledge, while significant, does not necessarily lead to just or equitable outcomes for those self-identifying as 'climate migrants', as Ioane Teitiota's experience demonstrates.

V. Conclusion

This chapter has focused on the case of Ioane Teitiota, and specifically on his self-identity as a 'climate migrant', and the implications of him doing so for how climate mobility is understood. Do climate mobility researchers have an ethical obligation to acknowledge those who self-identify as 'climate migrants', and do so by appealing to their lived experience of climate mobility? Can we even understand what is meant by climate mobility, and the life of this social category in the real world, without considering the stated lived experience, and self-identification, of people like Ioane Teitiota? His case is just one example of the way in which the concept of climate mobility has a social life beyond the science and the law. These sociological effects can and indeed should be a focus of research and policy going forward, independent of the outcome of causality debates, as long as representations of climate mobility continue in science, the media, policy and elsewhere.

Using social scientific methods such as praxiography, it is possible to shed light on the concept of the 'climate migrant' in new ways. Put simply, the case of Ioane Teitiota is interesting far beyond the outcome of his legal case. As, possibly, the first person to self-identify as a 'climate migrant', his case is significant, as it gives social scientists no option but to take the study of the social category of 'climate migration' seriously, regardless of its founding in causality, or standing in the law.

9

International Law, the Climate–Migration Nexus, and *Teitiota v New Zealand*

GIOVANNA LAURIA

I. Introduction

The relationship between climate change and human mobility has been of interest to international law scholars for quite some time. This is not surprising as the topic lies at the intersection of two sensitive global issues, which in turn belong to two politically contested areas of international law and governance: the climate change regime and the migration regime. Because of the political currency and evocative power of the 'climate refugee' label, the climate–migration nexus has been persistently framed within international legal scholarship as a problem in need of solutions. The contours of this problem have been fundamentally premised upon the existence of a 'normative gap' regarding people displaced by climate impacts. As a result, international legal analyses of the topic have centred on the possible role of international legal instruments and mechanisms to fill this gap.[1]

Notwithstanding the criticism raised against the reduction of the climate–migration nexus to a 'problem/solution' binary,[2] a recent jurisprudential development within the UN Human Rights Committee (HRC) has given new impetus to legal debates about the protection of displaced people in the context of climate

[1] See for instance Giovanni Sciaccaluga, *International Law and the Protection of 'Climate Refugees'* (London, Palgrave 2020); Fanny Thornton, *Climate Change and People on the Move: International Law and Justice* (Oxford, Oxford University Press 2018); Simon Behrman and Avidan Kent (eds), *Climate Refugees: Beyond the Legal Impasse?* (Abingdon, Routledge 2018); Jane McAdam, *Climate Change, Forced Migration, and International Law* (Oxford, Oxford University Press 2012); Angela Williams, 'Turning the Tide: Recognizing Climate Change Refugees in International Law' (2008) 30(4) *Law & Policy* 502, available at doi.org/10.1111/j.1467-9930.2008.00290.x.

[2] See, amongst many, Giovanni Bettini, 'And yet it Moves! (Climate) Migration as a Symptom in the Anthropocene' (2019) 14(3) *Mobilities* 336, available at doi.org/10.1080/17450101.2019.1612613; Andrew Baldwin and Giovanni Bettini, 'Introduction' in Andrew Baldwin and Giovanni Bettini (eds), *Life Adrift: Climate Change, Migration, Critique* (London, Rowman & Littlefield 2017) 5; Andrew

change and disasters. The HRC's views on the *Teitiota v New Zealand* case[3] (hereinafter the 'decision') have indeed already made history in this respect. The case concerned Ioane Teitiota, a national of the small-island state of Kiribati, who claimed that, by returning him to his country of origin, New Zealand had violated his right to life under Article 6 of the International Covenant on Civil and Political Rights (ICCPR) on the basis of environmental changes taking place in the island. While Mr Teitiota's claim was dismissed, the HRC has accepted in principle that the adverse effects of climate change may give rise to life-threatening risks or risks of ill-treatment, and thus trigger states' international protection obligations.

The decision was a contested one within the HRC, as reflected by two dissenting opinions. Its outcome has also prompted vivid discussions amongst international legal scholars: the HRC's decision has been praised for its progressive approach to international protection in the context of climate change impacts,[4] but it has also been criticised for the extremely high threshold set by the HRC in these types of claims.[5] In some respects, the simultaneous characterisation of the HRC's decision as both innovative in principle and conservative in its concrete effects is reflexive of the complex ethical and legal issues raised by the relationship between forced migration and climate change. In engaging with this complexity, the HRC has offered interesting insights on the way the climate–migration nexus should be framed in international law. In this chapter, rather than discussing the decision's prospects in terms of international law development in relation to the climate–migration nexus,[6] I analyse both the merits of the decision in advancing an accurate conceptualisation of this nexus and the pitfalls related to such conceptualisation. In particular, I will assess the way in which the HRC, either implicitly or explicitly, has dealt with what represents one of the most controversial knots of the climate–migration nexus, that is, the 'multicausality' issue.

The next section provides a brief outline of the concept of multicausality by considering both the problems and the opportunities it offers in respect

Baldwin, Christiane Fröhlich, and Delf Rothe, 'From Climate Migration to Anthropocene Mobilities: Shifting the Debate' (2019) 14 *Mobilities* 289, available at doi.org/10.1080/17450101.2019.1620510; Benoit Mayer, *The Concept of Climate Migration: Advocacy and its Prospects* (Cheltenham, Edward Elgar 2016).

[3] *Teitiota v New Zealand*, CCPR/C/127/D/2728/2016, UN Human Rights Committee, 7 January 2020.

[4] See for instance Katrien Steenmans and Aaron Cooper, 'Ioane Teitiota v New Zealand: A Landmark Ruling for Climate Refugees?' (2020) 25(2) *Coventry Law Journal* 2.

[5] Simon Behrman and Avidan Kent, 'The Teitiota Case and the Limitations of the Human Rights Framework' (2020) 75 *Questions of International Law* 25; Michelle Foster and Jane McAdam, 'Analysis of "Imminence" in International Protection Claims: Teitiota v New Zealand and Beyond' (2022) 71 *International & Comparative Law Quarterly* 975.

[6] About which several other and more authoritative scholars have already focused: see Jane McAdam, 'Protecting People Displaced by the Impacts of Climate Change: the UN Human Rights Committee and the Principle of Non-Refoulement' (2020) 114(4) *American Journal of International Law* 708; Amina Maneggia, 'Non-Refoulement of Climate Change Migrants: Individual Human Rights Protection or "Responsibility to Protect"? The Teitiota Case before the Human Rights Committee' (2020) 14(2) *Diritti Umani e Diritto Internazionale* 635.

to a consistent conceptualisation of the relationship between climate change and human mobility. In particular, it is claimed that while multicausality has often been considered a major obstacle to coherent discussions about the climate–migration nexus, it can also be a useful analytical tool to understand the nexus through the lens of disaster and climate vulnerability. On these theoretical grounds, the following sections focus on the *Teitiota* decision by assessing whether and to what extent the HRC has integrated the insights offered by the concept of multicausality into its conceptualisation of the climate–migration nexus. It is ultimately argued that, while the HRC has acknowledged the multicausality of migration, it has refrained from taking a clear position about the role of climate impacts within international human rights protection claims.

II. The Multicausality of Climate Mobility: A Perennial Conundrum?

Since the earliest academic debates about 'environmental refugees', scholars have always been aware that environmental conditions cannot be disentangled from a larger cluster of causes that induce people to migrate.[7] Empirical studies have observed, for instance, that slow-onset hazards, such as drought, influence people's decision to migrate because of the economic impact at the household level.[8] Other studies focusing on sudden-onset hazards have highlighted the role played by the broader political and economic context.[9] Even in highly vulnerable regions like small-island states in the Pacific, environmental degradation is rarely identified as the sole or even the main reason for migrating, especially for migrating internationally.[10] Environment and human mobilities are in fact linked by an indirect relationship, where the former interacts with other macro-level conditions of a socio-economic, cultural, and political nature that can altogether induce or suppress migration responses to environmental events.

The impossibility to establish a direct causal relationship between environmental pressures and population movement has long represented a major obstacle

[7] The introduction of multicausality in debates regarding environmental refugees was secured, in particular, by the 'minimalist' school – as opposed to the 'maximalist' school – composed mainly of migration scholars. For an overview of the maximalist-minimalist debate see Stephen Castles, 'Environmental Change and Forced Migration: Making Sense of the Debate' (2002) UNHCR Working Paper 70.

[8] Reiko Obokata, Luisa Veronis, and Robert McLeman, 'Empirical Research on International Environmental Migration: a Systematic Review' (2014) 36 *Population and Environment* 111, 119 ff.

[9] ibid.

[10] Robert Oakes and others, 'Climate Change and Migration in the Pacific: Links, Attitudes, and Future Scenarios in Nauru, Tuvalu and Kiribati' (Bonn, United Nations University Institute for Environment and Human Security 2017), available at collections.unu.edu/view/UNU:6515; Jane McAdam, 'Refusing Refuge in the Pacific: (de)Constructing Climate-Induced Displacement in International Law' in Étienne Piguet, Antoine Pécoud, and Paul de Guchteneire (eds), *Migration and Climate Change* (Cambridge, Cambridge University Press 2011) 102.

to normative arguments about the protection of 'climate migrants'. The problem of multicausality is also at the root of the absence of consensus over a definition of such migrants – an absence that, in turn, has repercussions on the identification of policy and legal solutions. The issue is, however, conceptual rather than definitional:[11] indeed, if it is highly problematic to single out and distinguish 'climate migrants' from other migrants, then it may arguably be concluded that any definition of the former category would ultimately appear arbitrary. At the same time, if climate change functions as a 'threat multiplier' by amplifying factors of migration, then it means that any migration could, to a lesser or greater extent, be related to climate change, which in turn would widen the category of 'climate migrants' to an indefinite class of persons.

Critical scholarship on climate mobility has repeatedly pointed out the contradiction underlying the 'multicausality' of 'climate displacement'.[12] Furthermore, Baldwin and Bettini have noted that '[t]he act of refusing climate reductive logic, while simultaneously reinforcing the explanatory value of climate, is a peculiar feature of the discourse on climate change and human migration'.[13] Along these lines, Nicholson has argued that, because of the paradox inherent in such mechanism, scholarship on the climate–migration nexus has produced a pattern of 'inconclusive conclusions'.[14] Indeed, if it is recognised that climate causality cannot fully capture the multiform dynamics inherent in the climate–migration nexus, then should we not refer more broadly to migration?[15] Why should we waste our efforts in trying to tease out a causal relationship that is impossible to determine?

These observations may suggest that multicausality precludes any meaningful discussion about climate mobility, especially if conducted in legal terms – where the identification of causation is often linked to the attribution of duties, rights, and responsibilities. Yet, multicausality may also represent a valuable analytical tool when it is used to shed light on the dynamics underpinning the relationship between environmental degradation, vulnerability to disasters, and human mobility. In this perspective, rather than identifying 'climate migrants' through the isolation of an environmental cause, the focus shifts to the wider social context in which climate adverse effects strike. A serious concern with multicausality becomes thus preoccupied with 'the dynamic relationships between a human population, its socially generated and politically enforced productive and allocative patterns,

[11] Mayer (n 2) 20.

[12] Baldwin and Bettini, 'Introduction' (n 2) 4; Benoit Mayer, 'Who Are "Climate Refugees"? Academic Engagement in the Post-Truth Era' in Simon Behrman and Avidan Kent (eds), *Climate Refugees: Beyond the Legal Impasse?* (Abingdon, Routledge 2018) 89, 94; Calum TM Nicholson, 'Climate Change and the Politics of Causal Reasoning: the Case of Climate Change and Migration' (2014) 180 *Geographical Journal* 151.

[13] Baldwin and Bettini 'Introduction' (n 2) 4.

[14] Calum TM Nicholson, '"Climate Mobility" is not a Proper Subject of Research and Governance', in Benoit Mayer and Alexander Zahar (eds), *Debating Climate Law* (Cambridge, Cambridge University Press 2021) 215.

[15] Baldwin and Bettini 'Introduction' (n 2) 4.

and its physical environment, all in the formation of patterns of vulnerability and response to disaster'.[16]

The importance of understanding the climate–migration nexus primarily by looking at the social dimension of natural hazards has indeed been increasingly recognised in the literature,[17] as well as within a number of human rights mechanisms.[18] It has also been observed that the importance attributed to climate causality has so far narrowed the scope of legal analyses in respect to the climate–migration nexus: indeed, the climate change spotlight 'has led to an excessive focus on understanding the hazards themselves from a physical and natural science point of view', to the detriment of a more nuanced consideration of human and social vulnerability.[19] As it has long been known by modern disaster scholars, 'there is no such thing as a natural disaster':[20] it is thus evident that, in order to fully integrate this caveat into the climate–migration nexus through a socially oriented perspective, multicausality comes into play. Indeed, as noted by Alexander Betts, what is crucial for a meaningful debate about the topic 'is not attributing causality to movement, which is both virtually impossible and also irrelevant, but rather identifying the sets of rights deprivations within a country of origin that entitle a person to seek substitute protection in another country'.[21]

A socially oriented reading of the climate–migration nexus becomes particularly salient when the climate–migration nexus is analysed through the lens of international human rights protection.[22] In fact, the appreciation of disasters as

[16] Anthony Oliver-Smith, '"What is a Disaster?" Anthropological Perspectives on a Persistent Question', in Anthony Oliver-Smith and Susanna Hoffman (eds), *The Angry Earth: Disaster in Anthropological Perspective* (Abingdon, Routledge 2020) 29, 38.

[17] See in particular Matthew Scott, *Climate Change, Disasters, and the Refugee Convention* (Cambridge, Cambridge University Press 2020); Carmen G Gonzalez, 'Climate Justice and Climate Displacement: Evaluating the Emerging Legal and Policy Responses' (2019) 36 *Wisconsin International Law Journal* 366.

[18] The Office of the High Commissioner for Human Rights, 'Addressing Human Rights Protection Gaps in the Context of Migration and Displacement of Persons across International Borders Resulting from the Adverse Effects of Climate Change and Supporting the Adaptation and Mitigation Plans of Developing Countries to Bridge the Protection Gap' (2018) UN Doc A/HRC/38/21 para 14; Committee on the Elimination of All Forms of Discrimination Against Women, 'General Recommendation No 37 on Gender-Related Dimensions of Disaster-Risk Reduction in the Context of Climate Change' (2018) UN Doc CEDAW/C/GC/37 paras 74–75.

[19] Sálvano Briceño, 'Foreword' in Ben Wisner, JC Gaillard, and Ilan Kelman (eds), *Handbook of Hazards and Disaster Risk Reduction* (Abingdon, Routledge 2011) p xxx. See also discussion in Giovanna Lauria, 'A Critical Appraisal of the Concept of Climate Migration' (2022) 9(3) *London Review of International Law* 375, 395, available at doi.org/10.1093/lril/lrab018.

[20] Gregory Squires and Chester Hartman (eds), *There is no Such Thing as a Natural Disaster: Race, Class, and Hurricane Katrina* (Abingdon, Routledge 2006).

[21] Alexander Betts, 'Survival Migration: A New Protection Framework' (2010) 16(3) *Global Governance* 361, 378.

[22] This has been recently recognised by the UNHCR: '[t]he assessment of claims for international protection made in the context of the adverse effects of climate change and disasters should not focus narrowly on the climate change event or disaster as solely or primarily natural hazards. Such a narrow focus might fail to recognize the social and political characteristics of the effects of climate change or the impacts of disasters or their interaction with other drivers of displacement. More broadly, climate change and disasters may have significant adverse effects on State and societal structures and

social phenomena challenges the conception of climate impacts as indiscriminate forces of nature, and of the persons affected as unfortunate victims. This is because:

> [t]he threat posed by a natural disaster is far more than the threat of the moment, the terror experienced when the Earth moves underfoot or when people face the hurricane's gale and advancing storm surge. It is incubated through a history of discrimination that may involve either active denial or inability to ensure fundamental rights[23]

On the grounds of the theoretical framework outlined so far, the remainder of the chapter analyses the way in which the twofold dimension of the multicausality concept is reflected in the HRC's approach to the climate–migration nexus.

III. *Teitiota v New Zealand*: Preliminary Outline

The legal hurdle concerning Mr Teitiota is well known to most scholars with an interest in the climate–migration nexus. Ioane Teitiota, a citizen of the small-island state of Kiribati, arrived in New Zealand in 2007 on a temporary work visa. After overstaying his visa, he applied for refugee status, which was denied by government officials. He challenged the decision before the New Zealand Immigration and Protection Tribunal, claiming refugee protection on the ground of adverse effects of environmental changes taking place in his country of origin. The Immigration and Protection Tribunal rejected the claim, which was also subsequently denied by the High Court and the Supreme Court, leading to Mr Teitiota being deported to Kiribati in 2015. Mr Teitiota filed a communication before the HRC claiming that by removing him to Kiribati, New Zealand had violated his right to life under Article 6 of the International Covenant on Civil and Political Rights (ICCPR).

Mr Teitiota's grievances were based on the adverse effects of sea-level rise caused by global warming identified, *inter alia*, 'in the scarcity of habitable space, which has in turn caused violent land disputes that endanger the author's life, and environmental degradation, including saltwater contamination of the fresh-water supply'.[24] After declaring the claim admissible, the HRC moved to assess the merits by analysing each element of Teitiota's claim separately. These regarded, in particular, four main sources of life-threatening risks: violent disputes due to scarce habitable land, access to drinking water, availability of means of subsistence and general risks originating from overpopulation. For each of these elements, the

individual well-being and the enjoyment of human rights'. UN High Commissioner for Refugees, 'Legal Considerations Regarding Claims for International Protection Made in the Context of the Adverse Effects of Climate Change and Disasters' (2021) 33 *International Journal of Refugee Law* 151, 154 (para 5).

[23] John C Mutter and Kye M Barnard, 'Climate Change, Evolution of Disasters and Inequality', in Stephen Humphreys (ed), *Human Rights and Climate Change* (Cambridge, Cambridge University Press 2010) 272, 295.

[24] *Teitiota v New Zealand* (n 3) para 3.

HRC found that the threshold required in order to establish the existence of a risk of irreparable harm – the relevant question in removal cases[25] – was not met in the case at issue. As such, it concluded that 'the facts before it do not permit it to conclude that the author's removal to Kiribati violated his rights under article 6(1) of the Covenant'.[26]

IV. The Conceptualisation of the Climate–Migration Nexus in the *Teitiota* Decision

The core of the HRC's reasoning in respect to the climate–migration nexus is contained in three sentences at paragraph 9.11, which warrant quoting at length:

> Both sudden-onset events (such as intense storms and flooding) and slow-onset processes (such as sea level rise, salinization, and land degradation) can propel cross-border movement of individuals seeking protection from climate change-related harm. The Committee is of the view that without robust national and international efforts, the effects of climate change in receiving states may expose individuals to a violation of their rights under articles 6 or 7 [right to be free from torture or cruel, inhuman or degrading treatment or punishment] of the Covenant, thereby triggering the *non-refoulement* obligations of sending states. Furthermore, given that the risk of an entire country becoming submerged under water is such an extreme risk, the conditions of life in such a country may become incompatible with the right to life with dignity before the risk is realized.[27]

Although the passage must be appreciated in its entirety, each sentence contained therein is amenable to critical analysis for the purposes of this chapter. Put into perspective, the three sentences provide food for thought in respect to a number of key issues related to the climate–migration nexus. The following two subsections analyse the first and last sentence of the quoted passage respectively in order to shed light on the advancements made by the HRC with regards to the appreciation of disaster impacts and of the concept of uninhabitability. Subsequently, in light of its critical content for the purposes of this chapter, the central sentence is analysed in a separate section.

A. The Rejection of Categories in Favour of the Holistic Appreciation of Disasters

In the opening sentence, the HRC notes that both sudden-onset and slow-onset events have harmful impacts and can give rise to scenarios of forced migration

[25] As recalled in ibid para 9.3.
[26] ibid para 10.
[27] ibid para 9.11.

with similar protection and assistance needs.[28] That the HRC was going to accept such a broad approach to hazards and their effects was not self-evident. Many legal analyses take as a starting point for the conceptualisation of climate mobility the categorisation of migration movements on the basis of the type of climate event triggering them. Within such categorisations, slow-onset processes are typically associated with voluntary forms of migration.[29] This perspective was also recalled by New Zealand's Immigration and Protection Tribunal, according to which Mr Teitiota's migration represented a 'voluntary adaptive migration' which, in spite of some degree of compulsion, cannot be considered 'forced'.[30] Leaving aside Mr Teitiota's specific case, the problem with this 'category-based' approach is that it distracts the point of enquiry from the appreciation of the actual local conditions where the disaster (broadly understood, including slow-onset event) strikes, to a decontextualised causal nexus between a specific type of movement and a given hazard. As a result, conceptualisations of the issue through the vehicle of categorisations – as well as of definitions – tend to 'suggest that nature is at fault, when in fact humans are deeply implicated in the environmental changes that make life impossible in certain circumstances'.[31]

Within disaster studies, it has long been recognised that disasters are hardly defined and determined by the category of natural hazard alone. Indeed, the variety of phenomena that can generate a disaster should be appreciated holistically: therefore, the (oft-heard) distinction between sudden and slow onset hazards is not tenable under this framework. This is because, as disasters are social processes rather than events, to understand what a disaster is, the primary concern is not the type and nature of natural hazards, but rather their effects – that is, the specific impacts on the social context in which they strike.[32] By considering slow and sudden-onset disasters equally harmful and capable of giving rise to international protection needs, the HRC has implicitly adhered to contemporary understandings of disasters while simultaneously rejecting preformulated assumptions about the climate–migration nexus. It is precisely on this basis that the HRC could elaborate on the applicability of international protection instruments and norms in the context of climate change and disasters.

B. The Issue of Uninhabitability

As a corollary to the recognition of climate change impacts' role in exposing people to life-threatening risks, the HRC noted that, in light of Kiribati's expected

[28] As suggested by the use of the expression 'individuals seeking protection from'.

[29] See, for instance, the well-known categorisation proposed by Kälin and discussion therein: Walter Kälin, 'Conceptualising Climate-Induced Displacement' in Jane McAdam (ed), *Climate Change and Displacement: Multidisciplinary Perspectives* (Oxford, Hart 2010) 81.

[30] *AF (Kiribati)* [2013] NZIPT 800413, para 49.

[31] Anthony Oliver-Smith, cited in Fanny Thornton, 'Climate Change, Displacement and International Law: Between Crisis and Ambiguity' (2012) 30 *Australian Yearbook of International Law* 147, 156.

[32] For analysis see Oliver-Smith, '"What is a Disaster?"' (n 16).

submersion under water, living conditions therein may become incompatible with human rights standards before the country is submerged.

This is where the decision touches upon the peculiar condition of small island states and their inhabitants, notoriously portrayed as the 'canaries in the coal mine' of climate change.[33] Because of their particular vulnerability to climate impacts, manifested first and foremost by the risk of submersion, scholars have been particularly drawn to the 'fascinating legal issues'[34] raised by 'sinking' states – ranging from the relocation of whole populations to the legal implications of state disappearance.[35] Yet, the 'sinking states' narrative, while rhetorically powerful, has a number of shortcomings.[36] For instance, it tends to crystallise the risk faced by low-lying atolls as one of territorial loss, which in turn 'works to erase from view the material, populated history of ocean island degradation'.[37] Furthermore, Barnett and Adger have argued that the fatalistic scenario encapsulated by the image of drowning states could be a self-realising prophecy, as it 'could … be brought about less by the physical impacts of climate change *per se*, and more by a common expectation of serious climate impacts leading to changes in domestic resource use and decreased assistance from abroad'.[38] It is thus evident that the situation of small island states represents a plastic exemplification of what is 'both a discursive and material phenomenon'.[39]

The language used by the HRC throughout the *Teitiota* decision suggests that the plight of low-lying atolls has been framed as, fundamentally, an issue of uninhabitability. The recurring references throughout the decision to the right to a life with dignity, which arguably entails the entitlement to minimum living conditions,[40] is indeed consistent with such a framing. From a legal standpoint, the focus on territorial habitability – as opposed to territorial loss – anticipates the moment at which a violation of the right to life may materialise and thus the point at which individuals might be considered in need of international protection against these risks. This is because the attention to uninhabitability welcomes

[33] Richard Benwell, 'The Canaries in the Coalmine: Small States as Climate Change Champions' (2011) 100(413) *The Round Table* 199; Matthew Offord and Kerry McCarthy, '*Small Island States are Canary in the Coalmine of Climate Change*' (*The Times*, 2021), available at www.thetimes.co.uk/article/small-island-states-are-canary-in-the-coalmine-of-climate-change-jsp6vphvl.

[34] McAdam (n 1) 119.

[35] Indeed, the topic of 'sea-level rise in relation to international law' has been recently included in the International Law Commission's programme of work.

[36] For a critique of this label, see Carol Farbotko, 'Wishful Sinking: Disappearing Islands, Climate Refugees and Cosmopolitan Experimentation' (2010) 51 *Asia Pacific Viewpoint* 47.

[37] Cait Storr, 'Islands and the South: Framing the Relationship Between International Law and Environmental Crisis' (2016) 27(2) *European Journal of International Law* 519, 534.

[38] Jon Barnett and W Neil Adger, 'Climate Dangers and Atoll Countries' (2003) 61 *Climatic Change* 321, 330.

[39] Carol Farbotko and Heather Lazrus, 'The First Climate Refugees? Contesting Global Narratives of Climate Change in Tuvalu' (2012) 22(2) *Global Environmental Change* 382, available at doi.org/10.1016/j.gloenvcha.2011.11.014.

[40] For discussion about the scope of states' obligations regarding the right to a life with dignity, particularly in respect to the socio-economic sphere, see Sarah Joseph, 'Extending the Right to Life under the

a more context-specific understanding of climate vulnerability. Indeed, through the uninhabitability lens, climate vulnerability is not only defined with reference to the existential threat represented by rising sea levels, but also by other, non-environmental pressures, such as weak infrastructures, political and economic instability, and social disorder.

The analysis so far has highlighted the ways in which the HRC has developed the conceptualisation of the climate–migration nexus by realigning it with a social and disaster-oriented perspective. It has been shown that the HRC has overcome the problems linked to some oft-heard assumptions regarding, specifically, the categorisation of hazards and related movements and the particular vulnerability of small island states. The HRC appears to have framed the issue of multicausality not only by offering an accurate representation of the dynamics underpinning the climate–migration nexus, but also by developing a concept that can more swiftly inform legal analysis. Nonetheless, the HRC's decision reproduces also, without addressing them, a number of internal contradictions linked to the 'reification' of the climate–migration nexus – that is, the exemplification of the elusive relationship between climate change and human mobility through the figure of the climate migrant.[41] Such contradictions are encapsulated by the central issue that the decision touches upon: the potential application of states' obligations to protect international migrants in the context of climate and disaster impacts. It is thus to such recognition that the remainder of this chapter turns to.

V. The Recognition of Climate Change Effects as Triggers of *Non-Refoulement* Obligations: Waltzing with Ambiguity

The second sentence of the previously quoted passage is the decision's most significant finding for practitioners and scholars advocating the protection of 'climate migrants'. Indeed, the HRC has admitted that climate change and related effects may expose individuals to unacceptable risks of harm, regardless of the acts or omissions of the state to which the individual is returned. In emphasising the implications of this statement, the HRC further affirmed that state parties have a 'continuing responsibility … to take into account in future deportation cases the situation at the time in Kiribati and new and updated data on the effects of climate change and rising sea levels thereupon'.[42] The HRC thus suggested that, while

International Covenant on Civil and Political Rights: General Comment 36' (2019) 19(2) *Human Rights Law Review* 347, available at doi.org/10.1093/hrlr/ngz003; Thomas M Antkowiak, 'A "Dignified Life" and the Resurgence of Social Rights' (2020) 18 *Northwestern Journal of Human Rights* 1.

[41] For critical discussion about the reification of the climate–migration nexus see Bettini (n 2).

[42] *Teitiota v New Zealand* (n 3) para 9.14.

Mr Teitiota's claim did not reach the required threshold, future claims may succeed as a result of further environmental degradation.

While representing the most celebrated and innovative part of the decision, the recognition of climate impacts' role in creating life-threatening risks or risks of ill-treatment has also put the conceptualisation of the climate–migration nexus elaborated by the HRC on a slippery slope. Indeed, what is not fully clear from the way in which the HRC has approached the relationship between climate change and migration is whether climate impacts can be considered, by themselves, as potential triggers of *non-refoulement* obligations, rather than as one of the factors reinforcing an international protection claim. As will be seen in the remainder of this section, the HRC's decision oscillates between two irreconcilable positions, which adds a layer of uncertainty as to the role that the HRC has attributed to climate causality.

A. The 'Restrictive' Interpretation: Climate Impacts as *Indirect* Triggers

In retrospective, the HRC's finding regarding the implications of the climate–migration nexus for the international protection of migrants can be traced from the evolution of human rights case law and doctrine in the preceding years. In 2018, in a General Comment on the right to life, the HRC had recognised not only that the right to life encompasses the enjoyment of a life with dignity, but also that 'environmental degradation, climate change and unsustainable development constitute some of the most pressing and serious threats to the ability of present and future generations to enjoy the right to life'.[43] In deciding Mr Teitiota's case, the New Zealand Supreme Court had emphasised that their decisions 'did not mean that environmental degradation resulting from climate change or other natural disasters could never create a pathway into the Refugee Convention or protected person jurisdiction'.[44] Indeed, the European Court of Human Rights has long admitted that conditions not related to acts of state or non-state actors may give rise to an international protection claim, for instance in its so-called 'medical' jurisprudence regarding the removal of seriously ill migrants.[45] Indeed, as a matter of human rights law, the central question concerns the *existence* of a real

[43] HRC, 'General Comment No 36 on Article 6 of the International Covenant on Civil and Political Rights, on the Right to Life' (2018) UN Doc CCPR/C/GC/36 para 62.

[44] *Teitiota v Chief Executive of the Ministry of Business, Innovation and Employment* [2015] NZSC 107, para 13.

[45] In the case of *D v the United Kingdom* App No 30240/96 (ECtHR, 2 May 1997) at para 49, the European Court of Human Rights recognised for the first time that, in light of the fundamental importance and absolute nature of Article 3 (right to be free from torture and other ill-treatment), a *non-refoulement* obligation might arise in cases where 'the source of the risk of proscribed treatment in the receiving country stems from factors which cannot engage either directly or indirectly

risk of irreparable harm in the receiving state, regardless of the *source* of such harm. As such, recognising that it would be contrary to human rights obligations to send a person back to a place where their life would be in danger is hardly a legal revolution.[46] In other words, the HRC has done nothing more than admitting that, if a threat to life or a risk of ill-treatment exists – regardless of the source of this risk – then the *non-refoulement* obligations of sending states will be activated.

Through this perspective, the (legal) relevance of the HRC's finding is clearly downsized. Indeed, besides its symbolic weight as an international precedent, the HRC adds little to the already existing human rights standards and their scope of application.[47] But beyond its legal implications, the 'restrictive' interpretation of the HRC's recognition of climate impacts' role in triggering international protection invites further reflections about the conceptual dimension related to the framing of the climate–migration nexus. A first observation is that such recognition does not amount to an endorsement of the 'climate refugee' category. The HRC has in fact applied to Mr Teitiota's communication the same standards that would have been employed to any removal case brought before it. Thus, for instance, the HRC has recalled that generally the risk of irreparable harm faced by the author must be personal, and that only in the most exceptional cases it can derive from the general conditions in the country of origin.[48] Accordingly, it has analysed whether the threats faced by the applicant were sufficiently serious by applying the high threshold that, in conformity with its case law, is required in order to establish that a real risk of irreparable harm exists.

A second and related observation is that, by applying such interpretation, the HRC has refrained from attributing to climate change a direct role in producing displacement or in creating specific vulnerabilities. Through this perspective, climate change impacts are conceived of as providing an overarching context for displacement, rather than as a separative drive of displacement. While potentially more consistent with a multicausal and in turn disaster-oriented reading of the climate–migration nexus, this approach is also more prone to criticism of 'conservatism': as Behlert has affirmed, '[d]ue to the deferential approach taken by the HRC, the ruling is not the unconditional assurance that human rights protect those most affected by climate change which many have been hoping for'.[49] Along similar lines, the HRC's 'insensitivity' to the threat posed by climate change has indeed been voiced in the dissenting opinion of Committee member Duncan Laki

the responsibility of the public authorities of that country, or which, taken alone, do not in themselves infringe the standards of that Article'.

[46] See Miriam Cullen, 'The UN Human Rights Committee's Recent Decision on Climate Displacement' (*Asylum Insight*, February 2020), available at www.asyluminsight.com/c-miriam-cullen.

[47] As has been noted by Behrman and Kent (n 5).

[48] *Teitiota v New Zealand* (n 3) para 9.3.

[49] Benedikt Behlert, 'A Significant Opening. On the HRC's Groundbreaking First Ruling in the Case of a "Climate Refugee"' (*Voelkerrechtsblog*, 30 January 2020), available at voelkerrechtsblog.org/a-significant-opening.

Muhumuza, who pointed out that 'the Committee needs to handle critical and significantly irreversible issues of climate change, with the approach that seeks to uphold the sanctity of human life'.[50]

Along a 'restrictive' interpretation underlying the indirect role of climate impacts, some of the HRC's statements appear to endorse a rather opposite understanding of climate causality, according to which climate impacts are posited in a direct relationship with the rise of international protection needs. It is to such understanding that the following paragraph turns to.

B. The 'Broad' Interpretation: Climate Impacts as *Direct* Triggers

A number of commentators have argued that the significance of the *Teitiota* decision lies in the 'explicit recognition that the impacts of climate change may themselves be a bar to deportation'.[51] Such a central role attributed to climate causality is reinforced by the message transpiring from the HRC's references to the 'international efforts' and the 'assistance of the international community' necessary in order to address climate change.[52] As Delval, for instance, has suggested, it is as though the HRC was warning states that, if they do not satisfy their obligations and duties under the climate regime, then they should be ready to undertake the responsibilities and obligations flowing from the human rights regime, including those related to *non-refoulement*.[53]

From this perspective, the HRC's reasoning seems to reinforce a deterministic reading of the climate–migration nexus – that is, one that frames climate change and human mobility respectively as a cause and an effect. From a legal viewpoint, such a reading extends the scope of states' obligations well beyond current international law standards. The attribution of a direct role to climate causality implies, in principle, a recognition that all nationals of a climate-vulnerable state might be entitled to international protection – provided that they have already crossed an international border. In an attempt to counterbalance the potentially far-reaching effects of such an enhanced *non-refoulement* regime, the HRC has appealed to the 10–15 years timeframe of the island's 'life expectancy' that could allow

[50] Individual Opinion of Committee member Duncan Laki Muhumuza (dissenting) in *Teitiota v New Zealand* (n 3), para 1.

[51] McAdam (n 6) 710.

[52] *Teitiota v New Zealand* (n 3), paras 9.11 and 9.12, respectively.

[53] See Eugénie Delval, 'From the U.N. Human Rights Committee to European Courts: which Protection for Climate-Induced Displaced Persons under European Law?' (*EU Migration Law Blog*, 8 April 2020), available at eumigrationlawblog.eu/from-the-u-n-human-rights-committee-to-european-courts-which-protection-for-climate-induced-displaced-persons-under-european-law; Lucia Rose, 'The World after Teitiota: What the HRC Decision Means for the Future of Climate Migration' (2021) 12 *San Diego Journal of Climate & Energy Law* 41, 53.

'the Republic of Kiribati, with the assistance of the international community, to take affirmative measures to protect and, where necessary, relocate its population'.[54] Beyond generating some confusion amongst scholars as to *when* a real risk of harm might materialise in climate-vulnerable contexts,[55] what seems to transpire from the HRC's reference to this time frame is a preoccupation with the tenability of its own finding. A broad extension of states' international protection obligations has important practical implications, which could lead to questions being raised about the HRC's legitimacy, while also prompting unpredictable and possibly adverse effects on domestic migration policies. In this connection, as Rive has pointed out,

> it is not inconceivable that domestic political responses to a material increase in successful climate change-related non-refoulement claims from Pacific nationals in sending states would include a careful review, and perhaps restriction, of existing temporary labour migration schemes which, through remittances, provide significant sources of income to residents of those states.[56]

This suggests two remarks in response. The first relates to the extent to which it is desirable that legal 'solutions' to the climate–migration nexus be achieved by courts rather than by other actors – such as political branches of the government or international negotiations.[57] The second goes back to the well-known critiques related to the unintended consequences of what Nicholson calls 'equivocal causal claims', of which 'climate migration' is a prime example.[58]

VI. Conclusion

This chapter has attempted to take stock of the way the HRC's decision in *Teitiota* has affected the conceptualisation of the climate–migration nexus. This has been done by focusing primarily on multicausality as one of the main controversial issues surrounding the topic. By offering a theoretical framework through which multicausality can be used as a valuable analytical tool to unravel the linkages between environmental degradation, disaster vulnerability, and human mobility, the analysis has assessed the extent to which the HRC has integrated a multicausal and disaster-oriented perspective into its reasoning. As has been argued, the HRC's

[54] *Teitiota v New Zealand* (n 3) para 9.12.

[55] See Michelle Foster and Jane McAdam, 'Analysis of "Imminence" in International Protection Claims: Teitiota v New Zealand and Beyond' (2022) 71 *International & Comparative Law Quarterly* 975.

[56] Vernon Rive, 'Is an Enhanced non-Refoulement Regime under the ICCPR the Answer to Climate Change-Related Human Mobility Challenges in the Pacific? Reflections on Teitiota v New Zealand in the Human Rights Committee' (2020) 75 *Questions of International Law* 7, 11.

[57] For further insights see Lys Kulamadayl, 'Between Activism and Complacency: International Law Perspectives on European Climate Litigation' (2021) 10(5) *European Society of International Law Reflection* 1.

[58] Nicholson (n 12).

conceptualisation of the climate–migration nexus reflects a valuable engagement with a more nuanced understanding of disaster and climate vulnerability, particularly in respect to the plight of low-lying atolls. However, it has also been claimed that the HRC's decision leaves open two different interpretations as to the role to be attributed to climate causality within international protection claims.

The HRC's incapacity to take a clear position in this respect calls for further reflection on the role of international law in addressing sensitive questions, oscillating between ethics and law. The anthropogenic basis of climate change and its increasing impacts on human societies are a constant reminder of developed states' long history of environmental exploitation and uncontrolled greenhouse gas (GHG) emissions to the detriment of local livelihoods in the world's poorest countries. In this perspective, it is evident that climate change 'is not a legally or ethically neutral environmental problem'.[59]

Should this, as a matter of ethics and law, create a duty upon states who have so far benefitted from the disruption of the climate system to help other less responsible and yet more affected countries to cope with such disruption? More specifically, if such a duty exists, should it also extend to individuals who have anticipated the worst effects of climate change by migrating, or who cannot or do not want to return to increasingly disaster-affected countries and worsening living conditions? The HRC's negative and yet sympathetic answer is in turn indicative of the difficulties that accompany any effort to situate the climate–migration nexus within the framework of international law.

[59] Maxine Burkett, Book Review (2012) 3 *Climate Law* 314.

10

De-Conceptualising 'Climate Migration'

BENOIT MAYER

I. Introduction

More than a decade ago, I was looking for a topic on which to write a master's thesis when I came across news reports on 'sinking' island states. The unfortunate plight of 'climate refugees' resonated with my interest in advancing the human rights of migrants. Further, I was under the impression that including a policy proposal in my thesis would facilitate its publication, which, in turn, could help when applying for doctoral studies. A year later, I published my first article, which proposed an 'international legal framework' for 'climate migrants' to 'be granted some protection in a third-party country as soon as their state becomes unable to protect their most fundamental human rights'.[1]

Yet, as I embarked on a doctoral programme in the following years, it became clearer to me that this argument was taking on water. The first leak I became aware of is the absence of normative ground for singling out 'climate migrants' as a category of individuals specifically worthy of protection. Instead of 'climate migrants', normative arguments bifurcate towards two alternatives: a 'solidarity' project for the protection of all vulnerable populations with similar needs (eg by addressing 'survival migration');[2] and a 'responsibility' project on addressing the harm resulting from climate change.[3] These arguments do not justify policies on 'climate migration' but, rather, broader reforms in *either* migration *or* climate governance.

[1] Benoit Mayer, 'The International Legal Challenges of Climate-Induced Migration: Proposal for an International Legal Framework' (2011) 22 *Colorado Journal of International Environmental Law and Policy* 357, 360.

[2] Alexander Betts, *Survival Migration: Failed Governance and the Crisis of Displacement* (Ithaca, Cornell University Press 2013).

[3] See Benoit Mayer, 'The International Legal Protection of Climate (or Environmental) Migrants: Fraternity, Responsibility and Sustainability' (2012) 56 *Supreme Court Law Review* 723, available at doi.org/10.2139/ssrn.1806760; Benoit Mayer, 'Climate Change and International Law in the Grim Days' (2013) 24(3) *European Journal of International Law* 947, 962–63, available at doi.org/10.1093/ejil/cht054; Benoit Mayer, 'Climate Change, Migration and the Law of State Responsibility', in Benoit Mayer and Francois Crépeau (eds), *Research Handbook on Climate Change, Migration and the Law* (Cheltenham, Edward Elgar 2017).

While troubling, the confusion of the normative arguments on 'climate migration' is not necessarily an obstacle to its political reception. Effective policy arguments often build opportunistically on what attracts public attention at a particular time. Rather than talking about 'economic refugees' or 'environmental refugees' as it once did, the 'solidarity' project might now seek to use the 'climate' brand as a way to capture public interest. Likewise, the 'responsibility' project could benefit from the political attention invested in international migration to flag the need for action to combat climate change. Either way, a value of a political argument does not depend on its logical cogency as much as its ability to change things for the better.

However, I soon realised that there was also another, more fundamental 'leak' in my argument – one that affected its central premise, namely, the existence of 'climate migrants'. The issue is that it is not possible to characterise any individual as a 'climate migrant' in any meaningful (ie non-arbitrary) way.[4] Climate change has fundamental consequences on global environmental systems, but it does not directly displace one person from one place to another. Whether an extreme weather event occurs depends only in part on climate change; and whether this event results in a disaster and whether it induces migration are contingent on local circumstances such as the successful implementation of risk-reduction strategies for disasters. Likewise, slow-onset environmental changes, such as sea-level rise, do not cause human mobility in abstraction from political, demographic, economic, and other social conditions. Depending on arbitrary choices in the way 'climate migrants' are accounted for, their number could be anywhere between zero and almost eight billion.

The flaws of my original argument became more difficult to ignore as I finally took the time to read the relevant literature in other (ie non-law) disciplines, including the writings of many contributors to this book.[5] Also, having relocated from Canada to Singapore for my doctoral studies, I had some opportunities to travel to would-be 'climate migration' hotspots in and around Southeast Asia. A field trip to Mongolia helped me better understand how climate change acts as an underlying factor rather than as a direct cause of migration. In that case, climate change resulted in an increase in snowfall in some years (*dzud*), which impeded grazing, hence also herders' livelihood, thus exacerbating various political, social, and economic factors inducing herders to move to the capital city, Ulaanbaatar.[6]

[4] See, for example, Benoit Mayer, 'Constructing "Climate Migration" as a Global Governance Issue: Essential Flaws in the Contemporary Literature' (2013) 9 *McGill International Journal of Sustainable Development Law and Policy* 87, 87, available at www.jstor.org/stable/24352635.

[5] See generally Calum TM Nicholson, 'Conceptualising "Climate Migration"', ch 1 in this volume; Ilan Kelman, 'Climate Change-Disaster-Migration: Manufacturing a Nexus', ch 2 in this volume; Gunvor Jónsson, '"Climate Migration"? Empirical Insights and Conceptual Cautions from Political Ecology and Migration Studies', ch 3 in this volume; and previous publications by these authors.

[6] See Benoit Mayer, 'The Rights of Mongolia's Internal Migrants under International Law: Climatic, Domestic and Commercial Responsibilities Student Contribution' (2014) 7 *Journal of East Asia and*

As a result, having begun by wondering why scholars in the 'Global South' were not more interested in 'climate migration',[7] I now found myself wondering why institutions in the 'Global North' were promoting this concept in the first place[8] – and, with some concern, I wondered what could result from advocacy based on such a misleading concept.[9]

Many years of observing the research community working on this issue has confirmed that I was not the only person to experience this struggle with the conceptual confusion of the topic. While I was shifting from enthusiastic advocacy for the rights of 'climate migrants' to a more critical and ultimately sceptical perspective, I observed with much dismay that many scholars kept making similar mistakes, arguing for law-and-policy responses to 'climate migration', without realising the lack of normative basis for singling out 'climate migration' and, overall, the practical impossibility of identifying the putative beneficiaries of such laws and policies. Proposals extended from a treaty on the protection of 'climate migrants' (or 'climate refugees'),[10] to alternative approaches expected to be more realistic or effective.[11] The literature, in particular in law and other governance-oriented

International Law 197; Benoit Mayer, 'Managing "Climate Migration" in Mongolia: The Importance of Development Policies', in Walter Leal Filho (ed), *Climate Change in the Asia-Pacific Region* (Basel, Springer 2015) 191; Benoit Mayer, 'Climate Migration and the Politics of Causal Attribution: A Case Study in Mongolia' (2016) 5(2) *Migration and Development* 234, available at doi.org/10.1080/21632324.2015.1022971. See also Benoit Mayer and others, 'Governing Environmentally Related Migration in Bangladesh: Responsibilities, Security and the Causality Problem' (2013) 22(2) *Asian and Pacific Migration Journal* 177, available at doi.org/10.1177/011719681302200202.

[7] See Benoit Mayer, 'Environmental Migration: Prospects for a Regional Governance in the Asia-Pacific Region' (2013) 16 *Asia Pacific Journal of Environmental Law* 77, available at ssrn.com/abstract=2495983; Benoit Mayer, 'Environmental Migration in the Asia-Pacific Region: Could we Hang out Sometime?' (2013) 3 *Asian Journal of International Law* 101, available at doi.org/10.2139/ssrn.1955818.

[8] Benoit Mayer, 'The Arbitrary Project of Protecting Environmental Migrants', in Robert McLeman, Jeanette Schade, and Thomas Faist (eds), *Environmental Migration and Social Inequality* (Basel, Springer 2016) 189; Benoit Mayer, 'La sécurisation du changement climatique comme stratégie politique', in Nicholas Clinchamps and others (eds), *Sécurité et environnement* (Bruxelles, Bruylant 2016) 239.

[9] Benoit Mayer, '"Environmental Migration" as Advocacy: Is it Going to Work?' (2012) 29(2) *Refuge: Canada's Journal on Refugees* 27, available at www.jstor.org/stable/48648723; Benoit Mayer, *The Concept of Climate Migration: Advocacy and its Prospects* (Cheltenham, Edward Elgar Publishing 2016).

[10] See, for example, Bonnie Docherty and Tyler Giannini, 'Confronting a Rising Tide: A Proposal for a Convention on Climate Change Refugees Symposium' (2009) 33(2) *Harvard Environmental Law Review* 349; Frank Biermann and Ingrid Boas, 'Preparing for a Warmer World: Towards a Global Governance System to Protect Climate Refugees' (2010) 10 *Global Environmental Politics* 60, available at doi.org/10.1162/glep.2010.10.1.60; Michel Prieur, 'Towards an International Legal Status of Environmentally Displaced Persons', in Simon Behrman and Avidan Kent (eds), *'Climate Refugees': Beyond the Legal Impasse?* (Abingdon, Routledge 2018) 233.

[11] See, for example, Camilla Schloss, 'Cross-Border Displacement Due to Environmental Disaster: A Proposal for UN Guiding Principles to Fill the Legal Protection Gap', in Behrman and Kent (n 10) 243 (advocating for a soft-law approach); Avidan Kent and Simon Behrman, *Facilitating the Resettlement and Rights of Climate Refugees: An Argument for Developing Existing Principles and Practices* (Abingdon, Routledge 2018) 123 (calling for an institutional framework of 'cross-governance' led by the UN Climate Secretariat); Patrícia Galvão Teles, 'Remarks by Patrícia Galvão Teles' (2021) 115 *Proceedings of the ASIL Annual Meeting* 158, 161 ('a mapping exercise, a stocktaking exercise to identify the protections, in terms of legal principles and rules, that already exist in the different relevant applicable legal frameworks'). See also Issa Ibrahim Berchin and others, 'Climate Change and Forced

disciplines, has remained, by and large, unable to address the flawed premises on which it had originally built.

Some scholars have turned away from simplistic policy proposals for granting a legal status to 'climate migrants' and sought somehow to 'mend' the argument.[12] Yet they have not *really* departed from the concept of 'climate migration'. What they have suggested was more a facelift or a rebranding than a solution to the fundamental normative and conceptual flaws highlighted above. Substituting 'climate migrants' with 'people displaced in the context of disasters and climate change',[13] 'people displaced by the impacts of climate change',[14] or 'affected populations in climate mobilities',[15] does nothing to address the problem that the object of concern does not exist – that the existence of individual migrants cannot be attributed to climate change. Likewise, replacing 'climate migration' with 'climate mobilities'[16] maintains the problematic suggestion that climate change causes a separate type of migration (or mobility), rather than merely affecting the prevalence of existing scenarios.[17] Either way, the argument has remained based on the (false) assumption that there are distinct populations of individuals who are migrating (or unable to migrate) *because of* climate change. The debate has evolved towards more convoluted phrases rather than towards clearer concepts or more cogent arguments.

Meanwhile, the argument for responses to 'climate migration' has gained ground in the world of policy-making. The New York Declaration for Refugees and Migrants, adopted by the UN General Assembly in 2016, asserted that '[s]ome people move … in response to the adverse effects of climate change'.[18] There, national governments 'commit[ed] to addressing the drivers that create or exacerbate large movements', including by 'combating … the adverse impacts of climate change'.[19] Two years later, the General Assembly adopted the Global Compact for Safe, Orderly and Regular Migration, in which states promised to '[c]ooperate to identify, develop and strengthen solutions for migrants compelled to leave their

Migrations: An Effort towards Recognizing Climate Refugees' (2017) 84 *Geoforum* 147, available at doi.org/10.1016/j.geoforum.2017.06.022 (calling for 'the legal acceptance of climate refugees' without specifying the form this acceptance could take).

[12] See, for example, Ingrid Boas and others, 'Climate Migration Myths' (2019) 9 *Nature Climate Change* 901, available at doi.org/10.1038/s41558-019-0633-3.

[13] Madeline Garlick, Marine Franck, and Erica Bower, 'Enhancing Legal Protection for People Displaced in the Context of Disasters and Climate Change', in Behrman and Kent (n 10).

[14] Jane McAdam, 'Protecting People Displaced by the Impacts of Climate Change: The UN Human Rights Committee and the Principle of *Non-Refoulement*' (2020) 114(4) *American Journal of International Law* 708, available at doi.org/10.1017/ajil.2020.31.

[15] Boas and others (n 12) 902.

[16] ibid 901.

[17] See generally Calum TM Nicholson, '"Climate Mobility" is not a Proper Subject of Research and Governance', in Benoit Mayer and Alexander Zahar (eds), *Debating Climate Law* (Cambridge, Cambridge University Press 2021) 215.

[18] New York Declaration for Refugees and Migrants (adopted 3 October 2016 UNGA Resolution 71/1) para 1.

[19] ibid para 43.

countries of origin owing to … the adverse effects of climate change'.[20] As in the most recent academic literature, these policy documents seek, but fail, to address the conceptual flaws of the discourse they rely on. For instance, these documents do not refer to 'climate migrants', but the convoluted phrases they use ('migrants compelled to leave their countries of origin owing to … the adverse effects of climate change') build on the same flawed concept: these documents assume that it is possible to attribute the movements of individual migrants to climate change. A 2022 Report of the Secretary-General recognises that '[t]he relationship between climate change and migration is complex', only then to discuss the situation of 'persons that move because of climate change'.[21]

This chapter seeks to understand the persistent disconnect between the law-and-policy discourse on 'climate migration' and what is known about the nature of the climate–migration nexus. Migration scholars have long shown the complexity of migration decisions and, more specifically, the impossibility of attributing migration to climate change. Yet, the chapter notes that a simplistic discourse on 'climate migration' continues to prevail not only in the media but also in specialised scholarship on 'climate migration' and, increasingly, in international policy documents. The analysis in this chapter is informed by a critical reading of the literature, and it also builds on my own experience – from my first article on the protection of 'climate migrants' to my present scepticism – to consider what could be the causes of this persistent disconnect and, ultimately, what could be the ways forward for academic research and for law and policy.

Section II focuses on understanding the impact of climate change on migration. It reviews the writings of migration scholars, discusses the possibility of attributing individual harm to climate change, and, more generally, reflects on the obstacles to causal claims in (quasi-)chaotic systems. Section III observes and seeks to explain the persistence of a loaded concept of 'climate migration' in some of the literature. Among other things, it considers scholars' political motivation as a potential cause for the persistence of a flawed conception of 'climate migration'. Lastly, section IV discusses possible ways forward for law- and policy-makers on the one hand and for scholars on the other hand.

II. Conceptualising the Impact of Climate Change on Migration

This section explores three ways of understanding the impact of climate change on migration. A first subsection retraces the way a literature focusing on the

[20] Global Compact for Safe, Orderly and Regular Migration (adopted 11 January 2019 UNGA Res 73/195) para 21(h).

[21] Report of the Secretary-General, 'The Impacts of Climate Change on the Human Rights of People in Vulnerable Situations' (6 May 2022) UN Doc A/HRC/50/57 para 12.

climate–migration nexus has evolved from a simplistic causal model of migration 'produced' by climate change to the recognition of the multicausal determination of migration. A second subsection considers how a 'science' of climate attribution has tried to attribute individual harm to climate change but argues that this endeavour is bound to fail. A third subsection points, more generally, to the limitations of causal attribution in chaotic systems.

A. The Integration of Climate Change in Migration Theory

Migration studies have never totally ignored the role the environment plays in influencing migration.[22] However, the focus has long been elsewhere. In the context of the Cold War, in particular, more emphasis was generally put on economic or political drivers. Even then, however, environmental protection advocates sought to highlight the benefits of environmental protection, among other things, by identifying the impacts of environmental degradation on human societies. In 1988, Jodi Jacobson of the Worldwatch Institute in Washington, DC, was among the first authors to suggest the existence of 'environmental refugees', which she described as 'a yardstick of habitability'.[23]

In the following years, this new concept was adopted by several scholars in environmental studies. Five years after Jacobson, Norman Myers, undertaking a study for the Climate Institute (also in Washington, DC) wrote that '[l]arge numbers of environmental refugees could be among the most significant of all upheavals entrained by global warming'.[24] He noted that the existence of large numbers of 'environmental refugees' could 'serve … as a powerful further rationale for policy measures to slow global warming while there is still time'.[25] And he predicted that 150 million 'environmental refugees' would be displaced within or across international borders by 2050.[26] However, Myers' methodology was rudimentary, boiling down to little more than counting the present populations living within exposed areas.[27] Among other things, his analysis appeared to confuse a stock of refugees at a given point in time with the total flow of refugees over a period of time.[28]

These early publications did not develop strong analytical tools to understand how climate change impacts human mobility. Neither Jacobson nor Myers made

[22] See Etienne Piguet, 'From "Primitive Migration" to "Climate Refugees": The Curious Fate of the Natural Environment in Migration Studies' (2013) 103 *Annals of the Association of American Geographers* 148, available at doi.org/10.1080/00045608.2012.696233.

[23] See Jodi L Jacobson, 'Environmental Refugees: A Yardstick of Habitability' (1988) 8(3) *Bulletin of Science, Technology & Society* 257, available at doi.org/10.1177/027046768800800304.

[24] Norman Myers, 'Environmental Refugees in a Globally Warmed World' (1993) 43(11) *BioScience* 752, 752, available at doi.org/10.2307/1312319.

[25] ibid 753.

[26] ibid 757.

[27] ibid 755.

[28] ibid 752.

any distinction between different scenarios of migration, or even between internal and international migration. The conspicuous goal of these alarmist reports was to highlight the connection of environmental degradation, in particular climate change, with social turmoil.[29] Rather than being seen as individuals in need of protection, 'environmental refugees' were largely approached as a symptom of environmental degradation. Thus, the First Assessment Report, published by the Intergovernmental Panel on Climate Change (IPCC) in 1990, mentions that '[e]ven a modest rise in global sea-levels could produce tens of millions of such [environmental] refugees'.[30] Both the choice of the word 'produce' and the emphasis on a single number are symptomatic of a lack of awareness of the different factors interacting with sea-level rise (eg development strategies to promote a sustainable human settlement) and of the depersonalisation of 'environmental refugees' in this early literature.

By the early 1990s, scholars in migration studies proposed a refined understanding of the impact of climate change on migration. These scholars opposed the use of terms such as 'environmental refugee' or 'climate refugee' on various grounds. One possible issue was that most 'climate migrants' would not fall within any legal definition of 'refugee'. However, legal definitions are not set in stone, and the definition of 'refugee' can evolve. A more important issue was that the term 'refugee' suggested forced migration, while, migration scholars pointed out, environmental factors could *influence* without necessarily *forcing* migration, and any individual migration decision should rather be situated on a continuum between 'voluntary' and 'forced' migration. More fundamentally, these scholars questioned the very concept of 'climate migration' as implying excessive simplification of migration decisions. Thus, Richard Bilsborrow, Steve Lonergan, JoAnn McGregor, and Astri Suhrke, among others, insisted that it would be unhelpful to approach migration as if it was 'produced' by environmental factors in a vacuum.[31] Environmental factors were part of a wider cluster of causes; little was gained, and much was lost, in approaching 'environmental migration' – and *a fortiori* 'climate migration' – in isolation from more direct social, economic, political, demographic, and cultural factors of migration.

Multiple analytical studies carried out and published since the 1990s have provided support to this critique.[32] Many environmental scholars acknowledged

[29] See James Morrissey, 'Environmental Change and Forced Migration: A State of the Art Review' (2009) Refugee Studies Centre Background Paper, available at perma.cc/RS9Y-MMU7.

[30] IPCC First Assessment Report, *Climate Change: The IPCC Impacts Assessment* (Canberra, Australian Governmental Publishing Service 1990) 5–10 (emphasis added).

[31] See Richard E Bilsborrow, 'Rural Poverty, Migration and the Environment in Developing Countries: Three Case Studies' (1992) *World Bank Policy Research Working Paper* 1017; JoAnn McGregor, 'Climate Change and Involuntary Migration: Implications for Food Security' (1994) 19(2) *Food Policy* 120, available at doi.org/10.1016/0306-9192(94)90065-5; Astri Suhrke, 'Environmental Degradation and Population Flows' (1994) 47(2) *Journal of International Affairs* 473, available at www.jstor.org/stable/24357292; Steve Lonergan, 'The Role of Environmental Degradation in Population Displacement' (1998) 4 *Environmental Change and Security Project Report* 5.

[32] See, for example, James Morrissey, 'Rethinking the "Debate on Environmental Refugees": From "Maximalists" to "Proponents" and "Critics"' (2012) 19 *Journal of Political Ecology* 36, available at

the consensus among migration scholars that climate change is rarely, if ever, a discrete factor of migration.[33] For instance, a 2011 study commissioned by the UK Government Office for Science, Foresight, concluded that 'the range and complexity of the interactions between [multiple] drivers [of migration] mean that it will rarely be possible to distinguish individuals for whom environmental factors are the sole driver'.[34] The report further insisted that '[m]igration decisions are complex, reflecting the interconnectedness of environmental factors with economic, social and political factors'.[35] The IPCC no longer suggests that climate change 'produces' refugees in abstraction from other factors. Rather, the Fifth Assessment Report noted that, 'given the complex motivations for all migration decisions, it is difficult to categorize any individual as a climate migrant'.[36] And the Sixth Assessment Report points out that, while '[c]limatic conditions, events and variability are important drivers of migration', 'migration responses to specific climate hazards [are] strongly influenced by economic, social, political and demographic processes'.[37] Gregory White's review of some of the most recent publications on climate change and migration reflects the general sense that the concept of 'climate migration … underplay[s] … more proximate causes' of migration 'such as repressive governments, poor policies, failing economies, complicated colonial and cold war legacies, uneven levels of economic development, and civil strife'.[38]

Rather than a single phenomenon, academic debates have identified several causal pathways through which climate change can affect human migration.[39]

doi.org/10.2458/v19i1.21712; Robert McLeman, 'Climate-Related Migration and its Linkages to Vulnerability, Adaptation, and Socio-Economic Inequality: Evidence from Recent Examples', in Mayer and Crépeau (n 3) 29.

[33] See Koko Warner and others, 'Where the Rain Falls: Climate Change, Food and Livelihood Security, and Migration' (United Nations University Institute for Environment and Human Security 2012), available at perma.cc/2XX9-GZ3A; Robert Oakes, Andrea Milan, and Jillian Campbell, 'Kiribati: Climate Change and Migration: Relationships Between Household Vulnerability, Human Mobility and Climate Change' (United Nations University Institute for Environment and Human Security 2016), available at perma.cc/HES2-DAJH; Jos Lelieveld and others, 'Strongly Increasing Heat Extremes in the Middle East and North Africa (MENA) in the 21st Century' (2016) 137 *Climatic Change* 245, available at doi.org/10.1007/s10584-016-1665-6; Richard Black, Dominic Kniveton, and Kerstin Schmidt-Verkerk, 'Migration and Climate Change: Toward an Integrated Assessment of Sensitivity', in Thomas Faist and Jeanette Schade (eds), *Disentangling Migration and Climate Change* (Basel, Springer 2013) 29.

[34] Foresight, 'Migration and Global Environmental Change: Final Project Report' (London, Government Office for Science 2011).

[35] ibid 9.

[36] W Neil Adger and others, 'Human Security', in IPCC Fifth Assessment Report, *Impacts, Adaptation, and Vulnerability, Part A: Global and Sectoral Aspects* (Cambridge, Cambridge University Press 2014) 755, 768 (FAQ 12.3).

[37] Guéladio Cissé and Robert McLeman, 'Health, Wellbeing and the Changing Structure of Communities', in IPCC Sixth Assessment Report, *Impacts, Adaptation and Vulnerability: Working Group II Contribution* (Cambridge, Cambridge University Press 2022) 1041, 1080.

[38] Gregory White, '"Climate Refugees" – A Useful Concept?' (2019) 19 *Global Environmental Politics* 133, 133.

[39] See, for example, Walter Kälin, 'Conceptualising Climate-Induced Displacement', in Jane McAdam (ed), *Climate Change and Displacement: Multidisciplinary Perspectives* (Oxford, Hart 2010) 81, 85–86; Mayer, *The Concept of Climate Migration* (n 9) 21–24; Cissé and McLeman (n 37) 1082.

These include migration triggered by natural disasters, to the extent that climate change makes these disasters more likely, as well as migration attributed to slow-onset environmental changes, to the extent that climate change causes these environmental changes. But climate change could also have more diffuse effects. For instance, it can reduce economic opportunities or the overall wealth of entire populations, thus altering existing economic 'push' and 'pull' factors of migration. Impacts of climate change can also exacerbate conflicts, in particular in situations where tensions relate to access to natural resources (eg arable land and fresh water); these conflicts, in turn, can affect migration. And any natural disaster, environmental change, economic development, conflicts, and migration in one place may affect events in other places, in various, often unpredictable ways. The effects of climate change thus extend *ad infinitum* so that, if one had sufficient information and time to analyse it, one could show that every migrant is, in a sense, a 'climate migrant'.

B. The Limits of Climate Attribution

The literature on 'climate migration' is part of broader academic and advocacy endeavours seeking to attribute personal events to climate change. Not infrequently has legal scholarship suggested the possibility of identifying 'climate victims' – that is, individuals who are injured as a result of climate change.[40] To the extent that migration constitutes or reflects a harmful experience, 'climate migrants' could be described as a subcategory of 'climate victims'.[41]

While the identification of victims is partly a political argument, it also has important legal implications. An individual could justify standing to seek various judicial or quasi-judicial remedies if she can demonstrate that she is the victim of the failure of a given legal person to take sufficient steps to mitigate climate change.[42] Thus, the UN Committee on the Rights of the Child held that the authors

[40] See, for example, Daniel A Farber, 'Basic Compensation for Victims of Climate Change' (2007) 155(6) *University of Pennsylvania Law Review* 1605, available at scholarship.law.upenn.edu/penn_law_review/vol155/iss6/5; Stephen Humphreys, 'Competing Claims: Human Rights and Climate Harms', in Stephen Humphreys (ed), *Human Rights and Climate Change* (Cambridge, Cambridge University Press 2010) 37, 52; Vesselin Popovski and Kieran G Mundy, 'Defining Climate-Change Victims' (2012) 7 *Sustainability Science* 5, available at doi.org/10.1007/s11625-011-0138-0; Margaretha Wewerinke-Singh, *State Responsibility, Climate Change and Human Rights under International Law* (Oxford, Hart 2019); Sumudu Atapattu, 'The Right to a Healthy Environment and Climate Change', in John H Knox and Ramin Pejan (eds), *The Human Right to a Healthy Environment* (Cambridge, Cambridge University Press 2018) 252, 256.

[41] See Giulio Bartolini, 'Introductory Remarks by Giulio Bartolini' (2021) 115 *Proceedings of the ASIL Annual Meeting* 155, 155–56, available at doi.org/10.1017/amp.2021.145, presenting 'climate change refugees' as a category of the 'persons affected by climate change and disasters'.

[42] I do not touch here on an additional difficulty, in justifying a victim status in legal proceedings, of attributing the personal injury to the wrongful conduct of a person or entity (eg a state) rather than to a phenomenon (climate change) resulting from the conduct, partly wrongful and partly justifiable, of many legal persons over a long period of time. See a brief discussion in Benoit Mayer,

of a complaint against five states had 'prima facie established that they ha[d] personally experienced a real and significant harm', thus appearing to 'justify their victim status'.[43] However, the Committee did not have the opportunity to confirm or reverse this *prima facie* finding as the case was dismissed on the ground of another condition of admissibility (the failure of the authors to exhaust national remedies). One obvious limitation of the Committee's *prima facie* reasoning is that, even if the authors of the complaint were victims of climate change, they were not necessarily victims of the failure of any individual state to take sufficiently ambitious steps to reduce its greenhouse gas (GHG) emissions.

At any rate, there are strong obstacles to attributing adverse personal events to climate change. Climate change is certainly harmful, but it does not affect *individuals* in a direct, proximate way. Rather, climate change is one of the best examples of a harm to ecosystems and society as a whole that only has a broad, diffuse, and indirect effect on individuals. The *climate*, after all, is itself a statistical concept – describing the 'average weather' over a period of time, generally agreed to be thirty years.[44] Climate *change* affects various components of the climate system – including the atmosphere (eg warming of the average temperature), the hydrosphere (eg thermal expansion of sea water), the cryosphere (eg melting of the ice sheet), and the biosphere (eg extinction of species) – but these impacts unfold slowly, when considered on the scale of human lives, and they are generally difficult to demonstrate without systematic and rigorous observation. Such impacts impoverish the environment in which we live in multiple ways, for instance by raising sea level and increasing the likelihood of strong storms, but this broad, diffuse harm does not directly affect anyone *in particular*.

The existence of 'climate victims' in general, or 'climate migrants' in particular, has been invoked in the context of two types of climate impacts: extreme weather events and slow-onset changes. With regard to extreme weather events, scholars have referred to 'the emergence of the science of attribute of extreme weather events' to claim that it is 'possible to attribute individual losses to human-caused climate change'.[45] Others, however, have shown that the findings of weather-event

'Attribution Science and the Fate of Climate Litigation' (2022) 13(5) *Global Policy* 831, available at doi.org/10.1111/1758-5899.13153.

[43] UN Committee on the Rights of the Child, Communication No 104/2019, *Chiara Sacchi v Argentina*, UN Doc CRC/C/88/D/104/2019, para 10.14. Similar claims to victimhood were dismissed in other cases. See, for example, *Greenpeace Nordic Association v Ministry of Petroleum and Energy* (2020) Case no 20-051052SIV-HRET, paras 167–68, 171 (dismissing claims based on the European Human Rights Convention because of the absence of actual and imminent risk); Bundesgericht [BGer] [Federal Supreme Court] May 5, 2020, 1C_37/2019, paras 5.4–5.5 (*Verein KlimaSeniorinnen Schweizet v Eidgenössisches Departement für Umwelt*) (Switz.).

[44] Robin JB Matthews and others, 'Glossary', in IPCC Sixth Assessment Report, *The Physical Science Basis: Working Group I Contribution* (Cambridge, Cambridge University Press 2021) 2215, 2222.

[45] Friederike EL Otto and others, 'Causality and the Fate of Climate Litigation: The Role of the Social Superstructure Narrative' (2022) 13(5) *Global Policy* 736, 737–38, available at doi.org/10.1111/1758-5899.13113. See also, for example, Sophie Marjanac and Lindene Patton, 'Extreme Weather Event Attribution Science and Climate Change Litigation: An Essential Step in the Causal Chain?' (2018)

attribution studies rely largely on arbitrary premises (eg the definition of the adverse event) and questionable methodological choices.[46] At any rate, weather attribution studies attribute events to climate change in a probabilistic manner rather than in a binary one. Saying that the risk of an intense storm increased by 50 per cent does not mean that the individuals affected by that storm are 'climate victims'.

Overall, the effect of extreme weather events on society is contingent to multiple non-physical factors. Whether an extreme weather event causes a disaster depends, among other things, on the social, economic, political, cultural, and demographic context in which this event takes place. Despite the increased frequency of extreme weather events in recent decades, the number of casualties from such disasters has steadily *decreased*, both in proportion of the world's population and in absolute terms – a conclusion that hold for any specific categories of weather-related disasters considered separately, such as drought, floods, storms, landslides, wildfires, and extreme temperatures.[47] Thus, whether someone dies in an extreme weather event depends far more on development and disaster-reduction policies implemented by the territorial state than on the extreme weather event itself, whose likelihood may be affected by climate change. The premise of disaster-risk reduction, after all, is that certain measures *can* reduce the impacts of physical events on society.[48]

There is little evidence to support the frequent assertion that the number of individuals migrating in response to disasters has increased, let alone that this putative increase is due to climate change.[49] Statistics on displacement in the context of disasters are far less advanced and less reliable than statistics on

36(3) *Journal of Energy & Natural Resources Law* 265, 288, available at doi.org/10.1080/02646811.2018.1451020; Elena Cima, 'The Right to a Healthy Environment: Reconceptualizing Human Rights in the Face of Climate Change' (2022) 31 *Review of European, Comparative & International Environmental Law* 38, 41–42, available at doi.org/10.1111/reel.12430.

[46] Mike Hulme, 'Attributing Weather Extremes to "Climate Change": A Review' (2014) 38(4) *Progress in Physical Geography: Earth and Environment* 499, available at doi.org/10.1177/0309133314538644; Mike Hulme, Saffron J O'Neill, and Suraje Dessai, 'Is Weather Event Attribution Necessary for Adaptation Funding?' (2011) 334(6057) *Science* 764; Greg Lusk, 'The Social Utility of Event Attribution: Liability, Adaptation, and Justice-Based Loss and Damage' (2017) 143 *Climatic Change* 201, available at doi.org/10.1007/s10584-017-1967-3; Kevin E Trenberth, John T Fasullo, and Theodore G Shepherd, 'Attribution of Climate Extreme Events' (2015) 5(8) *Nature Climate Change* 725, available at doi.org/10.1038/nclimate2657.

[47] See, for example, Hannah Ritchie, Pablo Rosado, and Max Roser, 'Natural Disasters' (*Our World in Data*, 2014), available at perma.cc/J96P-6AVU.

[48] See Kirsten Hagon, 'Protecting People in the Context of Climate Change and Disasters: Setting the Scene' (2021) 115 *Proceedings of the ASIL Annual Meeting* 156, 157, available at doi.org/10.1017/amp.2021.146, observing that 'adaptation/disaster risk reduction action works'.

[49] See, for example, Hagon (n 48) 156–57. The data to which Hagon refers show an increase in the number of 'climate and weather related' disasters between 1960 and 2000, but no increase – but possibly a slight decrease – from 2000 to 2019. See 'Come Heat or High Water: Tackling the Humanitarian Impacts of the Climate Crisis Together' (International Federation of Red Cross and Red Crescent Societies 2020) 22, available at www.ifrc.org/document/world-disasters-report-2020. This trend does not correlate with the impacts of climate change, that have intensified in the last two decades.

casualties, probably because of the greater difficulty of defining and accounting for displacement. The Global Internal Displacement Database, set up by the Internal Displacement Monitoring Centre in 2008, shows no increase in the number of people displaced by weather-related disasters or by any sub-categories thereof (rather, it suggests a slight decrease).[50] But even if the number of individuals displaced in weather-related disasters did increase, climate change would only be one of many factors that could explain this increased mobility. Among the multiple possible explanations would be an evolution of the way societies respond to hazardous events – for instance by setting up early-warning systems that enable people to 'migrate' out of harm's way.

By contrast to extreme weather events, it may appear easier to attribute injury and migration to climate change in relation to slow-onset impacts such as land degradation and sea-level rise. Surely, if a territory is to become uninhabitable between now and a point in future, populations will have to migrate during this period. This objection is often raised in relation to atolls, although it could also be stated about territories that are prone to land degradation and desertification.[51]

This objection, however, ignores the significance of the long timescale over which such impacts unfold. Over decades, it is difficult to disentangle the effect of slow-onset climate impacts from other (geo)political, social, and economic processes that affect human mobility. For now at least, John Cornell observes that 'contemporary environmental changes in most islands in the southwest Pacific' are 'more likely … responses to local stresses of various kinds, from geophysical to human, including tectonic movements, cyclones, seawall construction, and sand mining' than to climate change.[52] Likewise, Mortreux finds 'no empirical evidence' in the literature in support of the frequent 'assumption … that migration driven by climate change is already happening' from atolls.[53] In years to come, an accelerating rate of sea-level rise will exacerbate issues of land and fresh water scarcity. This, however, will manifest in an increasing cost of living on atoll islands[54] and, thus, a stronger economic incentive for migration. There is likely to be an increase in the number of individuals migrating on certain routes but many, if not all, of these individuals will be indistinguishable from other economic migrants.

[50] See 'Global Internal Displacement Database' (Internal Displacement Monitoring Centre, 2023), available at perma.cc/EWX5-KGVZ.

[51] Avidan Kent and Simon Behrman, 'An Alternative Introduction: An Interview with the Editors, Which Never took Place', in Simon Behrman and Avidan Kent (eds), *Climate Refugees: Global, Local and Critical Approaches* (Cambridge, Cambridge University Press 2022) 1, 9.

[52] John Connell, 'Vulnerable Islands: Climate Change, Tectonic Change, and Changing Livelihoods in the Western Pacific' (2015) 27 *The Contemporary Pacific* 1, 3, available at www.jstor.org/stable/24809812. See also Hans Portner and others, 'Technical Summary', in IPCC Sixth Assessment Report, *Impacts, Adaptation and Vulnerability: Working Group II Contribution* (n 37) 37, 66.

[53] Colette Mortreux and others, 'Climate Change and Migration from Atolls? No Evidence Yet' (2023) 60(101234) *Current Opinion in Environmental Sustainability* 1, 1, available at doi.org/10.1016/j.cosust.2022.101234.

[54] Michelle Mycoo and Morgan Wairiu, 'Small Islands' in IPCC Sixth Assessment Report, *Impacts, Adaptation and Vulnerability: Working Group II Contribution* (n 37) 2043, 2095–96.

A mere statistical increase in the number of migrants does not justify essentialising 'climate migration' as a distinct phenomenon. There may be more migrants in the real world than there would be in a counterfactual world without climate change, but this does not mean that there is a discrete population of 'climate migrants'. If, for instance, one could conclude that climate change has increased the number of migrants by 30 million, this does not mean that there is a population of 30 million migrants who can individually be attributed to climate change. In a sense, most, perhaps all, of the 280 million international migrants in today's world[55] could justify that climate change features somewhere in the centuries-long chain of events that influenced their decision to migrate. Most, perhaps all, would not have migrated – or not in the same way, not to the same destination, not for the same duration, not from the same place – were it not for some impacts of climate change, and for the other effects of activities causing climate change.

C. Causation in a Chaotic World

The two previous subsections have hinted to a more general issue with the attribution of migration (and other individual effects) to climate change and, *a fortiori*, to individual activities contributing marginally to causing climate change. This more fundamental issue is that any interference with complex physical, ecological, and social systems causes ripple effects *ad infinitum* in unpredictable yet potentially very significant ways. No individual circumstances would be identical today were it not, among many other things, for the economic development the Industrial Revolution brought about; for the geopolitical implications of fossil-fuel production; for the possibility of rapid long-distance transportation; or for the conversion of natural lands into artificial lands. A world without climate change, or without the activities causing it, would be unrecognisable.

Chaos theory can help understand this issue. Chaos, in its mathematical meaning, characterises a system where 'the high sensitivity to initial conditions makes it impossible to practically determine the future evolution of [this] system, because the initial conditions are never known with total precisions'.[56] True chaotic systems follow physical rules (ie they are not truly random) but, due to their extreme sensitivity to initial conditions, they are unpredictable (ie they *appear* to be random. Pierre-Simon Laplace famously suggested that, for an omniscient intelligence – one knowing the situation and forces affecting every single object in the universe – 'nothing would be uncertain, and the future, like the past, would be open to its

[55] 'World Migration Report 2022' (International Organization for Migration 2022), available at perma.cc/SW7A-XNVV, 3.

[56] Étienne Ghys, 'The Lorenz Attractor, a Paradigm for Chaos', in Bertrand Duplantier, Stéphane Nonnenmacher, and Vincent Rivasseau (eds), *Chaos: Poincaré Seminar 2010* (Basel, Springer 2013) 1, 2–3.

eyes'.[57] In practice, however, we are unable to collect and analyse sufficient information to make comprehensive predictions on the long-term evolution of chaotic systems, or that of systems influenced by unpredictable human decisions.

The weather system is an example of a chaotic system: it follows physical rules, but its sensitivity to initial conditions is such that prediction is practically impossible beyond a few days.[58] Even though social, political, economic, and psychological systems may not be fully determined by physical rules, they can be approached by analogy with chaotic systems, in the sense that small differences in initial conditions can cause vast ripple effects.[59] Small decisions can affect human life in important but unpredictable ways, from romantic encounters to accidental injuries, with compounding consequences over time. Think of the world we would be living in, had Adolf Hitler attended art school.

The high sensitivity of chaotic system to initial conditions implies a high sensitivity to any variation of these conditions. Edward Lorenz suggested that 'a small alteration … will cause subsequent states to differ greatly from the states that would have followed without the alteration'.[60] He famously illustrated this point by wondering whether 'the flap of a butterfly's wings in Brazil [could] set off a tornado in Texas'.[61] The offsetting of a tornado, he quickly added, is just an example: the flap of a butterfly's wing (and 'the activities of innumerable more powerful creatures') 'can equally well be instrumental in preventing a tornado', or in causing, or preventing, many other consequences.[62] As far as such chaotic systems are concerned, anything happening today could have extensive (but unpredictable) effects on anything that happens in the future. Your decision to turn the page of this book or to scroll down to next paragraph could cause – or, just as well, prevent – storms, famines, and wars for the centuries to come.

Humankind has certainly more direct influence on planetary systems than a butterfly's wings. Among other things, human activity has resulted in the emission of well over two trillion tonnes of carbon dioxide, which has significantly altered the radiative forcing of the Earth's atmosphere and caused major upheaval in our climate system.[63] The concept of the Anthropocene, as a new geological era, was coined to reflect the idea that humans are now the greatest force that alters planetary systems – as illustrated by climate change.[64]

From this perspective, it is obvious that many phenomena, including human mobility, are affected by our impacts on the planet. If the flap of a butterfly can set

[57] Pierre S Laplace, *A Philosophical Essay on Probabilities* (Frederick W Truscott and Frederick L Emory trans, New York, John Wiley & Sons 1902) 4.

[58] Edward N Lorenz, *The Essence of Chaos* (Seattle, University of Washington Press 1993) 77.

[59] See Alain Albert (ed), *Chaos and Society* (Washington, DC, IOS Press 1995).

[60] Lorenz (n 58) 206.

[61] ibid 181.

[62] ibid.

[63] Jim Skea and others, 'Summary for Policymakers', in IPCC Sixth Assessment Report, *Mitigation of Climate Change: Working Group III Contribution* (Cambridge University Press 2022) 6.

[64] Paul J Crutzen, 'The "Anthropocene"', in Eckart Ehlers and Thomas Krafft (eds), *Earth System Science in the Anthropocene* (Basel, Springer 2006).

off a tornado, surely, the emission of over two trillion tonnes of carbon dioxide – or the activities causing such emissions – can have similar effects. And, in turn, weather events affect complex social systems, including human mobility. The only question worth asking, therefore, is not *whether* global environmental changes are affecting human mobility – they obviously do – but *whether* and *how far* these effects can be predicted.

It is worth highlighting that the argument here does not deny the possibility any form of prediction. Some of the more direct consequences of human actions can be predicted in a reliable manner, in much the same way was a weather agency can predict the effects of a cold front. Many causal claims are situated in simple, non-chaotic systems, ignoring remote effects. In tort law, for instance, judges usually limit their consideration to the consequences of one's action that are relatively proximate and reasonably foreseeable.[65] Some other causal claims involve chaotic systems, but at a level of abstraction that allows the identification of significant statistical trends. For instance, the actual effect of the emission of a tonne of carbon dioxide is unpredictable – it might prevent a deadly storm just as well as cause one – but, on average, one can expect that the emission of a tonne of carbon dioxide will further exacerbate climate change.[66]

More harm occurs in a world with climate change compared with a world where the same human activities could have taken place without GHG emissions, and possibly also compared with a world where fewer GHG-emitting activities would have taken place. Yet, seeking to determine *which* harmful events would not have occurred were it not for the emission of two trillion tonnes of carbon dioxide, or were it not for some of GHG-emitting activities, is a vain endeavour. Any single activity that took place decades ago has irremediably transformed the evolution of multiple chaotic or quasi-chaotic socio-physical systems to date. It makes no sense to try to determine whether a given individual would have migrated in the absence of these two trillion tonnes of carbon dioxide emissions when that individual would likely not have been born, or would not have been at the same location at the same time, had these emissions not taken place.

It is worth emphasising that this is not an issue that more scientific research could address. Even a person with infinite knowledge would be unable to identify 'climate migrants' because the question simply does not make sense in a world profoundly altered by climate change. Ignoring this ontological issue has allowed arbitrary choices in the framing of 'climate migration'. For instance, the emphasis in the discourse has generally been on adverse 'push' factors, such as the effects of climate change on low-lying or drought-prone areas, rather than on potential 'pull' factors from climate impacts, for instance from new agricultural lands.

[65] Christian Witting, *Street on Torts*, 15th edn (Oxford, Oxford University Press 2018) 151.

[66] See Josep G Canadell and others, 'Global Carbon and Other Biogeochemical Cycles and Feedbacks', in IPCC Sixth Assessment Report, *The Physical Science Basis: Working Group I Contribution* (n 44) 673, 742, noting the 'near-linear relationship between cumulative emissions of CO_2 and the resulting global warming'.

More fundamentally, climate change cannot be addressed without regulating the activities causing these emissions, and these activities are also affecting migration patterns in multiple ways, for instance by facilitating transportation, accelerating economic development in some places, and causing geopolitical turmoil. To the extent that a discourse on 'climate migration' is deployed as a means to advocate for the regulation of GHG-emitting activities, it is artificial to consider the effects of these activities that are mediated by the climate system without also considering the more direct (and, at times, more positive) effects of these activities on societies.

III. The Persistent Discourse on 'Climate Migration'

This section observes and seeks to explain the persistence of a discourse on 'climate migration' despite the conceptual issues identified in the previous section. A first subsection presents evidence of the persistence of this discourse. The second subsection explores several explanations, one of which being that scholars are willing to ignore the conceptual flaws of a discourse which, they reckon, would help pursue political goals they support. The third subsection questions the political impact of a discourse on 'climate migration'.

A. Irresponsiveness to Critique

The issues with the concept of 'climate migration' have long been known.[67] Yet, political leaders and the media often keep referring to 'climate refugees' as if they were a definite population of migrants who have been – as the IPCC had put it in 1990 – '*produced*' by climate change.[68] Even some of the most reputable newspapers often ignore the findings of relevant analytical studies on the impact of climate change on migration in the last two or three decades.[69]

More surprisingly perhaps, a large part of the academic law-and-policy literature on the climate–migration nexus does the same. Many scholars simply assume that, as the impacts of climate change continue to unfold, 'whole populations of

[67] See, for example, Roger Zetter, 'Protecting People Displaced by Climate Change: Some Conceptual Challenges', in McAdam (ed) (n 39) 131; Mayer (n 4); Calum TM Nicholson, 'Climate Change and the Politics of Causal Reasoning: The Case of Climate Change and Migration' (2014) 180(2) *The Geographical Journal* 151, available at doi.org/10.1111/geoj.12062; White (n 38); Sarah L Nash, *Negotiating Migration in the Context of Climate Change: International Policy and Discourse* (Policy Press 2019) 6–8.

[68] See IPCC First Assessment Report (n 30). See, for example, John R Wennersten and Denise Robbins, *Rising Tides: Climate Refugees in the Twenty-First Century* (Bloomington, Indiana University Press 2017).

[69] See Edward Wong, 'Resettling China's "Ecological Migrants"' (*New York Times*, 25 October 2016), available at perma.cc/Y88K-7ZUJ; Coral Davenport and Campbell Robertson, 'Resettling the First American "Climate Refugees"' (*New York Times*, 3 May 2016), available at perma.cc/P3AW-CMUK.

"climate refugees" will be created'.[70] Scholars continue to advocate for protection of 'climate refugees', possibly through a treaty creating a status for 'climate refugees'[71] or for an extension of complementary protection mechanisms for 'their' benefits.[72] These include leading scholars such as François Gemenne, who argued that 'they' should be called 'climate refugees' on the ground of the political impact this word could have.[73] In three successive books published between 2018 and 2022, Simon Behrman and Avidan Kent advocated for a legal protection of 'climate refugees'.[74] In one of these books, Jolanda van der Vliet and Frank Biermann asserted that 'climate migrants have special protection needs that are not always similar to those of other migrants'.[75] In turn, this academic and media discourse influences the political discourse.[76]

In their latest book, Kent and Behrman sought to justify that climate change can be attributed to climate change. They claim that '*in some cases*, the link between climate change and migration is in fact very clear',[77] and they seek to demonstrate this with two examples. This objection needs to be considered.

The first example concerns 'the residents of Pacific Islands'.[78] The only evidence Kent and Behrman provide, however, is a study on the physical impact of sea-level rise and other climate effects on atoll islands, which demonstrates that atolls 'may be uninhabitable within decades'.[79] This study does not claim that 'climate refugees' can be identified today – as Kent and Behrman claim – or even in the future. The depopulation of islands over several decades can occur gradually, with climate impacts exacerbating economic factors of migration, so that – in populations that have long been very mobile – it would remain impossible to disentangle climate change from other factors of migration.[80] And even if a complete evacuation of

[70] Andrew T Guzman, *Overheated: The Human Cost of Climate Change* (New York, Oxford University Press 2013) 174. See also, for example, César Rodríguez-Garavito, 'Introduction', in César Rodríguez-Garavito (ed), *Litigating the Climate Emergency: How Human Rights, Courts, and Legal Mobilization Can Bolster Climate Action* (Cambridge, Cambridge University Press, 2023) 1, at 1, upholding a prediction that 'up to a billion human beings … may become climate refugees by 2050' from a news report.

[71] See Frank Biermann and Ingrid Boas, 'Towards a Global Governance System to Protect Climate Migrants: Taking Stock', in Mayer and Crépeau (n 3) 405.

[72] See Susan F Martin, 'Towards an Extension of Complementary Protection?', in Mayer and Crépeau (n 3) 449.

[73] See François Gemenne, 'The Refugees of the Anthropocene', in Mayer and Crépeau (n 3) 394.

[74] Behrman and Kent (n 10); Kent and Behrman (n 11); Behrman and Kent (n 51).

[75] Jolanda van der Vliet and Frank Biermann, 'Global Governance of Climate Migrants: A Critical Evaluation of the Global Compacts', in Behrman and Kent (n 51) 60, 81.

[76] See, for example, remarks made by the US President Barack Obama at the United Nations Summit on Climate Change, 'Obama Addresses Climate Change in UN Speech' (PBS News, 22 September 2009), available at perma.cc/84CQ-4UD7.

[77] Behrman and Kent (n 51) 9 (emphasis added).

[78] ibid.

[79] Curt D Storalazzi, Edwin PL Ellias, and Paul Berkowitz, 'Many Atolls May be Uninhabitable within Decades Due to Climate Change' (2015) 5 *Scientific Reports* 14546, available at doi.org/10.1038/srep14546.

[80] See discussion in Mortreux and others (n 53).

some inhabited atolls or atoll states becomes necessary due to sea-level rise and other factors (eg subsidence and environmental degradation), these evacuees would have little in common with other individuals whom Kent and Behrman consider as 'climate refugees' (eg individuals displaced by a natural disaster); rather, they would share similar needs with other non-climate-related evacuation scenarios (eg caused by volcanic eruption).[81]

The second example Kent and Behrman provide regards the migration of coastal communities in Bangladesh.[82] Yet, here again, Kent and Behrman misconstrue the evidence they rely on, that is, mainly, a study concluding that migration can be attributed '*in part*' to 'the adverse consequences of [soil] *salinity* on crop production'.[83] Soil salinity, itself, can partly be attributed to climate change, but also partly to local activities ranging from fresh water management to shrimp production.[84] The authors of the study do not claim that the probabilistic link they identify between salinity and migration permits the identification of individual 'salinity migrants', let alone 'climate refugees'. Neither of these examples shows that climate change can be 'a direct cause for migration' as Kent and Behrman claim.[85]

Overall, Kent and Behrman's reasoning builds on a simplistic conception of human migration. They assume that environmental factors will cause migration like dominos fall, rather than as part of a cluster of causes involving individual and political agency. This approach, once again, is reminiscent of the literature on 'environmental refugees' from the late 1980s and early 1990s,[86] before migration scholars entered the room. Indeed, Kent and Behrman rely on studies in physical science, but not on migration scholarship, in support of their claims about the way migration will be affected by climate change.[87]

Other attempts have been made to address the flaws of the discourse on 'climate migration', but merely with cosmetic fixes. For instance, the UN General Assembly referred not to 'climate migrants', but to 'migrants compelled to leave their countries of origin owing to … the adverse effects of climate change'.[88] Kent and Behrman (in an earlier book) appeared to dismiss the conceptual critique summarised above as merely relating to 'issues regarding nomenclature'.[89] There

[81] See Robert McLeman, *Climate Change and Human Migration: Past Experiences, Future Challenges* (Cambridge, Cambridge University Press, 2013), 201, drawing an analogy with the impact of a volcanic eruption on the British overseas territory of Monserrat.

[82] Behrman and Kent (n 51) 9.

[83] Joyce Chen and Valerie Muller, 'Coastal Climate Change, Soil Salinity and Human Migration in Bangladesh' (2018) 8 *Nature Climate Change* 981, 981, available at doi.org/10.1038/s41558-018-0313-8 (emphasis added).

[84] See, for example, Md Mahmuduzzaman and others, 'Causes of Salinity Intrusion in Coastal Belt of Bangladesh.' (2014) 4 *International Journal of Plant Research* 8, available at article.sapub.org/10.5923.s.plant.201401.02.html.

[85] Behrman and Kent (n 51) 9.

[86] See above text at nn 20–26.

[87] Behrman and Kent go on citing other studies, but none of them supports the existence of individuals whose migration can be attributed to climate change.

[88] Global Compact for Safe, Orderly and Regular Migration (n 20) para 21(h).

[89] Kent and Behrman (n 11) 41.

is no doubt, as Kent and Behrman insist, that a legal definition of 'refugee' could be extended – the question is to *whom* it should be extended, following their argument on climate change, if no individual migrant can be attributed to climate change. No terminological, nomenclatural, or definitional change can address the ontological issues barring the attribution of individual migrants to climate change: notwithstanding whether they are called 'climate refugees', 'climate migrants', or anything else, 'they' are approached as a distinct population 'produced' by climate change. Efforts to address 'climate migration' are in vain if one cannot pinpoint instances of such migration.

Some publications contain caveats acknowledging the complexity of the relation between climate change and migration but, as Calum Nicholson noted, these publications 'then go on to discuss "environmental migration" as if those caveats had not been made'.[90] The frequent recognition of the 'multicausality of climate migration'[91] reflects the self-contradicting nature of such caveats. If migration is multicausal, then it cannot be attributed fully to climate change.

Irremediably, any discussion of the law applicable to 'climate migrants' or 'climate migration' assumes that a discrete population or phenomenon can be singled out. Any attempt to identify a gap in how 'they' are protected by the Refugee Convention, any evaluation of whether laws and policies should encourage 'them' in their migration endeavour, any assessment of how 'their' rights are being affected through migration or at the place or destination, or any discussion on a possible status that could be applied to protect 'them' or alternative assistance or protection policies for 'their' benefit – any such discourse inevitably relies on the assumption that 'they', as a group, can be singled out from a broader population.

B. Possible Explanations

There are several factors that may contribute to explain the persistence of a conceptually flawed discourse on 'climate migration'. For one, the compartmentalisation of knowledge certainly plays a role. The law-and-policy literature, in particular, is often compartmentalised away from research in migration studies. It is striking how rarely legal publications on the climate–migration nexus reference studies in other disciplines, especially in social sciences such as migration studies. By and large, most modern universities do not live up to the mission, suggested by the

[90] Nicholson (n 67) 153. See also text above, at n 21, for a recent illustration.

[91] See, for example, Gervais Appave and others, 'Organizational Perspectives: IOM's Role and Perspectives on Climate Change, Migration and the Law', in Mayer and Crépeau (n 3) 288; Mariam T Chazalnoel and Dina Ionesco, 'Perspectives from the International Organization for Migration (IOM): Breaking New Ground on the Governance of Climate Migration', in Behrman and Kent (n 51) 103; Mariam T Chazalnoel and Diana Ionesco, 'Perspectives from the International Organization for Migration (IOM): Breaking New Ground on the Governance of Climate Migration', in Behrman and Kent (n 51) 41, 50; Beatriz F Pérez, 'Climate Migration and Its Inclusion in Mexican Legal and Political Frameworks', in Behrman and Kent (n 51) 183, 214.

etymology of the word 'university', of turning scholars from various backgrounds into a single community. Law students and scholars are more likely to hear about 'climate refugees' from the media than they are to learn about the diffuse impact of climate change on migration from migration scholars. The media is thus continuously directing a flow of new scholars and postgraduate students into research on 'climate migrants'.[92] A frequent presumption is that, if so many media and politicians keep referring to 'climate migration', there must be a thing behind the concept.[93] Incoming researchers seldom have or take the time to read what migration scholars have to say about the effects of climate change on migration, at least at the beginning of their research.

A second factor relates to path dependence. We, researchers, are generally reluctant to take new insights into account when these new insights would fundamentally alter the assumptions on which we have based our research. Publication incentives encourage us to publish documents that are not fully researched, even while knowing that we have kept large stones unturned. In my own case, I was not entirely unaware that what I discounted as mere 'definitional issue[s]'[94] in my master's thesis might have been, in fact, epistemological or ontological ones – but the work had to be completed, the thesis had to be handed over, and the publication had to be finalised. The process of applying for research funding may further lock us into research projects even when realising their flawed assumptions.

Yet there may also be a more fundamental cause: a certain confusion between academic and political endeavours. A political agenda, it seems, has led some researchers unwittingly to compromise academic rigour. Thus, despite formally acknowledging the many reasons *not* to speak about 'climate refugees', Gemenne promoted this term in academic publications conspicuously on the ground that this term would 'recognize … that these migrations are first and foremost the result of a persecution that we are inflicting to the most vulnerable'.[95] While Gemenne is particularly clear about it, personal experience over the last decade suggests that other scholars in the field view the concept of 'climate migration' as a tool for political advocacy too – whether they seek to protect of the environment or to advance the protection of the human rights of migrants. Instead of the ability to understand and explain what we observed in the world, the use of the concept of 'climate migration' is often justified based on its putative ability to bring about policy change; a concept that has more to do with advocacy than with scholarship.

[92] See, for example, Giovanni Sciaccaluga, *International Law and the Protection of 'Climate Refugees'* (London, Palgrave Macmillan 2020), xiii, recounting his first encounter with the concept of 'environmental refugees' through a television documentary. On the simplistic representations of the climate-migration nexus conveyed by mass media and other forms of entertainment, see also Gregory White, 'The "Others" in John Lanchaster's *The Wall*', ch 4 in this volume.

[93] See ibid at 43–44.

[94] Mayer (n 1) 368.

[95] See François Gemenne, 'The Refugees of the Anthropocene', in Mayer and Crépeau (n 3) 394.

Here is not the place to engage with the complex debate about the relationship between scholarship and activism.[96] Suffice it to note that, whether or not scholars believe that they can use their research to promote the political causes dear to them, there ought to be a red line. Rigour and honesty are among the bedrock principles of academic research, with utility to a political cause at most a secondary concern; for activism, however, the bedrock is – as the word suggests – action, and if a concern for rigour and honesty lead to complexity where action requires conclusions with the simplicity to have utility, then it is quite common for such inconvenient scruples to be side-lined entirely.

Publications that continue using the concept of 'climate migration' for purely political goals have a disturbing family resemblance with a more general trend in twenty-first century politics. 'Post-truth' was named the word of the year 2016 by the Oxford Dictionaries after being widely used in relation to the political campaigns leading to Brexit in the United Kingdom and to the election of President Donald Trump in the United States.[97] In the post-truth era, a memorialist of Russia's President Vladimir Putin wrote, 'no one even tries proving the "truth". You can just say anything.'[98] But while Trumpism/Putinism is an extreme form, the trend extends beyond politics and affect society as a whole, including academia. Post-truth politics stems largely from a technological evolution in modern societies, in particular the development of social media and homophilous sorting – that is, the creation of clusters of like-minded individuals to whom a catered 'version of truth', a set of unchallenged dogmas, can be served.[99] Post-truth politics may rely on direct lies but, more often, it is simply based on a truncated version of facts mixed with loaded concepts and tendentious arguments selected to fit the worldview of a particular audience. In that sense, post-truth politics is not confined to populist demagoguery and commercial news outlets but may certainly extend to academic echo chambers as well.

Modern societies have traditionally relied on a set of institutions to develop some relative consensus on what is most likely to be true, from the movement of planets around the sun all the way to the impact of emitting two billion tonne of carbon dioxide within a few decades. Academia plays a central role in the creation and ascertainment of knowledge in a society, in particular through schools and the media. One of our roles, as scholars, is thus 'to provide the best information possible as the basis for public policy'.[100] Certainly, as *The Economist* noted in a report

[96] See Tarunabh Khaitan, 'On Scholactivism in Constitutional Studies: Skeptical Thoughts' (2022) 20(2) *International Journal of Constitutional Law* 547, available at doi.org/10.1093/icon/moac039.

[97] See 'Word of the Year 2016' (*Oxford Languages*, 2016), available at perma.cc/Y86C-P5XT.

[98] 'The Post-Truth World: Yes, I'd Lie to you' (*The Economist*, 10 September 2016) citing Peter Pomerantsev, available at perma.cc/89CW-UJ4M.

[99] See Yochai Benkler, *The Wealth of Networks: How Social Production Transforms Markets and Freedom* (New Heaven, Yale University Press 2007); Henry Farrell, 'The Consequences of the Internet for Politics' (2012) 15 *Annual Review of Political Sciences* 35, available at doi.org/10.1146/annurev-polisci-030810-110815.

[100] Kathleen Higgins, 'Post-Truth: A Guide for the Perplexed' (2016) 540 *Nature* 9, available at doi.org/10.1038/540009a.

on post-truth politics, the 'truth-producing infrastructure' of modern societies 'is never close to perfect: it can establish as truth things for which there is little or no evidence; it is constantly prey to abuse by those to whom it grants privileges; and, crucially, it is slow to build but may be quick to break'.[101] Although we make mistakes, we, as scholars, have a moral duty to exert our expert authority with honesty and diligence – we must *try* not to make mistakes. Academia can thus be seen as a touchstone in public debates, providing the facts that help the people and their representatives, in light of their values, to make policy decisions.

In reality, however, one generally becomes a scholar in normatively asymmetrical fields like climate or migration law because one has a personal engagement for climate action or for the rights of migrants. Peer review, the main form of quality controls in academia, does not address the structural bias for scholarly communities in such fields because, often, peers are from a community sharing similar interests, especially in specialised publication venues. Thus, one can get away in a leading environmental law journal with unsubstantiated claims *for more ambition* needed in climate action,[102] but one would not get away with similarly unsubstantiated claims *against more ambition* (ie for the status quo) or, *a fortiori*, *for less such ambition*. Likewise, a community of peers appears to have formed progressively around the concept of 'climate migration' – validating one another's research without questioning its conceptual bases. In fact, there is even a societal expectation that a scholar in climate law would be an advocate for climate action – whereas a scholar in trade law would be an advocate for the protection of international trade, a scholar in energy law would be an advocate for the interests of energy companies, and so on. It is difficult to reconcile this fragmentation of academic research into goal-oriented communities with academia's objective of informing society holistically.

To be clear, my claim is not that we, as scholars, should play no role in political debates. Scholars *can* and perhaps even *should* promote enlightened policies and a better government. They should make policy proposals. In fact, scholars are potentially the strongest opposition to post-truth politics. However, there is a danger of *misusing* our scientific authority and, thus, eroding it. Our authority comes from our persistent effort to do what we are trusted for – 'to provide the best information possible as the basis for public policy'.[103] Developing or defending an analytical concept as a way of promoting a political goal in spite of its analytical defects does no good to this trust. This utilisation of scientific authority to frame a

[101] *The Economist* (n 98).

[102] See, for example, Laura Burgers, 'An Apology Leading to Dystopia: Or, Why Fuelling Climate Change is Tortious' (2022) 11 *Transnational Environmental Law* 419, 427–28. The desirability of a very fast rate of emission reduction is only obvious until one considers the price (not only economic, but also human and ecological) of such efforts. For a well-reasoned (yet still value-based) argument for moderation in global action on climate change mitigation, see William Nordhaus, 'Climate Change: The Ultimate Challenge for Economics' (2019) 109(6) *The American Economic Review* 1991, 2002, available at doi.org/10.1257/aer.109.6.1991.

[103] Higgins (n 100).

political debate comes to reinforce the notion that we have entered the post-truth era and that facts are for bargain; it fuels the decreasing trust of a growing part of society with the 'truth' produced by academic institutions.

C. Ineffective Advocacy

Scholars and advocates have used the concept of 'climate migration' (and analogous terms) with the view of supporting political causes. It is worth taking a moment to consider the effectiveness of this discourse from the perspective of political advocacy. Even if we accept that the end can justify the means – that using a loaded concept is justifiable as a way to advance political goals, not only for advocates, but also for scholars – this justification is relevant only if the means can indeed achieve the end. Yet the following shows that the concept of 'climate migration' is ill-equipped to achieve any of the objectives pursued by advocates and scholars in the field, whether this is the extension of migrants' rights or the reparation of climate harm.[104] Part of the issue is the remarkable (although hardly surprising) absence of 'climate migrants' in the debate about how the law should regulate 'their' situation. Such advocacy *in absentia* is unlikely to benefit any population. Further, it is vulnerable to being exploited by other policy entrepreneurs, in particular to foster repressive agendas.

The first political goal pursued through the concept of 'climate migration' is what I refer to (broadly) as a 'solidarity' argument.[105] This argument is about the protection of 'climate migrants' *as vulnerable individuals*. Yet, the argument is shaky. Rather than individuals displaced because of climate change, arguments for the protection of vulnerable individuals should apply to a category of individuals in a similar situation of vulnerability, whose situation can be improved by the implementation of a given set of response measures (eg at different levels of generality, migrants, forced migrants, internationally forced migrants, child migrants, temporarily displaced persons, or individuals displaced by natural disasters), notwithstanding the cause of this vulnerability. Whether the disaster forcing an individual to run for her life is related to climate change is entirely irrelevant in determining this person's need for, or right to, protection.

Thus, the solidarity argument for an extension of international protection beyond the narrow legal definition of a refugee is more convincingly made using Alexander Betts' concept of 'survival migration'[106] than by reference to 'economic migration', 'environmental migration', or 'climate migration'. Talking about 'climate migration' might be a way for migrants' rights activists to get public attention, but

[104] The following builds on a reflection first presented in Mayer, '"Environmental Migration" as Advocacy' (n 9).

[105] Mayer, 'International Legal Protection' (n 3); Mayer, *The Concept of Climate Migration* (n 9).

[106] Alexander Betts, 'Survival Migration: A New Protection Framework' (2010) 16(3) *Global Governance* 361, available at www.jstor.org/stable/29764952; Betts (n 2).

at the price of an ineffective framing of their argument. Were they to be successful, few if any migrants would benefit from a norm protecting only those individuals able to justify that their migration is due to climate change. By analogy, statutory provisions that provided for the international protection in the context of 'environmental disasters' were repealed on the ground that they were ineffective: not a single person appeared to have benefitted from the protection these provisions offered for well over a decade.[107] The irony is that much of the solidarity argument builds on a critique of the narrow scope of international refugee protection, being limited, in its conventional form, to individuals unable to return to their home country due to a fear of persecution in one of five specified grounds. Extending a protection of 'climate refugees' would do little to address the suggestion that refugee protection is the exception that confirms the rule, namely, the principle that states have every right to send back (and not to allow entry in the first place) someone to a country in which their life and other fundamental rights would be at risk.

A second political goal for the concept of 'climate migration' is to advocate for various conceptions of responsibility. In its most common form, the argument is that the countries that have caused most GHG emissions have a special duty to help those most affected as a result of climate change.[108] This argument is slowly unfolding, in international negotiations on climate change, under an agenda item on 'loss and damage',[109] where migration has largely been singled out as *the* single most pressing issue.[110]

Here again, however, migration does not readily fit within this argument. For one, migration is not necessarily harmful: rather than a loss or damage, it can just as well be a way for individuals to get out of harm's way – a desirable way to adapt to varying circumstances. And to the extent that it is a loss and damage, migration is neither the only, nor necessarily the worst form of it. As such, if it was possible to attribute harm suffered by individuals directly to climate change,[111] a responsibility argument should focus on 'climate victims' in general (eg casualties) rather

[107] See Matthew Scott and Russell Garner, 'Nordic Norms, Natural Disasters, and International Protection: Swedish and Finnish Practice in European Perspective' (2022) 91 *Nordic Journal of International Law* 101, at 122, concluding: 'attempts to formulate a new category of international protection for people displaced across borders in the context of disasters and climate change are likely to generate conceptual confusion and result in judgments that apply potentially even more restrictive criteria than what would otherwise be applied under existing international refugee law or international human rights law'.

[108] See, for example, Jodi L Jacobson, 'Environmental Refugees: A Yardstick of Habitability' (1988) 8(3) *Bulletin of Science, Technology & Society* 257; Gemenne, 'The Refugees of the Anthropocene' in Mayer and Crépeau (n 3).

[109] See Decision 1/CP.13, para 1(c)(iii); Conference of the Parties, Adoption of the Paris Agreement (Paris Agreement) (adopted 12 December 2015) UN Doc FCC/CP/2015/L.9/Rev/1, art 8.

[110] See, for example, Decision 3/CP.18, para 7(a)(vi); Decision 1/CP.21, para 49; Decision 3/CP.22, para 9; Decision 5/CP.23, para 8; Decision 10/CP.24, para 1; Decision -/CMA.4, 'Sharm el-Sheikh Implementation Plan', para 44. See also discussion in Benoit Mayer, 'Migration in the UNFCCC Workstream on Loss and Damage: An Assessment of Alternative Framings and Conceivable Responses' (2017) 6 *Transnational Environmental Law* 107, available at doi.org/10.1017/S2047102516000078.

[111] But see above, section II.B, on the impossibility of identifying individuals as 'climate victims'.

than on 'climate migrants' in particular. It is troubling that the disproportional emphasis on migration among the various forms of loss and damage coincides with developed states' interest in managing global migration by holding migrants in the Global South.[112] This coincidence suggests that, instead of promoting reparation for the benefit of the countries disproportionately affected by the impacts of climate change, the discourse on 'climate migration' is enabling developed countries to impose their own anti-migration agenda on recipient countries.

After several decades, it is more than time to ask whether the discourse on 'climate migration' has achieved anything in relation to the solidarity or responsibility agendas. Some references to climate migration' have admittedly been inserted in policy documents on the governance of migration, including at least two resolutions adopted by the UN General Assembly.[113] Yet it is doubtful that these documents have achieved any concrete policy change, or that they were ever likely to do so. States pledged to 'develop … solutions' for 'migrants compelled to leave their countries of origin owing to … the adverse effects of climate change … in cases where adaptation in or return to their country of origin is not possible'[114] – but this pledge is meaningless if such migrants cannot be identified in the first place. Another commitment, to support 'climate change mitigation and adaptation'[115] as a means to 'minimize the adverse effects and structural factors that compel people to leave their country of origin',[116] merely reiterates existing obligations under (binding) climate treaties in a non-binding instrument.[117] On the other hand, states perpetuated a loaded concept of 'climate migration' by committing to conduct 'joint analysis and sharing of information to better map, understand, predict and address migration movements, such as those that may result from … the adverse effects of climate change'.[118]

As noted, human mobility has also become an increasingly central concept in international climate negotiations, first with regard to adaptation,[119] then increasingly as 'loss and damage'.[120] For years, however, the loss and damage workstream

[112] On the non-entry paradigm in international migration governance, see Bhupinder S Chimni, 'The Geopolitics of Refugee Studies: A View from the South' (1998) 11(4) *Journal of Refugee Studies* 350, available at doi.org/10.1093/jrs/11.4.350-a.

[113] New York Declaration for Refugees and Migrants (n 18) para 43; Global Compact for Safe, Orderly and Regular Migration (n 20) para 21(h). See generally Matthew Scott, 'Migration/Refugee Law (2020)' (2022) 3 *Yearbook of International Disaster Law Online* 615.

[114] Global Compact for Safe, Orderly and Regular Migration (n 20) para 21(h).

[115] ibid para 18(b). See also ibid para 18(i).

[116] ibid para 18 ('objective 2').

[117] See, for example, UN, United Nations Framework Convention on Climate Change (adopted 9 May 1992) UN Doc FCCC/INFORMAL/84, art 4(1)(b), 4(2)(a); Paris Agreement (n 109) art 4(2). See generally Benoit Mayer, *International Law Obligations on Climate Change Mitigation* (Oxford, Oxford University Press 2022) 38–63.

[118] Global Compact for Safe, Orderly and Regular Migration (n 20) para 18(h).

[119] See Decision 1/CP.16, para 16(f).

[120] See, for example, Decision 3/CP.18, para 7(a)(vi); Decision 1/CP.21, para 49; Decision -/CMA.4, 'Funding Arrangements for Responding to Loss and Damage Associated with the Adverse Effects of Climate Change, including a Focus on Addressing Loss and Damage', para 6(b).

has stalled in a succession of action plans, work programmes, mechanisms, committees, and other task forces. States' agreement at COP27 to consider 'new funding arrangements for responding to loss and damage' has been presented as a major development.[121] Yet the prominent inclusion of 'displacement', 'relocation', and 'migration'[122] and more generally the focus on 'rehabilitation, recovery and reconstruction'[123] could as well be a Trojan horse for 'donor' countries to promote policies and measures aimed primarily at limiting South-North international migration. Funding aimed at preventing migration to developed countries would likely not be additional to what developed countries were willing to 'offer' at the first place, and it would do little to repair the structural harm suffered by some developing countries disproportionally affected by climate change.

While there is no evidence that 'climate migration' advocacy has led to a better protection of migrants' rights or to enhanced climate action, the discourse might however have fuelled repressive policies. For many, especially outside of academia, 'climate migrants' are perceived as a threat.[124] Thus, the concept of 'climate migration' has long been invoked as a justification for enhanced border control and military investments.[125] Unlike the argument for a protection of 'climate migrants', the security argument does not suffer from the absence of such individuals. While a legal status only applies to individuals falling within a definition, walls and other control devices nominally built against 'climate migrants' can also 'protect' destination countries just as well against any other migrant.

IV. Possible Ways Forward

So far, this chapter has shown that the concept of 'climate migration' continues to be used despite its flawed premises. This last section discusses ways to look at the climate–migration nexus without working from within it and thereby adopting its flaws. It first takes the perspective of law- and policy-makers, before reverting to academic research.

A. Ways Forward for Law and Policy

While climate change does not cause a *distinct* type of migration, there is no question that it has some significant influence for human mobility. Some migration

[121] Decision -/CMA.4 (n 120) para 2.
[122] ibid para 6(b).
[123] ibid para 1.
[124] See, for example, Mayer, *The Concept of Climate Migration* (n 9) 268–77.
[125] See, for example, Gregory White, *Climate Change and Migration: Security and Borders in a Warming World* (New York, Oxford University Press 2011); Ingrid Boas, *Climate Migration and Security: Securitisation as a Strategy in Climate Change Politics* (Abingdon, Routledge 2015); Todd Miller, *Storming the Wall: Climate Change, Migration, and Homeland Security* (San Francisco, City Lights Publishers 2017).

scenarios are and will be becoming more frequent than before as a proximate consequence of the unfolding of climate impacts. This may apply, for instance, to economic migration *from* areas affected by slow-onset environmental changes. Some other scenarios are and will be becoming less frequent, such as, presumably, economic migration *to* areas whose economy is adversely affected by slow-onset environmental changes.

Naturally, these changes can be relevant to national and local governments and their partners, including international organisations and non-governmental organisations. For instance, predicting long-term rural-to-urban migration is essential to informing predictions about the rate of urbanisation and, thus, to assessing the need for new urban infrastructures (eg subway lines). Likewise, preparing for changes in disaster-induced displacement could help plan for adequate emergency responses. On the other hand, none of this requires the development of a distinct concept of 'climate migration'; rather, this calls for considering various impacts of climate change as part of modelling tools aimed at predicting the evolution of human mobility, along with other demographic and social trends.

A similar argument can be made, more generally, about adaptation to climate change.[126] Predicting the impacts of climate change is relevant, for instance, when devising national or international strategies for the preservation of biological diversity, the conservation of wetlands, and the protection of cultural heritage, or when adopting measures to reduce risks of disaster, to manage fresh water, or to guarantee food security.[127] Yet, it would be absurd to develop *separate* law or policy frameworks to address climate-related impacts on biological diversity, wetlands, and cultural heritage, or to manage climate-related effects on disasters, fresh water, and food production. For instance, no country should build a water reservoir to store water to use in case of a climate-related drought in addition to a water reservoir to use in case of a non-climate-related drought. Rather, an increasing risk of drought should justify the extension of a single water-storage system. Indeed, instead of substantive frameworks,[128] states have generally mainstreamed consideration for climate change adaptation in existing laws and policies.[129]

Likewise, the adoption of a parallel protection regime is an unlikely way forward for law- and policy-makers informed by the literature on the climate–migration nexus. Far less glamorous, the way forward consists in including consideration for the various impacts of climate change, including on migration, in various decisions. At times, such consideration for the impacts of climate change may admittedly

[126] See generally Benoit Mayer, 'Climate Change Adaptation and the Law' (2021) 39 *Virginia Environmental Law Journal* 141.

[127] See Jan McDonald, 'Creating Legislative Frameworks for Adaptation', in Jean Palutikof and others, *Climate Adaptation Futures* (Chichester, Wiley-Blackwell, 2013) 126, at 129.

[128] The only statutory provisions the author is aware of are focused on procedural or financial aspects of adaptation, rather than on substantive questions. See, for example, Climate Change Adaptation Act 2018 (Japan), available at perma.cc/6ENC-PRVG.

[129] Xangbai He, 'Legal and Policy Pathways of Climate Change Adaptation: Comparative Analysis of the Adaptation Practices in the United States, Australia and China' (2018) 7(2) *Transnational Environmental Law* 347, 347, available at doi.org/10.1017/S2047102518000092.

tilt the balance and justify the adoption of substantive measures that would not otherwise have been adopted. For instance, if national authorities anticipate that a higher number of individuals will move from one low-lying region to cities, these authorities may decide in favour of a new urban development (eg a new subway line) that would have not otherwise been necessary. Similarly, with regard to climate change adaptation in general, anticipating an increasing risk of drought could justify building new reservoirs, especially when existing ones are already insufficient. However, this new subway line or these water reservoirs do not aim specifically at responding to climate change-induced migration or climate change-induced drought. Rather, they aim at responding to migration or drought in a context in which migration and drought are expected to become more frequent, among other things, because of climate change.

This, in fact, has largely been the direction followed by law- and policy-makers around the world, explaining the relative lack of prominence of 'climate migration' in *national* law-and-policy discourses.[130] Despite multiple academic proposals, some of which have been actively considered by some political institutions,[131] no country has adopted any law or policy specifically targeted at 'climate refugees'. To the contrary, Sweden and Finland, which had statutory provisions on the protection of individuals unable to return to their home country due to an environmental disaster, repealed these provisions on the ground that they were ineffective.[132] Instead, countries have sought to enhance action aimed at reducing disaster risks and human rights protection, including with international support for development and climate change adaptation.

In this regard, the decision of the Human Rights Committee in *Teitiota v New Zealand* has been vastly misconstrued as paving the road to an international legal protection for 'climate refugees'[133] (or 'people displaced by the impacts of climate change')[134] when, in fact, the critical components of the Committee's reasoning are not specific to climate change. In this case, the Human Rights Committee dismissed Mr Teitiota's claim that New Zealand had breached its obligation to protect his right to life by removing him to his country of origin, Kiribati. However, the Committee suggested that it could have decided otherwise in a case with a different set of facts. What would be instrumental, in the Committee's

[130] On the lack of concrete actions following the discourse on the climate–migration nexus, see David Durand-Delacre, 'Obstacles to Action on "Climate Migration": A Story of Persistent Analytical and Political Ambiguity', ch 5 in this volume.

[131] See, for example, Council of Europe Committee of Ministers, Resolution 2307(2019) on a legal status for 'climate refugees' (Adopted by the Assembly on 3 October 2019 at the 34th Sitting).

[132] See Scott and Garner (n 107); Sarah Louise Nash, 'The View from the Fortress: European Governance Perspectives on Climate Change and Migration', ch 6 in this volume.

[133] Gabriella Citroni, 'Human Rights Committee's Decision on the Case Ieoane Teitiota v New Zealand: Landmark or Will-o'-the-Wisp for Climate Refugees?' (2020) 75 *Questions of International Law* 1, 2.

[134] McAdam (n 14).

reasoning, is the living standard that Mr Teitiota was expected to encounter upon his return to Kiribati. The impacts of climate change may be a part of the equation; but, precisely, they may only be *a part* of the equation.[135]

Admittedly, the Committee did assert that individuals might move across borders 'seeking protection from climate change-related harm'.[136] This statement is somewhat speculative, even when applied to small island states.[137] It remains, however, that this sentence does not inform the Committee's overall reasoning; or, at least, it is not a necessary element to justify either the decision that the Committee arrived at, or that the that Committee signalled it might have arrived at based on a different set of facts. As a whole, the Committee put considerable emphasis on the multiple causes of the degradation of living conditions in Kiribati.[138] Noting that 'all relevant facts and circumstances [had to] be considered' in deciding whether Mr Teitiota's removal was consistent with New Zealand's human rights obligations,[139] the Committee carefully considered various political,[140] sanitary,[141] economic,[142] and demographic[143] factors before alluding to the impacts of climate change.[144] It was never a question, in the Committee's view, of treating climate change as a factor 'producing' individual harm in isolation from the social, economic, and political context.

In the case at issue, the Committee found that none of these factors justified an obligation not to remove Mr Teitiota to Kiribati. Against Mr Teitiota's claim that sea-level rise was 'likely to render Kiribati uninhabitable', the Committee opposed the political contingency of the scenario – the possibility of 'intervening acts by Kiribati, with the assistance of the international community, to take affirmative measures to protect and, where necessary, relocate its population'.[145] Overall, the Committee was rather ambivalent on the causes of environmental degradation that it observed: it mentioned not only the impacts of climate change on sea-level rise and extreme weather events, but also the effects of '[r]apid population growth and urbanization' and '[w]aste contamination',[146] among other things. The main issue Mr Teitiota invoked was the lack of available land in the island of South Tarawa, which has more to do with the rapid demographic growth and urbanisation

[135] See also Giovanna Lauria, 'International Law, the Climate–Migration Nexus, and *Teitiota v New Zealand*' ch 9 in this volume, noting at least an 'ambiguity' in the Committee's decision. Such ambiguity is likely the sign of different views among the members of the Committee.

[136] UNHRC, Communication No 2728/2016, *Ioane Teitiota v New Zealand (Teitiota v New Zealand)*, UN Doc CCPR/C/127/D/2728/2016, para 9.11.

[137] See text above at note 49.

[138] *Teitiota v New Zealand* (n 136) paras 2.1, 2.4.

[139] ibid para 9.3.

[140] ibid para 9.7.

[141] ibid para 9.8.

[142] ibid para 9.9.

[143] ibid para 9.10.

[144] ibid para 9.11.

[145] ibid para 9.12.

[146] ibid para 2.4.

– the island's population was multiplied by ten between 1963 and 2020[147] – than with sea level rise.

Two dissenting Committee members argued that New Zealand should be precluded from removing Mr Teitiota to Kiribati. Interestingly, these two members justified their dissent in different ways. Duncan Laki Muhumuza asserted that the degradation of the living standard in Kiribati was primarily due to 'the evils of climate change'.[148] By contrast, Vasilka Sancin did not seek to attribute the degrading living standard in Kiribati to climate change, but merely argued that Mr Teitiota, upon his return to Kiribati, may 'have no access to safe drinking water', which would pose an imminent threat to his life.[149] Vasilka Sancin's dissenting opinion is more convincing than Dancan Laki Muhumuza's: whether Mr Teitiota could lawfully be removed to Kiribati depended on the living conditions in Kiribati, not on any causal link these living conditions may have with climate change. While Mr Teitiota's claim was framed as that of a 'climate refugee', it could just as well – and as misleadingly – be characterised as a claim of refuge from the impacts of overpopulation, urbanisation, population growth, waste contamination, or underdevelopment – when in fact it was a claim based solely on the overall living standard in Kiribati.

B. Ways Forward for Academic Research

It follows from the critique developed above that there is no need for research on how the law could protect 'climate migrants' or, otherwise, address 'climate migration'. Any substantial policy proposal on 'climate migration' is irremediably flawed by its lack of object (eg the absence of a distinct population of 'climate migrants'). However, these remarks do not exclude the relevance of *other* research endeavours. The following highlights three of the areas related to the climate–migration nexus in which more research might be needed, with a focus on applied, policy-relevant research. This list is not exhaustive.

First, as noted above, there is certainly a need for prediction of the evolution of human migration or mobility along with other demographic and social trends. Such research should take into account the impacts of a changing climate among other factors affecting the evolution of human migration, and it could rely on modelling tools. Yet this research should not be on 'climate migration' – a concept that loads the focus – but just on 'migration'. Thus, this research would look at the reality and see what patterns emerge, rather than begin from an abstraction and

[147] Kiribati National Statistics Office, Kiribati Census Atlas (July 2022), available at perma.cc/7GK8-837B, 11.

[148] Individual opinion of Committee member Duncan Laki Muhumuza in *Teitiota v New Zealand* (n 136) para 6.

[149] Individual opinion of Committee member Vasilka Sancin in *Teitiota v New Zealand* (n 136) para 2.

seek out empirical evidence to 'flesh it out'. The outcomes of this research will help to inform various policies ranging from urban planning to infrastructural development. This research could build on more fundamental research, both theoretical and observational, aimed at a better understanding of the drivers of human mobility. If we better understand why people are moving today (eg how extreme weather events affect human mobility), we should also be able to better understand how human mobility will evolve over time (eg how more extreme weather events will shape human mobility).

Second, research needs to evaluate laws and policies applicable to human mobility. Policy proposals related to 'climate migration' have often relied on rather simplistic assumptions: (i) that states implement all the international norms on the protection of refugees; (ii) that they implement nothing beyond these norms; and (iii) that these norms are effective. None of these assumptions withhold scrutiny. Some major states are not parties to the Convention Relating to the Status of Refugees (eg India and Bangladesh) or systematically disregard their obligations under it. Many states extend protection beyond the narrow definition of the Refugee Convention.[150] And these norms are rather ineffective, if only because they only protect those individuals who are *already* in the territory of another state.[151] They may even be counterproductive to the extent that destination countries limit opportunities for international protection by preventing the entry of asylum seekers onto their territory at the first place. A better assessment of the effect of existing laws and policies, including their interactions, is essential to developing relevant reform proposals.

Third, precisely, research can propose new laws and policies applicable to human mobility. These proposals should rely on the prediction of the way human mobility may evolve, including in light of the impacts of climate change. They should also reflect an evaluation of existing laws and policies. More generally, if these standards are to be of any genuine policy relevance, they should meet certain standards of quality. As a touchstone, the more structural the proposal is, the stronger the argument needs to be. At one extreme, a preponderant argument is sufficient to support one of two equally plausible interpretations of a treaty (eg when the treaty is indecisive and judicial authorities are ambivalent or non-existent). At the other extreme, the argument for the adoption of a new treaty needs to satisfy a much higher standard. After all, there often are reasons why a proposed treaty has not already been adopted, discussed, or even proposed.

Academic proposals for new laws and policies could follow, as far as practicable, national guidelines on the evaluation of legislative proposals. For instance, guidelines applicable to the EU Commission require that legislative proposals be

[150] Jane McAdam, *Complementary Protection in International Refugee Law* (Oxford, Oxford University Press 2007).

[151] James C Hathaway and Michelle Foster, *The Law of Refugee Status*, 2nd edn (Cambridge, Cambridge University Press 2014) 17.

supported, among other things, by a comprehensive evaluation of existing laws and policies, an assessment of the impacts that the proposed legislation might have, and consultation with stakeholders.[152] The impact assessment 'involves verifying the existence of a problem, identifying its underlying causes, assessing whether … action is needed, and analysing the advantages and disadvantages of available solutions' with the aim of 'deliver[ing] the full benefits of policies at minimum cost'.[153] Conducting full-fledged public consultations would be exceedingly burdensome, but scholars willing to propose a law or policy change could realistically seek views from some interested individuals beyond academia, such as lawmakers, regulators, diplomats, international civil servants, activists, and corporate managers, as the case may be. Such consultation would differ from peer review, which is often carried out by like-minded scholars rather than by relevant stakeholders and, thus, may fail to raise relevant objections to academic reform proposals.

V. Conclusion

By and large, scholars focusing on the effect of climate change on migration, in particular migration scholars, have long identified fundamental flaws in the concept of 'climate migration' as a distinct form of migration. However, mutually reinforcing media, political, and academic discourses continue to suggest substantive policies aimed at addressing 'climate migration', in particular by protecting 'climate migrants'. If one cannot distinguish 'climate migrants' from other migrants, as thirty-one leading scholars recognised in a Comment aimed at debunking 'climate migration myths', how could one 'include affected populations in climate mobilities' in developing the 'solutions to the challenges posed by climate change', as these scholars suggest?[154] Who, after all, are the 'affected populations', and what are the concrete 'challenges' that ought to be solved?

This persistent disconnect of between two parts of the literature is mind-boggling. How can the same simplistic concept be reinvented again and again? How can such a loaded concept keep being used? This chapter sought to identify a few causes – the fragmentation of research, path-dependency in research, and the development of academic echo chambers where flawed assumptions remain largely unchallenged – but there might be others. The chapter ended with a short discussion of the possible ways forward for scholars and for law- and policy-makers. While there is no denial that various impacts of climate change could be relevant to various policies, it seems neither possible, nor indeed desirable, for policies to seek to address 'climate migration' as if it were a distinct object of governance. Time has come to de-conceptualise 'climate migration'.

[152] EU Commission, 'Better Regulation Guidelines' SWD(2021)305 final, 3.
[153] ibid 30. For a list of the 'questions that an impact assessment should answer', see ibid 31–33.
[154] Boas and others (n 12) 902.

Conclusion

CALUM TM NICHOLSON AND BENOIT MAYER

At first glance, the cover design of this book may appear wholly unrelated to the discussions that lie within. In a literal sense, this is true. As editors, we were keen to avoid a design that 'essentialised' a construct that the book spends several hundred pages critiquing, namely 'climate migration'.

Forbidden, then, was the usual suspect when it comes to imagery to illustrate 'climate migration': a photograph of real people. Typically, these depict individuals or groups either walking or travelling across desert-like conditions, or wading or paddling across shallow bodies of water, often with burdens held aloft.

To some audiences in the 'Global North' (who, inevitably, are an important audience for much of the academic and grey literature), such images can be shocking, particularly when associated with terminology like 'climate migration', as they appear to show people in distress, perhaps 'fleeing' what look (to the 'northern' gaze) like inhospitable climates.[1]

Such images may, however, elicit a different reaction from anyone who is from, or who has spent any time in, remote regions of the 'Global South'. Namely, they provoke no reaction at all, as they are unremarkable. What may look, from a 'Global North' perspective, like images of people in crisis might, from a 'Global South' point of view, appear to be simply images of ordinary people going about ordinary lives. Perhaps they *are* images of people migrating, but not necessarily because of climate change. But more likely, they are simply pictures of people commuting, perhaps to or from the local market.

Choosing such an image for the cover would only have acted to 'reify' or 'essentialise' the figure of the 'climate migrant'. So, instead, we chose a more figurative one. The image of the leafless branches of a tree, reaching towards (but not touching) the title 'Climate Migration', might pass as a metaphor for the 'climate migration' literature: it is, of course, a literature with an almost arboreal proliferation of concepts and case studies, all branching out from central interests in the migratory effects of climate change, or the climatic causes of migration, reaching hopefully toward the goal of something that is conceptual discrete and empirically substantiated, the better to guide law- and policy-making.

[1] See, for instance, the cover image of Kanta Kumari Rigaud and others, *Groundswell Africa: Deep Dive into Internal Climate Migration in Uganda* (World Bank Group, 2021).

Yet, as this book has argued, this goal has never been reached. What is 'climate migration' remains as elusive as it ever was and, as a consequence, any question of what ought to be done about 'it' is moot. For, without an object of discussion, how can we hope to know what impact 'it' has, still less what society can (let alone should) do about 'it'?

The purpose of this book has, therefore, been threefold, addressed in three parts. In part I, the volume has made the case that 'climate migration' remains elusive because it is intrinsically equivocal, being an ideational or conceptual reference without a real-world, empirical referent. In part II, it has demonstrated the dangers of such a concept maintaining a certain cultural and political cachet despite (or perhaps because of) its equivocal meaning. And, in part III, it has suggested ways forward if the law, policy, and research are to avoid at the same time the epistemic pitfalls and paradoxes as outlined in part I and the political use and abuse of the phrase 'climate migration' (and its numerous cognate categories) outlined in part II.

The critical perspectives collected in this book matter, not because climate change does not, but precisely because it does. If the empirical results of the natural and physical sciences may be seen as the weft of the tapestry of our understanding of climate change, the human sciences – sociology, anthropology, philosophy – are the warp. We require both if we are to weave a way of seeing the world that will hold its form, maintaining a coherent, legible picture of how that world really is, so that we may be guided in our actions within and upon that world, ensuring that these actions have their intended effect, and with a minimum of unintended ones.

As such, this volume has not furnished a range of prescriptions for law, policy, or research. Rather, it has put forward a series of cautions and caveats. The purpose has not been to suggest what to do, but to indicate the sheer range of considerations that any person – or any institution – interested in action must take into account if they are indeed interested in actions that will have intended rather than unintended consequences.

To return to where we began, the volume may be seen as an effort 'not to say what is, or what ought to be, but to provoke thought', and to '"slow down" our reasoning', in order to 'create an opportunity to arouse a slightly different awareness of the problems and situations mobilizing us'.[2] In this sense, we hope the book proves some small help in raising awareness of critical perspectives on 'climate migration' that have relevance, and perhaps even utility, for law, policy, and research.[3]

[2] Isabelle Stengers, 'The Cosmopolitical Proposal', in Bruno Latour and Peter Weibel (eds), *Making Things Public: Atmospheres of Democracy* (Cambridge, MIT Press 2005) 994, at 994.

[3] ibid.

BIBLIOGRAPHY

Books and Reports

Ahuja, Neel (2021). *Planetary Specters: Race, Migration and Climate Change in the Twenty-First Century* (Chapel Hill, University of North Carolina Press).

Akoka, Karen (2020). *L'asile et l'exil: Une histoire de la distinction réfugiés-migrants* (Paris, La Découverte).

Albert, Alain (ed) (1995). *Chaos and Society* (Washington, DC, IOS Press).

Alcoff, Linda M (2015). *The Future of Whiteness* (Cambridge, Polity).

Andreas, Peter, and Greenhill, Kelly M (eds) (2011). *Sex, Drugs, and Body Counts: The Politics of Numbers in Global Crime and Conflict* (New York, Cornell University Press).

Atwood, Margaret (2013). *MaddAddam* (Canada, McClelland & Stewart).

Babutsidze, Zakaria, and Nesta, Lionel (2018). 'Le changement climatique en france: Croyances, comportements, responsabilites' *Sciences Po*, 43 OFCE Policy Brief.

Bacigalupi, Paolo (2015). *The Water Knife* (New York, Vintage Books).

Baldwin, Andrew (2022). *The Other of Climate Change: Racial Futurism, Migration, Humanism* (Lanham, Rowman & Littlefield).

Baldwin, Andrew, and Bettini, Giovanni (eds) (2017). *Life Adrift: Climate Change, Migration, Critique* (Lanham, Rowman & Littlefield).

Baucom, Ian (2020). *History 4° Celsius: Search for a Method in the Age of Anthropocene* (Durham, Duke University Press).

Behrman, Simon, and Kent, Avidan (eds) (2018). *'Climate Refugees': Beyond the Legal Impasse?* (Abingdon, Routledge).

Behrman, Simon, and Kent, Avidan (eds) (2022). *Climate Refugees: Global, Local and Critical Approaches* (Cambridge, Cambridge University Press).

Benkler, Yochai (2007). *The Wealth of Networks: How Social Production Transforms Markets and Freedom* (New Heaven, Yale University Press).

Benner, Ann-Kathrin, and others (2019). *Violent Climate Imaginaries: Science-Fiction-Politics* (Institute for Peace Research and Security Policy at the University of Hamburg).

Berlin, Isaiah (1998). *The Proper Study of Mankind: An Anthology of Essays* (New York, Farrar, Straus and Giroux).

Betts, Alexander (2013). *Survival Migration: Failed Governance and the Crisis of Displacement* (Ithaca, Cornell University Press).

Biecker, Sarah, and Schlichte, Klaus (eds) (2021). *The Political Anthropology of Internationalized Politics* (Lanham, Roman and Littlefield).

Bilsborrow, Richard E (1992). 'Rural Poverty, Migration and the Environment in Developing Countries: Three Case Studies' World Bank Policy Research Working Paper 1017.

Bjola, Corneliu, and Kornprobst, Markus (eds) (2010). *Arguing Global Governance* (Abingdon, Routledge).

Black, Richard (1998). *Refugees, Environment and Development* (Abingdon, Routledge 1998).

Black, Richard (2001). 'Environmental Refugees: Myth or Reality' UNHCR Paper No 34.

Blaikie, Piers, and Brookfield, Harold (eds) (1991). *Land Degradation and Society* (Abingdon, Routledge).

Blake, Jonathan, Clark-Ginsberg, Aaron, and Balagna, Jay (2021). *Addressing Climate Migration: A Review of National Policy Approaches* (RAND Corporation).

Boardley, Samantha (2020). 'Where the Rain Falls Phase III' CARE France Final Evaluation Report.

Boas, Ingrid (2015). *Climate Migration and Security: Securitisation as a Strategy in Climate Change Politics* (Abingdon, Routledge).

Böcker, Anita, de Hart, Betty, and Michalowski, Ines (eds) (2004). *Migration and the Regulation of Social Integration* (IMIS-Beiträge).

Böhm, Steffen, and Sullivan, Sian (eds) (2021). *Negotiating Climate Change in Crisis* (Cambridge, Open Book Publishers).

Bonilla-Silva, Eduardo (2017). *Racism without Racists: Colour-Blind Racism and the Persistence of Racial Inequality in America*, 5th edn (Lanham, Rowman & Littlefield).

Boserup, Ester (1965). *The Conditions of Agricultural Growth: The Economics of Agrarian Change under Population Pressure* (Abingdon, Routledge).

Bower, Erica, and Weerasinghe, Sanjula (2021). 'Leaving Place, Restoring Home: Enhancing the Evidence Base on Planned Relocation Cases in the Context of Hazards, Disasters, and Climate Change' (Platform on Disaster Displacement).

Briggs, Daniel (2021). *Climate Changed: Refugee Border Stories and the Business of Misery* (Abingdon, Routledge).

Brooks, Geraldine (2022). *Horse* (New York, Viking).

Brooks, Nick (2006). 'Climate Change, Drought and Pastoralism in the Sahel' (World Initiative on Sustainable Pastoralism).

Brown, Lester R (ed) (1989). 'State of the World' (Washington, DC, Worldwatch Institute).

Brown, Lester R, McGrath, Patricia L, and Stokes, Bruce (1976). *Twenty-Two Dimensions of the Population Problem* (Washington, DC, World Watch Institute).

Brown, Oli (2008). 'Migration and Climate Change' (IOM World Migration Report Series).

Butler, Judith (1990). *Gender Trouble: Feminism and the Subversion of Identity* (Abingdon, Routledge).

Castles, Stephen (2002). 'Environmental Change and Forced Migration: Making Sense of the Debate' UNHCR Working Paper 70.

Castles, Stephen (2008). 'Understanding Global Migration: A Social Transformation Perspective' (Conference on Theories of Migration and Social Change, Oxford).

Castles, Steven, and Miller, Mark J (2009). *The Age of Migration: International Population Movements in the Modern World*, 4th edn (London, Palgrave Macmillan).

Clement, Viviane, and others (2021). 'Groundswell Part 2: Acting on Internal Climate Migration' (World Bank Group).

Clinchamps, Nicholas, and others (eds) (2016). *Sécurité et environnement* (Bruxelles, Bruylant).

Conrad, Joseph (2012). *Heart of Darkness* (London, Penguin Books).

Cooper, Melinda (2017). *Family Value: Between Neoliberalism and the New Social Conservatism* (Princeton, Zone Books).

Davis, Mike (2006). *City of Quartz: Excavating the Future in Los Angeles* (New York, Verso).

de Haas, Hein (2007). 'The Myth of Invasion Irregular Migration from West Africa to the Maghreb and the European Union' (International Migration Institute).

de Haas, Hein (2009). 'Mobility and Human Development', International Migration Institute Paper No 14.

Deleuze, Gilles, and Guattari, Felix (1987). *A Thousand Plateaus: Capitalism and Schizophrenia* (Brian Massumi trans, Minneapolis, University of Minnesota Press).

Dennery, Etienne (1931). *Asia's Teeming Millions and its Problems for the West* (Port Washington, Kennikat Press).

Donaldson, David S (2022). *Greenland* (New York, Amistad).

Doyen, Pauline, Piva, Annaëlle, and Sebillotte, Oriane (2021). 'Les oubliés du droit d'asile: Enquête sur les conditions de vie et d'accès aux droits des exilés fréquentant 5 structures d'accueil à Paris' (Fédération Solidarité).

Drezner, Daniel W (2014). *Theories of International Politics and Zombies* (Princeton, Princeton University Press).

Duplantier, Bertrand, Nonnenmacher, Stéphane, and Rivasseau, Vincent (eds) (2013). *Chaos: Poincaré Seminar 2010* (Basel, Springer).

Durand-Delacre, David (2022). *Epistemic Mobilities of Climate Migration: a French Case Study* (Doctoral thesis, Cambridge University).
EACH-FOR project (2008). 'Preliminary findings from the EACH-FOR project on Environmentally Induced Migration' (Environmental Change and Forced Migration).
EACH-FOR project (2009). 'Environmental Change and Forced Migration Scenarios' (Environmental Change and Forced Migration).
Ehlers, Eckart, and Krafft, Thomas (eds) (2006). *Earth System Science in the Anthropocene* (Basel, Springer 2006).
El-Hinnawi, Essam (1985). 'Environmental Refugees' (UNEP).
Ellis, Frank (2003). 'A Livelihoods Approach to Migration and Poverty Reduction' (Department for International Development).
EU Commission (2021). 'Better Regulation Guidelines' SWD(2021)305 final.
EU Commission (2022). 'Commission Staff Working Document: Addressing Displacement and Migration Related to Disasters, Climate Change and Environmental Degradation' SWD(2022) 201 Final.
European Border and Coast Guard Agency (2022). *Strategic Risk Analysis 2022*, SAMD/RAU/SFALEM/7782/2022.
Faist, Thomas, and Schade, Jeanette (eds) (2013). *Disentangling Migration and Climate Change* (Basel, Springer).
Faye, Papa, Ribot, Jesse, and Turner, Matthew (2019). 'Climate Change is not the Cause, Migration is Not the Problem: Local Representation and Precarious Young Farmers Leaving Senegal' Swedish International Centre for Local Democracy Research Report No 14.
Fiddian-Qasmiyeh, Elena (ed) (2019). *Refuge in a Moving World: Interdisciplinary Conversations* (London, UCL Press).
Fiddian-Qasmiyeh, Elena (ed) (2020). *Refuge in a Moving World: Refugee and Migrant Journeys across Disciplines* (London, UCL Press).
Fiddian-Qasmiyeh, Elena, and others (eds) (2016). *The Oxford Handbook of Refugee and Forced Migration Studies* (New York, Oxford University Press).
Fiennes, Leandra (2019). 'New Zealand's Climate Refugee Visa, a Framework for Positive Change: Creating a Regional Framework of Protections for Climate Migrants from the Pacific' (LLB thesis, University of Otago).
Filho, Walter Leal (ed) (2015). *Climate Change in the Asia-Pacific Region* (Basel, Springer).
Filho, Walter Leal, and others (eds) (2019). *Climate Action: Encyclopedia of the UN Sustainable Development Goals* (Basel, Springer).
Foresight (2011). 'Migration and Global Environmental Change: Final Project Report' (London, Government Office for Science).
Gammeltoft-Hansen, Thomas, and Sorensen, Ninna N (eds) (2013). *The Migration Industry and the Commercialization of International Migration* (Abingdon, Routledge).
Gardiner, Stephen M (2011). *A Perfect Moral Storm: Climate Change, Intergenerational Ethics and the Global Environmental Tragedy* (Oxford, Oxford University Press).
Gemenne, Francois (2009). 'Environmental Changes and Migration Flows: Normative Frameworks and Policy Responses' (PhD thesis, Institut d'Etudes Politiques de Paris).
Ghosh, Amitav (2017). *The Great Derangement: Climate Change and the Unthinkable* (Chicago, University of Chicago Press).
Gilroy, Paul (2005). *Postcolonial Melancholia* (New York, Columbia University Press).
Goldberg, David T (2015). *Are We All Postracial Yet?* (London, Polity).
Gramsci, Antonio (1995). *The Southern Question* (Pasquale Verdicchio trans, Indiana, Bordighera Press).
Gregory, Derek (2004). *The Colonial Present: Afghanistan, Palestine, Iraq* (Oxford, Blackwell Publishing).
Gupta, Akhil, and Ferguson, James (eds) (1997). *Anthropological Locations: Boundaries and Grounds of a Field Science* (Berkeley, University of California Press).
Guzman, Andrew T (2013). *Overheated: The Human Cost of Climate Change* (New York, Oxford University Press).

Hall, Nina (2016). *Displacement, Development, and Climate Change: International Organizations Moving beyond their Mandates* (Abingdon, Routledge).

Hall, Stuart (2017). *The Fateful Triangle: Race, Ethnicity, Nation* (Cambridge, Massachusetts, Harvard University Press).

Hammar, Tomas, and others (eds) (1997). *International Migration, Immobility and Development: Multidisciplinary Perspectives* (Oxford, Berg Publishers).

Hartmann, Betsy, Subramanium, Ranu, and Zerner, Charles (eds) (2005). *Making Threats: Biofears and Environmental Anxieties* (Lanham, Rowman & Littlefield).

Hathaway, James C, and Foster, Michelle (2014). *The Law of Refugee Status*, 2nd edn (Cambridge, Cambridge University Press).

Héran, François (ed) (2020). *Chiffrer les migrations: À quelles fins?* (De Facto).

Herring, Stephanie C, and others (eds) (2021). 'Explaining Extreme Events in 2020 from a Climate Perspective' (Bulletin of the American Meteorological Society).

Hewitt, Ken (ed) (1983). *Interpretations of Calamity: From the Viewpoint of Human Ecology* (New York, George Allen & Unwin).

Homer-Dixon, Thomas F, and Blitt, Jessica (eds) (1999). *Ecoviolence: Links among Environmental Population and Security* (Lanham, Rowman & Littlefield).

Höppner, Miriam, and others (eds) (2012). *Kritische Migrationsforschung? Da kann ja jeder kommen* (Institut für Sozialwissenschaften).

Hugo, Graeme (2008). 'Migration, Development and Environment' (Workshop on Migration and the Environment: Developing a Global Research Agenda, Munich).

Humphreys, Stephen (ed) (2010). *Human Rights and Climate Change* (Cambridge, Cambridge University Press).

Ignatiev, Noel (1995). *How the Irish Became White* (Abingdon, Routledge).

IOM (2009). 'Compendium on IOM's Activities in Migration, Climate Change, and the Environment' (IOM).

IOM (2009). 'Migration, Climate Change and Environmental Degradation' (IOM).

IOM (2022). 'World Migration Report 2022' (International Organization for Migration).IPCC (1990). IPCC First Assessment Report. *Climate Change: The IPCC Impacts Assessment* (Canberra, Australian Governmental Publishing Service).

IPCC (2007). IPCC Fourth Assessment Report. *Climate Change 2007: Impacts, Adaptation and Vulnerability* (Cambridge, Cambridge University Press).

IPCC (2013). IPCC Fifth Assessment Report. *Climate Change 2013: The Physical Science Basis, Working Group I Contribution* (Cambridge, Cambridge University Press).

IPCC (2014). IPCC Fifth Assessment Report. *Impacts, Adaptation and Vulnerability: Working Group II Contribution* (Cambridge, Cambridge University Press).

IPCC (2014). IPCC Fifth Assessment Report. *Impacts, Adaptation, and Vulnerability, Part A: Global and Sectoral Aspects* (Cambridge, Cambridge University Press).

IPCC (2021). IPCC Sixth Assessment Report. *Climate Change 2021: The Physical Science Basis: Working Group I Contribution* (Cambridge, Cambridge University Press).

IPCC (2022). IPCC Sixth Assessment Report. *Climate Change 2022: Impacts, Adaptation and Vulnerability* (Cambridge, Cambridge University Press).

IPCC (2022). IPCC Sixth Assessment Report. *Impacts, Adaptation and Vulnerability: Working Group II Contribution* (Cambridge, Cambridge University Press).

IPCC (2022). IPCC Sixth Assessment Report. *Mitigation of Climate Change: Working Group III Contribution* (Cambridge, Cambridge University Press).

Itäranta, Emmi (2014). *Memory of Water* (New York, Harper Voyager).

Jansen, Clifford (eds) (1970). *Readings in the Sociology of Migration* (Oxford, Pergamon Press).

Joannon, Barbara, and others (eds) (2022). *Les migrations dans l'œil des médias: Infox, influence et opinion* (Paris, De facto).

Jones, Reece (2021). *White Borders: The History of Race and Immigration in the United States from Chinese Exclusion to the Border Wall* (Boston, Beacon Press).

Jónsson, Gunvor (2008). 'Migration Aspirations and Immobility in a Malian Soninke Village' International Migration Institute Paper No 10.

Jónsson, Gunvor (2010). 'The Environmental Factor in Migration Dynamics: A Review of African Case Studies' International Migration Institute Paper No 21.

Jouzel, Jean, and Michelot, Agnès (2016). 'La justice climatique: enjeux et perspectives pour la france' (Conseil economique, social et environnemental).

Jouzel, Jean, and others (2007). *Réfugiés climatiques* (Paris, Infolio).

Kainz, Lena, and Le Coz, Camille (2022). 'The Winding Road to Marrakech: Lessons from the European Negotiations of the Global Compact for Migration' (Migration Policy Institute).

Kelman, Ilan, Mercer, Jessica, and Gaillard, Jean-Christophe (eds) (2017). *The Routledge Handbook of Disaster Risk Reduction Including Climate Change Adaptation* (Abingdon, Routledge).

Kent, Avidan, and Behrman, Simon (2018). *Facilitating the Resettlement and Rights of Climate Refugees: An Argument for Developing Existing Principles and Practices* (Abingdon, Routledge).

Khalil, Suhair S (1987). 'The Socio-Economic and Political Implications on the Environmental Refugees in the Vicinity of Omdurman' (Institute of Environmental Studies).

Klöck, Carola, and Fink, Michael (eds) (2017). *Dealing with Climate Change on Small Islands: Towards Effective and Sustainable Adaptation?* (Göttingen, Göttingen University Press).

Knaus, Gerald (2020). *Welche Grenzen brauchen wir? Zwischen Empathie und Angst: Flucht, Migration und die Zukunft von Asyl* (Munich, Piper).

Kniveton, Dominic, and others (2008). 'Climate Change and Migration: Improving Methodologies to Estimate Flows' (International Organization for Migration).

Knox, John H, and Pejan, Ramin (eds) (2018). *The Human Right to a Healthy Environment* (Cambridge, Cambridge University Press).

Kramb, Daniel (2012). *From Here* (London, Lonely Coot).

Labonte, Melissa, and Mills, Kurt (eds) (2018). *Human Rights and Justice: Philosophical, Economic, and Social Perspectives* (Abingdon, Routledge).

Laczko, Frank, and Aghazarm, Christine (eds) (2009). *Migration, Environment and Climate Change: Assessing the Evidence* (International Organization for Migration).

Lalami, Laila (2005). *Hope and other Dangerous Pursuits* (New York, Algonquin Books of Chapel Hill).

Lalami, Laila (2019). *The Other Americans* (New York, Pantheon Books).

Lalami, Laila (2020). *Conditional Citizens: On Belonging in America* (New York, Pantheon).

Lanchester, John (2019). *The Wall* (London, Faber & Faber).

Laplace, Pierre S (1902). *A Philosophical Essay on Probabilities* (Frederick W Truscott and Frederick L Emory trans, New York, John Wiley & Sons).

Latour, Bruno, and Weibel, Peter (eds) (2005). *Making Things Public: Atmospheres of Democracy* (Cambridge, Massachusetts, MIT Press).

Lentin, Alana (2020). *Why Race Still Matters* (Cambridge, Polity).

Lewis, James (1999). *Development in Disaster-prone Places: Studies of Vulnerability* (Intermediate Technology Publications).

Livingston, David (1992). *The Geographical Tradition: Episodes in the History of a Contested Enterprise* (Oxford, Blackwell Publishing).

Lodge, Martin, and Wegrich, Kai (2012). *Managing Regulation: Regulatory Analysis, Politics and Policy* (London, Red Globe Press).

Lorenz, Edward N (1993). *The Essence of Chaos* (Seattle, University of Washington Press).

Malm, Andreas (2016). *Fossil Capital: The Rise of Steam Power and the Roots of Global Warming* (London, Verso).

Malm, Andreas, and others (2021). *White Skin, Black Fuel: On the Danger of Fossil Fascism* (London, Verso).

Mayer, Benoit (2016). *The Concept of Climate Migration: Advocacy and its Prospects* (Cheltenham, Edward Elgar).

Mayer, Benoit (2022). *International Law Obligations on Climate Change Mitigation* (Oxford, Oxford University Press).

Mayer, Benoit, and Crépeau, Francois (eds) (2017). *Research Handbook on Climate Change, Migration and the Law* (Cheltenham, Edward Elgar).
Mayer, Benoit, and Zahar, Alexader (eds) (2021). *Debating Climate Law* (Cambridge, Cambridge University Press).
McAdam, Jane (2007). *Complementary Protection in International Refugee Law* (Oxford, Oxford University Press).
McAdam, Jane (2012). *Climate Change, Forced Migration, and International Law* (Oxford, Oxford University Press).
McAdam, Jane (ed) (2010). *Climate Change and Displacement: Multidisciplinary Perspectives* (Oxford, Hart).
McLeman, Robert (2013). *Climate Change and Human Migration: Past Experiences, Future Challenges* (Cambridge, Cambridge University Press).
McLeman, Robert, Schade, Jeanette, and Faist, Thomas (eds) (2016). *Environmental Migration and Social Inequality* (Basel, Springer).
Miller, Sam J (2018). *Blackfish City* (New York, Harper Collins).
Miller, Todd (2017). *Storming the Wall: Climate Change, Migration, and Homeland Security* (San Francisco, City Lights Publishers).
Mitchell, Timothy (2011). *Carbon Democracy: Political Power in the Age of Oil* (London, Verso).
Mol, Annemarie (2002). *The Body Multiple: Ontology in Medical Practice* (Durham, Duke University Press).
Moore, Jason W (ed) (2016). *Anthropocene or Capitalocene? Nature, History and the Crisis of Capitalism* (Dexter, PM Press).
Morrissey, James (2009). 'Environmental Change and Forced Migration: A State of the Art Review' (Refugee Studies Centre Background Paper).
Myers, Norman (2005). 'Environmental Refugees: An Emergent Security Issue' (13th Economic Forum, Prague).
Myers, Norman, and Kent, Jennifer (1995). *Environmental Exodus: An Emergent Crisis in the Global Arena* (Washington, Climate Institute).
Naser, Mostafa M (2022). *The Emerging Global Consensus on Climate Change and Human Mobility* (Abingdon, Routledge).
Nash, Sarah L (2019). *Negotiating Migration in the Context of Climate Change: International Policy and Discourse* (Bristol, Bristol University Press).
Oakes, Robert, and others (2017). 'Climate Change and Migration in the Pacific: Links, Attitudes, and Future Scenarios in Nauru, Tuvalu and Kiribati' (Bonn, United Nations University Institute for Environment and Human Security).
Oakes, Robert, Milan, Andrea, and Campbell, Jillian (2016). 'Kiribati: Climate Change and Migration: Relationships Between Household Vulnerability, Human Mobility and Climate Change' (Bonn, United Nations University Institute for Environment and Human Security).
Office of the High Commissioner for Human Rights (2018). 'Addressing Human Rights Protection Gaps in the Context of Migration and Displacement of Persons across International Borders Resulting from the Adverse Effects of Climate Change and Supporting the Adaptation and Mitigation Plans of Developing Countries to Bridge the Protection Gap', UN Doc A/HRC/38/21.
Oliver-Smith, Anthony, and Hoffman, Susanna (eds) (2020). *The Angry Earth: Disaster in Anthropological Perspective* (Abingdon, Routledge).
Palutikof, Jean, and others (2013). *Climate Adaptation Futures* (Chichester, Wiley-Blackwell).
Park, Lisa SH, and Pellow, David (2011). *The Slums of Aspen: Immigrants vs the Environment in America's Eden* (New York, New York University Press).
Peterson, Andrew, and others (eds) (2016). *The Palgrave International Handbook of Education for Citizenship and Social Justice* (London, Palgrave Macmillan).
Piguet, Etienne (2008). 'New Issues in Refugee Research: Climate Change and Forced Migration' (UNHRC Research Paper No 153).
Piguet, Étienne, Pécoud, Antoine, and de Guchteneire, Paul (eds) (2011). *Migration and Climate Change* (Cambridge, Cambridge University Press).

Plato (2018). *The Republic* (Benjamin Jowett trans, London, Arcturus Publishing).
Polunin, Nicholas (ed) (1998). *Population and Global Security* (Cambridge, Cambridge University Press).
Pott, Andreas, Rass, Christoph, and Wolff, Frank (eds) (2018). *Was ist ein Migrationsregime? What is a Migration Regime?* (Osnabrück, Springer).
Rigaud, Kanta K, and others (2018). 'Groundswell: Preparing for Internal Climate Migration' (World Bank Group).
Robbins, Paul (2004). *Political Ecology: A Critical Introduction* (Cornwall, Blackwell Publishing).
Robinson, Kim S (2020). *Ministry for the Future* (London, Orbit).
Rodríguez-Garavito, César (ed) (2023). *Litigating the Climate Emergency: How Human Rights, Courts, and Legal Mobilization Can Bolster Climate Action* (Cambridge, Cambridge University Press).
Rosenow-Williams, Kerstin, and Gemenne, François (eds) (2016). *Organizational Perspectives on Environmental Migration* (Abingdon, Routledge).
Rosina, Matilde (ed) (2022). *The Criminalisation of Irregular Migration in Europe: Globalisation, Deterrence, and Vicious Cycles* (Basel, Springer).
Ross, Andrew (2021). *Sunbelt Blues: The Failure of American Housing* (New York, Metropolitan Books).
Roth, Veronica (2014). *Divergent* (New York, Katherine Tegan Books).
Sciaccaluga, Giovanni (2020). *International Law and the Protection of 'Climate Refugees'* (London, Palgrave).
Scott, James C (1992). *Seeing Like a State: How Certain Schemes to Improve the Human Condition Have Failed* (New Haven, Yale University Press).
Scott, Matthew (2020). *Climate Change, Disasters and the Refugee Convention* (Cambridge, Cambridge University Press).
Secours Catholique (2020). 'Migrations environnementales: Note d'analyse et de positionnement' (Caritas France).
Selby, Jan, Daoust, Gabrielle, and Hoffmann, Clemens (2022). *Divided Environments: The International Political Ecology of Climate Change, Water and Security* (Cambridge, Cambridge University Press).
Sen, Amartya K (1981). *Poverty and Famines: An Essay on Entitlement and Deprivation* (New York, Oxford University Press).
Seshadri-Crooks, Kalpana (2000). *Desiring Whiteness: A Lacanian Analysis of Race* (Abingdon, Routledge).
Shapiro, Harry L (1939). *Migration and Environment* (Oxford University Press).
Sharpe, Christina (2016). *In the Wake: On Blackness and Being* (Durham, Duke University Press).
Simonelli, Andrea C (2015). *Governing Climate Induced Migration and Displacement: IGO Expansion and Global Policy Implications* (London, Palgrave Macmillan).
Spengler, Oswald (1932). *Decline of the West, Volume 1: Form and Actuality* (New York, Alfred A Knopf).
Squires, Gregory, and Hartman, Chester (eds) (2006). *There is no Such Thing as a Natural Disaster: Race, Class, and Hurricane Katrina* (Abingdon, Routledge).
Stojanov, Robert, and others (2014). 'Migration as Adaptation? Population Dynamics in the Age of Climate Variability' (Global Change Research Centre).
Stott, Philip A, and Sullivan, Sian (eds) (2000). *Political Ecology: Science, Myth and Power* (Oxford, Oxford University Press).
Sturridge, Caitlin, and Holloway, Kerrie (2022). 'Climate Change, Conflict and Displacement: Five Key Misconceptions' (Humanitarian Policy Group Briefing Note, September).
Táíwò, Olúfémi O (2022). *Reconsidering Reparations* (New York, Oxford University Press).
Terminski, Bogumil (2012). 'Environmentally-Induced Displacement: Theoretical Frameworks and Current Challenges', Centre d'étude de l'ethnicité et des migrations Research Paper.
Theroux, Marcel (2009). *Far North* (New York, Farrar, Straus and Giroux).
Thornton, Fanny (2018). *Climate Change and People on the Move: International Law and Justice* (Oxford, Oxford University Press).
Tickell, Crispin (1989). 'Environmental Refugees' (London, National Environmental Research Council Annual Lecture).

Timberlake, Lloyd (1983). *Environmental Wars and Environmental Refugees: The Political Background to the Cartagena Convention* (London, Earthscan).

Tirado, Cristina M (2011). 'Global Climate and Environmental Change: Implications for Food Production and Safety Systems' (American Association for the Advancement of Science Annual Meeting, Washington Convention Center).

United Nations Educational, Scientific and Cultural Organization (2013). *World Social Science Report* (Paris, UNESCO).

UnitedNations High Commissioner for Refugees (2006). 'The State of The World's Refugees 2006: Human Displacement in the New Millennium' (Geneva, UNHCR).

UnitedNations High Commissioner for Refugees (2009). 'Climate Change, Natural Disasters and Human Displacement' Policy Paper, August (Geneva, UNHCR).

UnitedNations High Commissioner for Refugees (2009). 'UNHCR and Climate Change: Involvement, Challenges and Responses' (Geneva, UNHCR).

Vallet, Elizabeth (ed) (2014). *Borders, Fences and Walls: State of Insecurity*? (Farnham, Ashgate Publishing).

Van der Geest, Kees (2008). 'Ghana: Case Study Report: Migration and Natural Resources Scarcity in Ghana' (2008) EACH-FOR Paper No 044468.

Wallace-Wells, David (2019). *The Uninhabitable Earth: Life after Warming* (New York, Tim Duggan Books).

Walter, Kathrin M (2022). 'Migration as a Security Threat in our Warming World? Frontex and the Securitisation of Climate Change-Induced Migration through Practices and Speech Acts' (LLM thesis, King's College London).

Warner, Koko, and others (2009). 'In Search of Shelter: Mapping the Effects of Climate Change on Human Migration and Displacement' (United Nations University).

Warner, Koko, and others (2012). 'Where the Rain Falls: Climate Change, Food and Livelihood Security, and Migration' (United Nations University Institute for Environment and Human Security).

Weheliye, Alexander G (2014). *Habeas Viscus: Racializing Assemblages, Biopolitics, and Black Feminist Theories of the Human* (Durham, Duke University Press).

Wennersten, John R, and Robbins, Denise (2017). *Rising Tides: Climate Refugees in the Twenty-First Century* (Bloomington, Indiana University Press).

Wewerinke-Singh, Margaretha (2019). *State Responsibility, Climate Change and Human Rights under International Law* (Oxford, Hart).

White, Gregory (2011). *Climate Change and Migration: Security and Borders in a Warming World* (New York, Oxford University Press).

Wilderson, Frank B (2020). *Afropessimism* (New York, Liveright).

Wisner, Ben, and others (2003). *At Risk: Natural Hazards, People's Vulnerability and Disasters*, 2nd edn (Abingdon, Routledge).

Wisner, Ben, Gaillard, JC, and Kelman, Ilan (eds) (2011). *Handbook of Hazards and Disaster Risk Reduction* (Abingdon, Routledge).

Witting, Christian (2018). *Street on Torts*, 15th edn (Oxford, Oxford University Press).

Articles

Adams, Vincanne, Murphy, Michelle, and Clarke, Adele E (2009). 'Anticipation: Technoscience, Life, Affect, Temporality' 28 *Subjectivity* 246.

Adger, W Neil, and Barnett, Jon (2005). 'Compensation for Climate Change Must Meet Needs' 436 *Nature* 328.

Ahmed, Bayes (2021). 'The Root Causes of Landslide Vulnerability in Bangladesh' 18 *Landslides* 1707.

Akoka, Karen (2018). 'Réfugiés ou migrants? Les enjeux politiques d'une distinction juridique' 1(25) *Nouvelle revue de psychosociologie* 15.

Alemu, Belachew Y (2013). 'Expropriation, Valuation and Compensation Practice in Ethiopia: The Case of Bahir Dar City and Surrounding' 31(2) *Property Management* 132.

Anderson, Bridget (2019). 'New Directions in Migration Studies: Towards Methodological De-Nationalism' 7(36) *Comparative Migration Studies* 1.
Antkowiak, Thomas M (2020). 'A "Dignified Life" and the Resurgence of Social Rights' 18 *Northwestern Journal of Human Rights* 1.
Appel, Hannah (2017). 'Toward an Ethnography of the National Economy' 32(2) *Cultural Anthropology* 294.
Arnall, Alex, and Kothari, Uma (2015). 'Challenging Climate Change and Migration Discourse: Different Understandings of Timescale and Temporality in the Maldives' 31 *Global Environmental Change* 199.
Ayeb-Karlsson, Sonja (2021). '"When We Were Children We Had Dreams, Then We Came to Dhaka to Survive": Urban Stories Connecting Loss of Wellbeing, Displacement and (Im)Mobility' 13 *Climate and Development* 348.
Ayeb-Karlsson, Sonja, Baldwin, Andrew W, and Kniveton, Dominic (2022). 'Who is the Climate-Induced Trapped Figure' 13(6) *Wiley Interdisciplinary Reviews Climate Change* 1.
Bakewell, Oliver (2008). 'Research Beyond Categories: The Importance of Policy Irrelevant Research into Forced Migration' 21(4) *Journal of Refugee Studies* 432.
Baldwin, Andrew (2013). 'Racialisation and the Figure of the Climate-Change Migrant' 45(6) *Environment and Planning A: Economy and Space* 1474.
Baldwin, Andrew (2017). 'Climate Change, Migration, and the Crisis of Humanism' 8(3) *Wiley Interdisciplinary Reviews: Climate Change* 1.
Baldwin, Andrew (2017). 'Resilience and Race, or Climate Change and the Uninsurable Migrant: Towards an Anthroporacial Reading of "Race"' 5(2) *Resilience* 129.
Baldwin, Andrew, and Erikson, Bruce (2020). 'Introduction: Whiteness, Coloniality, and the Anthropocene' 38 *Environment and Planning D: Society and Space* 3.
Baldwin, Andrew, Fröhlich, Christiane, and Rothe, Delf (2019). 'From Climate Migration to Anthropocene Mobilities: Shifting the Debate' 14(3) *Mobilities* 289.
Ballu, Valérie, and others (2011). 'Comparing the Role of Absolute Sea-Level Rise and Vertical Tectonic Motions in Coastal Flooding, Torres Islands (Vanuatu)' 108(32) *PNAS* 13019.
Barnett, Jon, and Adger, W Neil (2003). 'Climate Dangers and Atoll Countries' 61 *Climatic Change* 321.
Bartolini, Giulio (2021). 'Introductory Remarks by Giulio Bartolini' 115 *Proceedings of the ASIL Annual Meeting* 155.
Bassett, Thomas J, and Turner, Matthew D (2007). 'Sudden Shift or Migratory Drift? Fulbe Herd Movements to the Sudano-Guinean Region of West Africa' 35 *Human Ecology* 33.
Behrman, Simon, and Kent, Avidan (2020). 'The Teitiota Case and the Limitations of the Human Rights Framework' 75 *Questions of International Law* 25.
Bell, Ruth G (2006). 'What to do about Climate Change' 85 *Foreign Affairs* 105.
Belshaw, Cyril (1951). 'Social Consequences of the Mount Lamington Eruption' 21(4) *Oceania* 241.
Benwell, Richard (2011). 'The Canaries in the Coalmine: Small States as Climate Change Champions' 100(413) *The Round Table* 199.
Berchin, Issa I, and others (2017). 'Climate Change and Forced Migrations: An Effort towards Recognizing Climate Refugees' 84 *Geoforum* 147.
Bettini, Giovanni (2013). 'Climate Barbarians at the Gate? A Critique of Apocalyptic Narratives on "Climate Refugees"' 45 *Geoforum* 63.
Bettini, Giovanni (2019). 'And yet it Moves! (Climate) Migration as a Symptom in the Anthropocene' 14(3) *Mobilities* 336.
Bettini, Giovanni, Nash, Sarah L, and Gioli, Giovanna (2017). 'One Step Forward, Two Steps Back? The Fading Contours of (In)Justice in Competing Discourses on Climate Migration' 183(4) *The Geographical Journal* 348.
Betts, Alexander (2010). 'Survival Migration: A New Protection Framework' 16(3) *Global Governance* 361.
Betts, Alexander, and Pilath Angela (2017). 'The Politics of Causal Claims: The Case of Environmental Migration' 20(4) *Journal of International Relations and Development* 782.
Biermann, Frank, and Boas, Ingrid (2021). 'Preparing for a Warmer World: Towards a Global Governance System to Protect Climate Refugees' 10 *Global Environmental Politics* 60.

Bloomer, Julian (2009). 'Using a Political Ecology Framework to examine Extra-Legal Livelihood Strategies: A Lesotho-Based Case Study of Cultivation of and Trade in Cannabis' 16 *Journal of Political Ecology* 49.

Boas, Ingrid, and others (2019). 'Climate Migration Myths' 9 *Nature Climate Change* 901.

Boas, Ingrid, and others (2022). 'Climate Mobilities: Migration, Im/Mobilities and Mobility Regimes in a Changing Climate' 14 *Journal of Ethnic and Migration Studies* 1.

Bosworth, Mary, and Vannier, Marion (2019). 'Blurred Lines: Detaining Asylum Seekers in Britain and France' 56 *Journal of Sociology* 53.

Box, Jason E, and others (2022). 'Greenland Ice Sheet Climate Disequilibrium and Committed Sea-Level Rise' 12 *Nature Climate Change* 808.

Brand, Anna (2022). 'The Sedimentation of Whiteness as Landscape' 40(2) *Environment and Planning D: Society and Space* 276.

Bronen, Robin (2008). 'Alaskan Communities' Rights and Resilience' 31 *Forced Migration Review* 30.

Broto, Vanesa C, and Robin, Enora (2021). 'Climate Urbanism as Critical Urban Theory' 42(6) *Urban Geography* 715.

Bryant, Raymond L (1992). 'Political Ecology: An Emerging Research Agenda in Third-World Studies' 11 *Political Geography* 12.

Bulkeley, Harriet, and others (2013). 'Climate Justice and Global Cities: Mapping the Emerging Discourses' 23(5) *Global Environmental Change* 914.

Burgers, Laura (2022). 'An Apology Leading to Dystopia: Or, Why Fuelling Climate Change is Tortious' 11 *Transnational Environmental Law* 419.

Buxton, Rebecca (2019). 'Reparative Justice for Climate Refugees' 94(2) *Philosophy* 193.

Calabrese, Laura (2018). 'Faut-il dire migrant ou réfugié? Débat lexico-sémantique autour d'un problème public' 210(2) *Langages* 105.

Callon, Michel, and Rabeharisoa, Vololona (2003). 'Research "in the Wild" and the Shaping of New Social Identities' 25(2) *Technology in Society* 193.

Carr, Edward R (2005). 'Placing the Environment in Migration: Environment, Economy, and Power in Ghana's Central Region' 37(5) *Environment and Planning* 925.

Castagnoli, Giuliana C, and others (2002). 'Solar Radiation Variability in the Last 1400 Years Recorded in the Carbon Isotope Ratio of a Mediterranean Sea Core' 29(12) *Advances in Space Research* 1989.

Cazenave, Anny, and Le Cozannet Goneri (2014). 'Sea Level Rise and its Coastal Impacts' 2(2) *Earth's Future* 15.

Chambers, Jonathan (2020). 'Global and Cross-Country Analysis of Exposure of Vulnerable Populations to Heatwaves from 1980 to 2018' 163 *Climatic Change* 539.

Chand, Savin S, and others (2022). 'Declining Tropical Cyclone Frequency under Global Warming' 12 *Nature Climate Change* 655.

Chen, Jiqua, Franklin, Jerry F, and Spies, Thomas A (1993). 'Contrasting Microclimates among Clearcut, Edge, and Interior of Old-Growth Douglas-Fir Forest' 63 *Agricultural and Forest Meteorology* 219.

Chen, Joyce, and Muller, Valerie (2018). 'Coastal Climate Change, Soil Salinity and Human Migration in Bangladesh' 8 *Nature Climate Change* 981.

Chimni, Bhupinder S (1998). 'The Geopolitics of Refugee Studies: A View from the South' 11(4) *Journal of Refugee Studies* 350.

Cima, Elena (2022). 'The Right to a Healthy Environment: Reconceptualizing Human Rights in the Face of Climate Change' 31 *Review of European, Comparative & International Environmental Law* 38.

Citroni, Gabriella (2020). 'Human Rights Committee's Decision on the Case Ieoane Teitiota v New Zealand: Landmark or Will-o'-the-Wisp for Climate Refugees?' 75 *Questions of International Law* 1.

Clarke, Peter U, and others (2016). 'Consequences of Twenty-First-Century Policy for Multi-Millennial Climate and Sea-Level Change' 6 *Nature Climate Change* 360.

Collier, Stephen, and Cox, Savanah (2021). 'Governing Urban Resilience: Insurance and the Problematization of Climate Change' 50(2) *Economy and Society* 275.

Connell, John (2015). 'Vulnerable Islands: Climate Change, Tectonic Change, and Changing Livelihoods in the Western Pacific' 27 *The Contemporary Pacific* 1.
Connell, John (2016). 'Last Days in the Carteret Islands? Climate Change, Livelihoods and Migration on Coral Atolls' 57 *Asia Pacific Viewpoint* 3.
Cottier, Fabien, and others (2022). 'Framing the Frame: Cause and Effect in Climate-Related Migration' 158 *World Development* 1.
Cournil, Christel (2006). 'Les refugiés écologiques: quelle(s) protection(s), quel(s) statut(s)?' 4 *Revue du droit public et de la science politique* 1035.
Cox, Heather M, and others (1999). 'Drowning Voices and Drowning Shoreline: A Riverside View of the Social and Ecological Impacts of the St. Lawrence Seaway and Power Project' 10(2) *Rural History*.
Crawley, Heaven, and Skleparis, Dimitris (2018). 'Refugees, Migrants, Neither, Both: Categorical Fetishism and the Politics of Bounding in Europe's "Migration Crisis"' 44 *Journal of Ethnic and Migration Studies* 48.
de Bruijn, Mirjam, and van Dijk, Han (2003). 'Changing Population Mobility in West Africa: Fulbe Pastoralists in Central and South Mali' 102(407) *African Affairs* 285.
de Haan, Arjan (1999). 'Livelihoods and Poverty: The Role of Migration – A Critical Review of the Migration Literature' 36(2) *Taylor & Francis Journals* 1.
Denis, Marine (2018). 'IOM and UNHCR Beyond Their Mandates: Legal and Administrative Functions in the Protection of Environmentally Displaced People' 16 *Medzinarodne vztahy* (Journal of International Relations).
Desai, Bina, and others (2021). 'Addressing the Human Cost in a Changing Climate' 372(6548) *Science* 1284.
DeSilva, Sanjaya, and Elmelech, Yuval (2012). 'Housing Inequality in the United States: Explaining the White-Minority Disparities in Homeownership' 27 *Housing Studies* 1.
Diekjobst, Rouven (2022). 'Book review: Climate Refugees: Global, Local and Critical Approaches' *South African Journal of International Affairs* 394.
Dixon, George IJ (1950). 'Land and Human Migrations' 9(2) *The American Journal of Economics and Sociology* 223.
Docherty, Bonnie, and Giannini, Tyler (2009). 'Confronting a Rising Tide: A Proposal for a Convention on Climate Change Refugees Symposium' 33(2) *Harvard Environmental Law Review* 349.
Doney, Scott C, and others (2020). 'The Impacts of Ocean Acidification on Marine Ecosystems and Reliant Human Communities' 45 *Annual Review of Environment and Resources* 83.
Dugmore, Andrew J, Keller, Christian, and McGovern, Thomas H (2007). 'Norse Greenland Settlement: Reflections on Climate Change, Trade, and the Contrasting Fates of Human Settlements in the North Atlantic Islands' 44 *Arctic Anthropology* 12.
Durand-Delacre, David (2022). '(Mis)Representing Climate Mobilities: Lessons from Documentary Filmmaking' 48(14) *Journal of Ethnic and Migration Studies* 3397.
Entman, Robert M (2006). 'Framing: Toward Clarification of a Fractured Paradigm' 43(4) *Journal of Communication* 51.
Estes, Jack, and Shaw, Dennis (1985) 'Popular Culture and Mt. St. Helens: A Study of a Response' 18(4) *The Journal of Popular Culture* 135.
Ezra, Markos (2001). 'Demographic Responses to Environmental Stress in the Drought-and Famine-Prone Areas of Northern Ethiopia' 7(4) *International Journal of Population Geography* 259.
Ezra, Markos, and Kiros, Gebre-Egziabher (2001). 'Rural Out-Migration in the Drought Prone Areas of Ethiopia: A Multilevel Analysis' 35(3) *International Migration Review* 749.
Farber, Daniel A (2007). 'Basic Compensation for Victims of Climate Change' 155(6) *University of Pennsylvania Law Review* 1605.
Farbotko, Carol (2010). 'Wishful Sinking: Disappearing Islands, Climate Refugees and Cosmopolitan Experimentation' 51 Asia Pacific Viewpoint 47.
Farbotko, Carol (2022). 'The Spectre of Mass Migration Across International Borders: Dismantling an Unscientific Expectation' 5(8) *One Earth* 841.
Farbotko, Carol, and Lazrus, Heather (2012). 'The First Climate Refugees? Contesting Global Narratives of Climate Change in Tuvalu' 22(2) *Global Environmental Change* 382.

Farbotko, Carol, Stratford, Elaine, and Lazrus, Heather (2016). 'Climate Migrants and New Identities? The Geopolitics of Embracing or Rejecting Mobility' 17(4) *Social and Cultural Geography* 533.
Farbotko, Carol, and others (2022). 'A Climate Justice Perspective on International Labour Migration and Climate Change Adaptation among Tuvaluan Workers' 2 *Oxford Open Climate Change* 1.
Farbotko, Carol, and others (2022). 'Climate Mobilities, Rights and Justice: Complexities and Particularities' *Frontiers in Climate Mobility*. Farrell, Henry (2012). 'The Consequences of the Internet for Politics' 15 *Annual Review of Political Sciences* 35.
Faulkingham, Ralph H, and Thorbahn, Peter F (1975). 'Population Dynamics and Drought: A Village in Niger' 29(3) *Population Studies* 463.
Ferris, Elizabeth (2020). 'Research on Climate Change and Migration Where Are We and Where Are We Going?' 8(4) *Migration Studies* 612.
Filindra, Alexandra, and Kolbe, Melanie (2022). 'Latinx Identification with Whiteness: What Drives it, and What Effects Does it Have on Political Preference?' 103(6) *Social Science Quarterly* 1424.
Findley, Sally E (1994). 'Does Drought Increase Migration? A Study of Migration from Rural Mali during the 1983–1985 Drought' 28(3) *International Migration Review* 539.
Foster, Michelle, and McAdam, Jane (2022). 'Analysis of "Imminence" in International Protection Claims: Teitiota v New Zealand and Beyond' 71 *International & Comparative Law Quarterly* 975.
Gaillard, Jean-Christophe (2010). 'Vulnerability, Capacity, and Resilience: Perspectives for Climate and Disaster Risk Reduction' 22(2) *Journal of International Development* 218.
Galtung, Johan (1969). 'Violence, Peace, and Peace Research' 6(3) *Journal of Peace Research* 167.
Gemenne, François (2011). 'Why the Numbers Don't Add Up: A Review of Estimates and Predictions of People Displaced by Environmental Changes' 22 *Global Environmental Change* 541.
Gemenne, François (2015). 'One Good Reason to Speak of "Climate Refugees"' 49 *Forced Migration Review* 70.
Gonin, Patrick, and Lassailly-Jacob, Véronique (2002). 'Les réfugiés de l'environnement: Une nouvelle catégorie de migrants forcés?' 18(2) *Revue européenne des migrations internationales* 139.
Gonzalez, Carmen G (2019). 'Climate Justice and Climate Displacement: Evaluating the Emerging Legal and Policy Responses' 36 *Wisconsin International Law Journal* 366.
Gonzalez, Carmen G (2021). 'Racial Capitalism, Climate Justice, and Climate Displacement' 11 *Oñati Socio-Legal Series* 108.
Granjou, Celine, Walkder, Jeremy, and Salazar, Juan F (2017). 'The Politics of Anticipation: On Knowing and Governing Environmental Futures' 92 *Futures* 5.
Graves, Philip E (1979). 'A Life-Cycle Empirical Analysis of Migration and Climate, by Race' 6 *Journal of Urban Economics* 135.
Graves, Philip E (1980). 'Migration and Climate' 20(2) *Journal of Regional Science* 227.
Green, Michael (2016). 'Contested Territory' 6(9) *Nature Climate Change* 817.
Greve, Ralf and Chambers, Christopher (2022). 'Mass Loss of the Greenland Ice Sheet until the Year 3000 under a Sustained Late-21st-century Climate' 68(269) *Journal of Glaciology* 618.
Hagon, Kirsten (2021). 'Protecting People in the Context of Climate Change and Disasters: Setting the Scene' 115 *Proceedings of the ASIL Annual Meeting* 156.
Hampshire, Kate, and Randall, Sara (1999). 'Seasonal Labour Migration Strategies: Coping with Poverty or Optimising Security?' 5(5) *International Journal of Population Geography* 367.
Hardin, Garrett (1968). 'The Tragedy of the Commons' 162(3859) *Science* 1243.
Hardin, Garrett (1974). 'Lifeboat Ethics: The Case Against Helping the Poor' 5 *The Hastings Center* 4.
Harris, Cheryl L (1993) 'Whiteness as Property' 106(8) *Harvard Law Review* 1707.
Hartmann, Betsy (2010). 'Rethinking Climate Refugees and Climate Conflict: Rhetoric, Reality and the Politics of Policy Discourse' 22(2) *Journal of International Development* 233.
Hartmann, Betsy (2014). 'Converging on Disaster: Climate Security and the Malthusian Anticipatory Regime for Africa' 19(4) *Geopolitics* 757.
Hauer, Mathew E (2017). 'Migration Induced by Sea-Level Rise Could Reshape the US Population Landscape' (2017) 7 *Nature Climate Change* 321.
Haurin, Donald R (1980). 'The Regional Distribution of Population, Migration and Climate' 95(2) *The Quarterly Journal of Economics* 293.

He, Xangbai (2018). 'Legal and Policy Pathways of Climate Change Adaptation: Comparative Analysis of the Adaptation Practices in the United States, Australia and China' 7(2) *Transnational Environmental Law* 347.

Hedegaard, Troels F (2022). 'Attitudes to Climate Migrants: Results from a Conjoint Survey Experiment in Denmark' 45 *Scandinavian Political Studies* 25.

Helbling, Marc (2020). 'Attitudes towards Climate Change Migrants' 160 *Climatic Change* 89.

Henning, Karla, Steimanis, Ivo, and Vollan, Björn (2022). '(Climate) Migrants Welcome? Evidence from a Survey Experiment in Austria' 22 *Regional Environmental Change* 108.

Henry, Sabine, and others (2004). 'Descriptive Analysis of the Individual Migratory Pathways According to Environmental Typologies' 25(45) *Population and Environment* 397.

Hermann, Elfriede, and Kempf, Wolfgang (2017). 'Climate Change and the Imagining of Migration: Emerging Discourses on Kiribati's Land Purchase in Fiji' 29(2) *The Contemporary Pacific* 231.

Higgins, Kathleen (2016). 'Post-Truth: A Guide for the Perplexed' 540 *Nature* 9.

Hodell, David A (2019). 'The Smoking Gun of the Ice Ages' 354 *Science* 1235.

Hoffmann, Roman, Sedova, Barbora, and Vinke, Kira (2021). 'Improving the Evidence Base: A Methodological Review of the Quantitative Climate Migration Literature' 71 *Global Environmental Change* 4.

Homer-Dixon, Thomas F (1991). 'On the Threshold: Environmental Change as Causes of Violent Conflict' 16(2) *International Security* 76.

Homer-Dixon, Thomas F (1994). 'Environmental Scarcities and Violent Conflict: Evidence from Cases' 19 *International Security* 5.

Hourcade, Renaud, and Wagener, Albin (2021). 'Le climatoscepticisme: Une approche interdiscursive' 127 *Mots: Les langages du politique* 9.

Hulme, Mike (2014). 'Attributing Weather Extremes to "Climate Change": A Review' 38(4) *Progress in Physical Geography: Earth and Environment* 499.

Hulme, Mike, O'Neill, Saffron J, and Dessai, Suraje (2011). 'Is Weather Event Attribution Necessary for Adaptation Funding?' 334(6057) *Science* 764.

Hunter, Lori M, Luna, Jessie K, and Norton, Rachel M (2015). 'Environmental Dimensions of Migration' 41 *Annual Review of Sociology* 377.

Hwang, Sean-Shong, and others (2007). 'Anticipation of Migration and Psychological Stress and the Three Gorges Dam Project, China' 65 *Social Science & Medicine* 1012.

Jacobson, Jodi L (1988). 'Environmental Refugees: A Yardstick of Habitability' 8(3) *Bulletin of Science, Technology & Society* 257.

Jinnah, Sikina (2011). 'Climate Change Bandwagoning: The Impacts of Strategic Linkages on Regime Design, Maintenance, and Death' 11(3) *Global Environmental Politics*.

Johnson, Gregory C, and Lyman, John M (2020). 'Warming Trends Increasingly Dominate Global Ocean' 10 *Nature Climate Change* 757.

Joseph, Sarah (2019). 'Extending the Right to Life under the International Covenant on Civil and Political Rights: General Comment 36' 19(2) *Human Rights Law Review* 347.

Kelley, Colin P, and others (2015). 'Climate Change in the Fertile Crescent and Implications of the Recent Syrian Drought' 112(11) *Earth, Atmospheric, and Planetary Sciences* 3241.

Kelman, Ilan (2019). 'Imaginary Numbers of Climate Change Migrants?' 8(5) *Social Sciences* 131.

Khaitan, Tarunabh (2022). 'On Scholactivism in Constitutional Studies: Skeptical Thoughts' 20(2) *International Journal of Constitutional Law* 547.

Kirksey, Eben (2015). 'Species: A Praxiographic Study' 21(4) *Journal of the Royal Anthropological Institute* 758.

Klepp, Silja, and Herbeck, Johannes (2016). 'The Politics of Environmental Migration and Climate Justice in the Pacific Region' 7 *Journal of Human Rights and the Environment* 54.

Kobayashi, Audrey, and Peake, Linda (2000). 'Racism out of Place: Thoughts on Whiteness and an Antiracist Geography in the New Millennium' 90(2) *Annals of the Association of American Geographers* 392.

Korsmo, Fae L (1993). 'Swedish Policy and Saami Rights' 11 *Northern Review* 32.

Kulamadayl, Lys (2021). 'Between Activism and Complacency: International Law Perspectives on European Climate Litigation' 10(5) *European Society of International Law Reflection* 1.

Kunz, Egon F (1973). 'The Refugee in Flight: Kinetic Models and Forms of Displacement' 7(2) *International Migration Review* 125.

Lane, Lucille R, Tobin, Graham A, and Whiteford Linda M (2003). 'Volcanic Hazard or Economic Destitution: Hard Choices in Baños, Ecuador' 5 *Environmental Hazards* 23.

Lauria, Giovanna (2022). 'A Critical Appraisal of the Concept of Climate Migration' 9(3) *London Review of International Law* 375.

Lelieveld, Jos, and others (2016). 'Strongly Increasing Heat Extremes in the Middle East and North Africa (MENA) in the 21st Century' 137 *Climatic Change* 245.

Lentin, Alana (2018). 'Beyond Denial: "Not Racism" as Racist Violence' 32(4) *Continuum* 400.

Lonergan, Steve (1998). 'The Role of Environmental Degradation in Population Displacement' 4 *Environmental Change and Security Project Report* 5.

Lowry, Daniel P, and others (2021). 'The Influence of Emissions Scenarios on Future Antarctic Ice Loss is Unlikely to Emerge this Century' 2 *Communications Earth & Environment* 221.

Lubkemann, Stephen C (2018). 'Involuntary Immobility: On a Theoretical Invisibility in Forced Migration Studies' 21(4) *Journal of Refugee Studies* 454.

Lunstrum, Elizabeth, Bose, Pablo, and Zalik, Anna (2015). 'Environmental Displacement: The Common Ground of Climate Change, Extraction and Conservation' 48(2) *Area* 130.

Lusk, Greg (2017). 'The Social Utility of Event Attribution: Liability, Adaptation, and Justice-Based Loss and Damage' 143 *Climatic Change* 201.

Mahmuduzzaman, Md, and others (2014). 'Causes of Salinity Intrusion in Coastal Belt of Bangladesh' 4 *International Journal of Plant Research* 8.

Maneggia, Amina (2020). 'Non-Refoulement of Climate Change Migrants: Individual Human Rights Protection or "Responsibility to Protect"? The Teitiota Case before the Human Rights Committee' 14(2) *Diritti umani e diritto internazionale* 635.

Marjanac, Sophie, and Patton, Lindene (2018). 'Extreme Weather Event Attribution Science and Climate Change Litigation: An Essential Step in the Causal Chain?' 36(3) *Journal of Energy & Natural Resources Law* 265.

Marx, Werner, Haunschild, Robin, and Bornmann, Lutz (2021). 'Heat Waves: A Hot Topic in Climate Change Research' 146 *Theoretical and Applied Climatology* 781.

Massey, Douglas S (1990). 'Social Structure, Household Strategies, and the Cumulative Causation of Migration' 56 *Population Index* 3.

Mather, John R (1954). 'The Effect of Climate on the New World Migration of Primitive Man' 10(3) *Southwestern Journal of Anthropology* 304.

Mayer, Benoit (2011). 'The International Legal Challenges of Climate-Induced Migration: Proposal for an International Legal Framework' 22 *Colorado Journal of International Environmental Law and Policy* 357.

Mayer, Benoit (2012). '"Environmental Migration" as Advocacy: Is it Going to Work?' 29(2) *Refuge: Canada's Journal on Refugees* 27.

Mayer, Benoit (2012). 'The International Legal Protection of Climate (or Environmental) Migrants: Fraternity, Responsibility and Sustainability' 56 *Supreme Court Law Review* 723.

Mayer, Benoit (2013). 'Climate Change and International Law in the Grim Days' 24(3) *European Journal of International Law* 947.

Mayer, Benoit (2013). 'Constructing "Climate Migration" as a Global Governance Issue: Essential Flaws in the Contemporary Literature' 9 *McGill International Journal of Sustainable Development Law and Policy* 87.

Mayer, Benoit (2013). 'Environmental Migration in the Asia-Pacific Region: Could we Hang out Sometime?' 3 *Asian Journal of International Law* 101.

Mayer, Benoit (2013). 'Environmental Migration: Prospects for a Regional Governance in the Asia-Pacific Region' 16 *Asia Pacific Journal of Environmental Law* 77.

Mayer, Benoit (2014). 'The Rights of Mongolia's Internal Migrants under International Law: Climatic, Domestic and Commercial Responsibilities Student Contribution' 7 *Journal of East Asia and International Law* 197.

Mayer, Benoit (2016). 'Climate Migration and the Politics of Causal Attribution: A Case Study in Mongolia' 5(2) *Migration and Development* 234.
Mayer, Benoit (2017). 'Migration in the UNFCCC Workstream on "Loss and Damage": An Assessment of Alternative Framings and Conceivable Responses' 6 *Transnational Environmental Law* 107.
Mayer, Benoit (2021). 'Climate Change Adaptation and the Law' 39 *Virginia Environmental Law Journal* 141.
Mayer, Benoit (2022). 'Attribution Science and the Fate of Climate Litigation' 13(5) *Global Policy* 831.
Mayer, Benoit, and others (2013). 'Governing Environmentally Related Migration in Bangladesh: Responsibilities, Security and the Causality Problem' 22(2) *Asian and Pacific Migration Journal* 177.
McAdam, Jane (2020). 'Protecting People Displaced by the Impacts of Climate Change: the UN Human Rights Committee and the Principle of *Non-Refoulement*' 114(4) *American Journal of International Law* 708.
McGregor, JoAnn (1994). 'Climate Change and Involuntary Migration: Implications for Food Security' 19(2) *Food Policy* 120.
McGuire, Bill (2010). 'Potential for a Hazardous Geospheric Response to Projected Future Climate Changes' (2010) 368(1919) *Philosophical Transactions of the Royal Society A: Mathematical, Physical and Engineering Sciences* 2317.
McLeman, Robert, and others (2021). 'Conceptual Framing to Link Climate Risk Assessments and Climate-Migration Scholarship' 165 *Climatic Change* 24.
McMichael, Clia, and others (2021). 'Rising Seas, Immobilities, and Translocality in Small Island States: Case Studies from Fiji and Tuvalu' 43 *Population and Environment* 82.
McNamara, Karen E, and Combes, Helene JD (2016). 'Planning for Community Relocations due to Climate Change in Fiji' 6 *International Journal of Disaster Risk Science* 315.
Mercer, Jessica (2010). 'Disaster Risk Reduction or Climate Change Adaptation: Are we Reinventing the Wheel?' 22(2) *Journal of International Development* 247.
Meze-Hausken, Elisabeth (2000). 'Migration Caused by Climate Change: How Vulnerable are People in Dryland Areas? A Case Study in Northern Ethiopia' 5(4) *Mitigation and Adaptation Strategies for Global Change* 379.
Morrissey, James (2008). 'Rural-Urban Migration in Ethiopia' 31 *Forced Migration Review* 28.
Morrissey, James (2012). 'Rethinking the "Debate on Environmental Refugees": From "Maximalists" to "Proponents" and "Critics"' 19 *Journal of Political Ecology* 36.
Morrissey, James (2021). 'How Should we Talk about Climate Change and Migration?' 9 *Migration Studies* 150.
Mortreux, Colette, and others (2023). 'Climate Change and Migration from Atolls? No Evidence Yet' 60(101234) *Current Opinion in Environmental Sustainability* 1.
Mounkaila, Harouna (2002). 'De la migration circulaire à l'abandon du territoire local dans le Zarmaganda (Niger)' 18(2) *Revue européene des migrations internationales* 161.
Myers, Norman (1993). 'Environmental Refugees in a Globally Warmed World: Estimating the Scope of What Could Well Become a Prominent International Phenomenon' 43(11) *Bioscience* 752.
Myers, Norman (1997). 'Environmental Refugees' 19 *Population and Environment* 167.
Myers, Norman (2001). 'Environmental Refugees: A Growing Phenomenon of the 21st Century' 357(1420) *Philosophical Transactions of the Royal Society* 609.
Nash, Sarah L (2018). 'From Cancun to Paris: An Era of Policy Making on Climate Change and Migration' 9 *Global Policy* 53.
Nash, Sarah L (2018). 'Knowing Human Mobility in the Context of Climate Change: The Self-Perpetuating Circle of Research, Policy, and Knowledge Production' 4 *movements. Journal for Critical Migration and Border Regime Studies* 67.
Neef, Andreas, and Benge, Lucy (2022). 'Shifting Responsibility and Denying Justice: New Zealand's Contentious Approach to Pacific Climate Mobilities' 22(3) *Regional Environmental Change* 1.
Neumayer, Eric (2006). 'An Empirical Test of a Neo-Malthusian Theory of Fertility Change' 27(4) *Population and Environment* 327.
Nicholson, Calum TM (2014). 'Climate Change and the Politics of Causal Reasoning: The Case of Climate Change and Migration' 180(2) *The Geographical Journal* 151.

Nicholson, Calum TM (2021). 'Review of Negotiating Migration in the Context of Climate Change: International Policy and Discourse' 34(4) *Journal of Refugee Studies* 4594.

Nier, Charles L (1999). 'Perpetuation of Segregation: Toward a New Historical and Legal Interpretation of Redlining Under the Fair Housing Act' 32(3) *John Marshall Law Review* 617.

Nordhaus, William (2019). 'Climate Change: The Ultimate Challenge for Economics' 109(6) *The American Economic Review* 1991.

Nunn, Patrick D, and Carson, Mike (2015). 'Collapses of Island Societies from Environmental Forcing: Does History Hold Lessons for the Future?' 8 *Global Environment* 110.

Obokata, Reiko, Veronis, Luisa, and McLeman, Robert (2014). 'Empirical Research on International Environmental Migration: A Systematic Review' 36 *Population and Environment* 111.

Ollitrault, Sylvie (2010). 'De la sauvegarde de la planète à celle des réfugiés climatiques: L'activisme des ONG' 4 *Revue Tiers Monde* 19.

Oltmer, Jochen (2016). 'Das aushandeln von migration: Historische und historiographische perspektiven' 14(3) *ZSE zeitschrift für staats- und europawissenschaften* 333.

Park, Robert E (1928). 'Human Migration and the Marginal Man' 33(6) *American Journal of Sociology* 881.

Parsons, Laurie (2018). 'Structuring the Emotional Landscape of Climate Change Migration: Towards Climate Mobilities in Geography' 43(4) *Progress in Human Geography* 670.

Pedersen, Jon (1995). 'Drought, Migration and Population Growth in the Sahel: The Case of the Malian Gourma: 1900–1991' 49 *Population Studies* 111.

Otto, Friederike EL, and others (2022). 'Causality and the Fate of Climate Litigation: The Role of the Social Superstructure Narrative' 13(5) *Global Policy* 623.

Perry, Ronald W (1979). 'Evacuation Decision-Making in Natural Disasters' 4 *Mass Emergencies* 25.

Petersen, William (1958). 'A General Typology of Migration' 23(3) *American Sociological Review* 256.

Pieterse, Jan N (2000). 'Globalization and Human Integration: We are all Migrants' 32(5) *Futures* 385.

Piguet, Etienne (2013). 'From "Primitive Migration" to "Climate Refugees": The Curious Fate of the Natural Environment in Migration Studies' 103 *Annals of the Association of American Geographers* 148.

Piguet, Etienne (2021). 'Linking Climate Change, Environmental Degradation, and Migration: An Update After 10 Years' 13 *Wiley Interdisciplinary Reviews: Climate Change* 1.

Piguet, Etienne, Kaenzig, Raoul, and Guélat, Jérémie (2018). 'The Uneven Geography of Research on "Environmental Migration"' 39(4) *Population and Environment* 357.

Popovski, Vesselin, and Mundy, Kieran G (2017). 'Defining Climate-Change Victims' 7 *Sustainability Science* 5.

Poulin, Eric G (2022). 'Mirabel Airport: In the Name of Development, Modernity, and Canadian Unity' *Economic Anthropology*.

Pulido, Laura (2000). 'Rethinking Environmental Racism: White Privilege and Urban Development in Southern California' 90 *Annals of the Association of American Geographers* 12.

Radel, Claudia, and others (2018). 'Toward a Political Ecology of Migration: Land, Labor Migration, and Climate Change in Northwestern Nicaragua' 108 *World Development* 263.

Ramphal, Shridath S (1987). 'The Environment and Sustainable Development' 135(5376) *Journal of the Royal Society of Arts* 879.

Ramstein, Gilles, and others (1997). 'Effect of Orogeny, Plate Motion and Land-Sea Distribution on Eurasian Climate Change over the Past 30 Million Years' 386 *Nature* 788.

Rein, Martin, and Schön, Donald (1996). 'Frame-Critical Policy Analysis and Frame-Reflective Policy Practice' 9 *Knowledge and Policy* 85.

Rice, Jennifer L, Long, Joshua, and Levenda, Anthony (2021). 'Against Climate Apartheid: Confronting the Persistent Legacies of Expendability for Climate Justice' 5(2) *Environment and Planning E: Nature and Space* 1.

Richmond, Anthony H (1993). 'Reactive Migration: Sociological Perspectives on Refugee Movements' 6 *Journal of Refugee Studies* 7.

Rive, Vernon (2020). 'Is an Enhanced non-Refoulement Regime under the ICCPR the Answer to Climate Change-Related Human Mobility Challenges in the Pacific? Reflections on Teitiota v New Zealand in the Human Rights Committee' 75 *Questions of International Law* 7.

Romanello, Marina, and others (2021). 'The 2021 Report of the Lancet Countdown on Health and Climate Change' 398 *The Lancet* 1619.

Rose, Lucia (2021). 'The World after Teitiota: What the HRC Decision Means for the Future of Climate Migration' 12 *San Diego Journal of Climate & Energy Law* 41.

Ruela, Rui, and others (2020). 'Global and Regional Evolution of Sea Surface Temperature under Climate Change' 190 *Global and Planetary Change* 103190.

Russo, Katherine, and Wodak, Ruth (2019). 'Introduction: The Representation of "Exceptional Migrants" in Media Discourse: The Case of Climate-Induced Migration' 21(2) *Anglisticaj*.

Sajjad, Tazreena (2018). 'What's in a Name? "Refugees", "Migrants" and the Politics of Labelling' 60(2) *Race & Class* 40.

Scherschel, Karin (2011). 'Who is a Refugee? Reflections on Social Classifications and Individual Consequences' (2011) 8 *Migration Letters* 67.

Schiller, Nina G, and Salazar, Noel B (2013). 'Regimes of Mobility across the Global' 39(2) *Journal of Ethnic and Migration Studies* 183.

Scott, Matthew (2023). 'Migration/Refugee Law (2020)' 3 *Yearbook of International Disaster Law Online* 615.

Scott, Matthew, and Garner, Russel (2022). 'Nordic Norms, Natural Disasters, and International Protection: Swedish and Finnish Practice in European Perspective' 91 *Nordic Journal of International Law* 101.

Selby, Jan, and others (2017). 'Climate Change and the Syrian Civil War Revisited' 60 *Political Geography*.

Steenmans, Katrien, and Cooper, Aaron (2020). 'Ioane Teitiota v New Zealand: A Landmark Ruling for Climate Refugees?' 25(2) *Coventry Law Journal* 2.

Stojanov, Robert, and others (2021). 'Climate Mobility and Development Cooperation' 43(2) *Population and Environment* 209.

Storalazzi, Curt D, Ellias, Edwin PL, and Berkowitz, Paul (2015). 'Many Atolls May be Uninhabitable within Decades Due to Climate Change' 5 *Scientific Reports* 14546.

Storr, Cait (2016). 'Islands and the South: Framing the Relationship Between International Law and Environmental Crisis' 27(2) *European Journal of International Law* 519.

Strauss, Sarah (2012). 'Are Cultures Endangered by Climate Change? Yes, but …' 3(4) *Wiley Interdisciplinary Reviews Climate Change* 371.

Suhrke, Astri (1993). 'A Crisis Diminished: Refugees in the Developing World' 48(2) *International Journal* 191.

Suhrke, Astri (1994). 'Environmental Degradation and Population Flows' 47(2) *Journal of International Affairs* 473.

Sultana, Farhana (2021). 'Climate Change, COVID-19, and the Co-Production of Injustices: A Feminist Reading of Overlapping Crises' 22(4) *Social & Cultural Geography* 447.

Svart, Larry M (1976). 'Environmental Preference Migration: A Review' 66(3) *Geographical Review* 314.

Syphard, Alexandra D, Brennan, Teresa J, and Keeley, Jon E (2017). 'The Importance of Building Construction Materials Relative to Other Factors Affecting Structure Survival during Wildfire' 21 *International Journal of Disaster Risk Reduction* 140.

Tacoli, Cecilia (2009). 'Crisis or Adaptation? Migration and Climate Change in Context of High Mobility' 21(2) *Environment and Urbanization* 513.

Taylor, Zac J, and Aalbers, Manuel B (2022). 'Climate Gentrification: Risk, Rent and Restructuring in Greater Miami' 112(6) *Annals of the American Association of Geographers* 1685.

Teles, Patrícia G (2021). 'Remarks by Patrícia Galvão Teles' 115 *Proceedings of the ASIL Annual Meeting* 158.

Thornton, Fanny (2012). 'Climate Change, Displacement and International Law: Between Crisis and Ambiguity' 30 *Australian Yearbook of International Law* 147.

Tilley, Lisa, and others (2022). 'Race and Climate Change: Towards Anti-Racist Ecologies' *Politics*.

Tirado, Cristina M, and others (2010). 'Climate Change and Food Safety: A Review' 43 *Food Research International* 1745.

Trenberth, Kevin E, Fasullo, John T, and Shepherd, Theodore G (2015). 'Attribution of Climate Extreme Events' 5(8) *Nature Climate Change* 725.

Tuana, Nancy (2019). 'Climate Apartheid: The Forgetting of Race in the Anthropocene' 7 *Critical Philosophy of Race* 1.

UN High Commissioner for Refugees (2021). 'Legal Considerations Regarding Claims for International Protection Made in the Context of the Adverse Effects of Climate Change and Disasters' 33 *International Journal of Refugee Law* 151.

Valluy, Jérôme (2012). 'De l'asile aux répulsions: La radicalisation des frontières' *Le sujet dans la cité* 84.

Venturini, Tommaso, Gemenne, François, and Severo, Marta (2012). 'Des migrants et des mots: Une analyse numérique des débats médiatiques sur les migrations et l'environnement' 88 *Cultures & conflits* 133.

Verhoeven, Harry (2014). 'Gardens of Eden or Hearts of Darkness? The Genealogy of Discourses on Environmental Insecurity and Climate Wars in Africa' 19(4) *Geopolitics* 784.

Watts, Nick, and others (2018). 'The Lancet Countdown on Health and Climate Change: From 25 Years of Inaction to a Global Transformation for Public Health' 391(10120) *The Lancet* 581.

White, Gregory (2019). '"Climate Refugees": A Useful Concept?' 19(4) *Global Environmental Politics* 133.

Whyte, Kyle, Talley, Jared L, and Gibson, Julia D (2019). 'Indigenous Mobility Traditions, Colonialism, and the Anthropocene' 14(3) *Mobilities* 319.

Wiegel, Hanne, Boas, Ingrid, and Warner, Jeroen (2019). 'A Mobilities Perspective on Migration in the Context of Environmental Change' 10(6) *Wiley Interdisciplinary Reviews: Climate Change* 451.

Williams, Aleatra P (2015). 'Lending Discrimination, the Foreclosure Crisis, and the Perpetuation of Racial and Ethnic Disparities in Homeownership in the U.S.' 6(2) *William and Mary Business Law Review* 601.

Williams, Angela (2008). 'Turning the Tide: Recognizing Climate Change Refugees in International Law' 30(4) *Law & Policy* 502.

Wimmer, Andreas, and Schiller, Nina G (2002). 'Methodological Nationalism and Beyond: Nation-State Building, Migration and the Social Sciences' 2(4) *Global Networks* 301.

Wolpert, Julian (1966). 'Migration as an Adjustment to Environmental Stress' *Journal of Social Issues* 92.

Wynter, Sylvia (2003). 'Unsettling the Coloniality of Being/Power/Truth/Freedom: Towards the Human, After Man, its Overrepresentation – an Argument' 3(3) *CR: The New Centennial Review* 257.

Yates, Olivia E, and others (2022). '"There's so Much More to That Sinking Island!": Restoring Migration from Kiribati and Tuvalu to Aotearoa New Zealand' *Journal of Community Psychology* 1.

Yelfaanibe, Augustine, and Zetter, Roger (2017). 'Policies and Labels for Negotiating Rights Protection for the Environmentally Displaced in Ghana: The Dagara Farmer in Perspective' 37(2) *African Geographical Review* 83.

Zammit-Mangion, Andrew, and others (2014). 'Resolving the Antarctic Contribution to Sea-Level Rise: A Hierarchical Modelling Framework' 25(4) *Environmetrics* 245.

Zhu, Jiaojun, and others (2007). 'Microclimate Regimes following Gap Formation in a Montane Secondary Forest of Eastern Liaoning Province, China' 18(3) *Journal of Forestry Research* 167.

INDEX

www.ingramcontent.com/pod-product-compliance
Ingram Content Group UK Ltd.
Pitfield, Milton Keynes, MK11 3LW, UK
UKHW021909150926
475560UK00003B/262